READY CHECK GO!

Put this book to work for you and your family today. Use "Ready, Check, Go!" to help you plan a healthier life.

Self-care is something you do <u>every day.</u> This book will help with many health problems — both routine and emergency — during the year. But these first pages have tips you can use <u>right now.</u> It takes just a few minutes to do the "Ready, Check, Go!" checklist. And what you learn may add years to your life.

What You'll Need

- A pencil
- A bathroom scale
- A tape measure
- Your *Mayo Clinic Guide to Self-Care*

Get Started

"Ready, Check, Go!" asks some basic questions about living a healthy life. If you breeze through them, you're probably already very healthy. If not, you'll have a good idea of what changes to make. First, make sure that you don't have a medical condition that might make it unsafe or unwise for you to make lifestyle changes.

Check All That Apply

Do you have a significant medical condition for which you see a doctor regularly or take daily medication (examples include cancer, diabetes, heart disease, significant arthritis, asthma)?

Yes _____ → Go ahead and answer the "Ready, Check, Go!" questions, but before you follow the recommendations in this book, get your doctor's OK. In addition, look through "Specific Conditions" beginning on page 157 for more on your condition.

No _____ → Go to the next question.

For women: Are you pregnant?

Yes or not sure _____ → Talk with your doctor first. And read the pregnancy information in this Guide, beginning on page 154.

No _____ → Go to the next question.

Do you have a condition for which you follow a special diet or that might be worsened by losing weight or exercising?

Yes _____ → Answer the questions, but before starting a weight-loss or exercise program, get your doctor's OK. Also look for information on your condition in "Common Problems," beginning on page 49.

No _____ → You're ready to go!

Step 1

Do You Use Tobacco?

Do you smoke or use spit tobacco?

Yes _____ → Tobacco use is a tough habit to break, but stopping could be the single most important health change you make. Smoking causes heart disease, stroke and cancer. It's never too late to stop. See pages 192 to 194 for how to stop smoking.

No _____ → Go to the next question.

Basic Tobacco Quit Plan
1. List your top five reasons for quitting.
2. Set a quit date.
3. Get rid of all tobacco on your quit date.
4. Get support from family, friends and co-workers.
5. Find alternatives to the habit — nicotine replacement, lifestyle changes.

Tobacco Fact: More than 400,000 Americans die of tobacco-related illness each year. Smoking can significantly increase your yearly health care costs. If you smoke a pack a day and you quit, you'll save about $1,500 a year.

How's Your Weight?

Find out your body mass index (BMI) and your waist circumference to see whether you're in the healthy weight zone. To do this, you'll need a bathroom scale and a tape measure.

First, determine your BMI. To do this, use the handy BMI chart on page 207 and write your BMI here. _____

Next, measuring at the narrowest part of your abdomen, determine your waist circumference and write it here. _____

If your BMI is less than 19, talk with your doctor — you may be underweight.
If your BMI is between 19 and 24.9, you're at a healthy weight.
If your BMI is 25 or greater, consider starting a weight-loss program (see page 208).

An ideal waist circumference is 40 inches or less for men and 35 inches or less for women.

Basic Weight-Loss Plan

1. Set a weight-loss goal of 1 to 2 pounds a week.
2. Eat five or more servings of fruits and vegetables a day.
3. Increase your physical activity so you're doing at least 30 minutes a day.
4. Recruit a friend or family member for support.

Weight Facts: More than two-thirds of all Americans are overweight. Being overweight increases the risk of diabetes, arthritis, heart disease and sleep disorders. Slow, steady weight loss is the best way to get to a healthy weight.

Good Nutrition

How many servings of:
Fruits do you eat each day? → _____
Vegetables do you eat each day? → + _____
= _____ *Total*

If your total is five or greater, go to the next step.
If not, see "Eating Well" on page 210 for tips on good nutrition.

Serving Size

Vegetables
- 1 cup broccoli
- 2 cups raw, leafy greens

Visual Cue
1 baseball
2 baseballs

Fruits
- ½ cup sliced fruit
- 1 small apple or medium orange

Visual Cue
Tennis ball

Carbohydrates
- ½ cup whole-grain pasta, brown rice or dried cereal
- ½ whole-wheat bagel
- 1 slice whole-grain bread

Visual Cue
Hockey puck

Protein and Dairy
- 2½ ounces chicken or fish
- 1½ ounces beef

Visual Cue
Deck of cards
½ deck of cards

Fats
- 2 ounces hard cheese
- 2½ teaspoons peanut butter
- 1 teaspoon butter or margarine

Visual Cue
4 dice
2 dice
1 die

For a guide to selecting servings, see "The Mayo Clinic Healthy Weight Pyramid" on page 211.

Basic Healthy Nutrition Plan

1. Add one additional fruit or vegetable serving each week until you're getting five or more servings most days.
2. Try at least one new healthy recipe each week.
3. Make sure you eat three healthy meals — including breakfast — every day.

Nutrition Facts: Eating the right foods can make you healthier and prevent disease. Fiber — found in fruits, vegetables and whole grains — may lower your risk of colon cancer. Vitamins and other nutrients in fresh or frozen fruits and vegetables may reduce your risk of other cancers and cardiovascular disease. Replacing butter, lard and other solid fats with healthier substitutes like olive, canola and peanut oils can help lower your risk of heart disease.

Prevent Disease or Find It Early

Here are recommendations — according to how old you are — for having a preventive checkup with your doctor. See where you fit and then answer the question.

Age	
20 to 29	At least once every five years
30 to 39	At least once every three to four years
40 to 49	At least once every two to three years
50 to 59	At least once every two years
60 and older	Yearly

Have you had a preventive checkup in the time frame for your age?

Yes _____ → Go to the next question.

No _____ → Make an appointment for a checkup.

Basic Preventive Care Plan

1. Call your doctor to schedule a preventive checkup.
2. Use a birthday or anniversary to remind you to make your appointment.
3. Know your blood pressure, cholesterol and blood sugar numbers after your checkup, and keep track of those and other numbers that are important to your health.

Screening Facts: Cancer is the leading cause of death among Americans in their 40s and 50s. Heart disease is the leading cause of death for Americans over age 65. Your doctor can screen for breast, colon, cervical and prostate cancers. Cholesterol and blood pressure screenings can help you detect and manage heart disease. (See "Adult Screening Tests and Procedures" on page 223.)

How's Your Mood?

For at least the past two weeks, have you persistently felt down, depressed or hopeless?

Yes _____ → Talk with your doctor.

No _____ → Go to the next question.

For at least the past two weeks, have you had little interest or pleasure in doing things?

Yes _____ → Talk with your doctor. In addition, see pages 200 to 202 for more on depression and the blues.

No _____ → Go to the next question.

Basic Stress Management Plan

1. Exercise at least 30 minutes most days of the week.
2. Try for an average of eight hours of sleep a day.
3. Stay connected with family and friends.

Mood Facts: Stress and a depressed mood contribute to an increased risk of heart disease and can intensify your physical symptoms.

Get Moving and Keep Moving

How many minutes a week do you spend doing moderate or vigorous physical activities? Check the time that comes closest.

(*Note:* For most people, moderate or vigorous includes activities such as brisk walking, dancing, biking, swimming and running).

0 to 30 minutes _____ → You're just getting started. If there are health reasons why you're not more active, ask your doctor about an exercise plan that's right for you.

30 to 90 minutes _____ → Good for you! You've got a good start. Make a goal to gradually increase the amount of time you exercise.

90 to 120 minutes _____ → You're well on your way to maintaining a good fitness program. If you're doing vigorous activity, you've reached a reasonable goal when you're doing 90 minutes or more a week.

120 minutes or more _____ → You're an active person and probably at a good level of fitness. If your exercise is moderate, you should be doing at least 30 minutes most days of the week. If weight loss is part of your plan, you'll likely need at least 200 minutes a week of moderate physical activity.

See "Physical Activity and Fitness" starting on page 217 for more on getting and staying fit.

Basic Activity Plan
1. Aim to do something nearly every day of the week.
2. Set a goal of a specific number of minutes or steps a week.
3. Keep a log to help remind you and track your progress.
4. Recruit a friend or family member to keep you company.
5. Build up slowly, but steadily. If you're having difficulty or not feeling well while doing physical activities, see your doctor.

Fitness Facts: More than 60 percent of American adults aren't physically active on a regular basis, and 25 percent aren't active at all. Even a modest walking program (see pages 219 to 220) can help increase your heart health, reduce stress and give you the extra energy to do the things you enjoy.

Safety

Do you wear a seat belt every time you drive or ride in a motor vehicle?

Yes _____ → Go to the next question.

No _____ → Buckle up! Check out page 231.

If you own firearms, do you lock them up and have trigger locks on them?

Yes _____ → Go to the next question.

No _____ → Keep firearms and ammunition under lock and key.

Have you done a home-safety survey in the past six months?

Yes _____

No _____ → Use the home-safety checklist "Reduce Your Risk at Home" on page 231 to make your home safer.

Basic Safety Plan

1. Always wear your seat belt when traveling in a motor vehicle.
2. Do a home-safety review at least once a year.

Safety Fact: If you're under age 45, the biggest threat to your life is a motor vehicle accident.

The Bottom Line

Threats to Your Health

Why is it important to know what threatens your health? It's not to scare you, but rather to help guide you in the choices you make about your health and safety. The news is full of stories about avian flu and bioterrorism, crashes, floods and explosions. They're important, and we have a section on emergency preparedness on pages 229 to 230. But what should you spend most of your time working to avoid? Check out the table below for the biggest risks to your health and well-being.

Top 5 Leading Causes of Death and Lost Productive Years in the United States

RANK	Causes of Most "Lost Productive Years of Life"	Most Common Causes of Death in All Ages	Causes of Death in Infants	Causes of Death in Children 1-14	Causes of Death in Young Adults 15-44	Causes of Death in Adults 45-64	Causes of Death in Adults 65 and older
1	Cancer 23%	Heart Disease	Complications of Birth (Perinatal Death)	Motor Vehicle Accidents	Motor Vehicle Accidents	Cancer	Heart Disease
2	Heart Disease 22%	Cancer	Birth Defects	Other Accidents	Cancer	Heart Disease	Cancer
3	Motor Vehicle Accidents 5%	Stroke	Sudden Infant Death Syndrome (SIDS)	Cancer	Other Accidents	Diabetes	Stroke
4	Stroke 5%	Chronic Lung Disease	Accidents	Birth Defects	Heart Disease	Stroke	Lung Disease
5	Chronic Lung Disease 4%	Diabetes	Lung Disease	Homicide	Suicide	Lung Disease	Alzheimer's Disease

Modified from Centers for Disease Control and Pevention and National Center for Health Statistics Information, 2002-2003

MAYO CLINIC
Guide to
SELF-CARE

Answers for Everyday Health Problems

Philip Hagen, M.D.
Medical Editor in Chief

Martha Millman, M.D.
Associate Medical Editor

Fifth Edition

Mayo Clinic
Rochester, Minnesota
Jacksonville, Florida
Scottsdale, Arizona

Published by Mayo Clinic Health Information, Rochester, Minn.

Library of Congress Control Number: 2006922989

ISBN-13: 978-1-893005-42-6
ISBN-10: 1-893005-42-9

Printed in the United States of America

Fifth Edition

1 2 3 4 5 6 7 8 9 10

Preface

Dr. Martha Millman, the associate medical editor for this book, and I have the privilege of taking care of people in the Mayo Clinic Division of Preventive and Occupational Medicine. We understand the devastating effect that a stroke or cancer can have on patients and their families. But we also understand the effect that a child with a fever can have on a working parent. We, and our colleagues at Mayo Clinic, have learned a lot about how to prevent illness and care for people who are sick. And one of the most important lessons we've learned is that self-care is key!

Self-care is something each of us practices every day. It may be doing the obvious things such as taking our medications, eating right, getting a checkup or exercising. Or it may be doing the less obvious, such as taking time to meet a new person, building a supportive family, checking our home for safety or taking steps to be prepared in the event of a disaster.

We invite you to use this book to help build your self-care skills. Don't put it on the shelf until you've paged through it first! We've added a new section, "Ready, Check, Go!," that nearly everyone can use as a quick health check. Use it and in just a few minutes, you'll be started on your personal self-care program. Then scan the rest of the book so that you know where to look when specific health concerns arise.

Having a good doctor is an important part of your health care. But as health care costs rise, it's important to know when to go see your doctor, and when to manage a problem yourself. The *Mayo Clinic Guide to Self Care* is designed to help you do that. For example, five minutes spent reading the section on back pain, cough or fever may save you a trip to the doctor and pay for this book many times over.

How We Prepared This Book

In planning this book, we asked people throughout the United States what they'd like to find in this book. Here's what they told us:

"Discuss common problems in simple language. Provide tips on prevention and self-care. Address important children's health concerns. And don't forget the workplace. Work is where we spend a third of our waking lives."

It was a tall order. We began by reviewing the top 200 reasons why adults and children visit a doctor. Then we talked to Mayo Clinic nurses who respond to telephone calls from people with questions about health and illness. We consulted with health care providers, employers and managers of corporate health programs to learn what illnesses and injuries are common in the workplace.

Then we looked at health care costs. We reviewed our experience at Mayo Clinic, which includes providing care annually to more than 500,000 patients and 47,000 employees at our three major locations in Rochester, Minn., Scottsdale, Ariz., and Jacksonville, Fla., and our regional community-based health care practices.

Using all of this information, we focused on how to prevent illness, how to detect illness before it becomes a serious, costly problem, and how to avoid unnecessary trips to the clinic or emergency room.

New in This Fifth Edition

Our colleagues have reviewed every page of this edition and added much new information. Have you heard of automatic electronic defibrillators, or AEDs? They're in many public places now. Learn about them on page 3. Did you know there are ways to lower your "bad cholesterol" without medication? See the chart on page 215. Diabetes is on the rise. We explain how to reduce your risk. If you spend hours a day at your computer, push back for three minutes and do the office stretches on page 240. We've revised immunization guidelines, including who should get the new tetanus booster that contains the whooping cough (pertussis) vaccine. We've enhanced tips for travelers, added new travel first-aid kit suggestions, and included some tips if you're traveling to parts of the world where avian flu or other infections are a concern. And we've updated a wide variety of information and quick-care tips.

Please use this book for improving your health. Salud!

Philip Hagen, M.D.
Medical Editor in Chief

Editorial Staff

Editor in Chief
Philip Hagen, M.D.

Associate Medical Editor
Martha Millman, M.D.

Managing Editor
Richard Dietman

Publisher
Sara Gilliland

**Editor in Chief,
Books and Newsletters**
Christopher Frye

Editorial Research
Anthony Cook

Danielle Gerberi
Deirdre Herman
Michelle Hewlett

Proofreading
Miranda Attlessey
Donna Hanson

Contributing Writers
Harvey Black
Katie Colón
Terry Jopke
Lynn Madsen
Lee Ann Martin
Catherine LaMarca Stroebel
Doug Toft
Jeremiah Whitten

Creative Director
Daniel Brevick

Art Director
Stewart Koski

Medical Illustration
John Hagen

Illustration
Kent McDaniel
Christopher Srnka

Indexing
Larry Harrison

Administrative Assistants
Beverly Steele
Terri Zanto-Strausbauch

Contributing Editors and Reviewers

Julie Abbott, M.D.
Steven Altchuler, M.D.
Gregory Anderson, M.D.
Patricia Barrier, M.D.
Brent Bauer, M.D.
Lisa Buss, Pharm.D.
Gerald Christenson, R.Ph.
Matthew Clark, Ph.D.
David Claypool, M.D.
Maria Collazo-Clavell, M.D.
Bradford Currier, M.D.
Albert Czaja, M.D.
Diane Dahm, M.D.
Lowell Dale, M.D.
Lisa Drage, M.D.
Joseph Duffy, M.D.
Brooks Edwards, M.D.
Martin Ellman, D.P.M.
Mary Gallenberg, M.D.
Gerald Gau, M.D.
James Graham, D.P.M.
Peg Harmon, R.N.
J. Taylor Hays, M.D.
Donald Hensrud, M.D.
David Herman, M.D.
W. Michael Hooten, M.D.
Daniel Hurley, M.D.
Richard Hurt, M.D.
Robert Jacobson, M.D.

Mary Jurisson, M.D.
Kevin Kaufman
Stephen Kopecky, M.D.
Debra Koppa, C.P.N.P.
Lois Krahn, M.D.
Barbara Kreinbring, R.N.
James Li, M.D.
Charles Loprinzi, M.D.
Lois McGuire, R.N.
Irene Meissner, M.D.
Linda Miller, M.D.
Sara Miller, R.N.P.
Robin Molella, M.D.
Margaret Moutvic, M.D.
Debra Mucha, C.P.N.P.
Jennifer Nelson, R.D.
Deborah Newman, M.D.
Eric Olson, M.D.
David Patterson, M.D.
Ronald Petersen, M.D.
Gregory Poland, M.D.
Carroll Poppen, P.A.
Donna Rasmussen, R.N.
Randall Roenigk, M.D.
Julia Rosekrans, M.D.
Teresa Rummans, M.D.
Priya Sampathkumar, M.D.
Arnold Schroeter, M.D.
Phillip Sheridan, D.D.S.

Jay Smith, M.D.
Ray Squires, Ph.D.
James Steckelberg, M.D.
Robert Stroebel, M.D.
Jerry Swanson, M.D.
Jill Swanson, M.D.
Sandra Taler, M.D.
Kristin Vickers Douglas, Ph.D.
Abinash Virk, M.D.
Stacey Vlahakis, M.D.
Gerald Volcheck, M.D.
Karen Wallevand

Introduction

Mayo Clinic Guide to Self-Care provides reliable, practical, easy-to-understand information on more than 200 common medical conditions and issues relating to your health.

No book can replace the advice of your doctor or other health care providers. Instead, our intent is to help you manage some common medical problems safely at home or at work. The information you'll find may allow you to avoid a trip to the clinic or emergency room. And you'll learn when you need to visit a medical professional.

How the Book Is Organized

Most chapters in *Mayo Clinic Guide to Self-Care* begin with a general discussion of the health topic, sometimes including signs and symptoms and a summary of the cause. Next, look for self-care and prevention suggestions highlighted in blue shading. Under the heading "Medical Help," you're advised when to see a doctor or other health care provider and what kind of treatment you might expect. When there's special information for children, you'll see a "Kids' Care" heading. Finally, articles with gray shading contain information on related medical topics.

Listed below are summaries of the eight sections that make up *Mayo Clinic Guide to Self-Care.*

Urgent Care

Emergencies are rare and usually require the care of a medical professional. However, there are some things that you can do before medical help arrives to stabilize the person who's in the emergency situation and prepare him or her for treatment. Areas covered include how to perform cardiopulmonary resuscitation (CPR) and how to help someone who's choking or having a heart attack. How to deal with a variety of common problems, such as bleeding, animal bites, frostbite and puncture wounds, also is covered.

General Symptoms

General symptoms are medical conditions that tend to affect your entire body rather than a specific body part or system. General symptoms might include dizziness, fatigue, fever, pain, sleeplessness, sweating and unexpected weight changes. In this section, the common causes for each of these seven general symptoms are explained and self-care information is provided.

Common Problems

This section, the largest single section of the book, examines common problems in areas such as your eyes, ears, nose, skin, stomach, throat, back and limbs. You'll also find information on men's and women's health issues. Simple remedies for problems such as a sore throat, cold, stomachache, ingrown toenail and black eye are offered.

Specific Conditions

In this section, we offer general guidelines on the prevention and management of common conditions for which there's a significant opportunity for self-care. If you have any of these conditions, see your health care provider for proper diagnosis and treatment.

Mental Health

Here you'll find helpful information on how to deal with a variety of mental health issues, such as addiction and anxiety, domestic abuse and memory loss. The difference between depression and the blues, how to cope with the loss of a loved one and how to tell whether someone may be contemplating suicide also is discussed.

Staying Healthy

This section is filled with practical information on how to establish and maintain a healthy lifestyle. You'll find tips on nutrition, weight control, exercise, stress management, prevention of injury and illness.

(continued next page)

Your Health and the Workplace

This section focuses on ways to improve your health and well-being at your place of employment.

We begin by addressing common problems such as back pain and carpal tunnel syndrome, then we deal with issues of safety and injury prevention. We deal with burnout and co-worker conflict. We address time management and anger management. You'll find ways to handle a demanding workload and tips on listening more effectively. There's also a page of stretches you can do in the workplace.

Technology in the workplace is on the increase. We help you cope with some of the health-related challenges posed by routine use of a computer.

The Healthy Consumer

In this section, we give you tips on topics such as how to talk to your doctor, what you can learn from your family's medical history, using home medical testing kits and what you should include in a home first-aid kit. We also discuss the use of common medications, and we provide easy-to-understand descriptions of cold remedies and over-the-counter pain medications.

Do you travel for business or pleasure? This section ends with a comprehensive review of what you need to know before you pack your bags.

Children and Adolescent Health

The major medical conditions likely to affect your child during his or her preteen years are addressed throughout this book. But the book is not a comprehensive resource for every childhood illness. You'll find short segments titled "Kids' Care," which provide information regarding specific concerns. Well-child immunizations are summarized in the Staying Healthy section and many safety tips for children are found in various locations in the book. How to identify and cope with alcohol and tobacco use in teenagers also is discussed. If you have a question about an issue dealing with your child's health, check the index. You'll probably find an entry that can help.

A Few Words About How We Speak

When doctors talk to their patients, doctors understand clearly the message they intend to convey. But sometimes their patients do not. In this book, we use conversational English because it's the way people talk to each other. You won't find many technical terms.

One term you will see is "health care provider." This phrase is used because, in addition to "doctor" and "physician," the term health care provider includes medical personnel such as physician assistants, nurse practitioners and certified nurse-midwives.

About Mayo Clinic

Mayo Clinic evolved from the frontier practice of Dr. William Worrall Mayo and the partnership of his two sons, Drs. William J. and Charles H. Mayo, in the early 1900s. Pressed by the demands of their busy practice in Rochester, Minn., the Mayo brothers invited other doctors to join them, pioneering the private group practice of medicine. Today, with more than 3,000 physicians and scientists at its three major locations in Rochester, Minn., Jacksonville, Fla., and Scottsdale, Ariz., and its regional community-based health care practices, Mayo Clinic is dedicated to providing comprehensive diagnoses, accurate answers and effective treatments.

With this depth of knowledge, experience and expertise, Mayo Clinic occupies an unparalleled position as a health information resource. Since 1983, Mayo Clinic has published reliable health information for millions of consumers through a variety of award-winning newsletters, books and online services. Revenue from the publishing activities supports Mayo Clinic programs, including medical education and research.

Table of Contents

Urgent Care

- CPR
- Choking
- Heart Attack
- Stroke (Brain Attack)
- Poisoning Emergencies
- Severe Bleeding
- Shock
- Allergic Reactions
- Bites and Stings
- Burns
- Cold Weather Problems
- Cuts, Scrapes and Wounds
- Eye Injuries
- Food-Borne Illness
- Heat-Related Problems
- Poisonous Plants
- Tooth Problems
- Trauma

Emergencies don't happen often, but when they do there's not much time to react. To be effective, you must know what to do when a person appears injured, seriously ill or in distress. Your skills may never be needed. However, you could someday save a life.

Take a certified first-aid training course to learn life-saving skills such as CPR, the Heimlich maneuver and dealing with a heart attack, shock and traumatic injury. Check with your local Red Cross, county emergency services, public safety office or the American Heart Association for information on first-aid courses in your community.

CPR

Cardiopulmonary resuscitation (CPR) involves a combination of mouth-to-mouth rescue breathing and chest compression. CPR keeps oxygenated blood flowing to the brain and other vital organs until appropriate medical treatment can restore a normal heart rhythm.

Before starting CPR on an adult, call for emergency help. If you can't leave the scene, have someone else call for medical assistance. (If the victim is an infant or a child, and you are alone, do CPR for two minutes first before calling for help.) Then assess the situation. Is the person conscious or unconscious? If the victim appears unconscious, tap or shake his or her shoulder and ask loudly, "Are you OK?" If the person doesn't respond, think of the ABCs:

A: Airway. Your first action is to open the airway, which may be blocked by the back of the tongue (see steps 1, 2 and 3 below).

B: Breathing. Mouth-to-mouth rescue breathing is the quickest way to get oxygen into a person's lungs (see step 4 below). Take normal breaths before giving rescue breaths. You must perform chest compressions anytime you do rescue breathing.

C: Circulation. Chest compressions replace the heartbeat when it has stopped. Compressions help maintain some blood flow to the brain, lungs and heart (see step 5 on page 3). You must perform rescue breathing anytime you do chest compressions.

The following five steps and illustrations demonstrate the CPR technique.

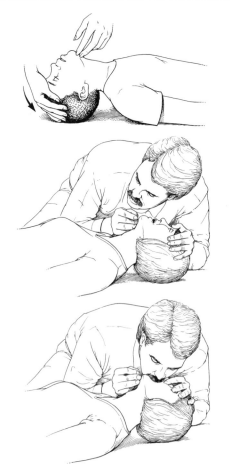

1. *Position the person so you can check for signs of breathing by laying the victim flat on a firm surface.*

2. *Open the person's airway; put your palm on the person's forehead and gently push down. Then with your other hand, gently lift the chin forward to open the airway.*

3. *Take five to 10 seconds (no more than 10 seconds) to determine whether the person is breathing normally by simultaneously listening for breath sounds, feeling for air motion on your cheek and ear, and looking for chest motion.*

4. *If the victim isn't breathing normally, pinch the person's nostrils closed and make a seal around the mouth. Give two full, slow breaths. Each should take about one second. If the victim's chest doesn't rise after the first rescue breath, the airway is probably blocked. Attempt to reopen the airway by tilting the head and lifting the chin, then breathe into the victim's mouth again.*

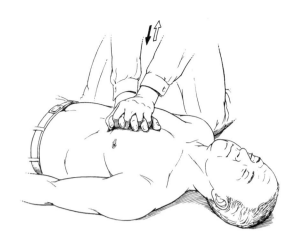

5. *Begin chest compressions. The heel of one hand should be located over the center of the person's chest, in the middle of the breastbone between the nipples. Place the heel of your other hand on top of your first hand. Keep your elbows straight and your shoulders positioned directly above your hands. Push hard straight down on (compress) the chest 1 ½ to 2 inches. Give 30 compressions at a rate of two a second, allowing the chest to re-expand completely after each compression. After 30 compressions, tilt the head back and lift the chin to open the airway. Pinch the nose shut and give two rescue breaths (about one second for each breath). Recheck for signs of normal breathing about every two minutes. Continue CPR until there are signs of breathing or until emergency medical personnel take over.*

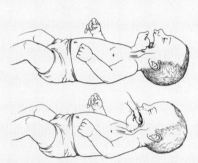

CPR for Infants

First, shout and gently tap the infant on the shoulder to see if the baby responds. If no response in five to 10 seconds (but no more than 10 seconds), place the baby on his or her back on a firm, flat surface. Gently tilt the head back to open the airway (top image above). Look for signs of breathing. Also look into the baby's mouth for food or foreign objects. If visual inspection reveals food or a foreign object, remove it with a sweep of your finger (bottom image above). Be careful not to push the food or object deeper into the child's airway.

To perform CPR, cover the mouth and nose with your mouth. Give two gentle breaths to make the chest rise. Check for signs of breathing, coughing or movement. If there are no signs, put one hand on the infant's forehead to keep the airway open (see image above). Place the tips of two fingers of your other hand on the center of the baby's chest on the breastbone just below the nipple line, then compress the chest $\frac{1}{3}$ to $\frac{1}{2}$ the depth of the chest at least 100 times a minute. Give two breaths for every 30 compressions. If alone, do this for two minutes before calling for emergency medical help.

Using an AED

If you're trained to use an automatic external defibrillator (AED) — a computerized medical device — and one is available, open it, turn it on and follow the voice prompts for operation. If you're in a public place such as an airport or shopping mall, have someone call 911. Have someone else contact security to see if there's an AED and a trained staff person who can help.

People using an AED will also need to do CPR when prompted by the AED. This device has voice prompts, lights and text messages that tell the rescuer what to do. If you're not trained to use an AED but one is available, the 911 operator may be able to guide you in its use. The AED will advise the rescuer when a shock is needed and when to resume CPR.

AEDs are recommended for use on children one year of age and older. Special pediatric pads should be used if available.

Choking

Choking occurs when the respiratory passage in the throat or windpipe is blocked. This situation requires emergency treatment to prevent unconsciousness or death. Choking, heart disease or other conditions may cause the heart and breathing to stop. To save the life of the person, breathing and blood circulation must be restored immediately (see previous section on CPR).

Recognizing and Clearing an Obstructed Airway

Choking is often the result of inadequately chewed food becoming lodged in the throat or windpipe. Most often, solid foods such as meats are the cause.

Commonly, people who are choking have been talking while simultaneously chewing a chunk of meat. False teeth also may set the stage for this problem by interfering with the way food feels in the mouth while it is being chewed. Food cannot be chewed as thoroughly with false teeth as with natural teeth because less chewing pressure is exerted by false teeth.

Panic is an accompanying sensation. The choking victim's face often assumes an expression of fear or terror. At first, he or she may turn purple, the eyes may bulge, and he or she may wheeze or gasp.

If some food "goes down the wrong pipe," the coughing reflex often will resolve the problem. In fact, a person isn't choking if he or she is able to cough freely, has normal skin color and is able to speak. If the cough is more like a gasp and the person is turning blue, the individual is probably choking.

A person who is choking is unable to communicate except by hand motions. Often the hand and arm motions are uncoordinated. It's important to remember that the universal sign for choking is hands clutched to the throat, with thumbs and fingers extended.

If in doubt, ask the choking person whether he or she is choking. If the person nods yes, he or she needs help. A person who is choking is unable to communicate except by hand or head motions. If the person is capable of speech, then the windpipe is not completely blocked and oxygen is reaching the lungs.

The universal sign for choking is a hand clutched to the throat, with thumb and fingers extended. A person who displays this requires emergency treatment and should never be left unattended.

The Heimlich Maneuver

The Heimlich maneuver is the best known method of removing an object from the airway of a person who is choking. You can use it on yourself or someone else. These are the steps:

1. Stand behind the choking person and wrap your arms around his or her waist.

2. Make a fist with one hand and place it slightly above the person's navel.

3. Grasp your fist with the other hand and press hard into

the abdomen with a quick, upward thrust. Repeat this procedure until the object is expelled from the airway or until the person loses consciousness.

If you must perform this maneuver on yourself, position your own fist slightly above your navel. Grasp your fist with your other hand and thrust upward into your abdomen until the object is expelled, or lean forward over the back of a chair to produce this effect.

Heart Attack

If you think you're having a **heart attack**, call for emergency help immediately. Most people who have a heart attack wait two hours or longer after the onset of symptoms before seeking treatment. About 170,000 Americans die each year of a heart attack. Among those who survive, most of the permanent damage to the heart occurs during the first hour.

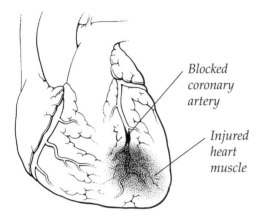

Blocked
coronary
artery

Injured
heart
muscle

A heart attack occurs when arteries supplying your heart with blood and oxygen become blocked. With each passing minute, more tissue is deprived of oxygen and deteriorates or dies. Restoring blood flow within the first hour, when most damage occurs, is critical to survival.

Why Is the First Hour Critical?

A heart attack is injury to heart muscle caused by a loss of blood supply. An attack occurs when arteries supplying your heart with blood and oxygen become blocked.

A blood clot that forms in an artery narrowed by buildup of cholesterol and other fatty deposits usually causes the blockage. Without oxygen, cells are destroyed, causing pain or pressure, and heart function is impaired.

A heart attack is not a static, one-time event. It's a dynamic process that typically evolves over four to six hours. With each passing minute, more tissue is deprived of oxygen and deteriorates or dies.

Minutes Matter

The main way to prevent progressive damage is to treat the condition early with clot-dissolving (thrombolytic) medications or angioplasty. "Clot busters," such as the tissue plasminogen activator, dissolve the clot and restore blood flow, preventing or limiting heart muscle damage. The sooner these medications are started, the more good they do. To be most effective, the medications need to be given within the first 60 to 90 minutes after the onset of heart attack symptoms.

Angioplasty, also called cardiac catheterization, uses balloons or devices called "stents" to unblock the artery. As with clot-dissolving drugs, if angioplasty is delayed beyond 90 minutes, benefits are reduced.

A heart attack can also trigger ventricular fibrillation. This unstable heart rhythm produces an ineffective heartbeat, causing insufficient blood flow to vital organs. Without immediate treatment, ventricular fibrillation can lead to sudden death.

Be Alert to Symptoms

During a heart attack, many people waste precious minutes because they don't recognize symptoms or they deny them. Many people also delay calling for help because they're afraid to risk the embarrassment of a false alarm, or they don't understand the importance of getting to a hospital right away.

A heart attack generally causes **chest pain** for more than 15 minutes. But a heart attack also can be "silent" and have no symptoms.

About half of heart attack victims have warning symptoms hours, days or weeks in advance. The earliest predictor of an attack may be recurrent chest pain that's triggered by exertion and relieved by rest.

The American Heart Association lists the following warning signs of a heart attack. Be aware that you may not have all of them and that symptoms may come and go. If you have diabetes, you may have fewer or more-atypical symptoms.

- Uncomfortable pressure, fullness or squeezing pain in the center of your chest or upper abdomen. The pain may last several minutes or may come and go. It may be triggered by exertion and relieved by rest.
- Discomfort or pain spreading beyond your chest to your shoulders, neck, jaw, teeth, and one or both of your arms.
- Shortness of breath.
- Lightheadedness, dizziness, fainting, sweating or nausea.

Emergency Treatment

In a heart attack emergency, you have to make crucial decisions under stress. Review the steps below so that you can act immediately. If you feel you may be having a heart attack, or that a person with you is having a heart attack, take these steps:

- **Call for emergency medical assistance first.** The 911 operator contacts the emergency medical services (EMS) system. In areas without 911 service, call the emergency medical response system. It's better to call these emergency numbers first. Calling your doctor may take unnecessary time.

  When you call, describe the symptoms, such as severe shortness of breath or chest pain. This ensures a priority dispatch of EMS responders trained in basic and advanced cardiac life support. Many police and fire rescue units also carry portable defibrillators, emergency devices used to help restore normal heart rhythm by delivering electric shocks to the heart. These units may respond before an ambulance.
- **Chew aspirin.** Consider chewing aspirin if your doctor has recommended that you take an aspirin if you think you're having a heart attack. Aspirin inhibits blood clotting, which helps maintain blood flow through a narrowed artery. When taken during a heart attack, aspirin can decrease death rates by about 25 percent. Take a regular-strength aspirin and chew it to speed absorption. *Note:* While aspirin may help reduce blood clotting, call for help first before looking for aspirin.
- **Begin CPR.** If the person is unconscious, a 911 dispatcher may advise you to begin CPR (mouth-to-mouth breathing and chest compression). Even if you're not trained, most dispatchers can instruct you in CPR until help arrives. (See page 2 for more on CPR.)
- **Go to the nearest emergency department.** If there isn't any 911 service available, get to the nearest facility that's staffed with doctors trained to provide emergency care.

  Clot-dissolving drugs and angioplasty improve your chances of surviving a heart attack once treatment begins. But successful treatment begins early. Recognize symptoms and act quickly.

Stroke (Brain Attack)

In the United States, <u>stroke</u> is the third-leading cause of death and the leading cause of adult disability. Only cardiovascular disease and cancer cause more annual deaths. Every year, about 700,000 Americans have a stroke. About 160,000 of them die. Among adults over age 55, the lifetime risk of stroke is greater than one in six.

You can reduce your chances of having a stroke by recognizing and changing certain lifestyle habits. If you're at high risk, drugs such as aspirin and a surgical procedure called carotid endarterectomy (kuh-ROT-id end-ahr-tur-EK-tuh-me) may help prevent a major stroke.

If you have a stroke, early treatment may minimize damage to your brain and subsequent disability. About 50 percent to 70 percent of stroke survivors regain functional independence, but 15 percent to 30 percent become permanently disabled.

A 'Brain Attack'

A stroke is a "brain attack." Seek immediate medical assistance, just as you would for a heart attack. Every minute counts. The longer a stroke goes untreated, the greater the damage and potential disability. Success of treatment may depend on how soon care is given.

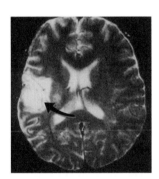

In this magnetic resonance imaging (MRI) scan, the arrow points to an area of brain tissue damaged by a stroke.

Your brain has 100 billion nerve cells and trillions of nerve connections. Although it's only 2 percent of your body weight, it uses approximately 25 percent of your body's oxygen and other nutrients. Because your brain can't store these nutrients as muscles can, it requires a constant flow of blood to keep working properly.

A stroke occurs when this blood supply is reduced and brain tissue is starved of blood. Within four minutes of being deprived of oxygen and essential nutrients, brain cells begin to die.

There are two main types of stroke:

- **Ischemic (is-KEM-ik).** About 80 percent of strokes are caused by buildup of cholesterol-containing fatty deposits called plaques (atherosclerosis). Growth of plaques roughen the inside of arteries. The irregular surface can cause turbulent blood flow around the buildup — like a boulder in a rushing stream — and trigger development of a clot. If the clot breaks loose, it can block blood flow to the brain.

  A transient ischemic attack (TIA) temporarily and, usually briefly, causes symptoms stemming from the disruption in blood supply to the brain. (For symptoms, see page 8.) During a TIA, your body may release enzymes that dissolve the clot quickly and restore blood flow.

- **Hemorrhagic (hem-uh-RAJ-ik).** This type of stroke occurs when a blood vessel in your brain leaks or ruptures. Blood from the hemorrhage spills into the surrounding brain tissue, causing damage. Brain cells beyond the leak or rupture are deprived of blood and also are damaged. The most common cause of a hemorrhagic stroke is high blood pressure (hypertension).

  Another cause of a hemorrhagic stroke is an aneurysm. This ballooning from a weak spot in a blood vessel wall develops with advancing age. Some aneurysms may form as a result of a genetic predisposition.

  Hemorrhagic strokes are less common than ischemic strokes — but more often fatal. Approximately 19 percent of people who have a hemorrhagic stroke die within 30 days, compared with about 7 percent for ischemic strokes. Strokes that occur in young adults are more likely to be hemorrhagic.

Can You Prevent a Stroke?

Although you can't change some risk factors for stroke, other factors are manageable with medications and changes in lifestyle. However, because some of these risk factors don't always cause symptoms, you may not know you have them.

Risk factors that can be controlled are described below:

- **High blood pressure.** People with high blood pressure (hypertension) have a four to six times greater risk of stroke than do people without high blood pressure. High blood pressure is defined as a systolic pressure of 140 millimeters of mercury (mm Hg) or higher or a diastolic pressure of 90 mm Hg or higher (see page 183).
- **Cigarette smoking.** Smoking almost doubles a person's risk of ischemic stroke and increases a person's risk of hemorrhagic stroke by up to 4 percent.
- **Cardiovascular disease.** In addition to atherosclerosis, heart conditions such as congestive heart failure, a previous heart attack, atrial fibrillation and heart valve disease or valve replacement increase your risk of stroke.
- **TIA.** Most TIAs last a few minutes, but some last up to 24 hours, and cause only slight symptoms. About one-third of people who have a stroke had one or more previous TIAs. The more frequent the TIAs, the greater the possibility of a stroke.
- **Diabetes.** People with diabetes have three times the risk of stroke compared with people without diabetes.
- **Undesirable blood cholesterol levels.** High blood levels of low-density lipoprotein (LDL) cholesterol increase your risk of atherosclerosis. In contrast, high levels of high-density lipoprotein (HDL) cholesterol are protective because they may prevent accumulation of plaques.

Know the Warning Signs

If you notice one or more of these signs, get emergency medical care immediately. They may be signaling a possible stroke or TIA:

- Sudden weakness or numbness in your face, arm or leg on one side of your body
- Sudden dimness, blurring or loss of vision, particularly in one eye
- Loss of speech, or trouble talking or understanding speech
- Sudden, severe headache — a "bolt out of the blue" — with no apparent cause
- Unexplained dizziness, unsteadiness or a sudden fall, especially if accompanied by any of the other symptoms

Some Risk Factors Are Beyond Your Control

You can't change these risk factors for stroke. But knowing you're at risk can motivate you to change your lifestyle to reduce your risk.

- **Family history.** Your risk is greater if one of your parents, a brother or a sister has had a stroke or TIA. It's not clear whether the in-creased risk is genetic or due to family lifestyles.
- **Age.** Generally, your risk of stroke increases as you get older.

- **Sex.** Men have a 1.25 times higher risk of stroke than women do. But more women die of stroke. That's because women are generally older than men when they have their strokes.
- **Race.** Blacks are more likely to have a stroke than are other groups. The increase is partly because of their greater risk of high blood pressure and diabetes.

Poisoning Emergencies

Many conditions mimic the symptoms of poisoning, including seizures and insulin reactions. If there's no indication of poisoning, don't treat the person for poisoning, but call the poison information hot line (800) 222-1222 or emergency medical help.

Call the poison control center immediately, even if the person looks and feels fine. Don't wait to see if symptoms arise before calling. Many toxins have delayed life-threatening effects. Early treatment may be important.

Children under age 5 are often exposed to poisons because they're curious. If infants and toddlers dwell in or visit your home:
- Keep potential poisons in cabinets located up high, or with safety locks.
- Keep the poison information line phone number (800) 222-1222 handy.

Emergency Treatment

Swallowed poison
Remove anything remaining in the person's mouth. Unless the victim is unconscious, having a seizure, or can't swallow, give about 2 ounces of water to drink. Don't administer ipecac syrup or do anything to induce vomiting. The American Academy of Pediatrics has advised against using ipecac syrup saying there's no good evidence of effectiveness and that it can do more harm than good.

Poison in the eye
Gently flush the eye for 10 minutes using slightly warm water. Pour a stream of water from a clean glass held about three inches above the eye.

Poison on the skin
Remove any contaminated clothing. Rinse the skin with large amounts of water for 10 minutes.

Inhaled poison
Get to fresh air as soon as possible. Avoid breathing the fumes.

If the poisoned person is unconscious, confused or having seizures or trouble breathing, immediately call emergency medical help (911). If the person is going to the hospital emergency department, bring the container or any information about the poison with you.

Medications as Poisons

Lifesaving medications can be killers. Overdoses of seemingly harmless medications such as aspirin and acetaminophen take many lives each year. Numerous other over-the-counter drugs are dangerous when taken in large doses.

Severe Bleeding

To stop a serious bleeding injury, follow these steps:

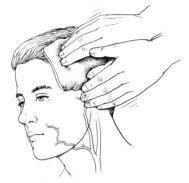

To stop bleeding, apply pressure directly to the wound using gauze or a clean cloth.

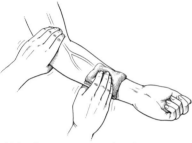

If bleeding continues despite pressure applied directly to the wound, maintain pressure and also apply pressure to the nearest major artery.

1. Lay the affected person down. If possible, the person's head should be slightly lower than the trunk, or the legs should be elevated. This position reduces the chances of fainting by increasing blood flow to the brain. If possible, elevate the site of bleeding.
2. Remove any obvious debris or dirt from the wound. Don't remove any objects pierced into the victim. Don't probe the wound or attempt to clean it at this point. Your principal concern is to stop the loss of blood.
3. Apply pressure directly on the wound with a sterile bandage, clean cloth or even a piece of clothing. If nothing else is available, use your hand.
4. Maintain pressure until the bleeding stops. When it does, bind the wound dressing tightly with adhesive tape or a bandage. If none is available, use a piece of clean clothing.
5. If the bleeding continues and seeps through the gauze or other material you're holding on the wound, don't remove it. Rather, add more absorbent material on top of it.
6. If the bleeding doesn't stop with direct pressure, you may need to apply pressure to the major artery that delivers blood to the area of the wound. In the case of a wound on the hand or lower arm, for example, squeeze the main artery in the upper arm against the bone. Keep your fingers flat; with the other hand, continue to exert pressure on the wound itself.
7. Immobilize the injured body part once the bleeding has been stopped. Leave the bandages in place and get the injured person to the emergency room as soon as possible.

Detecting Internal Bleeding

In the event of a traumatic injury, such as an automobile crash or fall, internal bleeding may not be immediately apparent. Look for the following signs:

- Bleeding from the ears, nose, rectum or vagina, or the vomiting or coughing up of blood
- Bruising on the neck, chest or abdomen
- Wounds that have penetrated the skull, chest or abdomen
- Abdominal tenderness, perhaps accompanied by hardness or spasm of the abdominal muscles
- Fracture

Internal bleeding may produce shock. The volume of blood in the body becomes inadequate, and the person may feel weak, thirsty and anxious. The skin may feel cool. Other symptoms of shock that may indicate internal bleeding include shallow and slow breathing, a rapid and weak pulse, trembling and restlessness. The person may faint and lose consciousness when standing or seated but recovers when allowed to lie down.

If you suspect internal bleeding, request emergency assistance. Treat the person for shock (see page 11). Keep the person lying quietly and comfortably. Loosen clothing but don't give the person anything to eat or drink.

Internal bleeding, especially in the abdomen, head or chest, is extremely serious and can be life-threatening. Blood loss can be considerable, even if there's no evident external bleeding.

Shock

Shock may result from trauma, heat, allergic reaction, severe infection, poisoning or other causes. Various symptoms appear in a person experiencing shock:

- The skin may appear pale or gray. It's cool and clammy.
- The pulse is weak and rapid, and breathing is slow and shallow. Blood pressure is reduced.
- The eyes lack luster and seem to stare. Sometimes the pupils are dilated.
- The person may be conscious or unconscious. If conscious, the person may feel faint or be very weak or confused. Shock sometimes causes a person to become overly excited and anxious.

Even if a person seems normal after an injury, take precautions and treat the person for shock by following these steps:

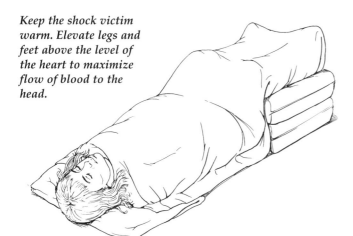

Keep the shock victim warm. Elevate legs and feet above the level of the heart to maximize flow of blood to the head.

1. Get the person to lie flat on his or her back. Keep the person from moving unnecessarily. Observe for the signs of shock noted above.
2. Keep the person warm and comfortable. Loosen tight clothing and cover the person with a blanket. Don't give the person anything to drink.
3. If the person is vomiting or bleeding from the mouth, place the person on his or her side to prevent choking.
4. Treat any injuries (such as bleeding or broken bones) appropriately.
5. Summon emergency medical assistance immediately.

Anaphylaxis Can Be Life-Threatening

The most severe allergic response is called **anaphylaxis**. It can produce shock and be life-threatening. Although it is infrequent, each year several hundred Americans die of the reaction.

The anaphylactic response occurs rapidly. Almost any allergen can cause the response, including insect venoms, pollens, latex, certain foods and drugs. Some people have anaphylactic reactions of unknown cause.

If you're extremely sensitive, you may notice severe hives and severe swelling of your eyes or lips or inside your throat that causes difficulty with breathing and shock. Dizziness, mental confusion, abdominal cramping, nausea or vomiting also may accompany a severe reaction.

Many people who know their specific allergies carry medication with them as an antidote to an allergic reaction. Epinephrine (adrenaline) is the most commonly used drug. The effects of the medication are only temporary, however, and you must seek further medical attention immediately.

If you observe an allergic reaction with signs of anaphylaxis, call emergency medical assistance. Check to see if the person is carrying special medication (to inhale, swallow or inject) to counter the effects of the allergic attack. Have the person lie flat on his or her back. If there's vomiting or bleeding from the mouth, turn the person on his or her side to prevent choking. Loosen tight clothing. Perform CPR as a lifesaving measure if there's no breathing (see pages 2 and 3).

Allergic Reactions

An allergy is a reaction to a foreign substance (allergen) by the body's immune system. The reaction may take many forms, including rashes, nasal congestion, asthma and, rarely, shock or death. Common allergens include pollen (see Respiratory Allergies, page 158) and insect venom (see Bites, page 14). This section covers food and drug allergies.

■ Food Allergies

Food allergies may be the most misunderstood of all allergies. About one in three Americans believe they're allergic to specific foods. However, only about 2 percent of adults and up to 8 percent of children have true food allergies. Most children eventually outgrow the allergy.

Ninety percent of food allergies are caused by certain proteins in cow's milk, eggs, peanuts, wheat, soy, fish, shellfish and tree nuts. Other foods that can cause problems include berries, corn, beans and gum arabic (a thickener used in processed foods). Chocolate, long thought to cause allergies (particularly among children), is actually seldom a cause.

Signs and symptoms of food allergies include the following:
- Abdominal pain, diarrhea, nausea or vomiting
- Hives or swelling of the lips, eyes, face, tongue or throat (see page 123)
- Fainting
- Nasal congestion and asthma

Emergency Treatment
- Avoidance is the best way to prevent an allergic reaction.
- Read labels carefully and look for substances derived from foods to which you're allergic. Example: Whey and casein are milk products used as additives.
- When choosing substitute foods, be careful to select foods that provide the necessary replacement nutrients.
- If you have had a severe reaction, wear an alert bracelet or necklace, available in most drugstores. Ask your doctor about carrying emergency medications, such as self-injectable epinephrine (EpiPen), and know when and how to use it.
- Learn rescue techniques, and teach them to family members and friends.

Medical Help

Food allergies can be diagnosed through a careful process that includes the following five steps:

1. History of your symptoms, including when they occur, which foods cause problems and the amount of food needed to trigger symptoms.
2. Food diary to track eating habits, symptoms and medication use.
3. Physical examination.
4. Testing. Skin prick tests using food extracts and a blood test that measures an antibody called immunoglobulin E (IgE) can help. Neither test is 100 percent accurate, and may be more helpful in determining foods to which you're not allergic.
5. Food elimination-trials are controlled challenges to your system and are considered the gold-standard food allergy test. However, food challenges shouldn't be used if you have a severe reaction to a particular food.

For mild reactions, your doctor may prescribe antihistamines or skin creams.

See back cover for online resource

| Caution | Severe reactions such as anaphylaxis (see page 11) or acute asthma can be life-threatening. Such reactions are rare. Most reactions are limited to rashes and hives. However, this doesn't mean they can be ignored. |

| Kids' Care | Food allergies are more common in children than in adults. As the digestive system matures, it's less apt to allow absorption of foods that trigger allergies. Children typically outgrow allergies to milk, eggs, wheat and soy. Severe allergies and those due to peanuts, tree nuts, fish and shellfish are more likely to be lifelong. |

■ Drug Allergies

If you have a drug allergy, carry appropriate identification at all times. Drug-alert necklaces and bracelets are available at drugstores.

Almost any drug can cause an adverse reaction in some people. Reactions to most drugs aren't common, but they can range from merely irritating to life-threatening. Some reactions (such as rashes) are true allergic responses. Most, however, are side effects of a particular drug, typified by dry mouth or fatigue. Some are toxic effects of the drugs, such as liver damage. Still other reactions are poorly understood. Your doctor will determine the nature of the reactions and what to do about them.

Penicillin and its relatives are responsible for many drug allergy reactions, ranging from mild rashes to hives to immediate anaphylaxis. Most reactions are minor rashes.

Other drugs most likely to cause reactions include sulfas, barbiturates and anticonvulsants. These are all common, effective, useful medications. Reactions occur in a minority of people. If you're taking one of them and not having problems, don't stop using it. In addition, contrast dyes used in some X-ray studies to help outline major organs may cause an allergic reaction.

Signs and symptoms of allergic reactions to drugs include the following:
● Rash, hives, generalized itching
● Wheezing and difficulty breathing
● Shock

| Self-Care | ● Avoid drugs that cause an allergic response.
● If you have a severe reaction, learn the names of related drugs.
● Wear a drug-alert necklace or bracelet to indicate your allergy.
● Alert physicians of your sensitivity before treatment.
● Report possible reactions to your doctor. Reactions can occur days after stopping use of a drug.
● Ask your doctor for emergency medication. |

| Medical Help | See your doctor if you develop a rash, itching, hives or if you suspect other symptoms you're having might be due to a drug you're taking. |

Bites and Stings

■ Animal Bites

Domestic pets cause most animal bites. Dogs are more likely to bite than cats. But cat bites are more likely to cause infection, and should be assessed by a doctor.

Self-Care

- If the bite only breaks the skin, treat it as a minor wound. Wash the wound thoroughly with soap and water. Apply an antiseptic cream to prevent infection, and cover the wound with a clean bandage.
- Establish whether you have had a tetanus shot within the past five years. If not, get a booster shot with any bite that breaks the skin.
- Report suspicious bites to local health authorities.
- Follow veterinary guidelines for immunization of your pets.

Medical Help

If the bite creates a deep puncture or the skin is badly torn and bleeding, apply pressure to stop the bleeding and see your doctor. If you haven't had a recent tetanus shot, seek medical care. Watch for signs of infection. Swelling, redness around the wound or in a red streak extending from the site, pus draining from the wound, or pain should be reported immediately to your doctor.

The Risk of Rabies

Bats, foxes, raccoons and other wild animals may carry rabies, but so can dogs, especially if they run in the woods. Farm animals, especially cows, may carry rabies, although farm animals rarely transmit rabies to humans.

Rabies is a virus that affects the brain. Transmitted to humans by saliva from the bite of an infected animal, the rabies virus has an incubation period (the time from a bite until symptoms appear) of three to seven weeks.

Once the incubation period is over, a tingling sensation usually develops at the site of the bite. As the virus spreads, foaming at the mouth may occur because of difficulty with swallowing. Uncontrolled irritability and confusion may follow, alternating with periods of calm.

In the event of a bite by a domestic dog, cat or ferret, the animal should be confined and observed for seven to 10 days. Contact a veterinarian if the animal shows any sign of sickness. If a wild animal has bitten you, it should be killed and tested for rabies.

■ Human Bites

There are two kinds of human bites. The first is what is usually thought of as a "true" bite — an injury that results from flesh being caught between the teeth. The second kind, called a "fight bite," occurs when a person is cut on the knuckles by an opponent's teeth. Treatment is the same in both cases. Human bites are dangerous because of the risk of infection. The human mouth is a breeding ground for bacteria.

Self-Care

- Apply pressure to stop bleeding, wash the wound thoroughly with soap and water, and bandage the wound. Then visit an emergency room. Your health care provider may prescribe antibiotics to prevent infection or update your tetanus shot if you haven't had one for more than five years.

■ Snakebites

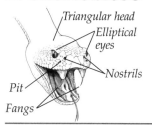

Triangular head
Elliptical eyes
Nostrils
Pit
Fangs

Most snakes aren't venomous. However, because a few are (including rattlesnakes, coral snakes, water moccasins and copperheads), avoid picking up or playing with any snake unless you're properly trained.

If you're bitten by a snake, it's important to determine whether the snake is venomous. Most venomous snakes have slit-like (elliptical) eyes. Their heads are triangular, with a depression or pit midway between the eyes and nostrils.

Self-Care

- If the snake isn't venomous, wash the bite thoroughly, cover it with an antiseptic cream and bandage it. In general, a snakebite is more scary than dangerous.
- Check on the date of your last tetanus shot. If it has been more than five years and the bite broke the skin, get a tetanus booster.

Medical Help

If you suspect that the snake is venomous, seek emergency medical assistance immediately. Don't cut the wound or attempt to remove the venom. Don't use a tourniquet or apply ice. Immobilize the bitten arm or leg, elevate it if possible, and try to stay as calm as possible until medical help arrives.

■ Insect Bites and Stings

Some bites or stings cause little more than an itching or stinging sensation and mild swelling that disappears within a day or so. But each year up to 5 percent of the population develops severe allergic reactions to insect venom. Bees, wasps, hornets, yellow jackets and fire ants are the most troublesome. Mosquitoes, ticks, biting flies and some spiders also cause problems, but these are generally milder reactions.

Symptoms of an allergic reaction usually appear within a few minutes after the sting or bite occurs. But some take hours or even days to appear. If you're mildly sensitive to the venom, hives, itchy eyes, pain and intense itching around the site of the sting or bite are common. With a delayed reaction, you may experience fever, painful joints, hives and swollen glands.

Severe allergic reactions can be life-threatening. You may have severe hives and swelling of your eyes, lips or inside your throat; the swelling of the throat can cause breathing difficulty. Dizziness, mental confusion, abdominal cramping, nausea, vomiting or fainting also may accompany a severe reaction.

West Nile virus is carried by mosquitoes and can cause illness. In severe cases, signs and symptoms include severe headache, confusion and light sensitivity. Severe infection may cause inflammation of the brain and membranes and fluid surrounding the brain. Such symptoms require prompt medical attention. To reduce your risk, avoid unnecessary outdoor activity when mosquitoes are most active, such as at dawn, dusk and early evening. In addition, wear long-sleeved shirts and long pants when outdoors, and use mosquito repellent.

Self-Care

- Scrape or brush off the stinger with a straight-edged object. Don't try to pull out the stinger with a tweezers or your fingers. This may release more venom.
- To reduce pain and swelling, apply ice or a cold pack.
- Apply 0.5 or 1 percent hydrocortisone cream, calamine lotion or a baking soda paste to the bite or sting several times daily until your symptoms subside.
- Take an antihistamine (Benadryl, Chlor-Trimeton, others).

If you've experienced a severe reaction in the past, obtain a medical-alert bracelet and always carry an allergy kit containing epinephrine.

Medical Help

If your reaction to an insect bite is severe (shortness of breath, tongue or throat swelling, hives), see your doctor or go to the emergency room immediately.

The most severe allergic reactions to bee stings can be life-threatening. If you experience any breathing problems, swelling of the lips or throat, faintness, confusion, rapid heartbeat or hives after a sting, seek emergency care. Less-severe allergic reactions include nausea, intestinal cramps, diarrhea or swelling larger than 2 inches in diameter at the site. See your doctor promptly if you experience any of these symptoms.

Your doctor may prescribe shots that can help desensitize your body to insect venom, and an emergency kit containing antihistamine tablets and a syringe filled with epinephrine (adrenaline). Pressure injector units are available that deliver a pre-measured dose. Keep the medicine fresh. Regularly check its shelf life.

■ Spider Bites

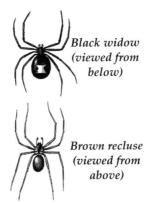

Black widow (viewed from below)

Brown recluse (viewed from above)

Only a few spiders are dangerous to humans. Two are the black widow (*Latrodectus mactans*), known for the red hourglass marking on its belly, and the brown recluse (*Loxosceles reclusa*), with its violin-shaped marking on its top.

Both prefer warm climates and dark, dry places where insects are plentiful. They often live in closets, drawers and outdoor toilets. Signs and symptoms of a black widow bite include muscle spasms, nausea and vomiting, swelling and redness around the bite, headache, dizziness and confusion. A brown recluse bite can cause a severe reaction at the site of the bite. Other symptoms include mild fever, rash, nausea and blood in the urine.

If bitten, seek emergency care immediately. In the meantime, wash the bite with soap and water and apply a cloth dampened with cold water or filled with ice. If the bite is on a limb, you may slow the venom's spread by placing a snug bandage above the bite and applying ice.

■ Tick Bites

By and large, ticks are harmless, but they can be a threat to human health. Some ticks carry infections, and their bite can transmit bacteria that cause illnesses such as **Lyme disease** (caused by the deer tick, see below) or Rocky Mountain spotted fever. Your risk of contracting one of these diseases depends on what part of the United States you live in, how much time you spend in wooded areas and how well you protect yourself.

Self-Care

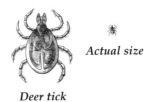

Actual size

Deer tick

Actual size

Wood tick

- When walking in wooded or grassy areas, wear shoes, long pants tucked into socks and long-sleeved shirts. Avoid low bushes and long grass.
- Tick-proof your yard by clearing brush and leaves; keep woodpiles in sunny areas.
- Check yourself and your pets often for ticks after being in wooded or grassy areas. Showering immediately after leaving these areas is a good idea, because ticks often remain on your skin for many hours before biting.
- Insect repellents often repel ticks. Use products containing DEET or permethrin. Be sure to follow label precautions.
- If you find a tick, remove it promptly with tweezers by gently grasping it near its head or mouth. Don't squeeze or crush the tick, but pull carefully and steadily. Once you have the entire tick removed, apply antiseptic to the bite area.
- If you've developed a rash or are sick after a tick bite, bring the tick to your doctor's office.
- When you discard a tick, bury, burn or flush it.

See back cover for online resource

Burns

Burns can be caused by fire, the sun, chemicals, hot liquids or objects, steam, electricity and other means. They can be minor medical problems or life-threatening emergencies.

Burn Classifications

Distinguishing a minor burn from a more serious burn involves determining the degree of damage to the tissues of the body. The following three classifications and illustrations will help determine your response.

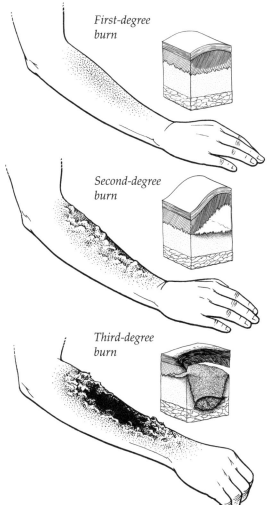

First-degree burn

Second-degree burn

Third-degree burn

First-Degree

The least serious burns are those in which only the outer layer of skin (epidermis) is burned. The skin is usually reddened, and there may be swelling and pain, but the outer layer of skin hasn't been burned through. Unless such a burn involves substantial portions of the hands, feet, face, groin, buttocks or a major joint, it may be treated as a minor burn with the self-care remedies listed on page 18. Chemical burns may require additional follow-up. If the burn was caused by exposure to the sun, see Sunburn, page 19.

Second-Degree

When the first layer of skin has been burned through and the second layer of skin (dermis) also is burned, the injury is termed a second-degree burn. Blisters develop, and the skin takes on an intensely reddened appearance and becomes splotchy. Severe pain and swelling are accompanying symptoms.

If a second-degree burn is limited to an area no larger than 2 to 3 inches in diameter, follow the home remedies listed on page 18. If the burned area of the skin is larger, or if the burn is on the hands, feet, face, groin, buttocks or a major joint, seek urgent care immediately.

Third-Degree

The most serious burns involve all layers of the skin. Fat, nerves, muscles and even bones may be affected. Usually some areas are charred black or appear a dry white. There may be severe pain or, if nerve damage is substantial, no pain at all. It's important to take immediate action in all cases of third-degree burns.

Emergency Treatment: All Major Burns

Seek emergency medical treatment immediately for major burns. Until an emergency unit arrives, follow these steps:
- **Don't remove burned clothing,** but do make sure that the victim is no longer in contact with smoldering materials.
- **Make certain that the burn victim is breathing.**
- **Cover the area of the burn** with a cool, moist sterile bandage or with a clean cloth.

Self-Care: **Minor Burns Only**	For minor burns, including second-degree burns limited to an area no larger than 2 to 3 inches in diameter, take the following action: ● **Cool the burn.** Hold the burned area under cold running water for 15 minutes. If this step is impractical, immerse the burn in cold water or cool it with cold compresses. Cooling the burn reduces swelling by carrying heat away from the skin. ● **Consider a lotion.** Once a burn is completely cooled, a lotion, such as one that contains aloe vera, or moisturizer prevents drying and increases your comfort. For sunburn, try 1 percent hydrocortisone cream or an anesthetic cream. ● **Bandage a burn.** Cover the burn with a sterile gauze bandage. (Fluffy cotton may be irritating.) Wrap it loosely to avoid putting pressure on burned skin. Bandaging keeps air off the area, reduces pain and protects blistered skin. ● **Take over-the-counter pain relievers** (see page 258). ● **Watch for signs of infection.** Minor burns will usually heal in about one to two weeks without further treatment, but watch for indications of infection.
Caution	**Don't use ice.** Putting ice directly on a burn can cause frostbite and further damage your skin. **Don't break blisters.** Fluid-filled blisters protect against infection. If blisters break, wash the area with mild soap and water, then apply an antibiotic ointment and a gauze bandage. Clean and change dressings daily.

■ Chemical Burns

Self-Care	● **Make sure the cause of the burn has been removed.** Flush the chemicals off the skin surface with cool running water for 20 minutes or more. If the burning chemical is a powder-like substance such as lime, brush it off your skin before flushing. ● **Treat the person for shock (see page 11).** Symptoms include fainting, pale complexion or breathing in a notably shallow fashion. ● **Remove clothing or jewelry** that has been contaminated by the chemical. ● **Wrap the burned area** with a dry, sterile dressing (if possible) or a clean cloth. ● **Rewash the burn** for several more minutes if the victim complains of increased burning after the initial washing. **Prevention** ● When using chemicals, always wear protective eyewear and clothing. ● Know about the chemicals you use. ● At work, read appropriate Material Safety Data Sheets, or call your local poison control center listed in your telephone book to learn more about the substance.
Medical Help	Minor chemical burns usually heal without further treatment. However, seek emergency medical assistance (1) if the chemical burned through the first layer of skin and the resulting second-degree burn covers an area more than 2 to 3 inches in diameter or (2) if the chemical burn occurred on the hands, feet, face, groin, buttocks or a major joint. If you're unsure if a given compound is toxic, call a poison control center.
Caution	Common household cleaning products, particularly those that contain ammonia or bleach, and garden chemicals can cause serious harm to the eyes or skin. Read labels. They contain instructions for proper use and treatment recommendations.

Sunburn

Although the sun provides a welcome change from gray winter months, it can damage your skin and increase your risk of skin cancer. Symptoms of sunburn usually appear within a few hours after exposure, bringing pain, redness, swelling and occasional blistering. A sunburn can also cause headache, fever and fatigue.

Self-Care

- Take a cool bath or shower. Adding $\frac{1}{2}$ cup of cornstarch, oatmeal or baking soda to your bath may provide some relief.
- Leave water blisters intact to speed healing and avoid infection. If they burst on their own, apply an antibacterial ointment on the open areas.
- Take an over-the-counter anti-inflammatory pain reliever, such as ibuprofen or aspirin. Not only will they help relieve pain but they can lessen the extent of the damage (see page 258).
- Avoid products containing benzocaine (an anesthetic) because they can cause allergic reactions in many people.

Prevention

- Try to avoid being outside from 10 a.m. to 3 p.m. when the sun's ultraviolet (UV) radiation is at its peak. Cover exposed areas, wear a broad-brimmed hat and use a sunscreen with a sun protection factor (SPF) of at least 15.
- Protect your eyes. Sunglasses that block 95 percent of UV radiation are adequate. You may need lenses that block 99 percent if you spend long hours in the sun, have had cataract surgery or are taking medication that increases your sensitivity to UV radiation.

Medical Help

If your sunburn begins to blister or you feel ill, see your physician. Oral cortisone such as prednisone is occasionally helpful.

Caution

A lifetime of overexposure to the sun's UV radiation can damage your skin and increase your risk of skin cancer. If you have severe sunburn or immediate complications (rash, itching or fever), contact your health care provider. Sunburn may also be accompanied by heat illness, such as heatstroke.

Electrical Burns

Any electrical burn should be examined by a doctor. A burn may appear minor, but the damage can extend into deep tissues. A heart rhythm disturbance, cardiac arrest or other internal damage can occur if the amount of electrical current that passed through the body was large. Sometimes the jolt of electricity can cause a person to be thrown or to fall, causing fractures or other injuries. If the person who has been burned is in pain, is confused, or is experiencing changes in breathing, heartbeat or consciousness, call for emergency medical assistance.

While waiting for medical help:
1. Don't touch the person. He or she may still be in contact with the electrical source.
2. Turn off the source of electricity. If that's not possible, move the source away from the person with a nonconducting object made of wood, cardboard or plastic.
3. Check for breathing or movement. If absent begin cardiopulmonary resuscitation (CPR) immediately.
4. Prevent shock. Have the person lie down flat.

Cold Weather Problems

■ Frostbite

Cover your face if you feel the effects of frostbite.

Frostbite can affect any area of your body. Your hands, feet, nose and ears are most susceptible because they are small and often exposed.

In subfreezing temperatures, the tiny blood vessels in your skin tighten, reducing the flow of blood and oxygen to the tissues. Eventually, cells are destroyed.

The first sign of frostbite may be a slightly painful, tingling sensation. This often is followed by numbness. Your skin may be deathly pale and feel hard, cold and numb. Frostbite can damage deep layers of tissue. As deeper layers of tissue freeze, blisters often form. Blistering usually occurs over one to two days.

People with "hardening of the arteries" (atherosclerosis) or who are taking certain medications may be more susceptible to frostbite.

Self-Care

- Carefully and gently rewarm frostbitten areas. Get out of the cold, if possible. If you're outside, place your hands directly on the skin of warmer areas of your body. Warm your hands by tucking them into your armpits. If your nose, ears or face is frostbitten, warm the area by covering it with your warm hands (but try to keep them protected).
- If possible, immerse your hands or feet in water that's slightly above normal body temperature (100 to 105 F) or that feels warm to someone else.
- Don't rub the affected area. Never rub snow on frostbitten skin.
- Don't smoke cigarettes. Nicotine causes your blood vessels to constrict and may limit circulation.
- If your feet are frostbitten, elevate them after rewarming.
- Don't use direct heat (such as heating pads).
- Don't rewarm an affected area if there's a chance that it'll refreeze.

Follow-Up

Frostbitten areas will turn red and throb, or they'll burn with pain as they thaw. Even with mild frostbite, normal sensation may not return immediately. A nonprescription anti-inflammatory medication, such as ibuprofen, will help with pain and may lessen the damage. When frostbite is severe, the area will probably remain numb until it heals completely. Healing can take months, and the damage to your skin can permanently change your sense of touch. In severe cases, in which infection is present after the affected area has been rewarmed, antibiotics may be necessary. Bed rest and physical therapy may be appropriate. Don't smoke cigarettes during recovery. Once you've had frostbite — no matter how mild — you're more likely to have it again.

Emergency Treatment

If numbness remains during rewarming, you develop blisters or the damage appears severe, seek medical care. A person with frostbite on the extremities also may have hypothermia (see page 21).

Kids' Care

Watch for signs of chilling or cold injury while your child is outside. Watch for wet chin straps on caps or snowsuits because the skin under the strap can easily freeze. Teach your child to avoid touching cold metal with bare hands and licking cold metal objects.

How to Prevent Cold Weather Injuries

- **Stay dry.** Your body loses heat faster when your skin is dampened by rain, snow or perspiration.
- **Protect yourself from the wind.** Wind robs more heat from your body than does cold air alone. Exposed skin is particularly affected by wind.
- **Wear clothes that insulate, shield and breathe.** Layers of light, loosefitting clothing trap air for effective insulation. As an outer layer, wear something that's water repellent and wind-proof.

- **Cover your head, neck and face.** Wear two pairs of socks and boots tall enough to cover your ankles. Mittens protect your hands better than do gloves.
- **Rewarm yourself.** If a part of your body becomes so cold that it starts to feel numb, rewarm it before continuing your activity.
- **Don't touch metal with bare skin.** Cold metal can absorb heat quickly.
- **Plan for trips and outdoor activities.** Carry emergency equipment (see page 231).

■ Hypothermia

Under most conditions, your body maintains a healthy temperature. But when it's exposed for prolonged periods to cold temperatures or a cool, damp environment, its control mechanisms may fail to keep your body temperature normal. When more heat is lost than your body can generate, **hypothermia** can result. Wet or damp clothing can increase your chances of hypothermia.

Falling overboard from a boat into cold water is a common cause of hypothermia. An uncovered head or inadequate clothing in winter is another frequent cause.

The key symptom of hypothermia is a body temperature that drops to less than 94 F. Signs include shivering, slurred speech, an abnormally slow rate of breathing, skin that is cold and pale, a loss of coordination and feelings of tiredness, lethargy or apathy. The onset of symptoms is usually slow; there's likely to be a gradual loss of mental acuity and physical ability. The person experiencing hypothermia, in fact, may be unaware that he or she is in a state requiring emergency medical treatment.

Older adults, the very young and very lean people are at particular risk. Other conditions that may predispose you to hypothermia are malnutrition, heart disease, underactive thyroid, certain medications and excessive consumption of alcohol.

Emergency Treatment
- After getting the person out of the cold, change the victim into warm, dry clothing. If going indoors isn't possible, the person needs to be out of the wind, have the head covered and be insulated from the cold ground.
- Seek emergency medical assistance. While waiting for help to arrive, monitor the person's breathing and pulse. If either has stopped or seems dangerously slow or shallow, start CPR immediately (see page 2).
- In extreme cases, once the victim has arrived at a medical center, blood rewarming, similar to the procedure in a heart bypass machine, is sometimes used to restore normal body temperature quickly.
- If emergency care isn't available, warm the person with a bath at 100 to 105 F, which is warm to the touch but not hot. Give warm, nutritional liquids.
- Companions may be able to share body heat.

Caution
Don't give the person alcohol. Give warm nonalcoholic drinks, unless he or she is vomiting.

Cuts, Scrapes and Wounds

Everyday cuts, scrapes and wounds often don't require a trip to the emergency room. Yet proper care is essential to avoid infection or other complications. The following guidelines can help you in caring for simple wounds. Puncture wounds may require medical attention.

■ Simple Wounds

Self-Care

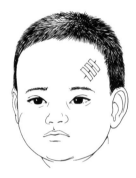

A few strips of surgical tape (Steri-Strips) may be used to close a minor cut. But if the mouth of the wound is not easily closed, seek a doctor's care. Proper closure will help minimize scarring.

- **Stop the bleeding.** Minor cuts and scrapes usually stop bleeding on their own. If not, apply gentle pressure with a clean cloth or bandage.
- **Keep the wound clean.** Rinse with clear water. Clean the area around the wound with soap and a washcloth. Keep soap out of the wound. Soap can cause an irritation. If dirt or debris remains in the wound after washing, use clean tweezers to remove the particles. Apply alcohol to the tweezers before use. If debris remains embedded in the wound after cleaning, contact your health care provider, and don't attempt to remove it by yourself. Thorough wound cleaning also reduces the risk of contracting tetanus (see page 23).
- **Apply hydrogen peroxide, iodine or an iodine-containing cleanser.** Such a substance may be used in the area around the wound but is not necessary. It's irritating to living cells and shouldn't be used in the wound itself.
- **Consider the source.** Puncture wounds or other deep cuts, animal bites or particularly dirty wounds put you at risk of tetanus infection (see page 23). If the wound is serious, you may require an additional tetanus booster even if you received your last one within the past 10 years. A booster is given for dirty or deep wounds if you haven't had one in the previous five years.
- **Prevent infection.** After you clean the wound, if desired, apply a thin layer of an antibiotic cream or ointment (such as Neosporin or Polysporin) to help keep the surface moist. The products don't make the wound heal faster, but they can discourage infection and allow your body's healing factors to close the wound more efficiently. Be aware that certain ingredients in some ointments can cause a mild rash in some people. If a rash appears, stop using the ointment.
- **Cover the wound.** Exposure to air will speed healing, but bandages can help keep the wound clean and keep harmful bacteria out. Blisters that are draining are vulnerable and should be covered until a scab forms.
- **Change the dressing to help prevent infection.** Do this at least once a day or whenever it becomes wet or dirty. If you're allergic to the adhesive used in most bandages, switch to adhesive-free dressings or sterile gauze, paper tape or pressure netting. These supplies generally are available at pharmacies.

Medical Help

If bleeding persists — if the blood spurts or continues to flow after several minutes of pressure — emergency care is necessary.

Are stitches needed? A deep (all the way through the skin), gaping or jagged-edged wound with exposed fat or muscle may require stitches to hold it together for proper healing. Strips of surgical tape may be used to close a minor cut, but if the mouth of the wound isn't easily closed, seek medical care. Proper closure will help minimize scarring (see page 23), speed healing and reduce risk of infection.

Caution   **Watch for signs of infection.** Every day that a wound remains unhealed, the risk of infection increases. See your health care provider if your wound isn't healing steadily or if you notice any redness, drainage, warmth or swelling.

A Shot in the Arm: Tetanus Vaccine

A cut, laceration, bite or other wound, even if minor, can lead to a tetanus infection. The result can be lockjaw that occurs days or weeks later. Lockjaw (tetanus) is a stiffness of the jaw and other muscles. Other symptoms may include breathing problems, convulsions and even death.

Tetanus bacteria usually are found in the soil but can occur virtually anywhere. If their spores enter a wound beyond the reach of oxygen, they germinate and produce a toxin that interferes with the nerves controlling your muscles.

Active immunization is vital for everyone in advance of an injury. The tetanus vaccine usually is given to children as a diphtheria, tetanus and pertussis (DTaP) shot. Adults generally need a tetanus booster every 10 years. If the wound is serious, your physician may recommend an additional booster even if your last one was within 10 years. A booster is given if you have a deep or dirty wound and your most recent booster was more than five years ago. Boosters should be given within two days of the injury.

■ Puncture Wounds

A puncture wound doesn't usually result in excessive bleeding. Often, in fact, little blood flows, and the wound seems to close almost instantly. These features don't mean that treatment is unnecessary.

A puncture wound — such as stepping on a nail or being stuck with a tack — can be dangerous because of the risk of infection. The object that caused the wound may carry spores of the tetanus or other bacteria, especially if the object has been exposed to soil. For a simple wound, follow the same self-care steps and advice on seeking medical help listed on page 22. A deep puncture wound may need to be cleaned by a doctor.

What About Scarring?

No matter how you treat them, all deep wounds that penetrate beyond the first layer of skin form a scar when healed. Even superficial wounds can form a scar or abnormal pigmentation if infection or re-injury occurs. Following the guidelines on page 22 may help avoid these complications.

When a healing wound is exposed to sunlight, it can darken permanently. This darkening can be prevented by covering the area with clothing or a sunblock (sunscreen protection factor more than 15) whenever you're outside during the first six months after the wound occurred.

A scar usually thickens about two months into the healing process. Within six months to a year, it should thin out and be even with your skin surface.

A large, jagged scar that continues to enlarge is called a keloid, an abnormal growth of scar tissue. Surgical incisions, vaccinations, burns or even a scratch can cause keloids. The tendency to develop keloids is often inherited, and they're more common on deeply pigmented skin than on white skin.

Keloids are harmless. But if they itch or look unattractive, doctors can remove small keloids by freezing them with liquid nitrogen, then injecting them with cortisone. Sometimes they stop growing, but they rarely disappear by themselves.

Ask a dermatologist or plastic surgeon to evaluate your scar and advise treatment if it looks unsatisfactory to you.

Eye Injuries

Consider some common objects in your home — paper clips, pencils, tools and toys. Used without care, they pose a threat to your windows on the world — your eyes.

The topic of eye injuries offers a "bad news-good news" scenario. Eye injuries are common, and some are serious. Fortunately, you can prevent most of these injuries by taking simple steps (see page 76 for common eye problems).

■ Corneal Abrasion (Scratch)

The most common types of eye injury involve the cornea — the clear, protective "window" at the front of the eye. The cornea can be scratched or cut by contact with dust, dirt, sand, wood shavings, metal particles or even an edge of a piece of paper. Usually the scratch is superficial, and this is called a corneal abrasion. Some corneal abrasions become infected and result in a corneal ulcer, which is a serious problem.

Everyday activities can lead to corneal abrasions. Examples are playing sports, doing home repairs or being scratched by children who accidentally brush your cornea with a fingernail. Other common injuries to the cornea include "splash accidents" — contact with chemicals ranging from antifreeze to household cleaners.

Because the cornea is extremely sensitive, abrasions can be painful. If your cornea is scratched, you might feel like you have sand in your eye. Tears, blurred vision, sensitivity to light, pain or redness around the eye can suggest a corneal abrasion.

Self-Care

In case of injury, seek prompt medical attention. Here are some immediate steps you can take:
- Run lukewarm tap water over the eye, or splash the eye with clean water. This is especially useful in a chemical splash accident. Many work sites have eye-rinse stations for this purpose. Rinsing the eye may wash out the offending foreign body. The technique is described on page 25.
- Blink several times. This movement may remove small particles of dust or sand.
- Pull the upper eyelid over the lower eyelid. The lashes of the lower eyelid can brush the foreign body from the undersurface of the upper eyelid.

Caution

- If abrasion was caused by an object in the eye, refer to page 25.
- Don't apply patches or ice packs to the eye. If you do get an object within the eye itself — typically when hammering metal on metal — don't press on the eyeball.
- Don't rub your eye after an injury. This action can worsen a corneal abrasion.

■ Chemical Splash

If a chemical splashes into your eye, flush it with water immediately. Any source of clean drinking water will do. It's more important to begin flushing than it is to find sterile water. Flushing water may dilute the chemical. Continue to flush the eye for at least 20 minutes, particularly if your eye is exposed to household cleaners that contain ammonia. After washing the eye thoroughly, close the eyelid and cover it with a loose, moist dressing. Then seek emergency medical assistance.

■ Foreign Object in the Eye

Children and adults alike occasionally get foreign objects in their eyes. You can take appropriate steps in some cases to remove the object. In other situations, you need to see a health care provider.

Clearing the Eye

To remove a small foreign object from your eye, flush the eye with a small amount of clean water using a small cup.

Your Own Eye

If no one is nearby to help you, try to flush the eye clear. Using an eyecup or small juice glass, wash your eye with clean water. Position the glass with its rim resting on the bone at the base of your eye socket and pour the water in, keeping the eye open. If you don't succeed in clearing the eye, seek emergency medical help.

Someone Else's Eye

- Do not rub the eye. Wash your hands before examining the eye. Seat the person in a well-lighted area.
- Locate the object in the eye visually. Examine the eye by gently pulling the lower lid downward and instructing the person to look upward. Reverse the procedure for the upper lid. Hold the upper lid and examine the eye while the person looks downward. If you find that the foreign object is embedded in the eyeball, cover the person's eye with a sterile pad or a clean cloth. Don't try to remove the object.
- If the object is large and makes closing the eye difficult, cover it with a paper cup taped to the face and forehead. Seek emergency medical assistance immediately.
- If the object is floating in the tear film or on the surface of the eye, you may be able to flush it out or remove it manually. While holding the upper or lower lid open, use a moistened cotton swab or the corner of a clean cloth to remove the object by lightly touching it. If you are unable to remove the object easily, cover both eyes with a soft cloth and seek emergency medical assistance.
- If you succeed in removing the object, flush the eye with an eye irrigating solution or with water.
- If pain, vision problems or redness persists, seek emergency medical care.

Common Sense Can Save Your Sight

- **Wear goggles** while working with industrial chemicals, power tools and even hand tools. Some of the most serious eye injuries occur while people are using hammers. Also wear a safety helmet when appropriate.
- **Wear safety glasses** for sports such as racquetball, basketball, squash and tennis. Also wear appropriate headgear, such as a batter's helmet for baseball and a face mask for hockey.
- **Carefully follow the instructions for using detergents, ammonia and cleaning fluids.** When using fluids that come in spray containers, point the nozzles away from your eyes at all times. Store household chemicals safely and out of children's reach.

- **Supervise children at play.** Remove toys that could lead to an eye injury. Examples are BB guns, plastic swords and spring-loaded toys that shoot darts. Don't allow children to have fireworks.
- **Don't lean over a car battery** when attaching jumper cables.
- **Pick up rocks and sticks** before mowing your lawn. While mowing, watch for trees with low-hanging branches.
- **Carefully follow instructions** for removing and applying contact lenses. Also, investigate any pain or eye reddening that occurs while you're wearing contact lenses.

Food-Borne Illness

Food-borne illness is a growing problem in the United States. The major reasons for this problem are an increase in restaurant dining and more centralized food processing.

All foods naturally contain small amounts of bacteria. But when food is poorly handled, improperly cooked or inadequately stored, bacteria can multiply in great enough numbers to cause illness. Parasites, viruses and chemicals also can contaminate food, but food-borne illness from these sources is less common.

If you eat contaminated food, whether you'll become ill depends on the organism, the amount of exposure, your age and your health. With age, immune cells may not respond as quickly and effectively to infectious organisms. Young children are at increased risk of illness because their immune systems haven't developed fully. If you're pregnant or you've had an organ transplant, you may be at higher risk. Conditions such as diabetes and AIDS and cancer treatment also reduce your immune response, making you more susceptible to food-borne illness.

Food poisoning can cause various ailments. If you become ill one to six hours after consuming contaminated food or water, you likely have a common form. Symptoms include nausea, vomiting, diarrhea, stomach pain and fever.

Self-Care

- Rest and drink plenty of liquids.
- Don't use antidiarrheal medications because they may slow elimination of the bacteria and toxins from your system.
- Mild to moderate illness often resolves on its own within 12 hours.

Medical Help

If symptoms last more than 12 hours, are severe, or you belong to one of the high-risk groups noted above, seek prompt medical attention to avoid dehydration.

Caution

Botulism is a potentially fatal food poisoning. It results from eating foods containing a toxin formed by certain spores in food. Botulism toxin is most often found in home-canned foods, especially green beans and tomatoes. Symptoms usually begin 12 to 36 hours after eating the contaminated food. Symptoms include headache, blurred or double vision, muscle weakness and eventually paralysis. Some people report nausea, vomiting, constipation, urinary retention and reduced salivation. These symptoms require immediate medical attention.

Handling Food Safely

- **Plan ahead.** Thaw meats and other frozen foods in the refrigerator, not on the countertop.
- **When shopping,** don't buy food in cans or jars with dented or bulging lids.
- **When preparing food,** wash your hands with soap and water. Rinse produce thoroughly or peel off the skin or outer leaves. Wash knives and cutting surfaces frequently, especially after handling raw meat and before preparing other foods. Launder kitchen items frequently.

- **When cooking,** use a meat thermometer. Cook red meat to an internal temperature of 160 F, poultry to 180 F. Cook fish until it flakes easily with a fork. Cook eggs until the yolks are firm.
- **When storing food,** check expiration dates. Use or freeze fresh red meats within three to five days after purchase. Use or freeze fresh poultry, fish and ground meat within one to two days. Refrigerate or freeze leftovers within two hours of serving.

Troublesome Bacteria and How You Can Stop Them

Keep hot food hot. Keep cold food cold. Keep everything — especially your hands — clean. Use soap when washing. If you follow these basic rules, you'll be less likely to become ill from the troublesome bacteria listed here.

Bacteria	How Spread	Symptoms	To Prevent
Campylobacter jejuni	Contaminates meat and poultry during processing if feces contacts meat surfaces. Other sources: unpasteurized milk, untreated water.	Severe diarrhea (sometimes bloody), abdominal cramps, chills, headache. Onset within 2 to 11 days. Lasts 1 to 2 weeks.	Cook meat and poultry thoroughly. Wash knives and cutting surfaces after contact with raw meat. Don't drink unpasteurized milk or untreated water.
Clostridium perfringens	Meats, stews, gravies. Commonly spread when serving dishes don't keep food hot enough or food is chilled too slowly.	Watery diarrhea, nausea, abdominal cramps. Fever is rare. Onset within 1 to 16 hours. Lasts 1 to 2 days.	Keep foods hot. Hold cooked meats above 140 F. Reheat to at least 165 F. Chill foods quickly. Store in small containers.
Escherichia coli O157:H7	Contaminates beef during slaughter. Spread mainly by undercooked ground beef. Other sources: unpasteurized milk and apple cider, human stool, contaminated water.	Watery diarrhea may turn bloody within 24 hours. Severe abdominal cramps, nausea, occasional vomiting. Usually no fever. Onset within 1 to 8 days. Lasts 5 to 8 days.	Cook beef to internal temperature of 160 F. Don't drink unpasteurized milk or unpasteurized apple cider. Wash hands after bathroom use.
Noroviruses (Norwalk-like viruses)	Consuming contaminated food or liquids; touching contaminated surfaces or objects.	Nausea, vomiting, diarrhea, stomach cramps, low-grade fever, chills. Lasts 1 to 2 days.	Wash hands after bathroom use. Wash fruits and vegetables. Disinfect surfaces.
Salmonella	Raw or contaminated meat, poultry, milk, egg yolks. Survives inadequate cooking. Spread by knives, cutting surfaces or an infected person with poor hygiene.	Severe diarrhea, watery stools, nausea, vomiting, temperature 101 F or more. Onset within 6 to 72 hours. Lasts 1 to 14 days.	Cook meat and poultry thoroughly. Don't drink unpasteurized milk. Don't eat raw or undercooked eggs. Keep cutting surfaces clean. Wash hands after bathroom use.
Staphylococcus aureus	Spread by hand contact, coughing and sneezing. Grows on meats and prepared salads, cream sauces, cream-filled pastries.	Explosive, watery diarrhea, nausea, vomiting, abdominal cramps, lightheadedness. Onset within 1 to 6 hours. Lasts 1 to 2 days.	Don't leave high-risk foods at room temperature for more than 2 hours. Wash hands and utensils before preparing food.
Vibrio vulnificus	Raw oysters and raw or undercooked mussels, clams, whole scallops.	Chills, fever, skin lesions. Onset 1 hour to 1 week. Fatal in 50 percent of cases.	Don't eat raw oysters. Make sure all shellfish is thoroughly cooked.
Listeria monocytogenes	Hot dogs, luncheon meats, unpasteurized milk and cheeses, unwashed raw vegetables.	Abdominal cramps, nausea, diarrhea, vomiting, fever.	Heat meats thoroughly. Avoid unpasteurized milk and milk products. Wash raw vegetables.

Heat-Related Problems

Under normal conditions, your body's natural control mechanisms — skin and perspiration — adjust to the heat. These systems may fail if you're exposed to high temperatures for prolonged periods.

Working out in hot or humid conditions can overstress your body's temperature-regulation system, causing an excessive increase in body temperature. Heat-related problems may include heat cramps, dehydration, heat exhaustion and heatstroke.

Heat Cramps

Heat cramps are painful muscle spasms. They usually occur after vigorous activity in a hot environment. They develop when sweating depletes your body of salt (sodium) and water. The muscles of the arms, legs and abdomen are most often affected.

Heat Exhaustion

Signs and symptoms of heat exhaustion include cool, clammy and pale skin, heat cramps, a weak pulse, nausea, chills and dizziness, weakness, or disorientation. You may have a headache and be short of breath.

Heatstroke

This condition can be life-threatening. Your skin becomes hot, flushed and dry. You stop perspiring, and your body temperature may rise above 106 F. You may feel confused and may even faint. Other signs include rapid heartbeat, rapid and shallow breathing, confusion and increased or reduced blood pressure. Young children, older adults and people who are obese are particularly at risk of **heatstroke.** Other risk factors include dehydration, alcohol use, heart disease, certain medications and vigorous exercise. People born with an impaired ability to sweat also are at higher risk.

Self-Care

To avoid heat-related conditions:
- Drink plenty of fluids, especially water and sports drinks. Avoid caffeine.
- Wear light-colored, loosefitting clothing made of breathable fabric.
- Exercise in the early morning or late evening. If possible, exercise in the shade.
- Allow yourself time to adjust to higher temperatures.
- Talk to your doctor if you take medications. Certain medications, such as diuretics and antihistamines may make you more susceptible to heat-related illness.

Medical Help

If you suspect a heat-related illness, get out of the heat, drink fluids, elevate your feet above your head, and either wet and fan your skin or immerse yourself in cool water. If you suspect heatstroke, seek emergency help immediately. Monitor the individual carefully until help arrives.

Tips to Beat the Heat

- **Stay out of the sun.** Avoid going outside during the hottest part of the day, noon to 4 p.m.
- **Limit activity.** Reserve vigorous exercise or activities for early morning or evening.
- **Dress properly.** Wear light-colored, lightweight, loosefitting clothing that breathes.
- **Drink lots of liquids.** Avoid alcohol and caffeine.
- **Avoid hot and heavy meals.**

See back cover for online resource

Poisonous Plants

Poison ivy

Poison oak

Poison sumac

When it comes to poison oak and ivy, it's wise to heed these words of advice: "Leaves of three, let them be."

With their leaves usually grouped three to a stem, poison ivy and poison oak are two of the most common causes of an allergic skin reaction called contact dermatitis.

Contact with poison ivy and poison oak usually causes red, swollen skin, blisters and severe itching. This reaction typically develops within two days after exposure, but it can develop within a few hours. The rash usually reaches its peak after about five days, and is usually gone within a week or two. It may leave scars.

The rash is caused by exposure to resin, a colorless, oily substance contained in all parts of these plants. Resin transfers easily from clothing or from pet hair to your skin. Burning the plants is also hazardous because inhaling the smoke can cause internal and external reactions.

It may take only a tiny amount of resin to cause a reaction. Sensitivity to poison ivy varies from person to person. Poison ivy and other rashes don't develop as a result of merely being near the plant, nor does the rash spread as a result of washing or scratching open rash blisters. The resin isn't present in blister fluid. However, it can be spread by accidentally rubbing the resin on other areas of the skin before all the resin is washed off.

Besides poison ivy and oak, other plants also can cause a reaction. They include sumac, heliotrope (found in the deserts of the Southwest), ragweed (both the leaves and pollen), daisies, chrysanthemums, sagebrush, wormwood, celery, oranges, limes and potatoes. Wild parsnip causes a burn-like reaction.

Self-Care

- Washing the harmful resin off the skin with soap within five to 10 minutes after exposure may avert a skin reaction.
- Don't try to remove the resin by taking a bath. Bathing can spread the resin to other areas of your body.
- Wash any clothing or jewelry that may have been in contact with the plant. *Note:* Footwear and shoelaces also should be washed.
- Try not to scratch. Take cool showers.
- Over-the-counter preparations (calamine lotion and hydrocortisone cream) can ease itching. Or apply a paste of baking soda or Epsom salts and water.
- Creams and lotions don't help much when the blisters open, but they can be used again when the blisters close.
- Don't apply alcohol because this tends to make the itching worse. Cover open blisters with a sterile gauze to prevent infection.
- To avoid exposure, learn to recognize poisonous plants and wear protective clothing when appropriate. Poison ivy leaves are oval or spoon-shaped. Poison oak leaves resemble oak leaves. The colors of the leaves of these plants change with the seasons, from green in the summer to orange and red in the fall.
- Avoid exposure to the sun after encountering wild parsnip.

Medical Help

If you have a severe reaction, or when your eyes, face or genital area is involved, contact your health care provider, who may prescribe cortisone or an antihistamine, either orally or topically. If you have an open cut that becomes infected, treatment with an antibiotic may be required. Reduce scarring by following the recommendations on page 23.

Tooth Problems

◼ Toothache

Dental cavities can lead to toothaches.

In most children and adults, tooth decay (cavities, also called caries) is the primary cause of toothaches. Tooth decay mainly is caused by bacteria and carbohydrates. Bacteria are present in a thin, almost invisible film on your teeth called plaque.

Tooth decay takes time to develop, often a year or two in permanent teeth but less in primary teeth. Decay can occur faster in people with dry mouth, who drink a lot of soft drinks, or who abuse methamphetamine.

Decay-producing acid — which forms within 20 minutes after you eat — forms in plaque and attacks the tooth's outer surface. The erosion caused by the plaque leads to the formation of tiny openings (cavities) in the tooth surface. The first sign of decay may be a sensation of pain when you eat something sweet, very cold or very hot.

Self-Care

Until you're able to get to the dentist, try these self-care tips:
- Try flossing to remove any food particles wedged between the teeth.
- Take an over-the-counter pain reliever.
- Apply a nonprescription antiseptic containing benzocaine directly to the irritated tooth and gum to relieve pain. Oil of cloves (eugenol) also may relieve pain.
- Prevention is the best way to avoid tooth decay and cavities.

Caution

Swelling, pain when you bite, a foul-tasting discharge and redness indicate infection. See your dentist as soon as possible. If you have fever with the pain, seek emergency care.

◼ Tooth Loss

Whenever a tooth is accidentally knocked out, appropriate emergency medical care is required immediately. Today, permanent teeth that are knocked out sometimes can be reimplanted if you act quickly. A broken tooth, however, cannot be reimplanted.

Emergency Treatment

If a permanent tooth is knocked out, save the tooth and consult your dentist immediately. If it's after office hours, call your dentist's emergency number. If he or she is unavailable, go to the nearest emergency room.

Successful reimplantation depends on several factors: prompt insertion (within 30 minutes if possible; no longer than two hours after loss) and proper storage and transportation of the tooth. Keeping it moist is essential.

Self-Care

To preserve the tooth and treat yourself until you get to the dentist:
- Handle the tooth by the top (crown) only.
- Do not rub it or scrape it to remove dirt.
- Rinse your mouth with water, and apply pressure to stop bleeding.
- Place the tooth in milk.
- Don't try to reinsert the tooth.

Trauma

Trauma is any injury sustained as a result of external force or violence. A broken bone, a severe blow to the head and a knocked-out tooth are all considered trauma.

Fractures, severe sprains, dislocations and other serious bone and joint injuries also are trauma emergencies and usually require professional medical care.

■ Dislocations

A dislocation is an injury in which the ends of bones in a joint are forced from their normal positions. In most cases, a blow, fall or other trauma causes the dislocation.

Indications of a dislocation include the following:

● An injured joint that's visibly out of position, misshapen and difficult to move
● Swelling and intense pain at a joint

The dislocation should be treated as quickly as possible, but don't try to return the joint to its proper place. Splint the affected joint in the position it's in. Treat it as you would a fracture. Seek immediate medical attention. Placing ice on the injured joint will help reduce swelling by controlling internal bleeding and buildup of fluids. For more information on dislocations, see page 93.

■ Fractures

A fracture is a broken bone. It requires immediate medical attention.

If you suspect a fracture, the proper approach is to protect the affected area from further damage. Don't try to set the broken bone. Instead, immobilize the area with a splint. Also keep joints above and below the fracture immobilized.

If bleeding occurs along with the broken bone, apply pressure to stop the bleeding. If possible, elevate the site of bleeding to lessen the blood flow. Maintain pressure until the bleeding stops.

If the person is faint, pale or breathing in a notably shallow, rapid fashion, use the treatment steps for shock: Lay the person down, elevate the legs and cover him or her with a blanket or something for warmth.

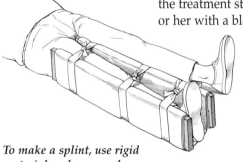

To make a splint, use rigid material such as wood, plastic or metal. The splint should be longer than the bone it's splinting and extend above and below the injury. Pad the splint wherever possible.

Signs and symptoms of a fracture are as follows:

● Swelling or bruising over a bone
● Deformity of the affected limb
● Localized pain that is intensified when the affected area is moved or pressure is put on it
● Loss of function in the area of the injury
● A broken bone that has poked through adjacent soft tissues and is sticking out of the skin

For more information on fractures, see page 89.

Sprains

A sprain occurs when a violent twist or stretch causes a joint to move outside its normal range. Sprains are the result of overstretched ligaments. Tearing of the ligaments may occur. The usual indications of a sprain are the following:

- Pain and tenderness in the affected area
- Rapid swelling and possible discoloration of the skin
- Impaired joint function

Most minor sprains can be treated at home. However, if a popping sound and immediate difficulty in using the joint accompany the injury, seek emergency medical care. For more information on sprains, see page 88.

Head Injuries

Approximately 1.4 million head injuries occur every year in the United States, and about 16 percent of cases require hospitalization. Most head injuries are minor. The skull provides the brain with considerable protection from injury. Simple cuts and bruises can often be treated with basic first-aid techniques.

Serious types of head injuries that require emergency medical care are listed below. In all cases of worrisome head injury, don't move the neck because it may have been injured. If the person must be moved, keep the head and neck stabile with your hands.

Concussion. When the head sustains a hard blow as the result of being struck or from a fall, a concussion may result. The impact creates a sudden movement of the brain within the skull. A concussion involves a loss of consciousness. Victims are often described as dazed. Loss of memory, dizziness and vomiting also may occur. Partial paralysis and shock are other possible symptoms.

Blood clot on the brain. This occurs when a blood vessel ruptures between the skull and the brain. Blood then leaks between the brain and skull and forms a blood clot (hematoma), which presses on the brain tissue. Symptoms occur from a few hours to several weeks after a blow to the head. There may be no open wound, bruise or other outward sign. Signs and symptoms include headache, nausea, vomiting, alteration of consciousness and pupils of unequal size. There may be progressive lethargy, unconsciousness and death if the condition isn't treated.

Skull fracture. This type of injury isn't always apparent. Look for the following:

- Bruising or discoloring behind the ear or around the eyes
- Blood or clear, watery fluids leaking from the ears or nose
- Pupils of unequal size
- Deformity of the skull, including swelling or depressions

Emergency Treatment

Seek emergency medical care if any of the following symptoms are apparent:

- Severe head or facial bleeding
- Change in level of consciousness, even if only briefly
- Irregular or labored breathing or stopping of breathing
- Confusion, loss of balance, weakness in an arm or leg, or slurred speech
- Vomiting

Caution

Until emergency help arrives, keep the person lying down and quiet in a dimmed room. Observe the person for vital signs: normal breathing and alertness. Begin CPR if no normal breathing. Stop any bleeding by applying firm pressure.

General Symptoms

- **Dizziness and Fainting**
- **Fatigue**
- **Fever**
- **Pain**
- **Sleep Disorders**
- **Sweating and Body Odor**
- **Unexpected Weight Changes**

Dizziness, fainting, fatigue, fever, pain, difficulty sleeping, sweating and unexpected weight changes. In medicine, these conditions are called general symptoms because they tend to affect your entire body rather than a particular body part or system. In this section, the common causes for each of seven general symptoms are explained, and self-care information and advice on when to seek medical care is provided.

Dizziness and Fainting

<u>Dizziness</u> has many causes. Fortunately, most dizziness is mild, brief and harmless. It can be caused by many things, including medications, infections and stress. The word *dizziness* actually describes various sensations.

Vertigo and Imbalance

Vertigo is the sensation that you or your surroundings are rotating. You may feel that the room is spinning, or you may sense the rotation within your own head or body. Vertigo usually is associated with problems in your inner ear. The inner ear has an ultrasensitive device for sensing movement. Viral illness, trauma or other disturbance can result in the device sending a false message to your brain.

Imbalance is the sensation that you must touch or hold on to something to maintain your balance. Severe imbalance may make it difficult to stand without falling.

Lightheadedness and Fainting

Lightheadedness includes feelings of being woozy, floating or near fainting. Fainting is a sudden, brief loss of consciousness. It occurs when your brain doesn't receive enough blood and the oxygen it carries. Although frightening, fainting generally isn't a reason for alarm. Once you're lying flat, blood flows to your brain and you regain consciousness within about a minute. Fainting may be caused by medical disorders, including heart disease, severe coughing spells and circulatory problems. In other cases, fainting may be related to the following:

- Medications for high blood pressure and erratic heartbeats
- Excessive sweating that results in loss of sodium and dehydration
- Extreme fatigue
- Upsetting news or an unexpected or unusual stress such as the sight of blood

A rapid drop in blood pressure, called *postural hypotension,* occurs when you get up quickly from a sitting or reclining position. Everyone experiences this reaction to a mild degree. You feel lightheaded or slightly faint, and it usually passes within seconds. The reaction may also occur after a hot bath or in people taking blood pressure medication. When it leads to fainting or blackouts, it's more serious.

Self-Care

If your vision darkens or you feel faint, lower your head. Lie down and elevate your legs slightly to return blood to the heart. If you can't lie down, lean forward and put your head between your knees.

Prevention

- Stand and change positions slowly — particularly when turning from side to side or when changing from lying down to standing. Before standing up in the morning, sit on the edge of the bed for a few minutes.
- Stand still for a minute or two before you start to walk.
- Pace yourself. Take breaks when you are active in heat and humidity. Dress appropriate to the conditions to avoid overheating.
- Drink enough fluids to avoid dehydration and assure good circulation.
- Avoid smoking, alcohol and illegal drugs.
- Don't drive a car or operate dangerous equipment if you feel dizzy.
- Don't climb or descend staircases.
- Check your medications. You may need to ask your doctor about adjustments.

Mild symptoms that persist for weeks or months may be due to nervous system diseases. Sudden nausea, vomiting, dizziness or vertigo and double vision are symptoms that require emergency attention, and may be due to bleeding in the hindbrain (cerebellum) or brainstem.

Because problems of dizziness and balance can have many different causes, a diagnosis usually requires a complete medical history and several tests. Treatments for sudden onset of vertigo may include medication and avoiding positions or movements that cause dizziness. Your doctor may also suggest an inner ear positioning treatment (vestibular rehabilitation).

Contact your health care provider in these situations:

- The condition is severe, prolonged (more than a few days or a week) or recurrent.
- You're taking medication for high blood pressure.
- You have black tarry stools, blood in your stools or other signs of blood loss.

Seek emergency medical care in these situations:

- You faint when you turn your head or extend your neck. Fainting or dizziness is accompanied by symptoms such as pain in the chest or head, trouble with breathing, numbness or continuing weakness, irregular heartbeat, blurred or double vision, confusion or trouble talking, nausea or vomiting.
- The signs and symptoms listed above are present on awakening.
- Someone faints without warning.
- This was the person's first fainting spell, and there were no obvious reasons for it.
- The person was injured during the faint.

Until medical help arrives, if the person is lying down, position him or her on the back. If you believe the person is about to vomit, roll him or her onto the side. Raise the legs above the level of the head. If a person faints and remains seated, quickly lay him or her flat. Loosen tight clothing. Listen for breathing sounds. If they're absent, the problem is more serious than fainting, and CPR must be started.

How Your Body Maintains Balance

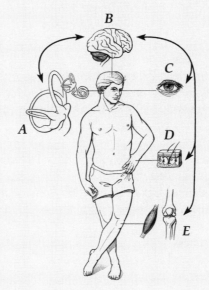

Maintaining balance requires a complex networking of several different parts of your body. To maintain balance, your brain must coordinate a constant flow of information from your eyes, muscles and tendons, and inner ear. All of these parts of the body work together to help keep you upright and provide you with a sense of stability when you're moving.

Many problems with dizziness are caused by problems within your inner ear. However, problems in any part of the system that controls your balance can cause dizziness and imbalance.

A. *The inner ear contains your primary balance structure.*

B. *The brain relays and interprets information to and from your body.*

C. *The eyes record your body's position and surroundings.*

D. *When you touch things, sensors in your skin give you information about your environment.*

E. *Muscles and joints report bodily movement to your brain.*

Fatigue

Almost everyone experiences fatigue at some time. After putting in a long weekend of yard chores or a hectic day with the children or at the office, it's natural to feel tired. This kind of physical and emotional fatigue is normal, and you can usually restore your energy with rest or exercise.

If you feel tired all the time, or if the exhaustion is overwhelming, you may begin to worry that your condition is more serious than just fatigue. When fatigue isn't accompanied by other symptoms, a specific cause often can't be determined. A common cause of chronic fatigue is lack of regular exercise (deconditioning). This problem can be remedied easily by gradually increasing your activity and beginning an exercise program.

Fatigue can be the result of physical or emotional problems. Physical fatigue is usually more pronounced later in the day, and it often resolves with a good night's sleep. Emotional fatigue often peaks first thing in the morning and gets better as the day progresses.

Common Causes

Common causes of physical fatigue include the following:
- Poor eating habits
- Lack of sleep
- Being out of shape
- Warm working or living quarters
- Carbon monoxide poisoning
- Over-the-counter medications, including pain relievers, cough and cold medicines, antihistamines and allergy remedies, sleeping pills and motion sickness pills
- Prescription drugs such as tranquilizers, muscle relaxants, sedatives, birth control pills and blood pressure medications
- Dehydration

Fatigue can also be an early symptom of these conditions:
- A low red blood cell count (anemia)
- Low thyroid activity (hypothyroidism)
- Various acute or chronic infections
- Heart disease
- Sleep disorder
- Electrolyte imbalance (when the levels of salts in your blood, such as sodium, potassium and other minerals, are too high or too low)
- Cancer
- Diabetes
- Alcoholism
- Rheumatoid arthritis

Many of these illnesses are accompanied by other signs and symptoms such as muscle aches, pain, nausea, weight loss, cold sensitivity and shortness of breath.

Common causes of emotional fatigue include:
- Overextending yourself, especially if you can't say no
- Boredom or lack of stimulation from family, friends or co-workers
- A major crisis (losing a spouse or a job), a move or a family difficulty
- Depression
- Loneliness
- Unresolved past emotional issues
- Repressing anger instead of expressing it

Self-Care

Before you talk to a health care provider, consider the possibility that your fatigue is related to an explainable cause that can be remedied with some of the following lifestyle changes:

- Get an adequate night's sleep — six to eight hours of uninterrupted sleep.
- Follow a sleep schedule. Go to bed and wake up at the same time each day.
- Give yourself a break. Ask others to pitch in.
- Organize your daily schedule, and prioritize activities.
- Rest and relax — unwind. Do something fun.
- Exercise more, starting gradually. Walk instead of watching television. If you're older than age 40, consult your doctor before beginning a vigorous exercise program.
- Increase your exposure to fresh air at home and at work.
- Eat a balanced diet. Steer clear of high-fat foods.
- Lose weight if you are overweight.
- Drink plenty of water (2 or more quarts a day to avoid dehydration).
- Review your medications (over-the-counter and prescription) to determine if fatigue is a side effect.
- Quit smoking.
- Reduce or eliminate your use of alcohol.
- If you have problems at your job, find ways to resolve them. (See Keeping Stress Under Control on page 225, and Stress Relievers on page 243.)

Medical Help

If fatigue persists even when you rest enough, and it lasts for two weeks or longer, you may have a problem that requires medical care. See your health care provider.

Kids' Care

Children and young adults rarely complain of fatigue. If they do, it's usually a sign that they have an acute infection or that one is developing. Consult a doctor.

What Is Chronic Fatigue Syndrome?

Chronic fatigue syndrome is a poorly understood, flu-like condition that can completely drain your energy and may last for years. People who were previously healthy and full of energy experience intense fatigue, pain in joints and muscles, painful lymph glands and headaches.

Experts haven't determined the causes of chronic fatigue syndrome, although there are likely to be many. Theories include infections, hormonal imbalances and psychological, immunological or neurological abnormalities. In one study, researchers found that some people with the syndrome had a low blood pressure disorder triggering the fainting reflex.

Treatment for chronic fatigue syndrome is aimed at relieving your symptoms. Anti-inflammatory pain relievers, such as ibuprofen, often are prescribed, but they rarely help. Low doses of certain antidepressants may help relieve pain and depression often present with a chronic illness, as well as promote better sleep. Because people with chronic fatigue syndrome may become out of shape, which perpetuates the fatigue, physical activity is crucial. It can help prevent or decrease muscle weakness caused by prolonged inactivity. You may benefit from counseling to help you deal with the illness and the limitations it creates.

Fever

Even when you're well, your temperature varies, and that variation is normal. We consider 98.6 F (37 C) a healthy body temperature. But, your personal normal temperature may differ by a degree or more.

In the morning your temperature is generally lower, and in the afternoon it's somewhat higher. Check your family members' temperatures when they're healthy. Discover their normal range.

What Is the Cause?

Fever itself isn't an illness, but it is often a sign of one. A fever tells you that something is happening inside your body.

Most likely, your body is fighting an infection caused by either bacteria or a virus. The fever may even be helpful in fighting the infection. Rarely, it's a sign of a reaction to a medicine, an immunization, an inflammatory condition or too much heat. Sometimes you don't know why you have a fever. But don't automatically try to lower your temperature. Decreasing it may mask symptoms, prolong an illness and delay identifying the cause.

You usually will know what caused a fever in a day or two. If you think it's something other than a viral illness, consult your health care provider. Other common causes of fever include the following:

- An infection, such as urinary tract infection (frequent or painful urination), strep throat or tonsillitis (often with a sore throat), sinus infection (pain above or beneath the eyes), bronchitis (cough and chest congestion) and dental abscess (tender area in the mouth)
- Infectious mononucleosis, accompanied by fatigue
- An illness you picked up in a foreign country
- Heat exhaustion or severe sunburn

Caution

Never give a child or young adult aspirin for a fever unless directed to do so by your doctor. Rarely, aspirin causes a serious or even fatal disease called Reye's syndrome if given during a viral infection.

Self-Care

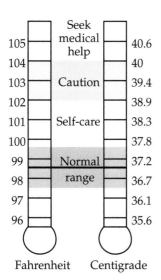

Drink plenty of water to avoid dehydration (because the body loses more water with a fever) and get enough rest.

- **For children and adults with temperatures less than 102 F (38.9 C):**
  - Normally, avoid using medicine for a new fever in this range.
  - Wear comfortable, light clothing and cover yourself with only a sheet or light blanket.
- **For children and adults with temperatures of 102 F (38.9 C) and above:**
  - Give adults or children acetaminophen (Tylenol, others) or ibuprofen (Advil, Motrin, others), according to the label instructions.
  - Adults may use aspirin instead. Don't give children aspirin.
- **For children and adults with temperatures more than 104 F (40 C):**
  - A sponge bath of lukewarm water may help to bring the temperature down.
  - Recheck the temperature every half-hour.

Medical Help

Call your health care provider about a fever in any of the following situations:

- A temperature of more than 104 F (40 C)
- A temperature of more than 102 F (38.5 C) for three or more days in anyone 3 months or older
- An older adult with a chronic medical condition and a fever

A fever is only one sign of the illness. Tell the doctor what contagious diseases people around you have had, including flu, colds, measles and mumps.

Call your health care provider **immediately** with fever in an infant, or if any of these symptoms accompany a fever:

- A baby 3 months or younger with a temperature of 100.4 F (38 C) or higher
- A bulging soft spot on a baby's head
- A severe headache or unusual eye sensitivity to bright light
- Severe swelling of the throat
- Significant stiff neck and pain when the head is bent forward
- Persistent vomiting
- Difficulty breathing
- Mental confusion or extreme listlessness or irritability

Kids' Care

An unexplained fever is a greater cause for concern in children than in adults. A rapid rise or fall in temperature causes a seizure in about 1 in 25 children younger than age 6. It generally lasts less than 10 minutes and usually causes no permanent damage. If a seizure occurs, lay your child on his or her side and hold the child to prevent trauma. Don't place anything in the mouth or try to stop the seizure. Promptly seek medical attention to determine the cause of the seizure and any necessary treatment.

Sometimes a fever accompanies teething. Fever with ear pulling often indicates a middle ear infection. Ask your doctor about fevers associated with shots.

It's usually easier to give medications in liquid form. For a small child, use a syringe (without the needle). Gently squirt the medicine in the back corners of the child's mouth.

Have your child drink water, juice or soda pop or suck on frozen fruit pops.

Taking Temperatures

There are several types of electronic digital thermometers and methods for taking your child's temperature. Mercury thermometers shouldn't be used and should be removed from the home to prevent accidental exposure to this toxin.

Rectal. Provides the best reading for a child 3 months to 4 years old.

- Clean end of thermometer with rubbing alcohol or soap and water. Place a small amount of lubricant, such as petroleum jelly, on the end.
- Lay the child on his or her stomach.
- Turn on the thermometer and carefully insert the end one-half to one inch into the anal opening.
- Hold the thermometer and child still for about one minute, until you hear the beep.
- Remove the thermometer and check the reading.

Oral. Generally the preferred method for children age 4 and older.

- Clean end of thermometer with rubbing alcohol or soap and water.
- Turn the switch on and place sensor under the tongue toward the back of the mouth.
- Hold the thermometer in place about one minute, until you hear the beep.
- Remove the thermometer and check the reading.

Ear. Tympanic thermometers, which measure temperature inside the ear, are an option for children 3 months or older.

- Gently place the end of the thermometer in the ear canal — placement needs to be correct to get an accurate reading.
- Press start button. Reading appears in seconds.

Pain

Physical pain is a part of life. Perhaps you've slammed your finger in a door, burned your hand touching the hot handle of a pan on the stove or twisted your ankle while playing your favorite sport. The result is a sensation of pain.

A great deal of the pain you experience in life may be intense, but it's usually short-lived. It may last only moments or might continue for days or weeks, depending on the severity of the injury and how long it takes to heal. Most of the time, however, the pain eventually does go away. This type of temporary pain is known as **acute pain.**

When pain lasts long after the normal healing process, or when there doesn't seem to be any past injury or bodily damage causing ongoing pain, it's known as **chronic pain.** Generally, chronic pain is considered to be pain that lasts more than three months. The American Pain Foundation estimates that more than 50 million Americans suffer from chronic pain, resulting in 50 million lost workdays each year, and a National Sleep Foundation study indicates about 20 percent of older adults have trouble sleeping a few nights a week due to pain.

Chronic pain can be overwhelming. But you can learn ways to manage your pain so that your life can be more fulfilling and enjoyable, and you can still carry out your daily activities. Your attitude about your pain, along with medications and therapies, can help you to control it. An important part of managing your pain is understanding it.

Why Doesn't the Pain Stop?

When your body is injured or infected, special nerve endings in your skin, joints, muscles or internal organs send messages to your brain telling it that there has been damage or an unpleasant stimulus to your body. Specialized nerve fibers instantaneously tell your brain where the pain is, how badly it hurts and the character of the pain (sharp, burning or throbbing). Your brain then "reads" these pain signals and sends back a message to stop you from doing whatever is causing the pain. If you're touching something hot, for example, your brain will send a message to your muscles to contract so that you will pull back your hand.

Your brain also sends a message to your nerve cells to stop sending pain signals once the cause of the pain goes away (for example, when your injury starts to heal). But sometimes this mechanism fails, like a gate that's blocked open. For some reason, your nervous system continues to fire pain signals to your brain for months or even years after the injury heals, or even when there has been no bodily damage. The result is chronic pain.

3. The brain interprets the message as pain, including its location, intensity and nature (burning, aching, stinging)

1. Pain source

2. Pain messages move through peripheral nerves up the spinal cord

4. The brain sends pain-suppressing chemicals to the pain source and triggers other responses

The Role of Emotions in Pain

Pain is an unpleasant sensory and emotional experience, typically associated with actual or potential tissue damage. Pain isn't only a physical experience but also an emotional one. Part of how you interpret and react to your pain is the result of your personal experience and upbringing.

Everyone perceives pain differently. If you learned to ignore or work through pain, it may have less of an effect on you than if you grew up in a family where people talked a lot about the pain they were in and how much they were suffering.

When you experience pain for a long time, it can cause frustration and irritability, and can lead to depression. You might also fall into a "sick role" — a feeling of being a victim of your pain that might bring you more attention and relieve you of some responsibilities. However, a sick role can cause you to become more inactive and isolated and even increase your perception of pain. Stress and unhappiness also tend to amplify pain and lessen your tolerance to it. Finding positive ways to cope with your pain can have both physical and emotional benefits.

■ Common Forms of Chronic Pain

Chronic pain can become debilitating, but there are many ways to effectively manage pain. The key to pain control is a careful review of causes and a coordinated approach to management. Early and effective treatment of acute pain, such as after an operation or after a bout of shingles, often can prevent chronic pain. If you already have chronic pain, various treatments exist. Some common forms of chronic pain are listed below.

Back pain. Low back pain is the most common cause of job-related disability in the United States and a leading contributor to missed work. Lingering back pain may be related to a variety of causes, including muscle strain and spasm, poor body mechanics, physical deconditioning, spinal changes, such as a herniated disk, and degenerative diseases, such as osteoarthritis. (See Back and Neck, page 50.)

Headache. The most common type of head pain is the so-called tension-type headache. However, doctors aren't certain it's caused by actual muscle tension. The start or worsening of tension headaches isn't always related to stressful events. The throbbing pain of a migraine may be related to changes in blood vessels located in your head. Genetics, medication, alcohol, certain foods, exertion, and anxiety or depression may provoke a migraine. (See Headache, page 82.)

Arthritis. Arthritis is the general name for an affliction of the joints. Osteoarthritis usually affects cartilage in joints of the knees, hands, hips and spine. Rheumatoid arthritis involves inflammation of tissue around and in the joints. It typically affects the hands and feet. (See Arthritis, page 161.)

Fibromyalgia. Fibromyalgia syndrome is a collection of symptoms that includes widespread pain and tenderness. It differs from arthritis in that the pain is in muscles and tissues near the joints instead of in the joints themselves. Symptoms may flare and then subside, but they usually don't disappear completely.

Neuropathy. Neuropathic pain is caused by damage to your nervous system. It may occur after an injury or as a result of a long-term disease, such as diabetes. It can be one of the most difficult types of pain to treat. Another form of pain related to nerve damage follows an attack of shingles, which usually affects older adults. It causes burning, searing pain.

Irritable bowel syndrome. This is a complex disorder of the lower intestinal tract that causes pain, bloating and recurrent bouts of diarrhea or constipation.

Stimulating Your Natural Painkillers

Studies show that aerobic exercise can stimulate the release of endorphins, your body's own natural painkillers. Endorphins are morphine-like pain relievers that send "stop pain" messages to your nerve cells. Duration of exercise seems to be more important than intensity. Doing low-intensity aerobic exercises for 30 to 45 minutes at a time five or six days a week may produce an effect. Be sure to build up slowly. Even three or four days of exercise a week may have some effect.

If you want to begin an exercise program that's more vigorous than walking, have a medical evaluation if:
- You're older than age 40
- You've been sedentary
- You have risk factors for coronary artery disease (see page 178)
- You have chronic health problems

Self-Care

After serious diseases have been excluded or treated, the following options may help you better manage chronic pain:

- **Stay active.** Focus on the things you can do. Try new hobbies and activities. Exercise daily. An activity that initially causes some pain doesn't necessarily cause further damage or worsen chronic pain. If you have arthritis, exercise can improve the range of motion in your joints. Exercises for your back and abdominal muscles may help relieve or even prevent back pain. Begin slowly. Work up to 20 to 30 minutes three or four times a week.
- **Focus on others.** When you pay more attention to the needs of others, you focus less on your own difficulties. Get involved in community, church or other volunteer activities.
- **Accept your pain.** Don't deny or exaggerate how you feel, but be clear and honest with others about your current capabilities. Be practical about what you can accomplish, and let people know when you're overcommitted.
- **Stay healthy.** Eat and sleep on a regular schedule.
- **Relax.** Muscle tension increases your awareness of pain. Traditional techniques such as massage or enjoying a whirlpool bath can promote muscle relaxation and general comfort. Learn relaxation skills, such as controlled-breathing exercises and visualization. (See Keeping Stress Under Control on page 225.)
- **Keep a pain diary.** A pain diary can be helpful when you're communicating with your doctor about pain.
  - Write a detailed description of your pain while you're having it.
  - Describe the location, intensity and frequency of your pain and what makes it better or worse.
  - Use words such as stinging, penetrating, dull, throbbing, achy, nagging or gnawing to describe the quality of your pain.
  - Note what days or time of day the pain is better or worse.

Medical Help

If your pain changes in character — for example, it escalates from mild to severe — or if you develop new symptoms — such as tingling or numbness — it might be a good idea to see your doctor to have your condition re-evaluated.

Using Pain-Relieving Medications Safely

Some over-the-counter medications can be effective for reducing chronic pain. Medications such as aspirin, ibuprofen and acetaminophen help control pain in various ways by interfering with the manner in which pain messages are developed, transmitted or interpreted.

For safe use of pain medications:

- Read the label and follow all instructions, cautions and warnings. Never use more than the maximum recommended dose.
- Unless a doctor recommends it, adults should not use pain medication for more than 10 days in a row. The limit for children and teenagers is five days.
- Don't take aspirin during the last three months of pregnancy unless your doctor recommends it. Aspirin can cause bleeding in both the mother and the child. Children shouldn't take aspirin unless directed to do so by a physician.
- If you're allergic to aspirin, check with your doctor or pharmacist about which pain relievers you can use safely.
- For more on pain medications, see page 258.

■ Chronic Pain Treatment Programs

Advances in medicine have created a wide range of options for managing chronic pain. Pain programs may use one or a combination of the following approaches:

Surgery. In some situations, surgery may help relieve or reduce the pain. Many times, though, surgery isn't an option.

Interventional approaches. For some forms of chronic pain, a doctor may attempt to control the pain with injections of medication at or near the site of the pain. Other interventional approaches include implanting small devices in your body, such as a nerve stimulator or medication pump, to help control pain.

Medication. Many types of drugs are used to help control chronic pain, based on the severity of the pain and the disease or disorder causing it.

Physical and occupational therapies. Physical therapy programs focus on reducing pain through a regular exercise program that includes flexibility, aerobic and strengthening exercises. Occupational therapy is primarily based on proper body mechanics — using your muscles and joints correctly to limit pain.

Cognitive and behavioral therapies. These approaches focus on understanding the behaviors, actions, feelings and relationship problems that often accompany chronic pain, and developing positive ways to deal with them.

Complementary and alternative therapies. These include a variety of practices such as yoga, massage, meditation and acupuncture.

Rehabilitation. Rehabilitation therapy may involve a specific program to regain motor function or assistance in learning new skills.

FOR MORE INFORMATION

- American Pain Society, 4700 W. Lake Ave., Glenview, IL 60025; (847) 375-4715, fax (877) 734-8758; *www.ampainsoc.org.*
- American Chronic Pain Association, P.O. Box 850, Rocklin, CA 95677; (800) 533-3231, fax (916) 632-3208; *www.theacpa.org.*

Sleep Disorders

■ Insomnia

The most common of 60 or more sleep disorders is **insomnia**. Insomnia includes difficulty going to sleep, staying asleep or going back to sleep when you awaken early. It may be temporary or chronic. Insomnia may be either a symptom of another disorder or, in some cases, a separate disease. Common causes include the following:

- Stress related to work, school, health or family concerns.
- Depression and anxiety.
- Use of stimulants (caffeine or nicotine), herbal supplements and over-the-counter and prescription medications.
- Alcohol.
- Change in environment or work schedule.
- Long-term use of sleep medications.
- Chronic medical problems, including fibromyalgia or complex diseases of the nerves and muscles.
- Behavioral insomnia, which may occur when you worry excessively about not being able to sleep well and try too hard to fall asleep. Most people with this condition sleep better when they're away from their usual sleep environment.

Sleep Cycle

Typically, you have four to five sleep cycles a night, lasting 70-90 minutes each. At the end of each cycle, you are nearly awake.

Light Sleep
Body movement decreases. Spontaneous awakening may occur.

Intermediate Sleep
Most of the night is spent in this stage. Helps refresh body.

Deep Sleep
Difficult to arouse. Most restorative stage, lasting 30-40 minutes in first few cycles, less in later cycles.

REM (Rapid Eye Movement)
Dreaming occurs. Heart rate increases. Lasts about 10 minutes in first cycle, 20-30 minutes in later cycles.

Self-Care

- Establish and follow a ritual for going to bed.
- Avoid afternoon or evening naps.
- Avoid strenuous exercise right before bedtime. Moderate exercise four to six hours before bedtime is preferable.
- Set aside a "worry time" during the day.
- Avoid taking work materials to bed or using the Internet right before bedtime.
- Take a warm bath one to two hours before bedtime.
- Drink a glass of milk, warm or cold. A light snack is fine, but don't eat a large snack or meal or consume alcohol close to bedtime.
- Keep your sleeping environment dark, quiet and comfortably cool. If necessary, use eye covers and earplugs.
- Try relaxation techniques (see page 227).
- Lower or eliminate use of stimulants. Avoid beverages and medications with caffeine.
- Do not smoke before bedtime.
- If you still can't sleep after 30 minutes, get up. Stay up until you feel tired, and then return to bed. But, as a result, do not shift your rising time.
- Keep a sleep diary. If, after a week or two, you still can't sleep, see your physician. Tests may uncover the cause of your insomnia.

Kids' Care

Bed-wetting (enuresis) is the most common reason children ages 3 to 15 wake up at night. Contact the National Kidney Foundation at (888) 925-3379, for suggestions.

Nightmares may be a response to stress or trauma that occurs during waking hours. Calmly reassure your child after an incident.

Night terrors generally occur between ages 3 and 5, and they tend to run in families. Sleepers may awaken screaming, with no recollection of a dream. Emotional tension increases night terrors.

Sleepwalking may include opening doors, going to the bathroom, dressing or undressing. This runs in families and is most common in children ages 6 to 12.

Should You Nap, or Not?

The urge for a midday snooze is built into your body's biological clock. This typically occurs between 1 p.m. and 4 p.m., as indicated by a slight dip in your body temperature.

Napping isn't a substitute for a full night's sleep. Don't nap if sleeping at night is a problem. If you find a nap refreshes you and doesn't interfere with nighttime sleep, try these ideas:

- **Keep it short.** A half-hour nap is ideal. Naps longer than an hour or two are more likely to interfere with your nighttime sleep.
- **Take a midafternoon nap.** Naps at this time produce a physically invigorating slumber.
- **If you can't nap, just rest.** Lie down for a short time and focus your mind on something else.

■ Other Sleep Disorders

Recurrent episodes of breathing stoppage during sleep (obstructive sleep apnea). People with this problem snore and stop breathing for short periods, from which they emerge with a jerk or gasp. If you have these symptoms, see your doctor. Relaxation of tissues of the soft palate, enlarged adenoids or nasal polyps may block an upper airway causing obstructive sleep apnea. Losing weight, sleeping on your stomach or side and avoiding alcohol before bedtime may improve symptoms. Your doctor may recommend a mask placed over your nose while you sleep to keep your airway open.

Grinding or clenching your teeth during sleep (bruxism) may be associated with stress. Your dentist can check whether your bite needs adjustment and provide you with a plastic guard to prevent further damage. Attempt to deal with the source of your tension. Learn relaxation skills (see page 227).

Excessive sleepiness may be controlled by getting plenty of sleep at night, taking a daytime nap and following a regular sleep schedule. Eat light or vegetarian meals and use caffeinated drinks (coffee, tea and colas) to keep you awake, especially before important activities. If you still need help, your physician may prescribe a stimulant.

Restless legs syndrome is the irresistible urge to move your legs and can occur shortly after you go to bed or throughout the night, interfering with your ability to sleep. Get up and walk around. Try muscle relaxation techniques and a warm bath before bedtime. See a doctor for severe symptoms.

FOR MORE INFORMATION

- National Sleep Foundation, 1522 K St. N.W., Suite 500, Washington, D.C. 20005; (202) 347-3471, fax (202) 347-3472; *www.sleepfoundation.org*.

General Symptoms

Sweating and Body Odor

Sweating is the body's normal response to the buildup of body heat. Sweating varies widely from person to person. Many women perspire more heavily during menopause. Drinking hot beverages, or those containing alcohol or caffeine, can cause temporary increases in sweating.

For most of us, sweating is only a minor nuisance. But for some people, sweaty armpits, feet and hands are a major dilemma. Sweat is basically odorless, but it may take on an unpleasant or offensive odor when bacteria multiply and break down the body's secretions into odor-causing byproducts. Sweating and odor may be influenced by mood, activity, hormones and some foods, such as caffeine.

A "cold sweat" is usually the body's response to a serious illness, anxiety or severe pain. A cold sweat should receive immediate medical attention if there are signs of lightheadedness or chest and stomach pains.

Self-Care

- **Wear clothing made of natural materials,** especially cotton, next to the skin.
- **Bathe daily.** Antibacterial soaps may help, but they can be irritating.
- **Try over-the-counter products,** such as antiperspirant sprays and lotions, that contain aluminum chlorohydrate or buffered aluminum sulfate.
- **For sweaty feet,** choose shoes made of natural materials that breathe, such as leather. Wear the right socks. Cotton and wool socks can help keep your feet dry because they absorb moisture. Change your socks or hosiery once or twice a day, drying your feet thoroughly each time. Dry your feet thoroughly after a bath. Microorganisms thrive in the damp spaces between your toes. Use over-the-counter foot powders to help absorb sweat. Air out your feet. Go without shoes when it's sensible. But when you can't, slip out of them from time to time. Women should try pantyhose with cotton soles.
- **For sweaty armpits,** use antiperspirants. If irritation remains a problem, a 0.5 percent hydrocortisone cream (available without prescription) can help.
- **Apply antiperspirants nightly** at bedtime to sweaty palms or soles of feet. Try perfume-free antiperspirants.
- **Try iontophoresis.** This procedure, in which a low current of electricity is delivered to the affected body part with a battery-powered device, may help. However, it may be no more effective than a topical antiperspirant.
- **Eliminate caffeine and other stimulants** from your diet, as well as foods with strong odors, such as garlic and onions.

Medical Help

Your doctor may recommend a prescription antiperspirant. In some cases, surgical removal of troublesome sweat glands may help. However, this is appropriate for only a few people who have persistent soreness and irritation caused by antiperspirants or excessive sweating. Repeated injections of botulinum toxin also may be used to decrease sweat gland activity.

Consult your doctor if there's an increase in sweating or nighttime sweating without an obvious cause. Infections, thyroid gland dysfunction and certain forms of cancer may produce unusual sweating patterns.

Excessive sweating associated with shortness of breath requires immediate action. This could be a sign of a heart attack.

Occasionally, a change in odor signals a disease. A fruity smell may be a sign of diabetes, or an ammonia-like smell could be a sign of liver disease.

Unexpected Weight Changes

In most cases, the reasons for change in weight are obvious. Changes in diet or activity are the usual explanations. Physical illness also can affect your weight. An unexpected weight change of 5 percent to 10 percent of your body weight (7½ to 15 pounds for a 150-pound person, or 3.4 to 6.8 kilograms for a 68-kilogram person) in six or fewer months is significant. If you lose or gain weight and can't point to a reason, or if you are losing or gaining weight very rapidly, talk to your health care provider.

■ Weight Gain

Weight gain is the most common scenario in adulthood. The increase in weight is usually a gradual creep — a few pounds a year. Careful diet and regular exercise can stop this trend.

If you've experienced a rapid gain, consider these possible causes:

1. **Diet changes.** Increased intake of alcohol or soda, a new favorite high-fat food such as ice cream, sweet rolls or fried foods, increased snacking, a switch to fast foods or prepared foods.
2. **Decrease in activity.** An injury restricting movement, a switch from an active to a sedentary job or a change in a routine such as using stairs or walking to work.
3. **New medication.** Some medicines can contribute to weight gain. Some antidepressants and some hormones, including estrogen, progesterone and cortisone, may produce weight gain.
4. **Changes in mood.** Excessive anxiety, stress or depression can affect activity and food intake. (See Depression and the Blues, page 200.)
5. **Fluid retention.** Medical conditions such as heart or kidney failure or thyroid conditions cause fluid buildup. Have you noted puffiness of the tissues — tight rings or shoes, progressive swelling of the ankles as the day progresses, unusual shortness of breath or new, frequent trips to the bathroom at night?

Self-Care

If item 1 or 2 listed above applies to you, change your diet and increase your activity. (See Weight: What's Healthy for You?, page 206, and Physical Activity: The Key to Burning Calories, page 209.) Wait four to six weeks to see if the changes work. If they don't, or if item 3, 4 or 5 applies to you, see your doctor.

■ Weight Loss

Unexplained weight loss of up to 10 percent of your body weight over six or fewer months often is cause for concern, but not always. Consider the following possibilities:

1. **A change in diet,** such as skipping meals, eating on the run, a significant reduction in fat intake, a change in meal preparation methods, a change in routines around mealtime or eating alone can cause weight loss.
2. **A change in activity,** such as a job change, a new exercise program, a busy or hectic schedule or a seasonal variation can cause weight loss.
3. **Decrease in appetite,** perhaps due to stress, anxiety or an underlying medical condition can cause weight loss.

4. **New medication,** including some antidepressants or stimulants — prescription or over-the-counter (caffeine, herbals).

5. **Mood changes,** such as depression, can cause weight loss (see page 198).

6. **Other conditions,** including dental problems; uncontrolled diabetes with thirst or increased urination; overactive thyroid gland (hyperthyroidism); digestive disorders, such as malabsorption or ulcer with abdominal pain; inflammatory bowel diseases, such as Crohn's or colitis, causing diarrhea and bloody stools; cancer; infections, such as human immunodeficiency virus (HIV), AIDS or tuberculosis.

Self-Care

If item 1 or 2 listed above applies to you, but none of the other items seem to fit, modify your diet. Eat three balanced meals. For snacks, or when you can't eat a good meal, try a nutritional supplement drink. Powders that you mix with milk are simple, fairly balanced and less expensive than ready-to-eat supplements. If you haven't reversed the weight loss trend in two weeks, or if item 3, 4, 5 or 6 seems to fit, see your doctor without delay.

Kids' Care

Weight loss or failure to grow in children may be caused by a digestive problem that prevents important nutrients from being digested or absorbed. Loss of these nutrients can lead to stunted growth and other problems. Your child also may have another underlying medical condition or an eating disorder. If your child has unexplained weight loss, consult your child's health care provider.

Eating Disorders: Anorexia Nervosa and Bulimia Nervosa

Anorexia nervosa is an eating disorder that can lead to severe weight loss as a result of self-imposed semi-starvation. A person with bulimia nervosa is often at normal weight but uses binge eating and purging (self-induced vomiting or laxative abuse) as a means of weight control. Both eating disorders are most common in adolescent girls and young women, but they can occur in males and older adults.

The number of people affected by anorexia and bulimia has increased as more emphasis is placed on being thin and attractive. Decreasing this emphasis and not placing unrealistic expectations on adolescents may be steps in curbing this trend. If you suspect an eating disorder in yourself or others, contact your health care provider.

Anorexia nervosa

Signs and symptoms:
- Misperception of body image — you see yourself as being fatter than you are
- Unrealistic fear of becoming fat
- Excessive dieting and exercise
- Significant weight loss or failure to gain weight during a period of growth
- Refusal to maintain a normal body weight
- Absence of menstrual periods
- Preoccupation with food, calories and food preparation

The cause of anorexia nervosa is unclear, but biological and psychological factors may be involved. Total recovery is possible if the disorder is diagnosed early. Left untreated, anorexia can lead to death. Treatment involves psychotherapy, diet counseling and family counseling in most cases. Hospitalization may be needed in severe cases.

Bulimia nervosa

Signs and symptoms:
- Recurrent episodes of binge eating
- Self-induced vomiting or laxative abuse
- Weight usually within fairly normal range
- Fear of becoming fat

Bulimia involves eating large amounts of food and then purging by vomiting or abusing laxatives. It's also a form of semistarvation. Purging depletes water and potassium from the body and can lead to death. People with bulimia often become depressed because they realize that their eating is abnormal. Treatment usually includes behavior modification, psychotherapy and, in some cases, antidepressant medication. Hospitalization may be needed if the disorder is out of control and there are complications.

See back cover for online resource

Common Problems

- Back and Neck
- Digestive System
- Ears and Hearing
- Eyes and Vision
- Headache
- Limbs, Muscles, Bones and Joints
- Lungs, Chest and Breathing
- Nose and Sinuses
- Skin, Hair and Nails
- Throat and Mouth
- Men's Health
- Women's Health

Most pains and ailments aren't serious. Often, simple remedies in combination with time can help resolve the problem and save you a trip to the doctor. Of course, if the problem persists or if simple remedies don't help, you need to seek medical care.

This section is mainly organized by body system. Each section includes several illnesses or symptoms with appropriate self-care advice and suggestions on when to see your doctor. Sidebar articles address related topics or offer insight into medical issues. Children's health is also addressed where appropriate throughout the section.

Back and Neck

Almost everyone has a back problem at some time. Back pain sends many people to health care providers each year. Fortunately, you can do things to prevent back problems. And you can do them most effectively if you know a little bit about your back.

Your back supports your body. It holds and protects your spinal cord and nerves that send signals back and forth from your brain to the rest of your body. And it serves as a place of attachment for muscles and ligaments of the back.

Anatomy

Your spine, or so-called backbone, isn't one bone, but many. If you look at a healthy spine from the side, it curves inward at the neck and lower back and outward at the upper back and pelvis.

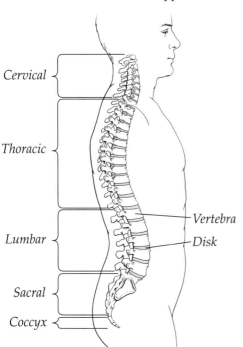

Cervical

Thoracic

Lumbar

Sacral

Coccyx

Vertebra

Disk

Vertebrae. The backbone, or vertebral column, is composed of bones called vertebrae, which are held together by tough, fibrous bands called ligaments. The normal adult vertebral column consists of seven cervical (neck) vertebrae, 12 thoracic (middle back) vertebrae, and five large lumbar (lower back) vertebrae. The lumbar vertebrae are the largest because they bear most of the body weight. The sacrum, made from five vertebrae that are fused together, is below the lumbar vertebrae. The last three vertebrae, also fused together, are called the coccyx, or tailbone.

Spinal cord. The spinal cord, part of the central nervous system, extends from the base of the skull to the lower back through the bony spinal canal. Two nerves (spinal nerves) are sent out at each vertebral level. In the upper lumbar part of the back where the spinal cord ends, a group of nerves (cauda equina) continue down the spinal canal. The spinal nerves exit from openings (foramina) on each side of the vertebrae, one leading to the right side of the body and the other to the left. In all, there are 31 pairs of these spinal nerves in the back and neck.

Disks. Between the vertebrae, and close to the point of exit of each pair of spinal nerves, are intervertebral disks. These disks prevent the hard and bony vertebrae from hitting one another when you walk, run or jump. They also allow the spine to move in all directions — twisting, bending and extending. A disk is made up of a ring of tough, fibrous tissue that has a jelly-like substance in the center. Damaged outer disk rings may cause the jelly-like interior to bulge outward — what's commonly know as a ruptured (herniated, or slipped) disk (see page 53). This may produce pressure on surrounding nerves or tissue, causing pain. (A disk doesn't actually slip because it's firmly attached between the vertebrae.)

Muscles. Muscles are like elastic bands up and down your back that support your spine. They contract or relax to help you stand, twist, bend or stretch. Tendons connect muscles to bones. The muscles of your abdomen and trunk support, protect and move your spine.

With age your spine may become stiff and lose its flexibility. Disks become worn, and the spaces between vertebrae may narrow. These changes are part of the aging process, but they're not necessarily painful. Vertebrae sometimes develop jutting bone spurs, which may or may not produce pain. As the cartilage that cushions joints wears out, bones can rub together, and you may experience the pain of arthritis. Often, though, it's hard to pinpoint the cause of back pain because of the back's complexity.

Common Back and Neck Problems

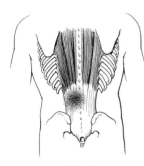

Your lower back, a pivot point for turning at your waist, is vulnerable to muscle strains.

Your lower back carries most of your weight. Among people age 40 and older, it's the site of most **back pain**. However, strains and sprains can injure any part of your neck or back.

Causes of back and neck pain include:
- Improper lifting (see Lifting Properly, page 54)
- A sudden, strenuous physical effort; an accident, sports injury or fall
- Lack of muscle tone
- Excess weight, especially around your middle
- Your sleeping position, especially if you sleep on your stomach
- Sitting in one position a long time; poor sitting and standing postures
- A pillow that forces your neck into an awkward angle
- Holding the telephone with your shoulder
- Carrying a heavy briefcase, purse or shoulder bag or backpack
- Sitting with a thick wallet in your back pocket
- Holding a forward-bending position for a long time
- Daily stress and tension
- Relaxation of muscles and ligaments during pregnancy

'No Pain, No Gain' — Not True!

You may become sore immediately after you've injured a muscle, or it may take several hours before it feels sore. An injured muscle may uncontrollably tighten or "knot up" (a muscle spasm). Your body is telling you to slow down and prevent further injury. A severe muscle spasm may last 48 to 72 hours, followed by days or weeks of less severe pain. Strenuous use of an injured muscle during the next three to six weeks may bring back the pain. However, most back pain is gone in six weeks.

As you age, muscle tone and strength tends to decrease, and your back is more prone to aches or injury. Maintaining your flexibility and strength and keeping your abdominal muscles strong are your best bets to avoid back problems. Spending 10 to 15 minutes a day doing gentle stretching and strengthening exercises can help.

Self-Care

Healing will occur most quickly if you can continue your usual activities in a gentle manner while avoiding what may have caused the pain in the first place. Avoid long periods of bed rest, which can worsen your pain and make you weaker.

With proper care of a strain or sprain, you should notice improvement within the first two weeks. Most forms of acute back pain improve in four to six weeks. Sprained ligaments or severe muscle strains may take up to 12 weeks to heal. Once you have back pain, you're more prone to experience repeated painful episodes.

Follow these home care steps:
- Use cold packs initially to relieve pain. Wrap an ice pack or a bag of frozen vegetables in a piece of cloth. Hold it on the sore area for 15 minutes four times a day. To avoid frostbite, never place ice directly on your skin.
- You may be most comfortable lying with your back on the floor, hips and knees bent and legs elevated. Get plenty of rest, but avoid prolonged bed rest — more than a day or two may slow recovery. Moderate movement keeps your muscles strong and flexible. Avoid the activity that caused the sprain or strain. Avoid heavy lifting, pushing or pulling, repetitive bending and twisting.

Common Problems

Self-Care

- After 48 hours, you may use heat to relax sore or knotted muscles. Use a warm bath, warm packs, a heating pad or a heat lamp. Be careful not to burn your skin with extreme heat. But if you find that cold provides more relief than heat, you can continue using cold, or try a combination of the two methods.
- Gradually begin gentle stretching exercises. Avoid jerking, bouncing or any movements that increase pain or require straining.
- Use over-the-counter pain medications (see page 258).
- Massage may be helpful, especially for muscle spasms, but avoid placing any pressure directly on your spine.
- If you must stand or sit much of the day, consider using a support brace or corset. Worn properly, they may relieve your pain and provide warmth, comfort and support. However, relying on this type of support for a long time prevents you from using, stretching and exercising your muscles.

Medical Help

Although uncommon, back or neck pain can result from serious problems such as cancer, infection, inflammatory arthritis and other diseases. Pain that worsens or remains constant for a month or more should be investigated by a doctor.

Seek medical care immediately if your pain:

- Is severe.
- Results from a fall or blow to your back. Don't try to move someone who has severe neck pain or can't move his or her legs after an accident. Moving the person can cause further injury.
- Produces weakness or numbness in one or both legs or arms.
- Is new and is accompanied by an unexplained fever.
- Results from an injury that causes pain from your neck to shoot down your arms and legs.
- Is accompanied by poorly controlled blood pressure, an abdominal aortic aneurysm, cancer or a sudden loss of bowel or bladder control.

The nerves to most of your body travel through your back. Sometimes, back or neck pain may be caused by a problem somewhere else in your body. Your doctor may do testing to determine the cause of your pain.

Kids' Care

Low back pain is unusual in children before their teen years. Common causes for back pain are sports injuries or falls. Be sure that your children's athletic programs:

- Use the proper protective equipment
- Have competent coaches
- Use sufficient warm-up and conditioning activities

If your injured child hasn't been unconscious, can move freely and has no numbness or weakness, use the self-care tips listed on page 51. Be careful to avoid excessive heat or cold. Check proper children's doses for over-the-counter medicines. Don't give children aspirin.

If the pain is unrelated to an injury or other known cause, your health care provider may want to check for an infection (especially if your child has a fever) or for factors in your child's development that may cause the pain. Girls often experience low back pain with their menstrual period.

Warning signs of serious back problems in children include constant pain that lasts for several weeks or occurs at night; pain that interferes with school, play or sports; and pain that occurs with stiffness and fever.

Other Common Back Problems

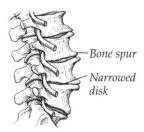

Osteoarthritis

- Bone spur
- Narrowed disk

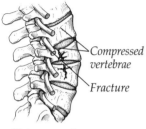

Osteoporosis

- Compressed vertebrae
- Fracture

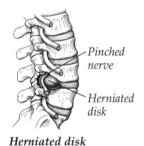

Herniated disk

- Pinched nerve
- Herniated disk

Back and neck problems often don't result from a single incident. They may be the product of a lifetime of stress and strain for your back and neck. If you have chronic back pain, your health care provider may look for the following conditions:

Osteoarthritis affects nearly 21 million Americans, mostly people age 45 and older. Aging causes the protective tissue that covers the surface of vertebral joints to deteriorate. Disks between vertebrae become worn, and the spaces between the bones narrow. Bony outgrowths called spurs also develop. Gradually, your spine can stiffen and lose flexibility.

Osteoporosis is the weakening of your bone structure as the amount of calcium in your bones decreases. Weakened vertebrae become compressed and fracture easily. Medication may slow or halt this process. Individuals over age 50, especially women, are at greatest risk.

Herniated, or slipped, disk occurs when normal wear and tear or exceptional strain causes a disk to rupture. Bulging of disks is common and often painless. It becomes painful when excessive bulging or fragments of the disk place pressure on nearby nerves. This condition may lead to pain in the sciatic nerve (sciatica), which extends down the back of the leg. Symptoms may resolve over days or weeks. Sometimes, the condition becomes chronic and may lead to weakness in the legs.

Fibromyalgia is a chronic syndrome that produces achy pain, tenderness and stiffness in the muscles and joints where tendons attach to your bones. Pain is usually worse after inactivity and improves with movement.

Surgery is usually reserved for times when a nerve is pinched and threatens to cause permanent weakness or is affecting bowel or bladder control. Back pain without nerve injury isn't usually treated with surgery. Leg weakness or pain (sciatica) that persists for more than six weeks despite other treatment can often be relieved with surgery.

Back Injuries in the Workplace

You can avoid many back problems by following these guidelines (see Exercises for Office Workers, page 239, and Coping With Technology, page 245, for other ideas):

- Change positions often.
- Avoid high heels. If you stand for long periods, rest one foot on a small box or stool from time to time.
- Use adjustable equipment. Find comfortable (rather than extreme) positions.
- Don't bend continuously over your work. Hold reading materials at eye level.
- Avoid excessive repetition. Take frequent, short breaks to stretch or relax — even 30 seconds every 10 to 15 minutes helps.
- Avoid unnecessary bending, twisting and reaching.
- Stand to answer your phone. If you're on the phone a lot, get a headset.
- Adjust your chair so your feet are flat on the floor. Change leg positions often.
- Use a chair that supports your lower back's curve or place a rolled towel or pillow behind your lower back. The seat of your chair shouldn't press on the back of your thighs or knees.
- Lift objects properly (see page 54) and carry them close to the body.
- Keep fit. Poor physical fitness and smoking are strong predictors of disability due to back pain.

Common Problems

■ Preventing Common Backaches and Neck Pains

Regular exercise is your most powerful weapon against back and neck problems. Proper exercise can help you:

- Maintain or increase flexibility of muscles, tendons and ligaments
- Strengthen the muscles that support your back
- Increase muscle strength in your arms, legs and lower body to reduce the risk of falls and other injuries and allow optimal posture for lifting and carrying
- Improve your posture
- Increase bone density
- Shed excess pounds that stress your back

If you're older than age 40 or have an illness or injury, check with your health care provider before you begin an exercise program. If you're out of condition, start slowly. Exercises that are good for your back include the following:

- Abdominal and leg strengthening exercises.
- Nonjarring exercise on a stationary bike, treadmill or cross-country skiing machine. Bicycling is good, but be sure your bike seat and handlebars are properly adjusted to keep you in a comfortable position.

If you have back problems or are out of shape, avoid activities that involve quick stops and starts and a lot of twisting. High-impact activities on hard surfaces — such as jogging, tennis, racquetball and basketball — may cause wear and tear to your back. Take precautions to avoid falling and avoid contact sports.

Lifting Properly

Follow these steps:
1. Position your feet firmly, toes pointed slightly outward, one foot slightly ahead of the other. Stand as close to the load as possible.
2. Bend from your knees, and use your powerful leg muscles to lift the load. Keep your back as upright as possible. As you lift, tighten the abdominal muscles that support your spine.
3. Hold the load close to your body. Avoid turning or twisting while holding the load. Avoid lifting heavy loads above your waist.

Proper Sleeping Positions

To avoid aggravating your backache when you sleep or lie down, sleep on your stomach only if your abdomen is cushioned by a pillow (top). If you sleep on your back, support your knees and neck with pillows (middle). Best option: Sleep on your side with your legs drawn up slightly toward your chest with a pillow between your legs (bottom).

■ Your Daily Back Routine

Here are exercises to stretch and strengthen your back and supporting muscles. The exercises should be comfortable and not cause pain. Do them for 15 minutes daily. (If you've hurt your back before or you have health problems such as osteoporosis, talk to your doctor before exercising.)

Shoulder blade squeeze. *Sit upright in a chair. Keep your chin tucked in and your shoulders down. Pull your shoulder blades together and straighten your upper back. Hold a few seconds. Return to starting position. Repeat several times.*

Knee-to-shoulder stretch. *Lie on your back on a firm surface with your knees bent and feet flat. Pull your left knee toward your chest with both hands. Hold for 15 to 30 seconds. Return to starting position. Repeat with opposite leg. Repeat with each leg three or four times.*

Half sit-up. *Lie on your back on a firm surface with your knees bent and feet flat. With your arms outstretched, reach toward your knees with your hands until your shoulder blades no longer touch the ground. Don't grasp your knees. Hold for a few seconds and slowly return to the starting position. Repeat several times.*

Cat stretch. *Step 1. Get down on your hands and knees. Slowly let your back and abdomen sag toward the floor.*

Cat stretch. *Step 2. Slowly arch your back away from the floor. Repeat steps 1 and 2 several times.*

Leg lifts. *Step 1. Lie facedown on a firm surface with a large pillow under your hips and lower abdomen. Keeping your knee bent, raise your leg slightly off the surface and hold about five seconds. Repeat several times with each leg.*

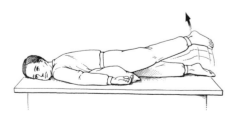

Leg lifts. *Step 2. With your leg straight, raise one leg slightly off the surface and hold for about five seconds. Repeat several times with each leg.*

Digestive System

Your digestive tract is an extremely complex system. Problems can occur anywhere along this tract, upsetting its delicate balance. Because of the complexity of this system, don't attempt to diagnose new problems, such as unexplained pain or bleeding, on your own.

Digestion begins when you chew your food. The food is broken into smaller pieces by your teeth and, at the same time, is mixed with saliva secreted by your salivary glands. Your saliva contains an enzyme that begins to change starches (carbohydrates) into sugars.

Food is propelled down your esophagus to the stomach and then on through the intestines by muscular contractions. This process, called digestion, is aided by digestive juices (acid, bile and enzymes) from the stomach, gallbladder and pancreas. They break down food and allow the nutrients to be absorbed. Undigestible food and bacteria are eliminated as feces from the rectum.

Gastrointestinal tract

Diaphragm

Liver

Gallbladder

Appendix

Esophagus
(food pipe)

Stomach

Pancreas

Large intestine
(colon)

Small intestine

Rectum

■ Abdominal Pain

Pain in your abdomen can occur anywhere along your digestive tract, from your mouth or throat to your pelvis and rectum. In some cases, pain can signal a mild problem such as overeating. In others, it can be an early warning sign of a more serious disorder that may require medical treatment.

Fortunately, many forms of discomfort respond well to a combination of self-care and supervised medical treatment. See the following pages if your pain accompanies any of these conditions: constipation, page 58; diarrhea, page 59; excessive gas, page 60; gastritis, page 61; or hemorrhoids, page 62.

Caution

Although most abdominal pains aren't serious, don't attempt to diagnose the source of new or unexplained pain. Seek medical attention if you experience any of the following: intense pain lasting longer than a minute or pain that seems to be worsening, pain accompanied by shortness of breath or dizziness, or pain accompanied by a temperature of 101 F or more.

What Is Appendicitis?

Your appendix is a worm-shaped structure that projects out from the large intestine. This tiny structure can become inflamed, swollen and filled with pus. This condition is called appendicitis.

Appendicitis typically causes acute pain that starts around your navel and settles in the lower right side of your abdomen. These symptoms generally progress over 12 to 24 hours. You may also experience a loss of appetite, nausea, vomiting and the urge to have a bowel movement or pass gas.

Although appendicitis can affect people of all ages, it usually occurs between the ages of 10 and 30.

An infected appendix may burst and cause a serious infection. Seek immediate medical attention if you suspect you have appendicitis.

Colic

Generations of families have dealt with colic. This frustrating and largely unexplainable condition affects babies who otherwise seem healthy. Colic usually peaks at six weeks of age and disappears in the baby's third to fifth month.

Colic is a difficult experience for everyone. One doctor describes colic as "when the baby's crying — and so is mom."

Although the term *colic* is used widely for any fussy baby, true colic is determined by the following:

- **Predictable crying episodes.** A colicky baby cries about the same time each day, usually in the evening. Colic episodes may last minutes or two or more hours.
- **Activity.** Many colicky babies pull their legs to their chests or thrash around during crying episodes as if they are in pain.
- **Intense or inconsolable crying.** Colicky babies cry more than usual and are extremely difficult — if not impossible — to comfort.

Doctors call colic a "diagnosis of exclusion," which means other possible problems are ruled out before determining the baby has colic. The parent of a colicky infant, therefore, can be assured that the crying is probably not a sign of a serious medical problem.

Studies of colic have focused on several possible causes: allergies, an immature digestive system, gas, hormones, mother's anxieties and handling. Still, it's unclear why some babies have colic and others don't.

Self-Care

If your health care provider determines that your baby has colic, these measures may help you and your child find some relief:

- Lay your baby tummy-down on your lap or arms and sway your baby gently and slowly. This may help him or her pass stool or gas.
- Rock, cuddle or walk your baby. Avoid fast, jiggling movements.
- Play a steady, uninterrupted "white noise" near your baby. Motors with soft noise, such as that in a clothes dryer, may work.
- Put your baby in an infant swing.
- Give your baby a warm bath or lay him or her tummy-down on a warm water bottle.
- Try singing or humming while walking with or rocking the baby. A soothing song can have a quieting effect on both parent and baby.
- Offer a pacifier. Even if you're breast-feeding, it's OK to try a pacifier.
- Experiment with food. Dietary changes can sometimes be helpful, but it's best to work with your doctor.
- Take your baby for a car ride.
- Leave your baby with someone else for 10 minutes and walk alone.

Medical Help

At this time, there are no medications to relieve colic safely and effectively. In general, consult with your health care provider before giving your baby any medication.

If you're worried that your baby is sick or if you or others caring for the baby are becoming frustrated or angry because of the crying, call your doctor or bring the baby to the doctor's office or emergency department.

Common Problems

■ Constipation

This common problem is often misunderstood and improperly treated. Technically speaking, constipation is the passage of hard stools fewer than three times a week. You also may experience a bloated sensation and occasional crampy discomfort. The normal frequency for bowel movements varies widely — from three bowel movements a day to three a week.

Like a fever, constipation is a symptom, not a disease. This problem can occur when one of many factors slows the passage of food through your large bowel. These factors include inadequate fluid intake, poor diet, irregular bowel habits, age, lack of activity, pregnancy and illness. Various medications also can cause constipation.

Although constipation may be extremely bothersome, the condition itself usually is not serious. If it persists, however, constipation can lead to complications such as hemorrhoids and cracks or tears in the anus called fissures.

Self-Care

To lessen your chances of constipation:
- Try to eat on a regular schedule, and eat plenty of high-fiber foods, including fresh fruits, vegetables and whole-grain cereals and breads
- Drink plenty of water or other liquids daily
- Increase your physical activity
- Don't ignore the urge to have a bowel movement
- Try fiber supplements such as Citrucel, Konsyl or Metamucil
- Don't rely on laxatives (see below)

Medical Help

Contact your doctor if your constipation is severe or it lasts longer than three weeks. In rare cases, constipation may signal more serious medical conditions such as cancer, hormonal disturbances, heart disease or kidney failure.

Kids' Care

Constipation isn't usually a problem among infants, especially if they're breast-feeding. A healthy breast-fed infant may have as few as one bowel movement a week.

Young children sometimes experience constipation because they neglect to take time to use the bathroom. Toddlers also may become constipated during toilet training because of a fear or unwillingness to use the toilet. However, as few as one bowel movement a week may be normal for your child.

If constipation is a problem, have your child drink plenty of fluids to soften stools. Warm baths also may help relax your child and encourage bowel movements.

Avoid use of laxatives in children unless advised by your doctor.

Excessive Use of Laxatives Can Be Harmful

Habitual or excessive use of laxatives can actually be harmful and make your constipation worse. Overusing these medications can:
- Cause your body to flush out necessary vitamins and other nutrients before they are absorbed. This process disrupts your body's normal balance of salts and nutrients.
- Interfere with other medications you're taking.
- Induce lazy bowel syndrome, a condition in which your bowels fail to function properly because they've begun to rely on the laxative to stimulate elimination. As a result, when you stop using laxatives, your constipation may worsen.

See back cover for online resource ⓘ

■ Diarrhea

Diarrhea affects adults an average of four times a year. Signs and symptoms include loose, watery stools, often accompanied by abdominal cramps.

Diarrhea has many causes, most of which aren't serious. The most common is a viral infection of your digestive tract. Bacteria and parasites also can cause diarrhea. These organisms cause your bowel to lose excess water and salts as diarrhea.

Nausea and vomiting may precede diarrhea that's caused by an infection. In addition, you may notice cramping, abdominal pain and other flu-like signs and symptoms, such as low-grade fever, achy or cramping muscles and headache. Bacterial or parasitic infestations sometimes cause bloody stools or a high fever.

Infection-induced diarrhea can be extremely contagious. You can catch a viral infection by direct contact with an infected person. Food and water contaminated with bacteria or parasites also spread diarrheal infections.

Diarrhea can be a side effect of many medications, particularly antibiotics. In addition, the artificial sweeteners sorbitol and mannitol found in chewing gum and other sugar-free products can cause bloating and diarrhea in some people, especially when consumed in excessive amounts. Chronic or recurrent diarrhea may signal a more serious underlying medical problem such as chronic infection or inflammatory bowel disease.

Self-Care

Although uncomfortable, diarrhea caused by infections typically clears on its own without antibiotics. Over-the-counter medications such as Imodium, Pepto-Bismol and Kaopectate may slow diarrhea, but they won't speed your recovery. Take these measures to prevent dehydration and reduce symptoms while you recover:

- Drink at least 8 to 16 glasses (2 to 4 quarts) of clear liquids, including water, clear sodas, broths and weak tea.
- Add semisolid and low-fiber foods gradually as your bowel movements return to normal. Try soda crackers, toast, eggs, rice or chicken.
- Avoid dairy products, fatty foods or highly seasoned foods for a few days.
- Avoid caffeine and nicotine.

Medical Help

Contact your health care provider if diarrhea persists beyond a week or if you become dehydrated (excessive thirst, dry mouth, little or no urination, severe weakness, dizziness or lightheadedness). Also seek medical attention if you have severe abdominal or rectal pain, bloody stools, a temperature of more than 101 F or signs of dehydration despite drinking fluids.

Your doctor may prescribe antibiotics to shorten the duration of diarrhea caused by some bacteria and parasites. However, not all diarrhea caused by bacteria requires treatment with antibiotics, and antibiotics don't help viral diarrhea, which is the most common kind of infectious diarrhea.

Kids' Care

Diarrhea can cause infants to become dehydrated. Contact your health care provider if diarrhea persists for more than 12 hours or if your baby:
- Hasn't had a wet diaper in eight hours
- Has a temperature of more than 102 F
- Has bloody stools
- Has a dry mouth or cries without tears
- Is unusually sleepy or drowsy or unresponsive

Excessive Gas and Gas Pains

Belching

Belching and burping are normal ways to get rid of the air you swallow every time you eat or drink. Belching removes **gas** from your stomach by forcing it into your esophagus and then out your mouth. Swallowing too much air can cause bloating or frequent belching. If you belch repeatedly when not eating, you may be swallowing air as a nervous habit.

Passing Gas

Most intestinal gas (flatus) is produced in the colon. Usually the gas is expelled during a bowel movement. All people pass gas (flatulence), but some people produce an excessive amount of gas that bothers them throughout the day. Intestinal gas is composed primarily of five substances: oxygen, nitrogen, hydrogen, carbon dioxide and methane. The foul odor usually is the result of small traces of other gases such as hydrogen sulfide and ammonia and other substances. Swallowed air makes up a small fraction of intestinal gas. Carbonated drinks may release carbon dioxide in the stomach and may be a source of gas.

Gas Pains

Sharp, jabbing or crampy pains in your abdomen may be caused by the buildup of gas. They're often intense, but brief (less than a minute). They often occur in the right lower and left upper abdomen and change locations quickly. You may notice a knotted feeling in your abdomen. Passing gas sometimes relieves these pains.

Any of the sources of intestinal gas or diarrhea can lead to **gas pains**. Gas pains can occur when your intestines have difficulty breaking down certain foods or when you have a gastrointestinal infection or diarrhea.

Self-Care

To reduce belching and bloating, try the following tips:
- Eat slowly and avoid gulping. Eat fewer rich, fatty foods.
- Avoid chewing gum or sucking on hard candy.
- Limit sipping through straws or drinking from narrow-mouthed bottles.
- Cut down on carbonated drinks and beer.
- Don't smoke cigarettes, pipes or cigars.
- Try to control stress, which may aggravate the nervous habit of swallowing air.
- Don't force yourself to belch.
- Avoid lying down immediately after you eat.

To reduce flatulence, try the following tips:
- Identify the foods that affect you the most. Try eliminating one of these foods for a few weeks to see if your flatulence subsides: beans, peas, lentils, cabbage, radishes, onions, brussels sprouts, sauerkraut, apricots, bananas, prunes and prune juice, raisins, whole-wheat bread, bran cereals or muffins, pretzels, wheat germ, milk, cream, ice cream and ice milk.
- Temporarily cut back on high-fiber foods. Add them back gradually over weeks.
- Reduce dairy products. Try Lactaid or Dairy Ease for lactose intolerance.
- Try adding Beano to high-fiber foods to reduce the amount of gas they make.
- Occasional use of over-the-counter anti-gas products containing simethicone (Mylanta, Mylicon, Riopan Plus) can help. Activated charcoal pills may help.

Gallstones

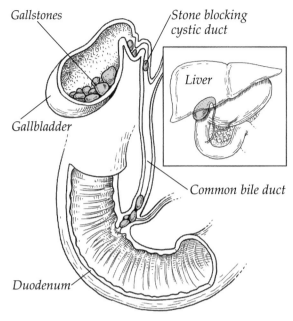

Gallstones · Stone blocking cystic duct · Liver · Gallbladder · Common bile duct · Duodenum

Gallstones may form in your gallbladder. If a stone obstructs your cystic duct, you may experience a gallbladder attack.

Approximately 10 percent to 15 percent of Americans are affected by **gallstones**. Most produce no symptoms. Stones that block the ducts linking your gallbladder with your liver and small intestine can be quite painful and potentially dangerous.

Your gallbladder stores bile, a digestive fluid produced in the liver. The bile passes through ducts from the gallbladder into the small intestine and helps digest fats. A healthy gallbladder has balanced amounts of bile acids and cholesterol. When the concentration of cholesterol becomes too high, gallstones may form.

Gallstones can cause intense and sudden pain that may last for hours. The pain usually begins shortly after eating. It begins in your right upper abdomen and may shift to your back or right shoulder blade. Fever and nausea also may accompany the pain. After your pain subsides, you may notice a mild aching sensation or soreness in your right upper abdomen. If a gallstone blocks your bile duct, your skin and the whites of your eyes may turn yellow (jaundice). You may also develop a fever or pass pale, clay-colored stools.

Older adults and women tend to be at higher risk, especially women who are pregnant or taking estrogen or birth control pills. Your risk may also be higher if:

- You're overweight or have recently lost weight
- You have a family history of this problem or a disorder of the small intestine

Self-Care	Avoid rich, fatty foods and eat smaller meals to reduce episodes of gallbladder pain.
Medical Help	Contact your health care provider if you have recurrent or intense pain. Seek prompt medical attention if you develop yellowing skin or a fever during an attack.

Gastritis (Burning or Sour Stomach)

Gastritis is inflammation of your stomach lining. Upper abdominal discomfort, nausea and vomiting are common symptoms. Gastritis may cause bleeding that appears in vomit or turns your stools black. Most often, gastritis is mild and poses no danger. Gastritis may occur when acid damages your stomach lining. Excessive smoking, alcohol and medications such as aspirin can cause gastritis. Some infections, such as *Helicobacter pylori* (*H. pylori*) infection, also can cause gastritis.

Self-Care	- Avoid smoking, alcohol and foods and drinks that irritate your stomach. - Try taking over-the-counter antacids or medicines such as Pepcid, Tagamet and Zantac. **Caution:** Excessive use of antacids containing magnesium can cause diarrhea. Calcium- or aluminum-based antacids can lead to constipation. - Use pain relievers that contain acetaminophen (see page 258). Avoid aspirin, ibuprofen, ketoprofen and naproxen sodium. They can cause or worsen gastritis.
Medical Help	If your discomfort lasts longer than one week, contact your health care provider.

Hemorrhoids and Rectal Bleeding

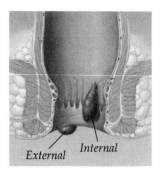

External   *Internal*

Internal hemorrhoids are usually painless but tend to bleed. External hemorrhoids may cause pain.

By age 50, about half of all people have experienced symptoms of <u>hemorrhoids</u> to some extent. Itching, burning and pain around the anus may signal their presence. You may also notice small amounts of bright red blood on your toilet tissue or in the toilet bowl.

Hemorrhoids occur when veins in your rectum become enlarged. They usually form over time as you strain to pass hard stools. Hemorrhoids may develop inside the anal canal or protrude outside the anal opening. Lifting heavy objects, obesity, pregnancy, childbirth, stress and diarrhea also can increase the pressure on these veins and lead to hemorrhoids. This condition seems to run in families.

In addition to hemorrhoids, bleeding from the rectum can occur for other reasons, some of which can be serious. Passing hard, dry stools may scrape the anal lining. An infection of the lining of the rectum or tiny cracks or tears in the lining of your anus called anal fissures also can cause rectal bleeding. With these types of problems, you may notice small drops of bright red blood on your stool, on your toilet tissue or in the toilet bowl.

Black, tarry stools, maroon stools or bright red blood in your stools also may signal more extensive bleeding elsewhere in your digestive tract. Small sacs that protrude from your large intestines (diverticula), ulcers, small growths (polyps), cancer and some chronic bowel disorders can all cause bleeding.

Self-Care

Although uncomfortable, hemorrhoids are not a serious medical condition. Most hemorrhoids respond well to the following self-care measures:

- Drink plenty of water each day and eat high-fiber foods such as wheat-bran cereal, whole-wheat bread, fresh fruit and vegetables.
- Bathe or shower daily to cleanse the skin around your anus gently with warm water. Soap isn't necessary and may aggravate the problem.
- Stay active. Exercise. If at work or home you must sit or stand for long periods, take quick walks or breaks from work.
- Try not to strain during bowel movements or sit on the toilet too long.
- Take warm baths.
- Apply ice packs.
- For flares of pain or irritation, apply over-the-counter creams, ointments or pads containing witch hazel or a topical numbing agent. Keep in mind that these products help relieve only mild itching and irritation.
- Try fiber supplements (Citrucel, Metamucil) to keep stools soft and regular.

Medical Help

Hemorrhoids become most painful when a clot forms in the enlarged vein. If your hemorrhoids are extremely painful, your health care provider may prescribe a cream or suppository containing hydrocortisone to reduce inflammation. Some troublesome internal hemorrhoids may require surgery or other procedures to shrink or eliminate them.

Diagnosing the cause of rectal bleeding can be difficult. See your health care provider for evaluation. Seek immediate emergency care if you notice large amounts of rectal bleeding, lightheadedness, weakness or rapid heart rate (more than 100 beats a minute).

See back cover for online resource

■ Hernias

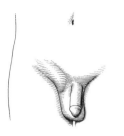

An inguinal hernia can cause a bulge at the junction of your thigh and groin. Bulges can be round or oval.

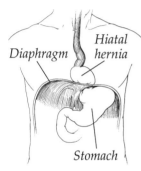

In hiatal hernia, a portion of the stomach protrudes through the diaphragm into the chest cavity.

A hernia occurs when one body part protrudes through a gap into another body area. Some hernias cause no pain or visible symptoms.

Types of Hernias

Inguinal hernia is the medical name for a hernia in the groin area. This type of hernia — which is more frequent in men than in women — accounts for about 75 percent of all hernias. An inguinal hernia occurs along the inguinal canal, an opening in the abdominal muscles. In men, the canal is the spermatic cord's passageway between the abdominal cavity and the scrotum. In women, it's the passageway for a ligament that helps hold the uterus in place. With an inguinal hernia, you may be able to see and feel the bulge created by the protruding tissue or intestine. It's often located at the junction of your thigh and groin. Sometimes in men the protruding intestine enters the scrotum. This can be painful and cause the scrotum to swell. The first sign of an inguinal hernia may be a bulge or lump in your groin. You may notice discomfort while bending over, coughing or lifting and a heavy or dragging sensation.

A *strangulated hernia* occurs when the tissue bulging through the abdominal wall becomes pinched and the blood supply is cut off. The affected tissue dies and then swells, causing extreme pain and a potentially life-threatening situation. Seek immediate medical attention if you think you have a strangulated hernia.

A hiatal hernia occurs at the spot called the hiatus, which is an opening in your diaphragm through which your food pipe (esophagus) passes into your stomach. If this opening is too large, your stomach may protrude (herniate) through it into your chest cavity, creating a hiatal hernia. Signs and symptoms include heartburn, belching, chest pain and regurgitation. Hiatal hernias are common, occurring most often in people older than 50. Most hiatal hernias are minor and show no symptoms. A hiatal hernia isn't painful in and of itself unless it's extremely large. Typically, the condition allows food and acid to back up into your esophagus, causing heartburn, indigestion and chest pain in some people. Obesity aggravates these symptoms.

Self-Care

For an inguinal hernia
You can neither prevent nor cure a hernia through self-care. Once you've had the lump evaluated and know it's a hernia and your hernia doesn't cause you discomfort, you don't need to take any special precautions. Wearing a corset or truss may give slight relief but won't reduce a hernia or fix it.

For a hiatal hernia
- Lose weight if you're overweight.
- Follow self-care precautions for heartburn on page 64.

Medical Help

If your hernia is painful or bothersome, contact your health care provider to discuss whether an operation is necessary.

Caution

If you cannot reduce the hernia by lying down and pushing on the lump, the blood supply to this segment of bowel may be cut off. Signs and symptoms of this complication include nausea, vomiting and severe pain. Left untreated, intestinal blockage or, in rare cases, a life-threatening infection may result. If you have any of these symptoms, contact your health care provider.

Common Problems

■ Indigestion and Heartburn

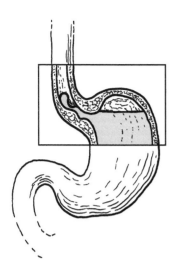

Heartburn occurs when stomach contents back up into your esophagus, causing irritation.

Indigestion is a nonspecific term used to describe discomfort in your abdomen that often occurs after eating. Indigestion isn't a disease. It's a collection of symptoms, including discomfort or burning in your upper abdomen, nausea and a bloated or full feeling that belching may relieve.

The cause of indigestion is sometimes difficult to pinpoint. In some people, eating certain foods or drinking alcohol may trigger it.

A common form of indigestion is the burning sensation called heartburn. As many as 10 percent of adults experience heartburn at least once a week. Technically called gastroesophageal reflux disease (GERD), heartburn occurs when stomach acids back up into your food pipe (esophagus). A sour taste and the sensation of food coming back into your mouth may accompany the burning sensation behind your breastbone.

Why do these acids back up? Normally, a circular band of muscle (sphincter) at the bottom of your esophagus closes off the stomach but it allows food to enter your stomach when you swallow. If the sphincter relaxes abnormally or becomes weakened, stomach acid can wash back up (reflux) into your esophagus and cause irritation.

Various factors can cause reflux. Being overweight puts too much pressure on your abdomen. Some medications, foods and beverages can relax the esophageal sphincter muscle or irritate the esophagus. Overeating or lying down after a meal also can lead to reflux.

Self-Care

Changing what and how you eat is the first step to prevent heartburn.
- Manage your weight. Slim down if you're overweight.
- Eat small, frequent meals.
- Avoid foods and drinks that relax the esophageal sphincter or irritate the esophagus (such as fatty foods, alcohol, caffeinated or carbonated beverages, decaffeinated coffee, peppermint, spearmint, garlic, onion, cinnamon, chocolate, citrus fruits and juices and tomato products).
- Stop eating two to three hours before you lie down or go to bed.
- Elevate the head of your bed.
- Quit smoking; eliminate nicotine use.
- Don't wear tight clothing and tight belts.
- Avoid excessive stooping or bending or heavy exertion for an hour after eating.
- Over-the-counter antacids can relieve mild heartburn by neutralizing stomach acids temporarily. However, prolonged or excessive use of antacids containing magnesium can cause diarrhea. Calcium- or aluminum-based products can lead to constipation.

Medications such as Pepcid, Tagamet and Zantac may relieve or prevent heartburn symptoms by reducing the production of stomach acid. These medicines are available in over-the-counter and prescription strengths.

Medical Help

Most problems with indigestion and heartburn are occasional and mild. But if you have severe or daily discomfort, don't ignore your symptoms. Left untreated, chronic heartburn can cause scarring in the lower esophagus. This can make swallowing difficult. In rare cases, severe heartburn can lead to a condition called Barrett's esophagus, which may increase your risk of cancer.

Heartburn and indigestion symptoms may signal the presence of a more serious underlying disease. Contact your health care provider if your symptoms are persistent or severe, or if you have difficulty swallowing.

See back cover for online resource ⓘ

■ Irritable Bowel Syndrome

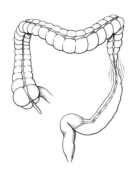

A spasm in the bowel wall may cause abdominal pain and other unpleasant symptoms commonly associated with IBS.

<u>Irritable bowel syndrome</u> (IBS), sometimes known as spastic bowel or spastic colon, is a common medical problem that's not completely understood. IBS is annoying, painful and sometimes embarrassing, but it isn't life-threatening. Some physicians rank the disorder with the common cold as the major cause of time lost from work.

IBS may affect up to 20 percent of Americans. Of this number, only a small percentage — 10 percent to 30 percent — seek medical care. Women experience the problem more than do men.

Although experts cannot pinpoint its exact cause, IBS may be related to abnormal muscle spasms in your stomach or intestines. Stress and depression are often blamed as causes of IBS. But these emotions only aggravate the condition.

Signs and symptoms may include abdominal pain, diarrhea, constipation, bloating, indigestion and gas. Although a bowel movement temporarily relieves the pain, you may feel as if you can't empty your bowels completely. Your stools can be ribbon-like and laced with mucus, or they can be hard, dry pellets. Often, diarrhea alternates with constipation.

Self-Care

Although no single treatment can eliminate IBS, simple diet and lifestyle measures can relieve your symptoms:

- Pay attention to what you eat. Avoid or eat smaller portions of foods that consistently aggravate your symptoms. Common irritants include tobacco, alcohol, caffeinated foods, beverages and medications, decaffeinated coffee, spicy foods, concentrated fruit juices, raw fruits and vegetables, fatty foods and sugar-free sweeteners such as sorbitol or mannitol.
- Eat high-fiber foods such as fresh fruits, vegetables and whole-grain foods. Add fiber gradually to minimize problems with gas and bloating.
- Drink plenty of fluids — at least eight to 10 glasses a day.
- Try using fiber supplements, such as Citrucel or Konsyl, to help relieve your constipation and diarrhea.
- Reduce your stress through regular exercise, sports or hobbies that help you relax.
- Try over-the-counter medications such as Imodium or Kaopectate to relieve diarrhea.

Medical Help

If self-care doesn't help, your health care provider may recommend prescription medications designed to relieve muscle spasms. If depression plays a role in your symptoms, treating this problem may be helpful.

Because the symptoms of IBS mimic those of more serious medical disorders such as cancer, gallbladder disease and ulcers, contact your health care provider for evaluation if simple self-care measures don't help within a couple of weeks.

Common Problems

■ Nausea and Vomiting

Nausea and vomiting are common and uncomfortable symptoms of a wide variety of disorders, most of which aren't serious.

Feeling queasy and throwing up usually signal a viral infection called gastroenteritis. Diarrhea, abdominal cramps, bloating and fever also may accompany this condition. Other causes include food poisoning, pregnancy, some medications and gastritis (see page 61).

Self-Care

If gastroenteritis is the culprit, nausea and vomiting may last from a few hours to two or three days. Diarrhea and mild abdominal cramping also are common. To keep yourself comfortable and prevent dehydration while you recover, try the following:

- Stop eating and drinking for a few hours until your stomach has settled.
- Try ice chips or small sips of weak tea, clear soda (Seven-Up or Sprite) and broths or noncaffeinated clear sports drinks to prevent dehydration. Consume 2 to 4 quarts (eight to 16 glasses) of liquid for no longer than 24 hours, taking frequent, small sips.
- Add semisolid and low-fiber foods gradually and stop eating if the vomiting returns. Try soda crackers, gelatin, toast, eggs, rice or chicken.
- Avoid dairy products, caffeine, alcohol, nicotine or fatty or highly seasoned foods for a few days.

Medical Help

Vomiting can lead to complications such as dehydration (if the condition is persistent), food in the windpipe (aspiration) or, in rare instances, a torn blood vessel in the food pipe that causes bleeding. Infants, older adults and people with suppressed immune systems are particularly vulnerable to complications. Contact your health care provider if you're unable to drink anything for 24 hours, if vomiting persists beyond two or three days, if you become dehydrated or if you vomit blood. Signs of dehydration include excessive thirst, dry mouth, little or no urination, severe weakness, dizziness or lightheadedness. Vomiting also can be a warning of more serious underlying problems such as gallbladder disease, ulcers or bowel obstruction.

Kids' Care

Spitting up is an everyday occurrence for babies and usually causes no discomfort. Vomiting, however, is more forceful and disturbing to your baby and can lead to dehydration and weight loss.

To prevent dehydration, let the baby's stomach rest for 30 to 60 minutes and then offer small amounts of liquid. If you're breast-feeding, let your baby nurse smaller amounts more frequently. Offer bottle-fed babies a small amount of formula or an oral electrolyte solution such as Pedialyte or Infalyte.

If the vomiting doesn't recur, continue to offer small sips of liquid or the breast every 15 to 30 minutes. Contact your health care provider if vomiting persists for more than 12 hours or if your child:

- Hasn't had a wet diaper in eight hours
- Has diarrhea or bloody stools
- Has a dry mouth or cries without tears
- Is unusually sleepy or drowsy or unresponsive

A few newborn babies have a disorder called pyloric stenosis, which can cause repeated and forceful vomiting. This condition usually appears after the third week of life. It requires medical care.

Ulcers

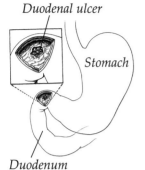

Duodenal ulcer

Stomach

Duodenum

The most common form of ulcer occurs in the duodenum and is called a duodenal ulcer.

Ulcers are sores in the inner lining of your esophagus or stomach or the uppermost section of your small intestine called the duodenum.

The cause of ulcers isn't fully known. Recent research suggests that bacteria called *Helicobacter pylori (H. pylori)* play an important role, especially for duodenal ulcers. Stomach ulcers can be caused by excessive use of aspirin or aspirin-like medications. Contrary to popular belief, there's no clear evidence that emotional stress causes ulcers.

Ulcers can cause considerable distress. Symptoms may include a burning feeling beneath your breastbone in your upper abdomen, gnawing hunger pangs or boring pain and nausea. At times, ulcers can also cause belching or bloating. These signs and symptoms typically occur when your stomach is empty. Although eating may relieve the symptoms, they often resume one to two hours later. In severe cases, ulcers may bleed and cause you to vomit blood or pass black, tarry stools. In rare cases, an ulcer may perforate the wall of your stomach or duodenum, causing severe abdominal pain.

Self-Care

Dietary, lifestyle and medication choices may help prevent or control ulcers.
- If you're using pain relievers, use acetaminophen. Aspirin, ibuprofen, ketoprofen and naproxen sodium can cause ulcers.
- Avoid alcohol and caffeinated foods, beverages and medications.
- Stop smoking.
- Eat small meals and avoid letting your stomach remain empty for long periods.
- Avoid spicy or fatty foods if they seem to make your symptoms worse.
- Take nonprescription antacids to neutralize stomach acids or medicines such as Pepcid, Tagamet or Zantac to stop the production of stomach acid.

Medical Help

Some ulcers disappear with self-care or with over-the-counter medication. If your symptoms don't improve after a week or if you have troublesome, recurrent ulcers, see your health care provider for further evaluation and treatment.

The diagnosis requires visualizing the ulcer with an X-ray or scope, although your doctor may treat you on the basis of your symptoms alone.

Bleeding ulcers can cause serious blood loss. Seek help immediately if you vomit blood, pass black, tarry stools or have severe pain.

Treatment for Peptic Ulcers

A two-drug combination has simplified the treatment of what was once a very misunderstood disease. Medications such as Prilosec, Prevacid, Aciphex or Protonix, which suppress stomach acid production, are used in combination with an antibiotic called Biaxin for the treatment of **peptic ulcers**.

The two drugs are used together for 14 days, followed by 14 days of treatment with the acid-suppressant alone. This treatment approach is an effort to cure a common illness that was once thought to be incurable.

FOR MORE INFORMATION
- National Digestive Diseases Information Clearinghouse, 2 Information Way, Bethesda, MD 20892; (800) 891-5389; *www.niddk.nih.gov/health/digest/nddic.htm.*

Common Problems

Ears and Hearing

There's more to the ear than meets the eye. The part of your ear that's visible — your outer ear — is connected inside your head to your middle ear and inner ear, which work together to allow you to hear and help you maintain balance.

How the Ear Works

Your ear is a finely tuned organ that's specially designed to send sound impulses to your brain. When sound waves travel through the ear canal, your eardrum and the three small bones to which it's attached vibrate. This vibration moves through the middle ear to your inner ear, triggering nerve impulses to your brain, where you perceive them as sound.

Air reaches your middle ear through the eustachian tube. The middle ear must maintain the same pressure as the air outside your ear to allow your eardrum and ear bones to vibrate freely and conduct sound waves. If the middle ear has fluid in it, the eardrum and the bones can't move well. This is why an ear infection can cause temporary hearing problems.

Some common causes of ear pain and ear problems are described in this section.

Eardrum

Inner ear

Middle ear

Eustachian tube

Outer ear

◼ Airplane Ear

The medical name for **airplane ear** is barotrauma or barotitis media. It means an injury caused by changes in pressure. It can occur if you fly or scuba dive with a congested nose, allergy, cold or throat infection. You may have pain in one ear, a slight hearing loss or a stuffy feeling in your ears. It's caused by your eardrum bulging outward or retracting inward as a result of a change in air pressure. Having a cold or ear infection isn't necessarily a reason to change or delay a flight, however.

Self-Care

- Try taking a decongestant an hour before takeoff and an hour before landing. This may prevent blockage of your eustachian tube.
- During flight, suck candy or chew gum to encourage swallowing, which helps open your eustachian tube.
- If your ears plug as the plane descends, inhale and then gently exhale while holding your nostrils closed and keeping your mouth closed. If you can swallow at the same time, it's more helpful.
- Consider using earplugs designed specifically to help prevent or reduce ear pain and discomfort during airplane travel.

Medical Help

If your symptoms don't disappear within a few hours, see your physician.

Kids' Care

For babies and young children, make sure they are drinking fluids (swallowing) during ascent and descent. Give the child a bottle or pacifier to encourage swallowing. Give acetaminophen 30 minutes before takeoff to help control discomfort that may occur. Decongestants in young children aren't generally recommended.

▊ Foreign Objects in the Ear

Objects stuck in your ear can cause pain and hearing loss. Usually you know if something is stuck in your ear, but small children may not be aware of it.

Self-Care

If an object becomes lodged in the ear, follow these steps:

- Don't attempt to remove the foreign object by probing with a cotton swab, matchstick or any other tool. To do so is to risk pushing the object farther into the ear and damaging the fragile structures of the middle ear.
- If the object is clearly visible, is pliable and can be grasped easily with tweezers, gently remove it.
- Try using the pull of gravity: Tilt the head to the affected side. Don't strike the victim's head, but shake it gently in the direction of the ground to try to dislodge the object.
- If the foreign object is an insect, tilt the person's head so that the ear with the offending insect is upward. Try to float the insect out by pouring mineral oil, olive oil or baby oil into the ear. It should be warm but not hot. As you pour the oil, you can ease the entry of the oil by straightening the ear canal. Pull the earlobe gently backward and upward. The insect should suffocate and may float out in the oil bath.
- Don't use oil to remove any object other than an insect. Don't use this method if there's any suspicion of a perforation in the eardrum (pain, bleeding or discharge from the ear).

Medical Help

If these methods fail or the person continues to experience pain in the ear, reduced hearing or a sensation of something lodged in the ear, seek medical assistance.

▊ Ruptured Eardrum

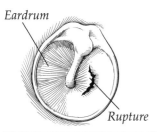

Eardrum

Rupture

An eardrum may rupture after an infection or from trauma. Signs of a ruptured (perforated) eardrum are earache, partial hearing loss and slight bleeding or discharge from your ear. With an infection, the pain often resolves once the eardrum ruptures, releasing infected fluid or pus. Usually, the rupture heals by itself without complications and with little or no permanent hearing loss. Large ruptures may cause recurring infections. If you suspect that you have ruptured an eardrum, see your doctor as soon as possible. Meanwhile, try the self-care tips listed here.

Self-Care

- Relieve pain with aspirin or another pain medication that is safe for you.
- Place a warm (not hot) heating pad over your ear.
- Don't flush your ear.

Medical Help

Your doctor may prescribe an antibiotic to make sure that no infection develops in your middle ear. Sometimes a plastic or paper patch is placed over your eardrum to seal the opening while it heals. Your eardrum will often heal within two months. If it hasn't healed in that time, you may require a minor surgical procedure to repair the tear.

■ Ear Infections

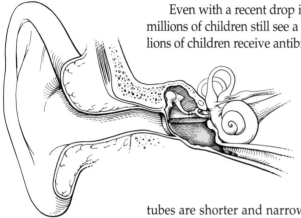

A fluid-filled middle ear creates an environment for growth of bacteria.

For many parents of young children, coping with ear infections is almost as routine as changing wet diapers. Approximately 75 percent of children will have at least one middle ear infection (otitis media) by age 3. Many have multiple episodes. Ear infections are one of the most common illnesses in babies and young children.

Even with a recent drop in the number of office visits for middle ear infections, millions of children still see a health care provider for this problem each year, and millions of children receive antibiotic prescriptions.

Most ear infections don't lead to permanent hearing loss. Some infections that aren't treated, however, can spread to other parts of the ear, including the inner ear. Infections of the middle ear can damage the eardrum, ear bones and inner ear structure, causing permanent hearing loss. An ear infection often begins with a respiratory infection such as a cold. Colds cause swelling and inflammation in the sinuses and eustachian tubes. Children's eustachian tubes are shorter and narrower than are adults'. This size makes it more likely that inflammation will block the tube completely, trapping fluid in the middle ear. This trapped fluid causes the discomfort of an earache and creates an ideal environment for bacteria to grow. The result is a middle ear infection.

Self-Care

- Consider an over-the-counter pain reliever such as ibuprofen or acetaminophen. If your child is younger than age two, consult your health care provider.
- Eardrops with a local anesthetic may help reduce pain. They won't prevent or stop an infection. They should **not** be used if there's drainage from the ear.
- To administer eardrops, warm the bottle slightly in water and place the child on a flat surface (not in your arms or on your lap) ear up, insert the eardrops and then insert a small cotton wick to retain the eardrops.
- Place a warm (not hot), moist cloth or heating pad (on lowest setting) over the ear.

Medical Help

Contact your child's health care provider if pain lasts more than a day or is associated with fever. Ear infections may be treated with antibiotics. Even if your child feels better after a few days, continue giving the medicine for the full length of time recommended (usually 10 days).

The Pros and Cons of Ear Tubes

Recurrent ear infections are sometimes treated by surgically inserting a small plastic tube through your eardrum, which allows pus to drain out of your middle ear.

For the procedure
- It usually results in fewer infections.
- Hearing is restored.
- The operation allows ventilation of the middle ear, which decreases the risk of permanent

changes in the lining of the middle ear that can occur with prolonged infection.

Against the procedure
- It requires brief general anesthesia.
- You must avoid getting water in your ear while the tube is in place.
- In rare cases, severe scarring or a permanent hole in the eardrum may result.

See back cover for online resource

Common Questions About Ear Infections in Kids

What are the risk factors for infections?

Although all children are susceptible to ear infections, those at higher risk are children who:

- Are male
- Have siblings with a history of recurrent ear infection
- Have their first ear infection before they're 4 months old
- Are in group child care
- Are exposed to tobacco smoke
- Are of American Indian, Alaskan or Canadian Eskimo descent
- Have frequent upper respiratory tract infections
- Were bottle-fed instead of breast-fed

What are the symptoms?

In addition to an earache or a feeling of pressure and blockage in the ear, some children may experience temporary hearing loss. Be aware of other signs of an ear infection such as irritability, a sudden loss of appetite, the development of a fever a few days after onset of a cold, nausea, vomiting or a preference for sleeping in an upright position. Your child may also have discharge in the ear or may tug at the ear.

Does your child need an antibiotic?

Because most ear infections clear on their own, your health care provider may first recommend a wait-and-see approach, especially if your child has few symptoms. In other cases, your doctor may opt to prescribe an antibiotic to treat the infection. Within two to three days of beginning the medication, symptoms usually improve.

Be sure to follow instructions carefully for giving the antibiotic. Continue to give the medication to your child for the entire recommended time. If you stop giving your child the antibiotic when symptoms improve, you may allow stronger remaining bacteria to multiply and cause another infection. Surviving bacteria may carry genes that make them drug resistant.

If symptoms don't go away or if your child is younger than 15 months, schedule a follow-up visit as recommended by your health care provider. If your child is older and symptoms have resolved, a recheck may not be necessary, especially if infections haven't been recurrent.

What can you do?

Although an ear infection isn't an emergency, the first 24 hours are often when your child's pain and irritability are the worst. Follow the self-care tips on page 70. To make your child more comfortable, don't underestimate the benefits of extra cuddling.

What about recurrent infections?

Time and the use of antibiotics usually resolve ear infections. But sometimes ear infections can become a chronic problem. If so, ask your health care provider about preventive antibiotic therapy. Persistent fluid buildup may cause temporary or even permanent hearing loss. This can lead to delayed speech development.

Can you prevent infections?

Preventing ear infections is difficult, but consider these approaches to help reduce your child's risk:

- Breast-feed rather than bottle-feed your baby for as long as possible.
- When bottle-feeding, hold your baby in an upright position.
- Avoid exposing your child to tobacco smoke.

Do children outgrow ear infections?

As your child matures, the eustachian tubes become wider and more angled, providing a better means of draining secretions and fluid out of the ear. Although ear infections still may occur, they probably won't develop as often as during the first few years of life.

What are medical researchers working on to help treat ear infections?

In addition to antibiotics, some approaches under investigation include the use of cortisone-like medication, such as prednisone, that would reduce inflammation (more research is needed to determine when this treatment is most effective); a one-shot approach using an injection of a particular antibiotic when oral drug therapy is impractical; and vaccines against the flu (influenza) virus.

Common Problems

■ Ringing in Your Ear

A ringing or buzzing in your ear when no other sounds are present can have many causes, including earwax, a foreign object, infection or exposure to loud noise. It also may be caused by high doses of aspirin or large amounts of caffeine. This condition, called **tinnitus**, uncommonly is a symptom of more serious ear disorders, particularly if it's accompanied by other symptoms such as hearing loss or dizziness.

Self-Care

- If aspirin was recommended to you in high doses (more than 12 a day), ask your doctor about alternatives. If you're taking aspirin on your own, try lower doses or another over-the-counter pain medication.
- Avoid nicotine, caffeine and alcohol, which may aggravate the condition.
- Try to determine a cause, such as exposure to loud noise, and avoid or block it if possible.
- Wear earplugs or some other form of hearing protection if you have excess noise exposure, such as when you're working with yard equipment (leaf blowers or lawn mowers).
- Some people benefit by covering up the ringing sound with another, more acceptable sound (such as music or listening to a radio as you fall asleep).
- Other people may benefit by wearing a masker, a device that fits in your ear and produces white noise.

Medical Help

If tinnitus worsens, persists or is accompanied by hearing loss or dizziness, consider evaluation by your health care provider. He or she may choose to pursue further evaluation. Although most causes of tinnitus are benign, it can be a difficult and frustrating condition to treat.

■ Swimmer's Ear

This is an infection of your outer ear canal. In addition to pain or itching, you may see a clear drainage or yellow-green pus and experience temporary hearing loss. **Swimmer's ear** is the result of having persistent moisture in the ear or, sometimes, from swimming in polluted water. Other similar inflammations or infections may occur from scraping your ear canal when you clean your ear or from hair sprays or hair dyes. Some people are prone to bacterial or fungal infections.

Self-Care

If the aching is mild and there's no drainage from the ear, do the following:
- Place a warm (not hot) heating pad over your ear.
- Take aspirin or another pain medication (be sure to follow the label instructions).
- To prevent swimmer's ear, try to keep ear canals dry, avoid substances that might irritate your ear and don't clean inside the ear canal unless you're instructed to do so by your health care provider.

Medical Help

Seek medical care if you have severe pain or swelling of the ear, a fever, drainage from the ear or an underlying disease. Your doctor may clean your ear canal with a suction device or a cotton-tipped probe. Your doctor also may prescribe eardrops or medications to control infection and reduce pain. Keep your ear dry while it's healing.

Wax Blockage

Earwax is part of the body's normal defenses. It traps dust and foreign objects, protects the ear canal and inhibits growth of bacteria. At times, you may produce too much earwax, blocking your ear canal, giving you an earache or causing a rattling in your ears. Earwax blockage also can cause gradual hearing loss as the wax accumulates.

Self-Care

- Soften earwax by applying a few drops of baby oil, mineral oil or glycerin with an eyedropper twice a day for several days.
- When the wax is softened, fill a bowl with water heated to body temperature (if it's colder or hotter, it may make you feel dizzy during the procedure).
- With your head upright, grasp the top of your ear and pull upward. With your other hand, squirt the water gently into your ear canal with a 3-ounce rubber-bulb syringe. Then, turn your head and drain the water into the bowl or sink.
- You may need to repeat this several times before the extra wax falls out.
- Dry your outer ear with a towel or a hand-held hair dryer.
- Earwax removers sold in stores also are effective.
- Other home wax removal methods also may be effective if wax buildup is a recurrent problem. But ask your doctor about these self-care remedies. For example, five to 10 drops of Colace, an over-the-counter medication (used for constipation in infants), can be very helpful but needs flushing (leave drops in for 30 minutes). Ear "flushers" are available in stores. A few drops of diluted vinegar (half-strength) after flushing returns the ear canal to an acid state, which suppresses bacteria growth after ears are wet. A commercial alcohol-boric acid preparation is available for the same purpose.

Caution

Your ear canal and eardrum are very delicate and can be damaged easily. Don't poke them with objects such as cotton swabs, paper clips or bobby pins.

Flushing wax out of the ears should be avoided if there has been a prior eardrum perforation or prior ear surgery, unless your doctor approves. If infection is a concern, don't flush your ears.

Medical Help

Even if the tips given above are followed, many people have difficulty washing wax out of their ears. It may be best to have this done by your health care provider. Excessive wax can be removed in a procedure similar to the one described above. A special instrument is used to either scoop the wax out of the ear or suction it out. If this is a recurring problem, your doctor may recommend using a wax-removal medication every four to eight weeks.

Common Problems

Mayo Clinic Guide to Self-Care **73**

■ Noise-Related Hearing Loss

Sound is measured in decibels. An average conversation is about 60 decibels. A loud conversation in a crowded building is about 70 decibels. Continual exposure to noise at 85 decibels or above can cause gradual hearing loss.

Self-Care

If you're exposed to loud power tools or engines, loud music, firearms or other equipment that produces loud noises, take the following precautions:

- Wear protective earplugs or earmuffs. Use commercially made protection devices that meet federal standards (cotton balls will not work, and they could get stuck in your ears). These bring most loud sounds down to acceptable levels. You can obtain custom-molded earplugs made of plastic or rubber to effectively protect against excessive noise.
- Have your hearing tested. Early detection of hearing loss can prevent future, irreversible damage.
- Use ear protection off the job. Protect your ears from any loud recreational activities, such as loud music or concerts, trapshooting or driving snowmobiles.
- Beware of recreational risks. Sensorineural hearing loss related to recreation is becoming more common. Activities with the greatest risk are trapshooting, driving snowmobiles and some other recreational vehicles and, particularly, listening to extremely loud music. If your son or daughter listens to loud music on a headset, use this simple test to determine whether the sound is too loud: If you can identify the music being played while your child is wearing the headset, it's too loud. Tell your child to save his or her ears for a lifetime of music enjoyment.

Maximal Job Noise Exposure Allowed by Law	
Duration, daily	Sound level, decibels
8 hours	90
6 hours	92
4 hours	95
3 hours	97
2 hours	100
90 minutes	102
60 minutes	105
30 minutes	110
15 minutes	115

Sound Levels of Common Noises	
Decibels	Noise
	Safe range
20	Watch ticking; leaves rustling
40	Quiet street noise
60	Normal conversation; bird song
80	Heavy traffic
	Risk range
85-90	Motorcycle; snowmobile
80-100	Rock concert
	Injury range
120	Ambulance siren
140	Jet engine at takeoff
165	Shotgun blast

Age-Related Hearing Loss

A decrease in hearing is common with age. This condition is called presbycusis. If you or a family member suspects you have more serious hearing loss, see a physician. You may be referred to a doctor who's an ear specialist or to a person trained in hearing evaluation (audiologist). <u>Hearing loss</u> can sometimes be restored with medical treatment or surgery, especially if the problem is in the outer ear or middle ear. If the problem is in the inner ear, however, it's usually not treatable. A hearing aid can improve your hearing. The advice given below may help you select a hearing aid.

Before You Buy a Hearing Aid, Here's Sound Advice

Of the 31 million Americans who have some degree of hearing loss, about 20 percent use hearing aids. The average cost of a hearing aid is around $1,000. But if it helps you hear better and improves your quality of life, it's worth the money. Of those who purchase hearing aids, approximately 68 percent are satisfied with the devices. Complaints range from improper fit to poor service to lack of hearing improvement.

Here are some tips for selecting a hearing aid:
- **Have a medical and hearing examination.** Before you buy a hearing aid, be examined by a physician, preferably an ear, nose and throat doctor (otolaryngologist). A Food and Drug Administration regulation says it's best to have this examination within six months before you buy a hearing aid. An examination can determine whether a medical condition will prevent you from using a hearing aid.
- **Buy from a reputable dispenser.** If you don't get a hearing test (audiogram) from a medical facility, a dispenser will give you one. This person then takes an impression of your ear, chooses the most appropriate aid and adjusts the device to fit well. These are complex tasks, and skills of dispensers vary. Also, contact the Better Business Bureau about a dispenser's complaint record. Be cautious of free consultations and dispensers who sell only one brand of hearing aid.
- **Be alert to misleading claims.** For years, a few manufacturers and distributors claimed their hearing aids allowed you to hear speech and eliminate background noise. But this technology doesn't exist. Some newer hearing aids subdue loud sounds and so make wearing a hearing aid in

noisy places more comfortable. But no hearing aid can filter out the voice you want to hear from other voices in a crowded room.
- **Ask about a trial period.** Have the dispenser put in writing the cost of a trial and whether this amount is credited toward the final cost of the hearing aid.
- **Obtain a second hearing test.** To determine if a hearing aid really helps you hear better, have another hearing test while wearing the aid.
- **Understand the warranty**. A warranty should extend for one to two years and cover both parts and labor.

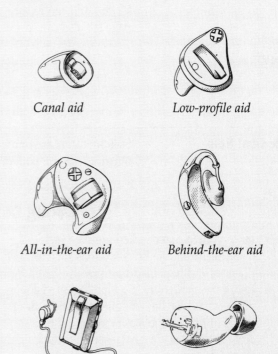

Canal aid

Low-profile aid

All-in-the-ear aid

Behind-the-ear aid

Body aid

Disposable hearing aid

Eyes and Vision

Because your eyes are crucial in so many activities, eye problems usually demand attention. Luckily, many eye problems are more bothersome than serious.

Almost everyone has vision changes with age. Age also increases your risk of developing more serious eye problems. Some eye problems can't be prevented, but medications or surgery can slow or stop progression. This section covers the more common eye problems and discusses some of the issues related to declining vision.

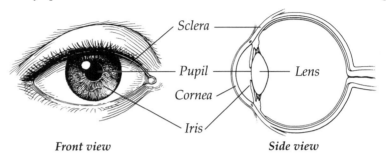

Front view   *Side view*

■ Black Eye

The so-called black eye is caused by bleeding beneath the skin around the eye. Sometimes a black eye indicates a more extensive injury, even a skull fracture, particularly if the area around both eyes is bruised or there has been head trauma. Although most injuries aren't serious, bleeding within the eye, called a hyphema, is serious and can reduce vision and damage the cornea. In some cases, glaucoma (see page 80) also can result.

Self-Care

- Using gentle pressure, apply ice or a cold pack to the area around the eye for 10 to 15 minutes. Take care not to press on the eye itself. Apply cold as soon as possible after the injury to reduce swelling.
- Be sure there's no blood in the white and colored parts of the eye.

Medical Help

Seek medical care immediately if you experience vision problems (double vision, blurring), severe pain or bleeding in the eye or from the nose.

Taking Care of Your Eyes

- Have your vision checked regularly.
- Control chronic health conditions such as diabetes and high blood pressure.
- Recognize symptoms. Sudden loss of vision in one eye, sudden hazy or blurred vision, flashes of light or black spots or halos or rainbows around lights may signal a serious medical problem such as acute glaucoma or a stroke.

- Protect your eyes against sun damage. Buy sunglasses with ultraviolet (UV) blocking lenses.
- Eat foods containing vitamin A and beta carotene, such as carrots, yams and cantaloupe.
- Optimize your vision with the right glasses.
- Use good lighting.
- If your vision is impaired, use low-vision aids, such as magnifiers and large-type books.

Dry Eyes

Dry eyes feel hot, irritated and gritty when you blink. They may become slightly red. Tear production decreases as you age. Dry eyes usually affect both eyes, especially in women after menopause. Some medicines (such as sleeping medications, antihistamines and some drugs for high blood pressure) can cause or worsen dry eyes. Some rare medical conditions may be associated with dry eyes.

Self-Care

- Use a preservative-free artificial tear preparation (Celluvisc, Refresh Plus).
- Because some over-the-counter eyedrops can cause drying, use them for no more than three to five days.
- Don't direct hair dryers (or other sources of air, such as car heaters or fans) toward your eyes.
- Wear glasses on windy days and goggles when swimming.
- Keep your home humidity between 40 percent and 55 percent.
- Seek medical care if the condition persists despite the self-care efforts.

Excessive Watering

Your eyes may actually water in response to dryness and irritation. Watery eyes also commonly occur with infections such as so-called pinkeye (see page 78). They can result from an allergic reaction to preservatives in eyedrops or contact lens solutions. Watery eyes can also result from a blockage in the ducts that drain tears to the inside of your nose. Overflowing tears can cause even more eye irritation and tearing.

Self-Care

- Apply a warm compress over closed eyelids two to four times a day for 10 minutes.
- Don't rub your eyes.
- Replace mascara every six months. Mascara can become contaminated with skin bacteria transferred by the applicator.
- If you wear contact lenses, follow directions for wearing, cleaning and disinfecting them.

Floaters (Specks in the Eye)

The jelly-like substance behind your lens (vitreous) is supported and distributed evenly within your eyeball by a framework of fine fibers (fibrils). As you age, these fibers thicken and gather in bundles, creating the appearance of specks, hairs or strings that move in and out of your vision. Floaters that appear gradually and become less noticeable over time are usually harmless and require no treatment. Floaters that appear suddenly may indicate a more serious eye disorder such as hemorrhage or retinal detachment. The retina is the light-sensitive layer of tissue at the back of the eye that transmits visual images to the brain.

Medical Help

If you see a cloud of spots or a spider web, especially accompanied by flashes of light, see your eye doctor (ophthalmologist). These symptoms can indicate a retinal tear or retinal detachment, which requires prompt surgery to prevent vision loss.

Common Problems

■ Pinkeye

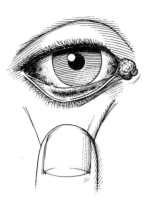

One or both eyes are pink or red in color and itchy. There may be blurred vision and sensitivity to light. You may have a gritty feeling in the eye or a discharge in the eye that forms a crust during the night.

All of these are signs of a bacterial or viral infection commonly known as pinkeye. The medical term is **conjunctivitis**. It's an inflammation of the membrane called the conjunctiva, which lines the inside of the eyelids and part of the eyeball.

The inflammation makes pinkeye an irritating condition, but it's usually harmless to sight. However, because it can be highly contagious, it must be diagnosed and treated early. Occasionally, pinkeye can cause eye complications.

Both viral and bacterial conjunctivitis are common among children and also affect adults. They're very contagious. Viral conjunctivitis usually produces a watery discharge, whereas bacterial conjunctivitis often produces a good deal of thick, yellow-green matter.

Allergic conjunctivitis affects both eyes and is a response to an allergen (such as pollen) rather than an infection. In addition to intense itching, tearing and inflammation of the eye, you may also experience some degree of itching, sneezing and watery discharge from the nose.

Self-Care

- Apply a warm compress to the affected eye or eyes. Soak a clean, lint-free cloth in warm water, squeeze it dry and apply it over your gently closed eyelids.
- Allergic conjunctivitis is often effectively soothed with cool compresses.

Prevention

Because pinkeye spreads easily and quickly, good hygiene is the most useful method for control. Once the infection has been diagnosed in you or a family member, the following steps may be useful to contain it:

- Keep your hands away from your eyes.
- Wash your hands frequently.
- Change your towel and washcloth daily; don't share them.
- Wear your clothes only once before washing.
- Change your pillowcase each night.
- Discard eye cosmetics, particularly mascara, after a few months.
- Don't use other people's eye cosmetics, handkerchiefs or other personal items.

Medical Help

If you have any symptoms of pinkeye, see your physician. He or she may culture the eye secretions to determine which form of infection you have. A physician may prescribe antibiotic eyedrops or ointments if the infection is bacterial. Viral conjunctivitis disappears on its own. If your doctor determines that you have allergic conjunctivitis, he or she may recommend medications to treat the allergy or your eye symptoms.

Kids' Care

Because the condition is contagious, keep your child away from other children. Many schools will send children with pinkeye home.

See back cover for online resource ⓘ

■ Sensitivity to Glare

Glare may result when light is scattered within the eyeball. Glare may be especially bothersome in low light when your pupils are enlarged (dilated) because light is allowed into your eyes at a wider angle. Sensitivity to glare may mean a developing cataract (see page 80). To evaluate your symptoms, your health care provider may measure your vision under low, medium and high levels of glare.

Self-Care

- Reduce daytime glare by wearing polarized sunglasses with wide frames that follow your brow and opaque side shields.
- Have accurate correction for your distance vision to help minimize glare.

■ Other Eye Problems

Drooping Eyelid

Your upper eyelid may droop if the muscles responsible for raising your eyelid weaken. Normal aging, trauma or disorders of the nerves and muscles can lead to drooping eyelid. If your eyelid interferes with vision, your ophthalmologist may recommend surgery to strengthen supporting muscles. **Caution:** A drooping eyelid that develops suddenly needs immediate evaluation and treatment. It may be associated with stroke or other acute problems of your nervous system.

Inflamed (Granulated) Eyelid

A chronic inflammation along the edges of your eyelids is called blepharitis. It may accompany dry eyes. Some people produce excess oil in glands near their eyelashes. Oil encourages growth of bacteria and causes your skin to be irritated, itchy and red. Tiny scales form along the edges of your eyelids, further irritating your skin. **Self-care:** Apply a warm compress over your gently closed eyelids two to four times a day for 10 minutes. Immediately afterward, wash away the scales with warm water or diluted baby shampoo. If the condition is caused by an infection, your health care provider may prescribe a medicated ointment or an oral antibiotic.

Twitching Eyelid

Your eyelid takes on a life of its own — twitching at random, driving you crazy. The involuntary quivering of the eyelid muscle usually lasts less than a minute. The cause is unknown, but some people report that the painless twitching is brought on by nervous tension and fatigue. Rarely, it can be a symptom of muscle or nerve disease. Twitching eyelid is usually harmless and needs no treatment. **Self-care:** Gentle massaging over the eyelid may help relieve the twitching.

Sty

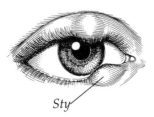

Sty

A <u>sty</u> is a red, painful lump on the edge of your eyelid. It's caused by inflammation or infection from a blocked gland in the eyelid. Sties usually fill with pus and then burst in about a week. For persistent infections, your health care provider might prescribe an antibiotic cream. **Self-care:** Apply a clean, warm compress four times a day for 10 minutes to relieve the pain and help the sty come to a point sooner. Let the sty burst on its own, then rinse your eye thoroughly.

■ Common Eye Diseases

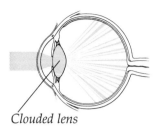

Clouded lens

Cataract

A <u>cataract</u> is a clouding of the normally clear lens of your eye. Lens clouding impairs vision. Some degree of cataract formation is normal as you grow older, but some exposures or conditions can accelerate the process. Long-term exposure to ultraviolet (UV) light, diabetes, a previous eye injury, exposure to X-rays and prolonged use of corticosteroid drugs increase your risk. Smoking may increase your risk of cataracts. If a cataract interferes with your daily activities, your cloudy lens can be surgically removed and replaced with a plastic lens implant. **Self-care:** Reduce glare. Prevent or slow cataracts by wearing UV-blocking sunglasses when outside in bright sun. Ensure adequate lighting.

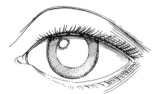 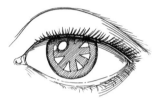

Cataracts take several forms. Illustrated here are a nuclear cataract (left) and a wheel-spoke pattern cataract (right).

Glaucoma

Glaucoma involves damage to the eye (optic) nerve caused by increased pressure within the eyeball. Pressure increases when tiny pores that normally allow fluid to drain from inside your eye become blocked. Damage to the optic nerve causes your side vision to diminish slowly. Untreated, glaucoma can lead to blindness. **Caution:** Because the early symptoms can be subtle, it's important to have regular eye examinations. If diagnosed and treated early, chronic glaucoma usually can be controlled with eyedrops, oral medications or surgery. If you have symptoms such as a severe headache or pain in your eye or brow, nausea, blurred vision or rainbows around lights at night, seek immediate evaluation. Treatment may require emergency laser surgery.

Macular Degeneration

Macular degeneration blurs central vision and reduces your ability to see fine detail. It doesn't affect side vision and usually doesn't lead to total blindness. The condition occurs when tissue in the center of the retina (macula) deteriorates. The vision impairment is irreversible. However, when the condition is diagnosed early, laser treatment may help reduce or slow the loss of vision.

Transportation Advice for the Vision-Impaired

- Don't drive if you fail to meet your state's vision requirements for drivers.
- Avoid stressful driving conditions — at night, in heavy traffic, in bad weather or on a freeway.
- Use public transportation or ask family members to help with night driving.
- Contact your local Area Agency on Aging for a list of vans and shuttles, volunteer driver networks or ride shares.
- Optimize the vision you have with the right glasses. Keep an extra pair in the car.

Problems Related to Glasses, Contact Lenses

Many people begin to notice a change in their vision around age 40. Close-up objects that were once easy to see become blurred. The print in newspapers and books begins to seem smaller, and you instinctively hold reading material farther away from your eyes. The condition is presbyopia. It refers to the difficulty with near vision that develops as the lenses in your eyes become thicker and more rigid. Another symptom is eyestrain, which may include a feeling of tired eyes and a headache.

If you're already farsighted, you may notice the changes somewhat earlier and will need to have stronger corrective lenses. Even if you're nearsighted, you'll experience the effects of presbyopia, and you may find yourself taking off your glasses to read small print. You may find that your eyes seem increasingly tired after reading.

Before trying over-the-counter reading glasses, first see an eye specialist to rule out other problems.

Medical Help

If you experience frequent headaches, see your ophthalmologist or optometrist, who will test your eyes and prescribe appropriate lenses, if needed.

Respond to warnings such as blurring of vision, yellowing of colors, increased sensitivity to light or loss of side vision, which could indicate cataracts or glaucoma.

Contact Lenses, Glasses and Laser Surgery

Contact lenses are improving, but they're not for everyone. Certain diseases of the eye (dry eyes, previous corneal ulcers or corneas that have a loss of sensation) make wearing contact lenses inadvisable. Insertion, removal and care of contacts may be impractical for people with arthritis of the hands, tremor from Parkinson's disease and physical disabilities from other disorders. In some cases, contacts are preferable to glasses. For example, contact lenses offer markedly improved vision to people who are born with a malformation of the cornea.

Laser, or refractive eye surgeries change the shape of the cornea, so it focuses more precisely. Laser-assisted in-situ keratomileusis (LASIK) involves making a thin, circular hinged cut into the cornea. The surgeon then lifts the flap and with a special laser reshapes the cornea. LASIK is good for correcting low to moderate astigmatism in people with nearsightedness. Results aren't as good in farsighted people with astigmatism.

Extended-wear and disposable soft contacts

If you use extended-wear contact lenses, remove and sterilize them most nights. If you wear disposable lenses, don't wear them beyond the time recommended by your eye specialist. Wearing contact lenses too long without removing them may deprive your corneas of oxygen. Lack of oxygen can cause blurred vision, pain, tearing, redness, sensitivity to light, and may make the cornea more susceptible to infection. Remove your lenses at once if any of these symptoms occur. Have regular eye examinations to avoid problems that may result from extended contact wear.

Common Problems

FOR MORE INFORMATION
- National Eye Institute, 2020 Vision Place, Bethesda, MD 20892; (301) 496-5248; *www.nei.nih.gov.*
- Lighthouse International, 111 E. 59th St., New York, NY 10022; (800) 829-0500; *www.lighthouse.org.*
- Local chapter of association or services for the blind and visually impaired.

Headache

Headaches are the most common reported medical complaint. They may point to a serious medical problem. But that situation is rare.

About 90 percent of all headaches have no underlying disease. These so-called primary headaches differ greatly. Researchers are learning more about what happens physically during a headache.

Types of Headaches

There are many recognized primary headache disorders. Three well-known types are:

Tension-type
- Affect men and women nearly equally
- Gradually produce a dull pain, tightness or pressure in neck, forehead or scalp

Migraine
- Produce moderate or severe and disabling pain, which is often pulsating
- Affect three times as many women as men
- May begin in your teens, less commonly after age 40
- May be preceded by a visual change, tingling on one side of face or body or a specific food craving
- Often associated with nausea (with or without vomiting) and sensitivity to light and noise

Cluster
- Produce steady, boring pain in and around one eye, occurring in episodes that often begin at the same time of day or night
- Cause eye watering and redness and nasal stuffiness on one side of the face
- May occur like clockwork and be linked to light or seasonal changes
- Frequently affect men, especially heavy smokers and drinkers
- May be misdiagnosed as a sinus infection or dental problem
- Usually last about 15 minutes to three hours

Migraine Theory

Research is focusing on various centers in the brain that may be involved in generating a migraine. Activity in these centers causes blood vessels inside the skull to dilate and possibly become inflamed. This causes painful impulses to travel along the trigeminal nerve into the brain. The result: a migraine.

When you don't feel pain:

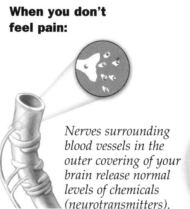

Nerves surrounding blood vessels in the outer covering of your brain release normal levels of chemicals (neurotransmitters).

When you have a migraine:

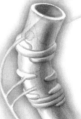

Nerves release higher levels of chemicals, which are irritating to the brain covering and other pain-sensitive structures. There may also be widening of blood vessels.

Self-Care	**For occasional tension-type headaches**

For occasional tension-type headaches

First, try massage, hot or cold packs, a warm shower, rest or relaxation techniques. If these measures don't work, try a low dose of aspirin (adults only), acetaminophen or ibuprofen. Moderate exercise may help a <u>tension-type headache</u>.

For recurrent headaches

- Keep a headache diary. Include these factors:
    - *Severity.* Is it disabling pain, or merely annoying?
    - *Frequency and duration.* When does the headache start? Does it begin gradually or strike rapidly? Does it occur at a certain time of day? In monthly or seasonal cycles? How long does it last? What makes it stop?
    - *Related symptoms.* Can you tell it's coming? Are you nauseated or dizzy? Do you see sparkling colors or blank spots?
    - *Location.* Is the pain usually on one side of your head? In your neck muscles? Around one eye?
    - *Family history.* Do other family members have similar headaches?
    - *Triggers.* Can you link your headache to any particular food, activity, weather, time frame or environmental factors? (See Avoiding Headache Triggers, page 84.)
- Avoid triggers, as possible. To do so may require lifestyle changes.
- Get adequate sleep and exercise.

Special migraine self-care

Begin treatment when you feel a <u>migraine</u> coming. This approach is your best chance to stop it early. Use acetaminophen, ibuprofen or aspirin (adults only) at the recommended dosage for pain relief. Some people can abort an attack by going to sleep in a darkened room or consuming caffeine (coffee or cola).

Medical Help

If self-care doesn't help after one or two days, see your health care provider. He or she will try to determine the type and cause of your headache, will try to exclude other possible sources of pain and may do tests. Your physician may prescribe one of many pain medications. Different medications are used for different types of headaches.

For severe migraines, your physician may prescribe a medication that mimics serotonin, a nerve chemical in your body. For frequent migraine attacks, your physician may prescribe a preventive medication to use on a daily basis.

Caution

Don't ignore unexplained headaches. Get medical attention right away if your headache:
- Strikes suddenly and severely
- Accompanies a fever, stiff neck, rash, mental confusion, seizures, double vision, weakness, numbness or speaking difficulties
- Begins or worsens after a head injury, fall or bump
- Is a new, significant problem or is worsening

Common Problems

Avoiding Headache Triggers

Does a particular food, drink or activity trigger your headaches? Some people can eliminate headaches by avoiding triggers. Triggers vary among individuals. Here are some common ones:

- Alcohol, red wine
- Smoking
- Stress or fatigue
- Eye strain
- Physical or sexual activity
- Poor posture
- Changing sleeping patterns or mealtimes

- Certain foods, such as:
  - fermented, pickled or marinated food
  - bananas
  - caffeine
  - aged cheeses
  - chocolate
  - citrus fruits
  - food additives (sodium nitrite in hot dogs, sausages or lunch meat, or monosodium glutamate in processed or Chinese foods) and seasonings
  - nuts or peanut butter

  - pizza
  - raisins
  - sourdough bread
- Weather, altitude or time zone changes
- Hormonal changes during your menstrual cycle or menopause, oral contraceptive use or hormone replacement therapy
- Strong or flickering lights
- Odors, including perfumes, flowers or natural gas
- Polluted air or stuffy rooms
- Excessive noise

Kids' Care

Recurrent headaches are common during late childhood and adolescence. They rarely represent a serious problem.

Headache is associated with many viral illnesses. However, if your child frequently complains of headache, even during times when he or she is otherwise well, consult your child's physician.

Migraines may occur in children and may be suspected if there's a family history of migraine. In children, this type of headache often is accompanied by vomiting, light sensitivity and sleep. Recovery follows within a few hours.

A headache may indicate stress with school, friends or family. It may be a reaction to a medication, particularly a decongestant.

If you think it's a tension-type headache, try the nonmedicating tips listed on page 83. If it occurs frequently, help your child keep a headache diary. Use acetaminophen or ibuprofen sparingly and briefly to avoid missing serious problems that the pain reliever may be masking.

If your child's headache persists, comes on suddenly without explanation or gets steadily worse, call your health care provider. Also call about headaches that follow recent ear infections, toothaches, strep throat or other infections.

Be sure to tell your physician if there's any family history of migraines. That information could help lead to a diagnosis.

The Link Between Caffeine and Headaches

That morning caffeine headache can be very real, especially if you consume four or more cups of caffeinated drinks during the day. It may be a withdrawal headache after a night without caffeine.

But, for some headaches, caffeine may be a cure. Some kinds of headaches cause blood vessels to widen. Caffeine temporarily causes them to narrow.

So, for adults, if aspirin or acetaminophen doesn't help, use a medicine that includes caffeine. But don't overdo. Too much caffeine can cause jitteriness, rapid heart rate, sweating and, yes, withdrawal headaches.

Limbs, Muscles, Bones and Joints

Your body is amazingly intricate. You don't think about your body much when it's working fine. Somehow, everything holds together, and you move about easily. But you usually do notice when there's a problem.

This section focuses on problems related to your limbs. Some conditions are common to many areas of your body, such as strains, sprains, broken bones, bursitis, tendinitis, fibromyalgia and gout. These conditions are addressed on pages 87 through 92. The remainder of the chapter provides additional information about problems related to specific joints: shoulder; elbow and forearm; wrist, hand and finger; hip; leg and knee; and ankle and foot. First, here is some general information.

Anatomy

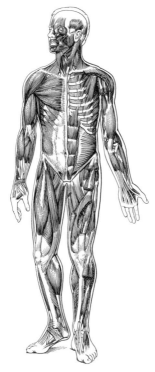

Many of your skeletal muscles are paired, enabling your body to move. Tendons connect these muscles to your bones.

Muscles and Tendons

Many of your 650 muscles help you move. Each skeletal muscle is attached to bones by bands called tendons. Pairs of muscles work together to move your joints by pulling on bones. One muscle relaxes as its partner tightens.

If you're active, your muscles enable you to run, walk, swim, jump, climb stairs, bike, dance or mow the lawn. Your muscles let you know when you've overdone it. They become sore and stiff.

Common causes of muscle injuries include accidents, strains, sudden movements, overuse and inflammation.

You can avoid many muscle and tendon aches by:
- Exercising regularly and moderately. Build up your activity gradually. You're not ready to run a marathon if you're not regularly running more than a few miles.
- Stretching your muscles gently before and after you exercise. For some people it's also helpful to use heat and massage to loosen their muscles before activity.
- Drinking plenty of water. Drinking six to eight glasses of water a day maintains good hydration. But you'll need more than that when you're active, especially in the heat of summer.
- Strengthening your muscles with resistance exercise.
- Supporting previously injured areas with elastic tape or a brace.
- Avoiding stressing your muscles when you are tired.
- Using appropriate ergonomic principles in the workplace.

Bones — Rigid, but Alive

You can't see it, but the 206 bones in your body change constantly. Proteins form the framework. Minerals, especially calcium and phosphate, fill in to give the bones strength. Because of this need for minerals, it's a good idea to consume mineral-rich milk and leafy green vegetables.

Common bone conditions include the following:
- Breaks, resulting from stress on a bone greater than it can withstand
- Bruising, usually from trauma
- Weakening through loss of minerals (osteoporosis)

A child's bones are more pliable than an adult's. When under strain or pressure, they're less likely to break. As you mature, your bones become more rigid.

Growing Pains Are Real

So-called growing pains can be very real during growth spurts. They usually occur in children's legs, often at night. They last a few hours and then go away. Growing pains usually don't hamper normal light activity.

If your child has growing pains:
- Use a warm heating pad for relief.

- Use recommended child's doses of acetaminophen or ibuprofen for pain. Don't give aspirin to children unless advised by your doctor to do so.
- Seek medical care if the area becomes swollen, hot and tender, or if your child develops a limp or unexplained fever.

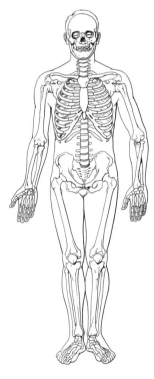

Your bones are living tissue and are always changing. They provide support for your body and function as your body's depository for important minerals.

Joints — Mechanical Masterpieces

Your bones come together at your joints. The end of each bone is covered by a layer of cartilage that glides smoothly and acts as a shock absorber. Tough bands of tissue (ligaments) hold your joints together.

Your body has several types of joints. This chapter discusses the following types:
- **Hinge joints** in the ends of your fingers or your knees, for example. They allow one kind of back-and-forth movement.
- **Ball-and-socket joints** in your shoulder or hip, for example. They allow a wide range of movement.

Causes of joint pain covered in this chapter include:
- Traumatic injuries or dislocation (when a joint is pushed out of place)
- Bursitis
- Fibromyalgia
- Gout
- Sprains

If your child has specific joint pain, you may want to see a health care provider. Contact your child's health care provider if your child has joint pain along with:
- A fever or rash
- Swelling, stiffness, abdominal pain or unexplained weight loss
- Enlarged and tender lymph glands in the neck
- Limping or impaired normal activity

Nerves — Lines of Communication

Most of this chapter focuses on bones, muscles and joints. However, all of your limbs are wired with nerves that carry messages to and from your brain. They sense pain and also help you locate its source. They direct your movement. They let you know when your muscles are tired or injured. They may keep a muscle from working properly.

Nerves help coordinate your movement. When your body is working properly, they're in constant contact with your brain. They also help you avoid many injuries.

It's easier for you or your health care provider to identify and treat pain if you can tell how it happened. Did it follow:
- An accident
- Prolonged overuse or repetitive motions
- Inflammation
- An illness or condition elsewhere in your body

Muscle Strains: When You've Overdone It

A muscle becomes strained or pulled — or may even tear — when it stretches unusually far or abruptly. This type of injury can also often occur when muscles suddenly and powerfully contract. A slip on the ice or lifting in an awkward position may cause a muscle strain.

Muscle strains vary in severity:

- **Mild.** Causes pain and stiffness when you move and lasts a few days.
- **Moderate.** Causes small muscle tears and more extensive pain, swelling and bruising. The pain may last one to three weeks.
- **Severe.** Muscle becomes torn apart or ruptured. You may have significant internal bleeding, swelling and bruising around the muscle. Your muscle may not function at all. Seek medical attention immediately.

Self-Care

- Follow the instructions for P.R.I.C.E. (see below). The earlier the treatment, the speedier and more complete your recovery.
- For extensive swelling, use cold packs several times each day throughout your recovery.
- Don't apply heat when the area is still swollen.
- Avoid the activity that caused the strain while the muscle heals.
- Use over-the-counter pain medications as needed (see page 258). Avoid using aspirin in the first few hours after the strain because aspirin may make bleeding more extensive. Don't give aspirin to children.

Medical Help

Seek medical help immediately if the area quickly becomes swollen and is intensely painful. Call your health care provider if the pain, swelling and stiffness don't improve in two to three days or if you suspect a ruptured muscle or broken bone.

P.R.I.C.E.: Your Best Tool for Muscle or Joint Injury

We refer to this information frequently throughout this section.

- **P: Protect** the area from further injury. Use an elastic wrap, sling, splint, cane, crutches or air splint.
- **R: Rest** to promote tissue healing. Avoid activities that cause pain, swelling or discomfort.
- **I: Ice** the area immediately, even if you're seeking medical help. Use an ice pack or slush bath for about 15 minutes each time you apply the ice. Repeat every two to three hours while you're awake for the first 48 to 72 hours. Cold reduces pain, swelling and inflammation in injured muscles, joints and connecting tissues. It may also slow bleeding if a tear has occurred.

- **C: Compress** the area with an elastic bandage until the swelling stops. Don't wrap it tightly or you may hinder circulation. Begin wrapping at the end farthest from your heart. Loosen the wrap if the pain increases, the area becomes numb or swelling is occurring below the wrapped area.
- **E: Elevate** the area above your heart, especially at night. Gravity helps reduce swelling by draining excess fluid.
- After 48 hours, if the swelling is gone, you may apply warmth or gentle heat. Heat can improve blood flow and speed healing.
- Apply cold to sore areas after a workout, even if you're not injured, to prevent inflammation and swelling.

Sprains: Damage to Your Ligaments

Strictly speaking, a sprain occurs when you overextend or tear a ligament. Ligaments are the tough, elastic-like bands that attach to your bones and hold your joints in place. However, the term *sprain* is commonly used to describe any instance in which a joint moves outside its normal range of movement.

Sprains frequently are caused by twisting. They occur most often in your ankles, knees or the arches of your feet. True sprains cause rapid swelling. Generally, the greater the pain, the more severe the injury. Sprains vary in severity:

- **Mild.** Your ligament stretches excessively or tears slightly. The area is somewhat painful, especially with movement. It's tender. There is not a lot of swelling. You can put weight on the joint.
- **Moderate.** The fibers in your ligament tear, but they don't rupture completely. The joint is tender, painful and difficult to move. The area is swollen and discolored from bleeding in the area.
- **Severe.** One or more ligaments tear completely. The area is painful. You can't move your joint normally or put weight on it. It becomes very swollen and discolored. The injury may be difficult to distinguish from a fracture or dislocation, which requires medical care. You may need a cast to hold the joint motionless, or an operation, if torn ligaments cause joint instability.

Self-Care

- Follow the instructions for P.R.I.C.E. (see page 87).
- Use over-the-counter pain medications (see page 258).
- Gradually test and use the joint after two days. Mild to moderate sprains usually improve significantly in a week, although full healing may take six weeks.
- Avoid activities that stress your joint. Repeated minor sprains will weaken it.

Medical Help

Seek medical care immediately if:

- You hear a popping sound when your joint is injured and you can't use it. On the way to your health care provider, apply cold.
- You have a fever and the area is red and hot. You may have an infection.
- You have a severe sprain, as described above. Inadequate or delayed treatment may cause long-term joint instability or chronic pain.

See your doctor if you're unable to bear weight on the joint after two to three days of self-care or if you don't experience much improvement in a week.

Preventing Sports Injuries

- Select your sport carefully. Don't jog if you have chronic back pain or sore knees.
- Warm up. Loosen, stretch and gradually increase your activity over five to 10 minutes. If you're prone to muscle pain, apply heat before you exercise.
- After exercising, cool down with muscle stretches.
- Begin a new sport gradually. Increase your level of exertion over several weeks.
- Use pain relievers with caution. It's easier to overexert and damage tissue without realizing it.
- Stop participating immediately if you think you may be injured, you become disoriented or dizzy or you lose consciousness, even briefly.
- Return gradually to full activity or switch sports until injuries heal.

See back cover for online resource

Broken Bones (Fractures)

If you suspect a bone is broken, get medical care. A broken bone may or may not poke through your skin. Open fractures break through the skin. Closed fractures do not. Closed fractures are classified according to the way the bone breaks. Several varieties are shown in the illustrations below.

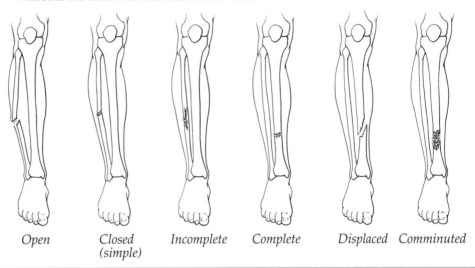

Open   Closed (simple)   Incomplete   Complete   Displaced   Comminuted

Emergency Treatment

After serious injury or trauma, seek medical care immediately if:
- The person is unconscious or can't be moved.
- The person isn't breathing or doesn't have a pulse. Begin CPR (see page 2).
- There's heavy bleeding.
- Even gentle pressure or movement produces pain.
- The limb or joint appears deformed, or the bone has pierced the skin.
- The part farthest from the heart is numb or bluish at the tip.

Self-Care

Take these precautions and seek medical care:
- Protect the area from further damage.
- If there's bleeding, try to stop it. Press directly on the wound with a sterile bandage, clean cloth or piece of clothing. If nothing else is available, use your hand. Keep pressing until the bleeding stops.
- Use a splint or sling to hold the area still. You can make a splint from wood, plastic or rolled newspaper. Place it on both sides of the bone, extending beyond the ends of the bone. Hold it firmly in place with gauze, cloth strips, tape or string, but not tight enough to stop the blood flow.
- Don't try to set the bone yourself.
- If ice is available, wrap the ice in cloth and apply it to the splinted limb.
- Try to elevate the injured area above the heart to reduce bleeding and swelling.
- If the person becomes faint or is breathing in short breaths, he or she may be in shock. Lay the person down with his or her head slightly lower than the rest of the body.

Kids' Care

The bones in your child's arms and legs have growth plates near the ends that allow bones to lengthen. If growth plates become damaged, the bone may not grow properly. Check out any possible fractures with your doctor.

Common Problems

■ Bursitis

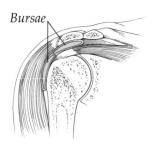

Bursae

You have more than 150 bursae in your body. These tiny, fluid-filled sacs lubricate and cushion pressure points for your bones, tendons and muscles near your joints. They help you move without pain. When they become inflamed, movement or pressure is painful. This condition is called **bursitis**. Bursitis is commonly caused by overuse, trauma, repeated bumping or prolonged pressure such as kneeling for an extended period. It may even result from an infection, arthritis or gout. Most often, bursitis affects the shoulder, elbow or hip joint. But you also can have bursitis at your knee, heel and even in the base of your big toe.

Self-Care

- Use over-the-counter pain medications (see page 258).
- Keep pressure off the joint. Use an elastic bandage, sling or soft foam pad to protect it until the swelling goes down.
- Simple bursitis usually disappears within two weeks. Ease the area back into activity slowly.

Prevention

- Strengthen your muscles to help protect the joint. Don't start exercising a joint that has bursitis until the pain and inflammation are gone.
- Take frequent breaks from repetitive tasks. Alternate repetitive tasks with rest or other activities. Follow ergonomic principles for desk work and lifting.
- Cushion the joint before applying pressure (such as with knee or elbow pads). For bursitis in a hip, cushion a hard mattress with a foam pad or soft mattress cover.

Medical Help

Seek medical care if the area becomes red and hot or doesn't improve, or if you also have a fever or rash.

■ Tendinitis

Tendinitis produces pain and tenderness near a joint. You can usually associate it with a specific movement (grasping, for example). It usually means you have an inflammation or a small tear of the tendon. Tendinitis is usually the result of overuse or a minor injury. It's most common around the shoulders, elbows and knees.

Pain may cause you to limit movement. Rest is important, but so is maintaining a full range of movement. If you don't treat tendinitis carefully, tendons and ligaments around your joint may gradually stiffen over several weeks. Movement may become limited and difficult.

Self-Care

- Follow the instructions for P.R.I.C.E. (see page 87).
- Gently move the joint through its full range four times a day. Otherwise rest it. A sling, elastic bandage or splint may help.
- Use an anti-inflammatory medication (see page 258).
- If soreness doesn't greatly improve in two weeks, see your health care provider.

Prevention

- Use warm-up and cool-down exercises and strengthening exercises.
- Apply heat to the area before you exercise, and apply cold afterward.
- Exercise on alternate days when starting an exercise program.

See back cover for online resource 🛈

Medical Help	Seek medical help immediately if you have a fever and the area is inflamed.

Sometimes doctors inject a drug into tissue around a tendon to relieve tendinitis. Cortisone injections reduce inflammation and can give rapid relief of pain. These injections must be used with care because repeated injections may weaken the tendon or cause undesirable side effects.

▮ Fibromyalgia

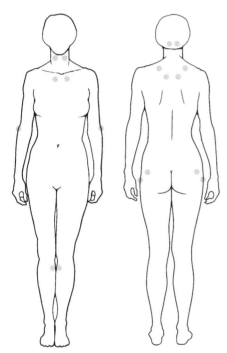

Common locations of fibromyalgia

Persistent pain and stiffness in your muscles may have many causes. In recent years, health care providers have increasingly diagnosed a condition called **fibromyalgia**.

Common symptoms that lead to the diagnosis include general aches and pain and stiffness in joints and muscles. The type of pain can vary. It often affects areas where tendons attach muscles to bones. Symptoms frequently include the following:

- Widespread aching, lasting more than three months
- Fatigue and nonrestful, nonrestorative sleep
- Morning stiffness
- Tender points on the body, usually at sites of muscle attachment (see illustration)
- Associated problems such as headaches (see page 82), irritable bowel syndrome (see page 65) and pelvic pain

Fibromyalgia is a "diagnosis of exclusion." There are no laboratory tests that can help make the diagnosis. Your doctor will do so after considering other causes for your symptoms. For some people, the condition resolves spontaneously. For others it becomes chronic.

Emotional tension or stress may increase your likelihood of having fibromyalgia. It's more frequent in women than in men. This difference may be partially due to the fact that men may be more reluctant to see a doctor about their symptoms.

Self-Care	<ul><li>Pace yourself. Reduce your stress and avoid long hours of repetitive activity. Develop a routine that alternates work with rest.</li><li>Develop a regular, low-impact exercise program such as walking, biking, swimming and plenty of stretching exercises. Improve your posture by strengthening supportive muscles, especially abdominal muscles (see page 55).</li><li>Improve your sleep naturally with daily physical activity. To avoid undesirable side effects, use sleep medications sparingly, if at all.</li><li>If necessary, use over-the-counter pain medications occasionally (see page 258).</li><li>Find a support group that emphasizes maintaining health.</li><li>Ask your family and friends for support.</li></ul>

Prevention

The best thing you can do to avoid or minimize fibromyalgia is to keep yourself in good physical condition, reduce stress and get adequate sleep.

- Try not to quit your job. Fibromyalgia seems to worsen in people who go on disability and eliminate activity entirely.
- Learn relaxation techniques. Try massage and warm baths.

Common Problems

■ Gout

<u>Gout</u> produces a sudden pain in a single joint, usually at the base of your big toe, although it may also affect joints in your feet, ankles, knees, hands and wrists. The joint becomes swollen and red. Genetics may play a role in the condition. A significant percentage of people with gout have a family history of it. Gout occurs when crystals of uric acid collect in a joint. Your risk of having gout increases if you're obese or have high blood pressure. Blood pressure medications that reduce your body's water content may provoke gout. Self-care measures include maintaining a reasonable weight, drinking plenty of water and avoiding heavy alcohol consumption. Seek medical care immediately if you have a fever and your joint is hot and inflamed. For more information, see page 162.

■ Shoulder Pain

Clavicle

Bursa

Tendon (torn)

Humerus

Ligament

Treatment of shoulder pain depends on its cause. Bursitis and tendinitis are common causes of shoulder pain (see page 90), as are acute injury and rotator cuff tears (see page 93). Take note of how the pain began and what makes the pain worse. This information can be helpful if you need medical care.

Most shoulder pain isn't life-threatening. Occasionally, though, shoulder pain may signal a heart attack. Call for emergency medical assistance right away if your pain:

- Starts as chest pain or pressure. The pain may occur suddenly or gradually. It may radiate to your shoulder, back, arms, jaw and neck.
- Is accompanied by excessive sweating, shortness of breath, faintness or nausea and vomiting.
- Is new and you have a known heart condition.

■ Acute Shoulder Pain

Acute shoulder pain centers on your upper arm, upper back or neck. Pain may suddenly limit arm movement. Possible causes include overuse or trauma. Your shoulder may become inflamed and swollen at the tip. It may be very painful to put on a coat, extend your arm straight out from your side or reach behind you.

Self-Care

- Use over-the-counter pain medications (see page 258).
- If the bone isn't broken or dislocated, it's important to move the joint through its full range four times a day to avoid stiffening or a permanent condition called frozen shoulder.
- Once pain has resolved, exercise your arm daily.

Medical Help

Seek medical care if:

- Your shoulders appear uneven or you cannot raise the affected arm
- You have extreme tenderness at the end of your collarbone
- An injury causes you to wonder if a bone is broken
- You have redness, swelling or fever
- Your shoulder isn't improving after a week of self-care

See back cover for online resource

■ Rotator Cuff Injury

The rotator cuff is formed by the attachment of several tendons to the shoulder. Because of the shoulder's complexity, many problems are simply diagnosed as rotator cuff injuries. The tendons in your shoulder may have tiny tears, be irritated or pinched between your bones (impingement). Pain may be more severe at night. This type of injury usually results from repetitive overhead motions, such as painting a ceiling, swimming or throwing a baseball, or from trauma, such as falling on your shoulder. In older adults, a **rotator cuff injury** may simply stem from degeneration of the shoulder tendons from a lifetime of use.

Self-Care

- Follow the instructions for P.R.I.C.E. (see page 87).
- Take anti-inflammatory medicines (see page 258).
- Do stretching exercises and put the shoulder through its full range of motion four times daily.
- Wait until the pain is gone before gradually returning to the activity that caused the injury. You may have to wait three to six weeks.
- Alter your technique in racket sports, pitching or golf.

Medical Help

Seek medical care if the area is hot and inflamed and you have a fever, if your shoulders are uneven or if you can't move your arm at all.

If the pain hasn't diminished in one week despite the use of self-care measures, see your doctor.

■ Elbow and Forearm Pain

Bursitis and tendinitis are common sources of pain in your elbow (see page 90). Bursitis may produce a small, egg-shaped, fluid-filled sac at the tip of your elbow. If the pain hasn't improved after a few days of treatment and the area is still very sensitive to pressure, or your arm or hand becomes numb, seek medical care. You may need an X-ray to determine whether a bone is broken.

A **dislocated elbow** may occur in a child if an adult suddenly pulls or jerks the child's arm. The elbow of a child — especially if younger than 6 years — cannot withstand this stress. **Dislocation** is very painful and limits movement. Seek medical treatment immediately. Your health care provider will return the bones to their proper position, which usually relieves the pain. An X-ray can rule out other problems.

A **hyperextended elbow** occurs when your elbow is pushed beyond its normal range of motion, often as a result of a fall or misplay during a tennis swing. Pain and swelling occur in your elbow and in the tissues beneath your elbow. Try P.R.I.C.E. (see page 87) and support your elbow with a splint or sling until the pain stops. If the pain hasn't improved in a week, see your health care provider.

Medical Help

Seek medical care immediately if:
- Your elbow seems deformed
- Your elbow is very stiff and has limited range of motion after a fall
- The pain in your arm is severe

Common Problems

■ Tennis Elbow or Golfer's Elbow

This recurrent pain is actually a form of tendinitis (epicondylitis). It affects the outside or inside of your elbow. Pain may extend down toward your wrist. It may result from repeated tiny tears (microtears) in tendons that attach muscles of your lower arm to your elbow, or by inflammation of tissues. Common causes of **tennis elbow** or golfer's elbow include swinging a racket or club, pitching a baseball, painting a house, using a screwdriver or hammer or any movement requiring twisting arm motions or repetitive gripping.

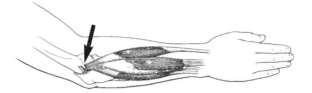

Tennis elbow produces pain on the outside of your forearm near your elbow when you exercise the joint. Tiny tears or inflammation (see arrow) causes the discomfort.

Self-Care

- Follow the instructions for P.R.I.C.E. (see page 87).
- Massage may speed healing by improving circulation in the area.
- Splinting your elbow and forearm at night may reduce pain.
- Take an anti-inflammatory medication (see page 258).
- It may take six to 12 weeks of treatment for the pain to disappear.

Prevention
- Prepare for repetitive work-related tasks by participating in fitness and strengthening routines.
- Prepare for any sport season with appropriate preseason conditioning. Do strengthening exercises with a hand weight by flexing and extending the wrists.
- Wear forearm support bands just below your elbow.
- Warm up properly. Gently stretch the forearm muscles before and after use.
- Try applying a warm pack for five minutes before activity and an ice pack after heavy use.

Medical Help

Seek medical care immediately if:
- Your elbow is hot and inflamed and you have a fever
- You can't bend your elbow at all or it looks deformed
- A fall or injury causes you to wonder if a bone is broken
  If the pain doesn't improve in a week or so, see your doctor to rule out other complications.

■ Wrist, Hand and Finger Pain

Think of all the things you do each day with your wrists, hands and fingers. You may not consider the many nerves, blood vessels, muscles and small bones that work together as you turn a key in the door — until the movement becomes painful.

Pain and swelling in your wrists, hands and fingers can result from injury or overuse. They can begin gradually or rapidly. They may be due to the following:

- A strain or sprain (see pages 87 and 88)
- Fracture, bursitis, tendinitis or gout (see pages 89, 90 and 92)
- Arthritis or fibromyalgia (see pages 91 and 161).

Self-Care

- Follow the instructions for P.R.I.C.E. (see page 87).
- Take over-the-counter pain medicines (see page 258).
- If an initial X-ray doesn't show a fracture and it's still quite painful a week later, ask your health care provider to check again. Some fractures may require special X-ray views or be invisible in the first few days.
- If pain continues, you may need further testing, a splint or cast or physical therapy.

Prevention

- Use tools with large handles so you don't have to grip them as hard.
- Remove your rings before manual labor. If you injure your hand, remove your rings before your fingers become swollen.
- Take frequent breaks to rest muscles you've used steadily. Vary your activities.
- Use flexibility and strengthening exercises.

Medical Help

Seek medical care immediately if:

- You suspect a fracture
- A fall or accident has caused rapid swelling and moving the area is painful
- The area is hot and inflamed and you have a fever
- Your fingers suddenly become blue and numb

■ Common Problems

A ganglion is a swelling beneath the skin. It's a fluid-filled cyst lined with tissue bulging from a joint or tendon sheath.

Ganglions are fluid-filled lumps that usually appear on the top of the wrist, but also may occur on the underside of the wrist, in the palm or over finger joints. They're filled with jelly-like material leaking from a joint or tendon, although they feel firm or solid. Ganglions are sometimes painful and, if bothersome, may require treatment. Seek medical care immediately if the lump becomes painful and inflamed or if the cyst breaks through the skin and drains (usually at the end of the fingers).

A **jammed finger** commonly occurs during sports activities. Pain may be caused by stretched ligaments (sprain) or a fracture involving the joint surface. Follow the P.R.I.C.E. guidelines on page 87. To protect it during use, "buddy tape" the injured finger to an adjacent finger. Seek medical care immediately if:

- Your finger appears deformed
- You cannot straighten your finger
- The area becomes hot and inflamed and you have a fever
- Swelling and pain are significant or persistent

Trigger finger is a condition that causes the finger to lock or catch in a bent position. It'll straighten with a visible sudden "snap," and if it's severe, the finger may not fully straighten. Triggering is more pronounced in the morning and after firmly grasping an object. The condition is caused by a binding "knot" in the palm that prevents smooth tendon motion. Change your habits to avoid overuse. Seek medical care immediately if your finger is hot and inflamed and you have a fever.

◼ Carpal Tunnel Syndrome

A narrow tunnel through your wrist (the carpal tunnel) protects your median nerve, which provides sensation to your fingers. When swelling occurs in the tunnel, the median nerve can become compressed, causing numbness and pain.

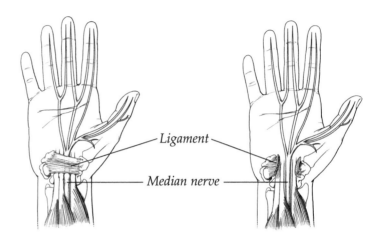

Ligament

Median nerve

Finger-bending (flexor) tendons and an important nerve pass through a tight space (carpal tunnel) as they enter the hand. Swelling in the tunnel or pressure in the palm may squeeze the nerve. Most problems occur without a clear cause. Swelling is more common in women than in men. **Carpal tunnel syndrome** occurs more frequently in people who are pregnant or overweight. Smoking and medical conditions such as diabetes, thyroid disease and arthritis also seem to play a role, as do occupations and hobbies that involve awkward wrist positions, pressure on the palm of the hand, and repetitive lifting or grasping actions.

Symptoms include the following:

- Tingling or numbness in your thumb, index and middle fingers (but not your little finger). This tingling may occur at night, and wake you from sleep, and may also occur while you're driving or holding the phone or a newspaper.
- Pain radiating or extending from your wrist into your forearm or down into your palm or fingers.
- A sense of weakness or clumsiness; dropping objects.
- If the condition is advanced, a constant loss of feeling in the affected fingers.

Self-Care

- Take breaks from heavy or repetitive activity, at least five minutes every hour.
- Vary your activities. Stretch your wrists and hands at least once every hour.
- Keep fit; watch your weight and don't smoke.
- If you have tingling in your hand or fingers that wakes you at night, or if you note numbness in your hand when you wake up in the morning, try wearing a wrist splint that holds your wrist straight at night. The splint should be snug but not tight.
- If the symptoms continue or worsen, see your health care provider.

Thumb Pain

Pain at the base of your thumb may be the first sign of osteoarthritis in your hands (see page 161) or tendinitis of the thumb (de Quervain's disease), a condition that more often affects younger individuals. You may notice pain and swelling at the base of your thumb when you write, open jars, turn your key in the door or ignition or try to hold small objects. With osteoarthritis of the hands, the pain may be limited to one joint or extend to many. It's more common in women than in men, usually occurring after age 40. The pain can be the result of a previous injury, repetitive activity or heredity.

Self-Care
- Modify behaviors and avoid activities that cause pain.
- Rest your thumb. Use a splint to stabilize the wrist and thumb. Remove the splint at least four times a day to move and stretch the joints to maintain flexibility.
- Use over-the-counter pain medications (see page 258).
- Exercise your thumb daily while your hands are warm. Move your thumb in wide circles. Bend it to touch each of the other fingers on your hand.
- Use tools specially designed for people with arthritis. Avoid pinching grips.

Medical Help
Seek medical care immediately if pain limits activities or is too severe to tolerate most days. Cortisone injections, arthritis medicine and, occasionally, an operation are effective in alleviating pain.

Hip Pain

Hip pain frequently follows a fall or accident. It may also occur after vigorous speed walking or aerobics. Common causes include bursitis, tendinitis and osteoarthritis (see pages 90 and 161, respectively) or strains and sprains (see pages 87 and 88). Only rarely is hip pain caused by having one leg shorter than the other, since differences in leg length of half an inch or more (1 to 2 centimeters) are common and normal.

Self-Care
- Follow the instructions for P.R.I.C.E. (see page 87).
- Avoid activities that aggravate the pain.
- Take over-the-counter pain medicines (see page 258).
- Strengthen the hip-group muscles (especially the hip abductors, which move the leg out from the body) to relieve pain and improve function in an arthritic hip.

Medical Help
Seek medical care immediately if:
- You have fallen or had an accident and wonder if your hip may be broken
- You have followed the self-care instructions above after an accident or fall and your hip is more painful the following day
- You have osteoporosis and have injured your hip in a fall

Common Problems

Leg Pain

Many leg difficulties result from a combination of overuse, deconditioning (poor strength and flexibility), being overweight, trauma and poor circulation. Lifestyle changes may improve your legs' comfort.

Use the following exercises to strengthen your muscles and avoid injuries:
- **Walk.** Begin with short strides. Lengthen your stride as your muscles loosen.
- **Bike.** Gradually increase your distance and speed over weeks.
- **Swim.** Stretch and tone your muscles.
- **Work paired muscles equally.** For example, exercise the quadriceps (the muscles on the front of the thigh) equally with the hamstrings (muscles on the back of the thigh).

Pulled Hamstring Muscle

Athletes often bruise or strain hamstring muscles, especially during sports such as soccer or track-and-field activities. You may suspect such an injury if you experience pain after a slip or rigorous activity.

Self-Care

- Follow the instructions for P.R.I.C.E. (see page 87). If symptoms don't begin to improve after a week of P.R.I.C.E. treatment, see your health care provider.

Prevention
To avoid hamstring injury, try this exercise called the lying hamstring stretch:
- Lie on your back with a towel around your foot. Raise your leg and pull on the towel to keep your knee as straight as possible. Your trunk stays relaxed. Hold for 30 seconds. Repeat, reversing leg positions. Don't lock your knee.

Pain, Cramps and Charley Horses

A cramp, sometimes called a charley horse, is actually a muscle spasm. Cramps commonly occur in an athlete who's overfatigued and dehydrated during sports, especially in warm weather. However, almost everyone experiences a _muscle cramp_ at some time. For most people, cramps are only an occasional inconvenience.

Self-Care

- Gently stretch and massage a cramping muscle.
- For lower leg (calf) cramps, put your weight on the leg and bend your knee slightly, or do the calf stretch illustrated on page 106.
- For upper leg (hamstring) cramps, straighten your legs and lean forward at your waist. Steady yourself with a chair. Or do the hamstring stretch described above.
- Apply heat to relax tense, tight muscles.
- Apply cold to sore or tender muscles.
- Drink plenty of water. Fluid helps your muscles function normally.
- If you have troublesome leg cramps, ask your health care provider about possible medication options.

Self-Care

Prevention

Stretch your leg muscles daily, using the following stretch for the Achilles tendon and calf (see the illustration on page 106):

- Stand an arm's length from a wall. Lean forward, resting your hands and forearms on the wall.
- Bend one leg at the knee and bring it toward the wall. Keep the other leg stiff. Keep both heels on the floor. Keep your back straight and move your hips toward the wall. Hold for 30 seconds.
- Repeat with the other leg. Repeat five times per leg.
- Stretch your muscles carefully and warm up before exercising vigorously.
- Stop exercising if a cramp begins.

■ Shin Splints

When pain occurs on the front, inside portion of the large bone of your lower leg (tibia), it may be the result of shin splints. <u>Shin splints</u> occur when tiny fibers of the membrane that attaches muscle to the tibia become irritated and inflamed, producing pain and sometimes swelling. Shin splints commonly occur in runners, basketball and tennis players and army recruits.

Self-Care

- Follow the instructions for P.R.I.C.E. (see page 87).
- Apply ice massage to the painful area.
- Try over-the-counter pain relievers (see page 258).
- Wait until the pain leaves before resuming the activity that caused it. The pain may last several weeks or even months. Meanwhile, bike or swim to maintain flexibility and strength.

Prevention

- Use stretching exercises before running to loosen the muscles in your legs and feet. Tap your foot up and down and side to side.
- A soft shoe insert may help cushion your leg.
- You may need a specially made insert (orthotic) to wear in your shoes, especially if you have flatfeet.
- A trainer can help evaluate and adjust your running style.

Medical Help

Seek medical care immediately if:

- Pain in your shin follows a fall or accident and is severe
- Your shin is hot and inflamed
- You have pain in your shin at rest or at night

Special X-rays may be used to look for a stress fracture.

■ Swollen Legs

Occasional swelling in your legs is a common problem and has many causes, including being overweight, sitting or standing for a long time, retaining fluids (common in pregnant or menstruating women), varicose veins, an allergic reaction and too much sun exposure.

Serious and ongoing swelling can be caused by these conditions:

- *Blood clot and inflammation in a vein (phlebitis).* Phlebitis usually occurs in the lower portion of a leg. It may affect either superficial or deep veins. The leg becomes sore, red and swollen. It often follows a period of inactivity, such as a long car or plane ride or after an operation. Phlebitis that occurs in a deep vein (deep vein thrombosis) is a serious medical condition. See your health care provider immediately.
- *Poor circulation (claudication).* A cramping pain occurs at about the same point each time you walk. It goes away when you stop and rest. It's caused by a narrowed or blocked area in your leg arteries. See your health care provider.
- *Heart failure.* If your heart is unable to keep up with the demands on it, you may retain fluid in your legs. This condition affects both legs at the same time and isn't painful. See your health care provider.
- *Liver or kidney disease.* See your health care provider.

Self-Care

For occasional swelling
- Lose weight and limit salt intake.
- Elevate your legs to a level above your heart for 15 to 20 minutes every few hours to let gravity help move fluid toward your heart.
- For prolonged sitting and travel, walk around frequently and stretch your legs.

For conditions that cause swelling
Although you cannot treat these conditions yourself, you can lower your risk if you do the following:
- Stop smoking.
- Control blood pressure.
- Exercise moderately and regularly.
- Attain a healthy weight.

Medical Help

Seek medical care immediately if you have unexplained, painful swelling in your legs or if a swollen leg becomes warm, red and inflamed.

■ Knee Pain

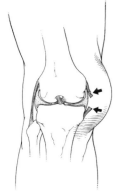

Arrows point to a torn ligament, a common form of knee injury. Swelling occurs and the joint becomes unstable.

Your knee is one of the largest joints in your body and is complex. The parts of your knee work together to support you each day as you bend, straighten, turn and walk.

Your knee is very susceptible to injury because of its exposed location. It's not designed to handle sideways stress, and it carries a lot of weight.

Knee injuries are often complex. Many are sports-related or result from trauma. Sometimes pain is simply a matter of wear and tear. You cannot accurately tell how severe a knee injury is by the extent of pain and swelling. It's more important that your knee can bear weight, feels stable and has its full range of motion.

Pain can be due to the following:
- **Strains and sprains** (see pages 87 and 88) from sudden twists or blows to your knee. A sprain will be on the opposite side of your knee from the side that took the blow. It may take days for swelling to develop fully.
- **Tendinitis** (see page 90), possibly as a result of intense bicycling or stair climbing. Runner's knee is a form of tendinitis. This overuse injury produces pain at the front of your knee. Your tendons become inflamed and it hurts to move your knee.
- **Fibromyalgia.** Knee pain is a common symptom of fibromyalgia (see page 91).
- **Bursitis** (see page 90).

- **Osteoarthritis** (see page 161). Arthritis often causes pain when you move or put weight on your knees.
- **Torn cartilage or ligaments** in your knee caused by twisting or impact. These are common injuries for skiers and basketball players, and in older adults.
- **Loose pieces** of your kneecap or cartilage floating around your joint. They may become pinched in your knee joint. This condition is painful and can cause your joint to lock.
- A tender, bulging **cyst** behind your knee (popliteal or **Baker's cyst**). It hurts to bend, squat or kneel.

Self-Care

- Follow the instructions for P.R.I.C.E. (see page 87).
- Take an anti-inflammatory medicine (see page 258). Remember that you may not feel injury-alerting pain after you take pain medicine.
- Flex and straighten your leg gently every day. If it's difficult to move your knee, have someone help you at first. Try to straighten it and keep it straight.
- If you use a cane, use it on the side that's not injured to take weight off your bad knee or leg.
- Avoid strenuous activity until your knee heals. Start nonimpact exercises slowly.
- Avoid squatting, kneeling or walking up and down hills.

Prevention

- Exercise regularly to strengthen your knee muscles. Bend your knee only to a 90-degree angle during exercise. Don't do deep knee bends.

Medical Help

Seek medical care immediately if:
- The injury produces intense, immediate pain, and your knee doesn't function properly.
- Your knee is very painful, even when you're not putting weight on it.
- The pain follows a popping sound or snapping or locking sensation. Torn knee ligaments may need surgical repair. Delay reduces the likelihood of success.
- Your knee locks rigidly in one position, or your kneecap is visibly deformed (dislocated).
- Your knee seems unusually loose or unstable.
- You have rapid, unexplained swelling or a fever.

If the pain isn't improving after one week of home treatment, see your health care provider.

Knee Supports and Braces

If your knees are unstable, try a brace or support bandage such as:
- A rubbery, neoprene sleeve. This slips over your knee and has a hole over your kneecap.
- An inexpensive, nonprescription knee brace. This may be hinged on the outer side or on both sides of your knee.

Caution: These devices appear to offer more support than they actually do. Although they don't protect your knee from injury, they may make it feel warm and secure and will protect it from scrapes. Use braces or supports under the direction of your doctor or therapist.

Common Problems

■ Ankle and Foot Pain

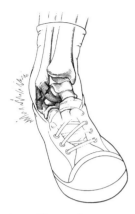

An ankle sprain occurs when ligaments that support your ankle are stretched or torn.

Your ankle is one of the most commonly injured joints. The ankle, where three bones meet, allows a wide-ranging foot movement and bears your full body weight. Common causes of foot or ankle pain include the following:

- **Strains and sprains** (see pages 87 and 88).
- **Fractures** (see page 89). High-impact activities such as basketball or aerobics can cause stress fractures. Stress fractures are really hairline cracks. They're often invisible on an X-ray for 10 to 21 days after the injury.
- **Bursitis and tendinitis** (see page 90).
- **Achilles tendinitis** occurs when the tendon that links your calf muscles to the bone at the back of your heel becomes inflamed. The tiny tears in the tendon may follow strenuous exercise. You'll feel a dull ache or pain, especially when you run or jump. The tendon may also be mildly swollen or tender.
- **Bunion.** Ill-fitting footwear or hereditary factors are often the cause of this condition. Your big toe bends toward the next toe, sometimes causing overlapping or underlapping of these toes. The base of your big toe extends beyond your foot's normal profile. That bump is called a bunion. The rubbing of shoes may cause corns, calluses and joint pain.

Self-Care

- Follow the instructions for P.R.I.C.E. (see page 87).
- Walking on an unstable joint may increase the damage, unless you stabilize it with an ankle brace, air splint or high, laced boots.

If you suspect a fracture, see your health care provider. If you have a **stress fracture:**
- Allow at least one month for healing. You usually won't need a cast.
- Avoid high-impact activities for four to six weeks.

If you have **Achilles tendinitis:**
- Wear soft-soled running shoes, and avoid running or walking up or down hills.
- Avoid any impact on your heel for several days.
- Use gentle calf stretches daily (see pages 99 and 106).

If you have **bunions:**
- Wear shoes with adequate toe width and soft leather. Wear sandals or light-weight shoes in the summer. Larger deformities may require special shoes.

Prevention
- Choose well-fitting, good-quality footwear. Shoes with a wider toe box will eliminate pressure on your toes. Avoid tight, thin-soled, high-heeled shoes.
- Stretch your Achilles tendon. Before exercise, follow the calf stretches outlined on pages 99 and 106.

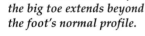

The bump of a bunion is caused when the base of the big toe extends beyond the foot's normal profile.

Medical Help

Seek medical care immediately if:
- Your foot pain is severe and the area is swollen after an accident or injury
- Your foot is hot and inflamed or you have a fever
- Your foot or ankle is deformed or bent in an abnormal position
- The pain is so severe that you can't move your foot
- You can't bear weight 72 hours after any injury

■ Flatfeet

All babies appear to have <u>**flatfeet**</u>. By the time children become teens, most of have developed arched feet. Arches go both from side to side and lengthwise and help distribute weight evenly across the foot.

Some people never develop arches. Others become flatfooted after they put many miles on their feet. But that isn't necessarily a problem.

Flatfeet can be a problem when:

- They place pressure on your foot's nerves and blood vessels
- They cause imbalance and joint problems in your ankles, knees, hips or lower back
- You carry excess body weight

Self-Care

- Arch supports in well-fitting shoes may give you a better weight-bearing position.
- See your health care provider if your flatfeet are continuously painful.

Kids' Care

Baby fat may make your infant's feet look flat. At about age 5 years, your child may begin to develop an arch. One in seven children never develops well-formed arches.

There are two kinds of flatfeet:

- **Flexible flatfeet** look flat only when your child stands up. Arches reappear if your child stands on tiptoe or takes weight off the foot. Flexible flatfeet are painless and tend to run in families. There's usually no need to treat them. Some health care providers recommend arch supports in firm shoes for increased comfort.
- **Fixed flatfeet** can be more difficult. If your child's feet are painful, stiff or extremely flat, special footwear or an operation may help.

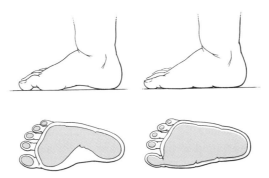

Flatfeet are feet that have little or no arch. Above at left (top and bottom) is a normal foot and footprint for a child age 5 or older. If your child's foot and footprint more nearly resemble the illustrations at right, then he or she may have flatfeet.

Common Problems

Burning Feet

Pain may be mild or severe burning or stinging. It may be constant or temporary. See a doctor if symptoms persist. This condition is most common in people older than age 65. The cause can be difficult to pinpoint and may include the following:

- Irritating fabrics
- Poorly fitting shoes
- A fungal infection such as Athlete's foot (see page 122)
- Exposure to a toxic substance like poison ivy

Suspect a nerve or blood vessel disorder if you have:

- Burning with prickling, tingling, weakness or a change of sensation or coordination in your legs; burning or tingling worse when at rest or in bed
- Burning with nausea, diarrhea, loss of urine or bowel control or impotence
- Other family members with the problem
- A persistent condition
- Diabetes

Self-Care

- Wear nonirritating cotton or cotton-synthetic blend socks and shoes of natural materials that "breathe." A specially fitted insole also may help.
- Eliminate aggravating activities, such as standing for long periods.
- Bathe your feet in cool water.
- Use over-the-counter pain medications (see page 258).

Hammertoe and Mallet Toe

Unlike a bunion, which affects the big toe, **hammertoe** may occur in any toe (most commonly the second toe). The toe becomes bent and may be painful. Generally, both joints in a toe are affected, giving it a claw-like appearance. Hammertoe can result from wearing shoes that are too short, but the deformity also occurs in people with long-term diabetes or other diseases that cause muscle and nerve damage. A **mallet toe** is deformed at the end of the toe.

Self-Care

- Special toe pads or cushions help protect the toe. Metatarsal pads may reduce pain in the ball of the foot behind the hammertoe.
- Your shoes should accommodate foot length and width and height of your toes.

Tips for Proper Shoe Fit

You can avoid many foot, heel and ankle problems with shoes that fit properly. Here's what to look for:

- Adequate toe room — height, width and length. Avoid shoes with pointed toes.
- Low heels will help you avoid back problems.
- Laced shoes are roomier and adjustable.
- Select comfortable athletic shoes, strapped sandals or soft pumps with cushioned insoles.

- Avoid vinyl and plastic shoes. They don't breathe when your feet perspire.
- Buy shoes in the afternoon and evening. Your feet are smaller in the morning and swell throughout the day. Measure both feet.
- As you age, your shoe size (length and width) may change.
- Have your shoe store stretch shoes in tight spots.

See back cover for online resource

■ Swelling

Most people have swollen feet occasionally. Causes include all of those noted in Swollen Legs on page 99.

Self-Care
- Reduce your salt intake.
- Exercise your legs.
- Lie down for 30 minutes at midday with your feet elevated higher than your heart.

Prevention
- Wear support stockings. They apply constant pressure and reduce foot and ankle swelling. Poorly fitting stockings (too tight in the calf) can cause swelling.
- Maintain a regular exercise program.

Medical Help

Seek medical care immediately if one foot becomes swollen rapidly, your foot is inflamed and you have a fever.

■ Morton's Neuroma

Morton's neuroma causes a sharp, burning pain in the ball of your foot. It may feel like you're walking on stones. Your toes may sting, burn or feel numb. Soft tissue grows around a nerve in your foot (neuroma), often between your third and fourth toes. It may not hurt early in the day, but only after you stand or walk in tight shoes.

Self-Care
- Wear well-fitting shoes with enough room in the toe box, or wear sandals.
- Shoe supports (orthotics) or a foot pad may help.
- Reduce high-impact activities for a few weeks.

Medical Help
- A cortisone injection may reduce pain.
- The growth may be surgically removed if pain is chronic and severe.

■ Heel Pain

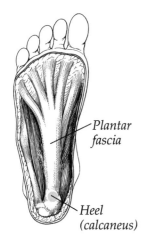

Plantar fascia

Heel (calcaneus)

Heel pain often results from stress on the plantar fascia.

Heel pain is irritating but rarely serious. Although it can result from a pinched nerve or a chronic condition, such as arthritis or bursitis, the most common cause is plantar fasciitis. This is an inflammation of the plantar fascia, the fibrous tissue along the bottom of your foot that connects to your heel bone (calcaneus) and toes.

The pain usually develops gradually, but it can come on suddenly and severely. It tends to be worse when you are getting out of bed in the morning, when the fascia is stiff. Although both feet can be affected, it usually occurs in only one foot.

The pain generally goes away once your foot limbers up. It can recur if you stand for a long time or get up from a sitting or lying position. Climbing stairs or standing on tiptoes also can produce pain. A bone spur (usually painless) may form from tension on your heel bone.

Plantar fasciitis can affect people of all ages. Factors increasing your risk include excess weight, improperly fitting shoes, foot abnormalities and activities that place added pressure on your feet. Treatment involves steps to relieve the pain and inflammation. Don't expect a quick cure. Relief may take six months or longer.

Self-Care

- Cut back on jogging or walking. Substitute exercises that put less weight on your heel, such as swimming or bicycling.
- Apply ice to the painful area for up to 20 minutes after activity.
- Stretching increases flexibility in your plantar fascia, Achilles tendon and calf muscles. Stretching in the morning before you get out of bed helps reverse the tightening of the plantar fascia that occurs overnight.
- Strengthening muscles in your foot can help support your arch.
- Buy shoes with a low to moderate heel (1 to 2 inches), good heel and arch support, and shock absorbency.
- Over-the-counter medications may ease the pain (see page 258).
- If you're overweight, shed excess pounds.
- Try heel pads or cups. They help cushion and support your heel.

These exercises stretch or strengthen your plantar fascia, Achilles tendon and calf muscles. Hold each for 20 or 30 seconds, and do one or two repetitions two or three times a day.

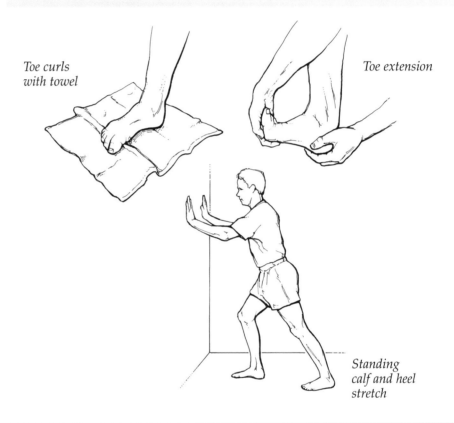

Toe curls with towel

Toe extension

Standing calf and heel stretch

Medical Help

If the self-care measures aren't effective, or if you believe your condition is due to a foot abnormality, see your doctor. Treatment options include the following:

- Custom orthotics.
- Night splints to keep tension on the tissue so it heals in a stretched position.
- Deep heat, which increases blood flow and promotes healing.
- A cortisone injection in your heel often can help relieve the inflammation when other steps aren't successful. But multiple injections aren't recommended because they can weaken and rupture your plantar fascia, as well as shrink the fat pad covering your heel bone.
- Doctors can detach your plantar fascia from your heel bone, but this is recommended only when all other treatments have failed.

Lungs, Chest and Breathing

Breathing is one of our most basic reflexes. We do it thousands of times a day. When we breathe in (inhale), we draw fresh oxygen into our lungs and bloodstream. When we breathe out (exhale), we remove the air from our lungs that contains carbon dioxide, a waste product of our bodies' activities. Breathing is something that most of us take for granted — until we have trouble with it.

■ Coughing: A Natural Reflex

A cough is a reflex — just like breathing. It's actually a way of protecting your lungs against irritants. When your breathing passages (bronchi) have secretions in them, you cough to clear the passages so that you can breathe more easily. A small amount of coughing is ordinary and even healthy as a way to maintain clear breathing passages.

Strong or persistent coughing can be an irritant to your breathing passages. Repeated coughing causes your bronchi to constrict. This change can irritate the interior walls of your breathing passages (membranes).

What Causes Coughing?

Coughing is frequently a symptom of a viral upper respiratory tract infection, which is an infection of your nose, sinuses and airways. A **cold** and **influenza** are common examples. Your voice box may become inflamed (**laryngitis**), causing hoarseness, which can affect your ability to speak. Coughing may also result from throat irritation caused by the drainage of mucus down the back of your throat, a condition called postnasal drainage.

The Cough

A cough begins when an irritant reaches one of the cough receptors in your nose, throat or chest (see dots). The receptor sends a message to the cough center in your brain, signaling your body to cough. After you inhale, your epiglottis and vocal cords close tightly, trapping air within your lungs. Your abdominal and chest muscles contract forcefully, pushing against your diaphragm. Finally, your vocal cords and epiglottis open suddenly, allowing trapped air to explode outward.

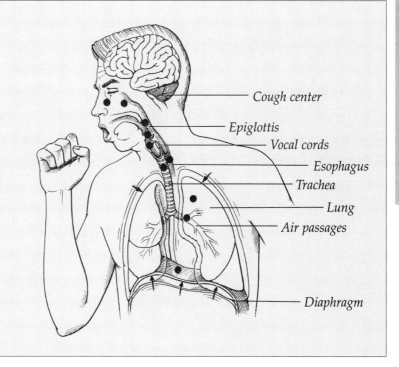

Cough center
Epiglottis
Vocal cords
Esophagus
Trachea
Lung
Air passages
Diaphragm

Common Problems

Coughing also occurs with chronic disorders. People with allergies and asthma have bouts of involuntary coughing, as do people who smoke. Irritants in the environment, such as smog, dust, secondhand smoke and cold or dry air, can cause coughing.

Sometimes coughing is caused by stomach acid that backs up into your esophagus or, in rare cases, your lungs. This condition is called gastroesophageal reflux (see page 64). Some people also develop a "habit" cough.

Self-Care

- **Drink plenty of fluids.** They help keep your throat clear. Drink water or fruit juices — not soda or coffee.
- **Use a humidifier.** The air in your home can get very dry, especially during the winter. Dry air irritates your throat when you have a cold. Using a humidifier to moisturize the air will make breathing easier (see below).
- **Honey, hard candy or medicated throat lozenges** may help to soothe a simple throat irritation and may help prevent coughing if your throat is dry or sore. Try drinking a cup of tea sweetened with honey.
- **Try sleeping with the head of your bed elevated 4 to 6 inches**, if your cough is caused by a backup of stomach acids. Also avoid food and drink within two to three hours of bedtime.

Medical Help

Contact a doctor if your cough lasts more than two or three weeks, or if it's accompanied by fever, increased shortness of breath or bloody phlegm. Managing a chronic cough requires careful evaluation.

Home Humidifiers — Help or Hazard?

When breathing dry indoor air makes you cough, increase the humidity. But don't let the remedy to one problem create another. Dirty humidifiers can be a source of bacteria and fungi. To minimize growth, the U.S. Consumer Product Safety Commission suggests the following:

- **Change the water every day.** Don't allow film and scale to develop inside. Empty the tank, dry the inside surfaces and refill with clean water. Follow the manufacturer's instructions.
- **Use distilled or demineralized water.** Tap water contains minerals that can create bacteria-friendly deposits. When released into the air, these minerals often appear as white dust on your furniture.

- **Clean your humidifier often during use.** Unplug the device before cleaning it. If chlorine bleach or another disinfectant is used, rinse the tank well afterward to avoid breathing harmful chemicals. Clean or replace sponge filters or belts when needed.
- **Keep the humidity between 30 percent and 50 percent.** Levels higher than 60 percent may create a buildup of moisture. When moisture condenses on surfaces, bacteria and fungi can grow. Periodically check the humidity with a hygrometer, available at your local hardware store.
- **Clean your humidifier before you store it.** Clean it again after summer storage and remove dust on the outside of it.

Bronchitis

Bronchitis is a common condition, much like the common cold. It usually is caused by a viral infection that spreads to the bronchi, producing a deep cough that, in turn, brings up yellowish-gray matter from your lungs. The bronchi are the main air passages of your lungs. When the walls that line the bronchi become inflamed, this condition is called bronchitis.

Self-Care

- Get plenty of rest. Drink lots of fluids. Use a humidifier in your room.
- Consider taking a nonprescription cold remedy (see page 259). Adults can take aspirin, another nonsteroidal anti-inflammatory drug (NSAID) or acetaminophen for a fever. Children should take only acetaminophen or ibuprofen.
- Avoid irritants to your airways, such as tobacco smoke.

Medical Help

Acute bronchitis usually disappears in a matter of days. Contact a doctor if you experience shortness of breath or a high temperature for more than three days. If your cough lasts for more than 10 days and the matter you spit up from your lungs (sputum) becomes yellow, gray or green, your doctor may prescribe an antibiotic.

Croup

Croup is caused by a virus that infects the voice box (larynx), windpipe (trachea) and bronchial tubes. Croup occurs most often in children between the ages of 3 months and 3 years. Because of a narrowing of the airway, a child with croup has a tight, brassy cough that may resemble the barking of a seal. The child's voice becomes hoarse, and it's difficult for the child to breathe. The child may become agitated and begin crying, actions that make breathing even more difficult. Croup typically lasts five or six days. During this period, it may go from mild to severe several times. The symptoms are usually worse at night.

Self-Care

- Give clear, warm fluids to help loosen thickened secretions.
- Keep the child away from smoke (it aggravates the symptoms).
- Expose the child to warm, humid air. Try one of the following methods:
  - Lay a wet washcloth loosely over your child's nose and mouth so that air moves easily in and out. (Don't do this if your child is in respiratory distress.)
  - Fill a humidifier with warm water and have your child put his or her face in or near the mist and breathe deeply through the mouth.
  - Have your child sit in a steamy bathroom for at least 10 minutes. Return as often as needed.
- Sometimes breathing fresh cool air helps. Wrap your child in a blanket and stand outside for a few minutes in the cool night air.
- Sleep in the same room as your child to be alert to worsening of the condition.

Medical Help

Occasionally, croup may cause nearly complete blockage of the airway. Get emergency help if you notice any of the following symptoms: drooling or difficulty swallowing, difficulty bending the neck forward, blue or dusky lips, worsening cough and more difficulty with breathing, and high-pitched noises when inhaling.

Common Problems

Wheezing

Wheezing occurs when you hear a high-pitched whistling sound coming from your chest as you breathe out. It's caused by a narrowing of the airways in the lungs and indicates breathing difficulty. In addition, your chest may feel tight.

Wheezing is a common symptom of **asthma**, **bronchitis**, smoking, allergies, **pneumonia**, **emphysema**, **lung cancer** and **congestive heart failure**. It can also stem from environmental factors, such as chemicals or air pollution. Wheezing requires medical attention. See a doctor if you have difficulty breathing and are wheezing.

Shortness of Breath

In general, unexpected shortness of breath is a symptom that needs medical attention. Shortness of breath can be caused by illnesses ranging from heart attacks to blood clots in the lung to **pneumonia**. It can also be caused by pregnancy.

In its chronic form, shortness of breath is a symptom of illnesses such as **asthma**, **emphysema**, other lung diseases and heart disease. All of these chronic conditions also require medical attention. Some exercises can help relieve shortness of breath if you have chronic lung disease (see below).

Simple Exercises Can Improve Your Breathing

Some simple breathing exercises may help you if you have emphysema or another chronic lung disorder. They help you control the emptying of your lungs by using your abdominal muscles. You can also increase the efficiency of your lungs. Ask your physician about them. Do them two to four times daily.

Diaphragmatic breathing
Lie on your back with your head and knees supported by pillows. Begin by breathing in and out slowly and smoothly in a rhythmic pattern. Relax.

Place your fingertips on your abdomen, just below the base of your rib cage. As you inhale slowly, you should feel your diaphragm lifting your hand.

Practice pushing your abdomen against your hand as your chest becomes filled with air. Make sure your chest remains motionless. Try this while inhaling through your mouth and counting slowly to three. Then purse your lips and exhale through your mouth while counting slowly to six.

Practice diaphragmatic breathing on your back until you can take 10 to 15 consecutive breaths in one session without tiring. Then practice it on one side and then on the other. Progress to doing the exercise while sitting erect in a chair, standing up, walking and, finally, climbing stairs.

Pursed-lip breathing
Try the diaphragmatic breathing exercises with your lips pursed as you exhale. With your lips puckered, the flow of air should make a soft "sssss" sound. Inhale deeply through your mouth and exhale. Repeat 10 times at each session.

Deep-breathing exercise
While sitting or standing, pull your elbows firmly backward as you inhale deeply. Hold the breath in, with your chest arched, for a count to 5 and then force the air out by contracting your abdominal muscles. Repeat the exercise 10 times.

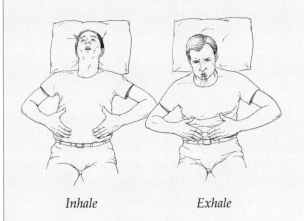

Inhale   *Exhale*

■ Chest Pain

Pain in your chest can be severe. It can also be difficult to interpret. <u>Chest pain</u> could be caused by something as simple as indigestion or by a serious medical situation.

Emergency Care

If pain in your chest persists, contact a health care provider immediately!

Heart attack. In addition to pain or pressure in your chest, you could experience pain in your face, arms, neck or back. Other symptoms of a <u>heart attack</u> may include shortness of breath, sweating, dizziness, nausea and vomiting. If you think you are having a heart attack, seek emergency medical assistance. If you go to a hospital, *do not drive yourself!*

Other Causes of Chest Pain

Here are common forms of chest pain that don't require immediate medical attention:

Chest wall pain. This is one of the most common forms of harmless chest pain. If probing the tender area with your finger causes the pain to return, then serious conditions, such as heart attack, are less likely. Chest wall pain usually lasts only a few days, and it can be treated with aspirin in adults. For children, treat with ibuprofen or acetaminophen. Apply low and intermittent heat to the area to help reduce the pain.

Heartburn. Symptoms are a warm or burning discomfort in the upper part of your abdomen and under your breastbone. You may also have an acid or sour taste in your mouth. <u>Heartburn</u> sometimes can be so painful that the symptoms are confused with the onset of a heart attack. Chest pain from heartburn usually can be relieved by belching or by taking an antacid.

Precordial catch. This is a condition that occurs most often in young adults. The symptom is a brief, sharp pain under the left breast that makes breathing difficult. There are no self-care measures. The condition goes away momentarily. The cause of this common condition is unknown, although it's apparently harmless.

Angina. Angina is the term used for chest pain, or pressure, associated with coronary artery disease. It's caused by a lack of oxygen reaching the heart muscle. It usually develops with physical exertion or when you're under emotional stress. When you've been diagnosed as having coronary artery disease, develop a treatment plan with your doctor.

- Don't try to "work through" an episode of angina. Stop and treat it.
- Angina usually is treated with rest and a medication such as nitroglycerin.
- If you have a change in your pattern of angina, such as increased frequency or nighttime attacks, see your doctor immediately.
- If you've tried measures to stop an angina attack but it lasts longer than 15 minutes or you're also having lightheadedness or palpitations, seek emergency medical help.

■ Palpitations

A palpitation is the feeling you have in your chest when it feels as if your heart skips a beat. Many people experience heart palpitations from time to time. Usually they're not dangerous, but check with your doctor to be sure. Palpitations can be caused by stress or by external factors such as consumption of caffeine and alcohol. Frequently, changes in lifestyle relieve the symptoms.

Common Problems

Nose and Sinuses

Your nose is the main gateway to your respiratory system. Normally, your nose filters, humidifies and warms the air you breathe as it moves from your nasal passage into your throat and lungs, 12 to 15 times a minute.

Occasionally, your nose is the site of conditions such as a nosebleed, cold, hay fever or a sinus infection. Luckily, most disorders of the nose and sinuses are temporary and easy to cure.

The following pages address the common disorders of the nose and its adjacent cavities, the sinuses. For information on respiratory allergies, see page 158.

■ Foreign Objects in the Nose

If a foreign object becomes lodged in the nose, follow these steps:
- Don't probe at the foreign object with a cotton swab or other tool. Don't try to inhale the object by forcefully breathing in; breathe through the mouth until the object is removed.
- Blow your nose gently to try to free the object, but don't blow hard or repeatedly.
- If the object protrudes from the nose and can be easily grasped with tweezers, gently remove it.

If these methods fail, seek emergency medical assistance.

■ Loss of Sense of Smell

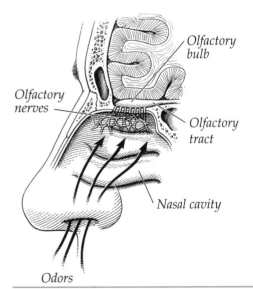

Olfactory bulb

Olfactory nerves

Olfactory tract

Nasal cavity

Odors

Your sense of smell and, to a large degree, your sense of taste begin with the olfactory nerve endings, which are found in the upper portion of your nose. The olfactory nerves contain very fine and sensitive fibers that transmit signals from the olfactory bulb to your brain.

Most people temporarily lose their sense of smell when they have a head cold. Usually, the sense of smell returns once the infection is gone.

However, when the sense of smell is lost without an apparent cause, the condition is called anosmia. Anosmia occurs from either an obstruction in your nose or nerve damage. An obstruction prevents odors from reaching the delicate nerve fibers in your nose. These nerves carry messages or signals to your brain. Nasal polyps, tumors, neurological conditions or swelling of the mucous membrane can cause obstruction. Viral infections, chronic nasal infections or allergies also can damage the nerves that allow you to smell.

Medical Help

If you lose your sense of smell and you don't have a cold, consult your doctor. He or she will check for polyps or tumors of the nasal passages. When the problem is caused by a virus, the sense of smell usually returns when the tissues of the olfactory area heal.

■ Nosebleeds

Nosebleeds are common. Most often they're a nuisance and not a true medical problem. But they can be both. Why do they start, and how can they be stopped?

Among children and young adults, nosebleeds usually begin on the septum, just inside the nose. The septum separates your nasal chambers.

In middle age and older, nosebleeds can begin on the septum, but they may also begin deeper in the nose's interior. This form of nosebleed is much less common. It may be caused by hardened arteries or high blood pressure. These nosebleeds begin spontaneously and are often difficult to stop. They require a specialist's help.

Self-Care

Use your thumb and index finger to squeeze together the soft portion of your nose, located between the end of your nose and the hard, bony ridge.

- **Sit or stand up.** By remaining upright, you reduce blood pressure in the veins of your nose. This action will discourage further bleeding.
- **Pinch your nose** with your thumb and index finger and breathe through your mouth. Continue the pinch for five to 10 minutes. This maneuver sends pressure to the bleeding point on the nasal septum and often stops the flow of blood.
- **Don't apply ice to the nose.** This is of little or no benefit. The cold only tightens blood vessels on the surface of the nose and does not penetrate deeply enough to help.
- **To prevent bleeding,** increase the humidity of the air you breathe in your home. A humidifier or vaporizer can help keep your nasal membranes moist. Lubricating your nose with petroleum jelly or other lubricants is often helpful.
- **To prevent re-bleeding after bleeding has stopped,** don't pick or blow your nose until several hours after the bleeding episode, and don't bend down. Keep your head higher than the level of your heart.
- **If re-bleeding occurs,** sniff in forcefully to clear your nose of blood clots, and spray both sides of your nose with a decongestant nasal spray, such as Afrin, Dristan or Neo-Synephrine. Pinch your nose again in the technique described above and call your doctor.

Medical Help

Seek medical care immediately if:
- The bleeding lasts for more than 15 to 30 minutes
- You feel weak or faint, which can result from the blood loss
- The bleeding is rapid or the amount of blood loss is great
- Bleeding begins by trickling down the back of your throat

If you experience frequent nosebleeds, make an appointment with your physician. You may need to have the blood vessel that is causing your problem cauterized. Cautery is a technique in which the blood vessel is burned with electric current, silver nitrate or a laser.

Kids' Care

Frequent nosebleeds in children can be a sign of a benign tumor. This condition occurs at puberty in boys and rarely in girls. It may shrink on its own after puberty, but it can grow rapidly, produce obstruction of nasal passages and sinuses and cause frequent and often severe nosebleeds. If the tumor doesn't shrink, a physician may suggest a procedure to remove it surgically.

Common Problems

■ Stuffy Nose

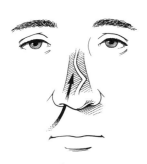

Your nasal septum separates your nasal chambers. A deviated septum may cause nasal obstruction.

Stuffy nose is a common medical complaint. A stuffy nose usually means nasal congestion or an obstruction that causes difficulty breathing. In most cases, a stuffy nose is a mere nuisance. Other causes of nasal obstruction are nasal polyps, tumors, enlarged adenoids and foreign objects in the nose.

Four causes of nasal obstruction and congestion are outlined below.

Common cold. See Aaachoo! Is It a Cold or the Flu? on page 115.

Deformities of the nose and the cartilage and bony partition separating your two nasal chambers (nasal septum) are usually due to an injury. The injury may have occurred years earlier, even in childhood. Deformities of the nose such as a deviated septum are fairly common problems. The deviation can also cause nosebleeds or sinusitis. For many people, a deviated septum poses few problems. However, if the condition makes breathing difficult, a surgical procedure may be the answer. The surgery, called septoplasty, realigns your septum.

Allergies. Allergic rhinitis, which means nasal inflammation from allergies, is the medical term for <u>hay fever</u>, rose fever, grass fever and other allergies. The allergic reaction is an inflammatory response to specific foreign substances that enter the nose, such as pollen, mold or house dust.

Vasomotor rhinitis. This form of inflammation is often episodic and associated with triggers such as smoke, air conditioning or vigorous exercise.

Self-Care

- For colds, see Aaachoo! Is It a Cold or the Flu? on page 115.
- Regularly and gently blow your nose if mucus or debris is present.
- Breathing steam can loosen the mucus and clear your head.
- Take a warm shower or sit in the bathroom with the shower running.
- Drink plenty of liquids.
- Use nonprescription nasal sprays or nose drops for no more than three or four days. Nonprescription oral decongestants (liquid and pills) may be helpful.
- Try saline drops.

Medical Help

If nose congestion persists for more than one to two weeks, consult your doctor, who will examine your nose for the cause of the obstruction, such as polyps or tumors. If your physician determines you have an allergy, he or she may prescribe a course of therapy that may include antihistamines and inhaled anti-inflammatory medications.

Beware of Nose Drop Addiction

Frequent use of decongestant drops and sprays can result in a condition called nose drop addiction. This is a vicious cycle requiring more frequent use of nose spray to keep your nasal passages clear.

Prolonged use of nasal sprays and drops can cause irritation of your mucous membrane, a stinging or burning in your nose and a chronic inflammation.

The only way to treat the problem is to stop using nose drops. You may want to take an oral decongestant instead. Your condition may become worse for a while, but over a period of weeks your breathing should become nearly normal as the ill effects of the nose drops wear off.

Remember, use decongestant drops or sprays for no more than three or four days.

■ Runny Nose

Runny nose commonly occurs early in a cold and in allergic irritation. Gently blowing your nose may be all the self-care you need. If the discharge is persistent and watery, an over-the-counter antihistamine may be helpful. If the discharge is thick, follow the recommendations for stuffy nose on page 114.

Aaachoo! Is It a Cold or the Flu?
Both are viral, upper respiratory tract infections

	Cold	Flu (Influenza)
Usual symptoms	• Runny nose, sneezing, nasal congestion • Sore throat (usually scratchy) • Cough • No fever or low fever • Mild fatigue	• Runny nose • Sore throat and headache • Cough • Fever (usually more than 101 F) and chills • Moderate to severe fatigue and weakness • Achy muscles and joints
Cause	One of more than 200 viruses typically causes two to four colds a year in adults and 6 to 10 a year in kids, especially preschoolers.	One of a few viruses from the influenza A or influenza B family. On average, adults have less than one infection a year.
Seriousness	Usually not serious except in people with lung disease or other serious illness.	Can be serious. A special concern in older adults and those with chronic health conditions.
Can I work?	Usually. Use care to avoid spreading a cold to others. Wash hands frequently. Cover sneezes.	No, not until fever, fatigue and all but the mild symptoms have resolved.
Preventable?	Possibly, through careful hand washing, not sharing food, towels or handkerchiefs and getting good nutrition and enough rest.	Usually, through vaccination. You need to be immunized every fall (see page 224).
Do antibiotics help?	No, not unless you also have a bacterial infection.	Sometimes. Antivirals are available, but work only if taken at the onset of the illness.
Self-care	• Drink plenty of warm liquids. Homemade chicken soup can help clear mucus. • Increase sleep and rest. • Use cold remedies cautiously (see page 259). • Try zinc gluconate lozenges (13.3 mg, one every two hours while awake). For adult uses only. Don't use if you're pregnant or immuno-compromised (cancer, AIDS, chronic disease).	• Drink plenty of fluids to avoid dehydration. • Increase sleep and rest. • Use over-the-counter pain relievers, cautiously, as needed (see page 258).
Seek medical help	• If you have difficulty breathing, faintness, change in alertness, severe sore throat, cough producing a lot of sputum or mucus (especially if green or yellow), pain in the face or a chronic health condition. • If symptoms haven't resolved in 10 days.	

A word about pneumonia

Pneumonia can occur after a cold or flu or on its own. Pneumonia can be caused by viruses, bacteria or other organisms. Typically, you will have a prominent cough that brings up a lot of phlegm. A fever is common. You may experience a sharp pain when you breathe deeply, called pleurisy. If you're concerned about pneumonia, see your health care provider. You may need a chest X-ray and antibiotics.

Common Problems

Sinusitis

Signs of <u>sinusitis</u> include pain about your eyes or cheeks, fever and difficulty breathing through your nose. Occasionally, tooth pain occurs with the condition, or it may mimic a migraine.

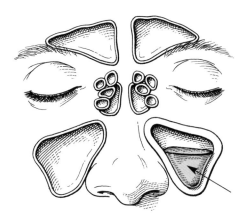

An infected maxillary sinus (arrow) is the most common site of sinusitis.

Your sinuses are cavities in the bones around your nose. They are connected to your nasal cavities by small openings. Normally, air passes in and out of your sinuses and mucus drains through these openings into your nose.

Sinusitis is an inflammation of the lining of one or more of these cavities. Usually, when your sinus is inflamed, the membranes of your nose also swell and cause a nasal obstruction. Swelling of the membranes of your nose may close off the opening of your sinus and thus prevent draining of pus or mucus. Pain in your sinus may result from the inflammation itself or from the pressure as secretions build up in your sinus.

The most frequent cause is a bacterial or viral respiratory tract infection, such as a common cold. Allergies and a fungal infection also can cause sinusitis.

Self-Care

- Stay indoors in an even temperature.
- Refrain from bending over with your head down — this movement usually increases the pain.
- Try applying warm facial packs, or cautiously inhale steam from a basin of boiling water.
- Drink plenty of liquids to help dilute the secretions.
- Gently and regularly blow your nose.
- Take pain relievers for discomfort.
- Use over-the-counter (OTC) decongestants and short-term decongestant sprays.
- Try OTC saltwater nose drops.
- If you're using OTC antihistamines, take care. They can do more harm than good by drying out your nose too much and thickening secretions. Use them only on the recommendation of your doctor, and follow instructions carefully.

Medical Help

Call your health care provider if you have a fever of more than 104 F (40 C) , a fever of 102 F (38.5 C) for three or more days, if the pain doesn't go away in 24 hours, or if the pain occurs repeatedly. X-rays and other examinations may be performed to discover the seriousness of the infection. If sinusitis is the result of a bacterial infection, you may be prescribed an oral antibiotic to be taken for seven to 14 days.

See back cover for online resource

Skin, Hair and Nails

Because your skin, hair and nails are an integral part of your appearance, changes and problems involving them are often distressing. External irritants, infections, aging and even emotional stress can affect your skin, hair and nails in many ways. Rarely, underlying medical conditions and allergies to foods or medications trigger abnormalities.

Fortunately, many of these problems are not serious and respond well to self-care measures. The following pages explain some of the more common disorders and offer some self-care tips to help you find relief. But first, here are some general guidelines for proper skin care.

■ Proper Skin Care

Regardless of your skin color or type or your age, monitoring your exposure to the sun — and its ultraviolet rays — can help prevent unnecessary damage and, eventually, skin cancer.

Dark skin can tolerate more sun than can fair skin. However, any skin can become blotchy, leathery and wrinkled from overexposure to the sun. Protective clothing, sunscreen preparations and daily lubrication or moisturizing can help.

Proper cleansing is another important strategy in protecting your skin. The best procedures and cleansing ingredients vary according to the type of skin you have — oily, dry, balanced or a combination of these.

Self-Care

- When washing your face, use comfortably cool (never hot) water and a washcloth or sponge to remove dead skin cells. Use a mild soap. A superfatted soap, such as Cetaphil, Dove or Vanicream, may be better for dry skin. You may need to clean oily skin two or three times each day.
- In general, avoid washing your body with very hot water or strong soaps. Bathing dries your skin. If you have dry skin, use soap only on your face, underarms, genital areas, hands and feet. After bathing, pat (rather than wipe) your skin dry, then immediately lubricate it with an oil or cream. Use a heavy, water-in-oil moisturizer rather than a light "disappearing" cream that contains mostly water. Avoid creams or lotions that contain alcohol. Keep the air in your home somewhat cool and humid.
- Shaving can be hard on the skin. If you shave with a blade razor, always use a sharp blade. Soften your skin by applying a warm cloth for a few seconds; then use plenty of shaving cream. Pass the blade over your beard only once, in the direction of hair growth. Reversing the stroke to obtain a close shave can cause a skin irritation. Electric razors are less irritating to your skin. Skin preparations are available to treat skin irritation.
- Match cosmetics to your skin type: An oil base is suitable for dry skin, and a water base is suitable for oily skin.
- For women, remove eye makeup before facial cleansing. Use cotton balls to avoid damaging the delicate tissue around your eyes.

Acne

It's a fear and frustration for teens, but <u>acne</u> can affect adults too. Acne is caused by plugged pores, hormonal changes and bacteria in the skin. Oil from glands combines with dead skin to plug the pores, also called follicles. Follicles bulge, producing pimples and other types of blemishes:

- **Whiteheads.** Clogged pores that have no opening
- **Blackheads.** Pores that are open and have a dark surface
- **Pimples.** Reddish spots that signal an infection by bacteria in plugged pores
- **Cysts.** Thick lumps beneath the surface of your skin, formed by the buildup of secretions

Nearly 85 percent of people ages 12 to 24 develop acne to some extent. It's most prevalent in adolescence because hormonal changes stimulate the sebaceous glands during these years. The sebaceous glands secrete a fatty oil called sebum, which lubricates your hair and skin. Menstrual periods or cortisone medications and stress may aggravate acne in later life.

Although a chronic problem for many people from puberty through adulthood, acne eventually clears in most cases.

Self-Care

- Identify factors that aggravate your acne. Avoid oily or greasy cosmetics, hair styling products or acne coverups. Use products labeled water-based or non-comedogenic.
- Wash problem areas daily with a cleanser that gently dries your skin.
- Try over-the-counter acne lotion (containing benzoyl peroxide or salicylic acid as the active ingredient) to dry excess oil and promote peeling.
- Keep your hair clean and off the face.
- Watch for signs of spreading infection beyond the edges of a pimple.
- Unless a food is clearly aggravating your acne, you don't need to eliminate it. Foods like chocolate, once thought to be a cause of acne, generally aren't the culprit.
- Don't pick or squeeze blemishes. Doing so can cause infection or scarring.

Medical Help

Persistent pimples, inflamed cysts or scarring may need medical attention and treatment with prescription drugs. Proper evaluation and treatment can prevent physical and psychological scarring of acne. In rare cases, a sudden onset of severe acne in an older adult may signal an underlying disease requiring medical attention.

Doctors may use cosmetic surgery to diminish scars left by acne. The main procedures are laser resurfacing or peeling of the skin by freezing or chemicals.

Peeling procedures eliminate superficial scars. Dermabrasion, usually reserved for more severe scarring, consists of abrading the skin with a rapidly rotating wire brush. Your doctor will use a local anesthetic or topical freezing of your skin during the procedure. Laser resurfacing involves use of an intense, pulsating beam of light to vaporize the outer layer of skin. General anesthesia and hospitalization ordinarily aren't required.

See back cover for online resource ⓘ

■ Boils

Boils are pink or red, very tender bumps under your skin that occur when bacteria infect one or more of your hair follicles. The bumps are usually larger than ½ inch in diameter. They typically grow rapidly, fill with pus and then burst, drain and heal. Although some boils resolve a few days after they appear, most burst and heal within about two weeks.

Boils can occur anywhere on your skin, but most often on the face, neck, armpits, buttocks or thighs. Poor health, clothing that binds or chafes and disorders such as acne, dermatitis, diabetes and anemia can increase your risk of infection.

Self-Care

To avoid spreading this infection and to minimize discomfort, follow these measures:
- Soak the area with a warm washcloth or compress for about 30 minutes every few hours. Doing so may help the boil burst and drain much sooner. Use warm salt water. (Add 1 teaspoon of salt to 1 quart of boiling water and let it cool.)
- Gently wash the sore twice a day with antibacterial soap. Cover the sore with a bandage to prevent spreading.
- Apply an over-the-counter antibiotic ointment, such as bacitracin.
- Never squeeze or lance a boil because you might spread the infection.
- Launder towels, compresses and clothing that have touched the infected area.

Medical Help

Contact your health care provider if the infection is located on your spine, groin or face, worsens rapidly or causes severe pain, hasn't disappeared within two weeks or is accompanied by fever or reddish lines radiating from the boil. In some cases, antibiotics or surgical drainage may be necessary to clear your infection.

■ Cellulitis

Cellulitis may appear gradually over a couple of days or rapidly over a few hours. It begins as a localized area of red, painful, warm skin. It may be accompanied by fever and swelling. This fairly common infection occurs when bacteria or fungus enters your body through a break in the skin and infects the deeper layers of your skin.

Good hygiene and proper wound care can help prevent this type of infection. However, bacteria can enter your skin through even tiny cuts or abrasions, such as a crack around your nostrils or a simple puncture wound.

Self-Care

To prevent cellulitis and other wound infections, follow these measures:
- Keep skin wounds clean.
- Cover the area with a bandage to help keep it clean and keep harmful bacteria out. Keep draining blisters covered until a scab forms.
- Change the bandage daily or whenever it becomes wet or dirty.

Medical Help

Contact your doctor if you have a fever and suspect you have cellulitis. Antibiotics can prevent the infection from spreading and causing severe damage.

Common Problems

Corns and Calluses

These thickened, hardened layers of skin commonly appear on your hands and feet. Corns often appear as raised bumps of hardened skin less than $\frac{1}{4}$-inch long. Calluses vary in size and shape. **Corns and calluses** are your skin's attempt to protect itself. Although they can be unsightly, treatment may be necessary only if they cause discomfort. For most people, eliminating the source of friction or pressure will help corns and calluses disappear.

Self-Care

- Wear properly fitted shoes, with adequate toe room. Have your shoe shop stretch your shoes at any point that rubs or pinches. Place pads under your heels if your shoes rub. Try to cushion or soften the corn while wearing shoes.
- Wear padded gloves when using hand tools, or try padding your tool handles with cloth tape or covers.
- Rub your corn or callus with a pumice stone or washcloth during or after bathing to gradually thin some of the thickened skin. This advice isn't recommended if you have diabetes or poor circulation.
- Try over-the-counter corn dissolvers containing salicylic acid. These are available in plaster-pad disks or solutions containing a thickener called collodion.
- Don't cut or shave corns or calluses with a sharp edge.
- Apply a moisturizer to your hands and feet to keep them soft.

Medical Help

If a corn or callus becomes very painful or inflamed, contact your health care provider.

Dandruff

Studies suggest a yeast-like organism may cause seborheic dermatitis, or **dandruff**. The malassezia species fungus causes irritation and increased sloughing of the top layer of skin cells on your scalp.

Self-Care

- Shampoo regularly. Start with a mild, nonmedicated shampoo. Gently massage your scalp to loosen flakes. Rinse thoroughly.
- Use medicated shampoo for stubborn cases. Look for shampoos containing zinc pyrithione, salicylic acid, coal tar or selenium sulfide in brands such as Head & Shoulders, Neutrogena T/Sal or T/Gel, Denorex or Selsun Blue. Use a dandruff shampoo each time you shampoo, if necessary, to control flaking.
- Kill dandruff-causing fungi that live on your scalp by using the antifungal shampoo Nizoral 1%. This shampoo is available over-the-counter or by prescription.
- If you use tar-based shampoos, use them carefully. They can leave a brownish stain on light-colored or gray hair and make scalp more sensitive to sunlight.
- Use a conditioner regularly. For mild dandruff, alternate dandruff shampoo with your regular shampoo.

Medical Help

If dandruff persists or your scalp becomes irritated or severely itchy, you may need a prescription shampoo. If your dandruff persists, you may have some other skin condition. See your doctor.

See back cover for online resource

■ Dryness

This is by far the most common cause of itching, flaking skin. Although dryness can be a problem any time of the year, cold air and low humidity can be especially tough on your skin. Dry skin due to the weather depends on where you live (for example, the Minnesota "winter itch" and the Arizona "summer itch").

Self-Care

- Take fewer baths or showers. Keep them short and use lukewarm water and minimal amounts of soap. Mild superfatted soaps such as Cetaphil, Dove or Vanicream will dry skin less. Add bath oils to your bath.
- Pat (rather than wipe) your skin dry after bathing.
- Apply an oil or cream to your skin immediately after drying. Use a heavy, water-in-oil moisturizer, not a light "disappearing" cream that contains mostly water.
- Avoid creams or lotions containing alcohol.
- Use a humidifier and keep room temperatures cool.

■ Eczema (Dermatitis)

Frequent locations of irritation from contact dermatitis, the most common form of dermatitis

The terms *eczema* and <u>dermatitis</u> are both used to describe irritated and swollen or reddened (inflamed) skin. Patches of dry, reddened and itchy skin are the major symptoms. Patches can thicken and develop blisters or weeping sores in severe cases.

Contact dermatitis results from direct contact with one of many irritants that can trigger this reaction. Common culprits include poison ivy (see Poisonous Plants, page 29), rubber, metals, jewelry, perfume and cosmetics.

Neurodermatitis can occur when something such as a tight garment rubs or scratches (or causes you to rub or scratch) your skin.

Seborrheic dermatitis (cradle cap in infants) can appear as a stubborn, itchy dandruff. You may notice greasy, scaling areas at the sides of your nose, between your eyebrows, behind your ears or over your breastbone.

Stasis dermatitis may cause the skin at your ankles to become discolored (red or brown), thickened and itchy. It can occur when fluid accumulates in the tissues just beneath your skin. This condition can lead to infection.

Atopic dermatitis causes itchy, thickened, fissured skin, most often in the folds of the elbows or backs of the knees. It frequently runs in families and is often associated with allergies.

Self-Care

- Try to identify and avoid direct contact with irritants.
- Follow the self-care tips to prevent dry skin (see above).
- Soak in cool to warm water for 20 to 30 minutes a day.
- Apply a moisturizing cream and an over-the-counter hydrocortisone cream.
- Avoid scratching whenever possible. Cover the itchy area with a dressing if you can't keep from scratching it. Trim nails and wear gloves when you sleep.
- Shampoo with an anti-dandruff product if your scalp is affected.
- Support hose may help relieve swelling (edema) with stasis dermatitis.
- Dress appropriate to conditions to help avoid excessive sweating.
- Wear smooth-textured cotton clothing.
- Avoid wool bedding and clothes and harsh soaps and detergents.
- Occasional use of over-the-counter antihistamines can reduce itching.

Common Problems

Fungal Infections

Fungal infections are caused by microscopic organisms that become parasites on your body. Mold-like fungi called dermatophytes cause __athlete's foot__, jock itch and ringworm of the skin or scalp. These fungi live on dead tissues of your hair, nails and the outer layer of your skin. Poor hygiene, moist skin and minor skin or nail injuries increase your susceptibility to fungal infections.

Athlete's foot usually begins between your toes, causing your skin to itch, burn and crack. Sometimes the sole and sides of the foot are affected, becoming thickened and leathery in texture. Although locker rooms and public showers are often blamed for spreading athlete's foot, the environment inside your shoes is probably more important. Athlete's foot becomes more common with age.

Jock itch causes an itching or burning sensation around your groin. In addition to the itching, you'll usually notice a red rash that may spread to the inner thighs, anal area and buttocks. This infection is mildly contagious. It can be spread by contact or sharing towels.

Ringworm affects children and adults. Symptoms are itchy, red, scaly, slightly raised, expanding rings on the trunk, face or groin and thigh fold. The rings grow outward as the infection spreads, and the central area begins to look like normal skin. This infection is passed from shared clothing, combs and barber tools. Pets also can transmit the fungus to humans.

Typical pattern of athlete's foot

Self-Care

General
- Practice good personal hygiene to prevent all forms of fungal infections.
- Use antifungal creams or drying powder two or three times a day until the rash disappears. Use medications that contain miconazole (Cruex, Desenex, Micatin) and clotrimazole (Lotrimin AF, Mycelex).

For Athlete's Foot
- Keep your feet dry, particularly the area between your toes.
- Wear well-ventilated shoes. Avoid shoes made of synthetic materials.
- Don't wear the same shoes every day, and don't store them in plastic.
- Change socks (cotton or polypropylene) twice a day if your feet sweat a lot.
- Wear waterproof sandals or shoes around public pools, showers and locker rooms.

For Jock Itch
- Keep your groin clean and dry.
- Shower and change clothes after exercise.
- Avoid clothes that chafe, and launder athletic supporters frequently.

For Ringworm
- Thoroughly clean brushes, combs or headgear that may have been infected.
- Wash hands before and after examining your child.
- Keep your child's linens separate from the rest of the family's.

Medical Help

See your health care provider if symptoms last longer than four weeks or if you notice increased redness, drainage or fever. You may require treatment with prescription medications.

See back cover for online resource ⓘ

Hives

Hives are raised, red, often itchy welts of various sizes that appear and disappear on the skin. They're more common on areas of the body where clothes rub your skin. Hives tend to occur in batches and last anywhere from a few minutes to several days.

Angioedema, a similar swelling, causes large welts below your skin, especially near your eyes and lips, but also on your hands and feet and inside your throat. Hives and angioedema result when your body releases a natural chemical called histamine in your skin. Allergies to foods, drugs, pollen, insect bites, infections, illness, cold and heat and emotional distress can trigger a reaction. In most cases, hives and angioedema are harmless and leave no lasting marks. However, serious angioedema can cause your throat or tongue to block your airway and cause loss of consciousness.

Self-Care

- Avoid substances that have triggered past attacks.
- Take cool showers. Apply cool compresses. Wear light clothing. Minimize vigorous activity.
- Use a lubricating cream or over-the-counter antihistamines such as diphenhydramine hydrochloride (Benadryl) or chlorpheniramine maleate (Chlor-Trimeton) to help relieve the itching.
- If you suspect that food may be causing the problem, keep a food diary.
- If hives persist and there is difficulty breathing, seek emergency care.

Medical Help

Seek emergency care if you feel lightheaded or have difficulty breathing or if hives continue to appear for more than a couple of days.

Impetigo

Impetigo is a common skin infection that usually appears on the face. The infection begins when staphylococcus or streptococcus bacteria penetrate your skin through a cut, scratch or insect bite. Impetigo is highly contagious and easily spread by contact.

The infection starts as a red sore that blisters briefly, oozes for a few days and forms a sticky, yellow crust. Scratching or touching the sores can spread this contagious infection to other people and other parts of your body.

Impetigo is more common among young children. In adults, it appears mostly as a complication of other skin problems such as dermatitis.

Self-Care

Good hygiene is essential for preventing impetigo and limiting its spread. For limited or minor infections that haven't spread to other areas, try the following:
- Keep the sores and skin surrounding them clean.
- Apply an antibiotic ointment three or four times daily. Wash the skin before each application, and pat the skin dry.
- Avoid scratching or touching the sores unnecessarily until they heal. Wash your hands after any contact with them. Children's fingernails should be trimmed.
- Don't share towels, clothing or razors with others. Replace linens often.

Medical Help

If the infection spreads, your health care provider may prescribe oral antibiotics such as penicillin or erythromycin or an ointment of mupirocin (Bactroban).

Common Problems

Itching and Rashes

Because so many things can cause itching and rashes, pinpointing the source of the problem can be difficult. For information about specific problems that cause itching and rashes, see the following segments in this book: Allergic Reactions, page 12; Lice, page 126; Insect Bites and Stings, page 15; Baby Rashes, see below; Common Childhood Rashes, page 125; Hives, page 123; Dryness, page 121; and Eczema (Dermatitis), page 121.

Baby Rashes

Cradle cap. Crusty, scaly skin on your baby's scalp. Wash your baby's hair only once a week with a mild shampoo and lukewarm water. Apply baby oil to the crusty areas and gently scrape off the scales with a soft brush after bathing. If the rash is red and irritated, apply a 0.5 percent hydrocortisone cream once a week.

Heat rash. Fine red spots or bumps, usually on the neck or the upper back, chest or arms. This harmless rash often develops during hot, humid weather, especially if your baby is dressed too warmly. It can also occur if your baby has a fever.

Milia. Tiny (pinpoint) white spots on the nose and cheeks. It's usually present at birth. The spots eventually disappear without treatment.

Infant acne. Red bumps that can appear during the first few months after birth. Gently wash your baby's face daily with plain water and once or twice weekly with a mild soap. Don't use acne creams or lotions on an infant or young child.

Drool rash. A red rash on the cheeks and chin that comes and goes. This rash is caused by contact with food, saliva and sputum. Cleaning and drying your baby's skin after feeding or spitting up usually helps clear this rash.

Diaper rash. Reddish, puffy skin in the diaper area, especially in the folds of the skin. This irritation usually is caused by moisture, the acid in urine or stool and chafing of diapers. Some babies also get a rash from detergent used to wash cloth diapers, plastic pants, elastic or certain types of disposable diapers and diaper wipes. Sometimes a yeast infection is the cause of diaper rash.

Self-Care for Recurrent Diaper Rash	• Change your baby's diapers frequently, placing the diaper loosely around the child, and expose the skin to air whenever possible. Avoid using plastic pants. • Use cloth diapers or disposable diapers without gathers. Wash cloth diapers in mild soap (Dreft or Ivory), and add 1 cup of white vinegar to the rinse cycle to help rid the diapers of bacteria. Avoid fabric softeners. • Wash and pat dry the area at each diaper change, using plain water or a mild soap and water. • Apply a thin layer of protective cream or ointment such as zinc oxide. • Try switching to a different brand of diapers if you use disposable diapers. • Avoid diaper wipes because many contain perfume and alcohol. • If the rash is particularly difficult to cleanse, place the baby in a sink of warm water with 2 ounces of white vinegar mixed in. • Don't apply cornstarch or talcum powder. It could worsen the condition.
Medical Help	See your health care provider if the above tips don't help; if the rash is purple or bruised-looking, crusty, blistered or weepy; or if the baby has a fever.

Common Childhood Rashes

Symptoms	Self-Care	Seek Medical Help

Chickenpox

Itchy, red spots on the face or chest that spread to the arms and legs. Spots fill with a clear fluid to form blisters, rupture and turn crusty. New spots generally continue appearing over four to five days. Fever, a runny nose or cough often accompanies chickenpox. Chickenpox seldom lasts for more than two weeks after the first spot appears. Symptoms usually appear 14 to 21 days after exposure. The child is contagious until the rash heals.

- Give child cool baths every three or four hours to reduce the itching. Sprinkle baking soda in the bath water for added relief.
- Apply a lubricating cream to the rash.
- Switch to a bland diet of soft foods, and avoid citrus fruits if blisters are present in the mouth.
- Trim fingernails. Put gloves on the child at night to prevent scratching.

- If the rash involves the eyes, or if you develop a cough or shortness of breath.
- If you're an older adult, have an impaired immune system or are pregnant and have not been previously exposed.
- An antiviral medication can shorten duration of the infection. In severe cases, a doctor may prescribe an antibiotic. A vaccine is available for children 12 months or older.

Roseola

Often begins with a high fever lasting about three days. When it subsides, a rash appears on the trunk and neck, lasting a few hours to a few days. Virus typically affects children, most often between 6 months and 3 years.

The rash causes little discomfort and disappears on its own without treatment. Acetaminophen and tepid sponge baths may help relieve the discomfort caused by the fever.

- If the rash lasts longer than three days.
- A child experiences a convulsion triggered by a high fever.

Measles

Typically begins with fever, often as high as 104 to 105 F, and a cough, sneezing, sore throat and inflamed, watery eyes. Two to four days later, a rash appears. It often begins as fine red spots on the face and spreads to the trunk, arms and legs. Spots may become larger and usually last about a week. Small white spots may appear on inside lining of the cheek.

- Bed rest, acetaminophen and an over-the-counter cough medication may help relieve the discomfort.
- Lukewarm baths, lubricant creams or Benadryl solution may relieve itching.

- If you suspect that you or a family member has measles. Measles has uncommon but potentially serious complications, such as pneumonia, encephalitis or a bacterial infection.
- A vaccine to prevent measles is given to children between 12 and 15 months and between 4 and 12 years of age.

Fifth disease

Bright red, raised patches appear on both cheeks. During the next few days, a pink, lacy, slightly raised rash develops on the arms, trunk, thighs and buttocks. Rash may come and go for up to three weeks. Often, there are no symptoms, or only mild, cold-like symptoms.

No specific treatment. Use acetaminophen to relieve the fever and any discomfort.

If you aren't sure whether a rash is fifth disease or if you are pregnant and suspect that you've been exposed.

■ Lice

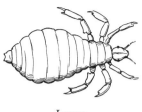

Louse

Lice are tiny parasitic insects. Head lice often are spread among children by contact, clothing or hairbrushes. Body lice are generally spread through clothing or bedding. Pubic lice — commonly called crabs — can be spread by sexual contact, clothing, bedding or even toilet seats.

The first sign of lice is intense itching. With body lice, some people have hives and others have abrasions from scratching. Head lice are found on the scalp and are easiest to see at the nape of the neck and over the ears. Small eggs (nits) that resemble tiny pussy willow buds can be found on the hair shafts. Body lice are difficult to find because they burrow into the skin, but they usually can be detected in the seams of underwear. Pubic lice are found on the skin and hair of the pubic areas. Lice live only three days off the body. Eggs hatch in about one week.

Self-Care

- Several lotions and shampoos, both prescription and over-the-counter, are available. Apply the product to all infected and hair parts of the body. Any remaining nits can be removed with tweezers or a fine comb. Repeat treatment with the lotion or shampoo in seven to 10 days.
- Your sexual partner should be examined and treated if infected.
- Keep infected children home until you complete this first treatment.
- Wash sheets, clothing and hats with hot, soapy water and dry them at high heat. Soak combs and brushes in very hot, soapy water for at least five minutes.
- Vacuum carpets, mattresses, pillows, upholstered furniture and car seats.

Medical Help

Consult your doctor before using products on a child younger than 2 months or if you're pregnant. The Food and Drug Administration (FDA) cautions that products containing lindane can cause serious side effects, even when used as directed.

■ Scabies

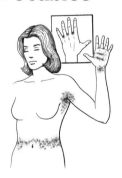

Almost impossible to see without a magnifying glass, scabies mites cause itching by burrowing under the skin. Itching is usually worse at night. The burrowing leaves tiny bumps and thin, irregular, pencil-like marks or tracks on your skin. They appear most often in the following areas: between your fingers, in your armpits, around your waist, along the insides of your wrists, on the back of your elbows, on your ankles and soles of your feet, around your breasts and genitals and on your buttocks. Almost any part of the skin may be involved.

Close physical contact and, less often, sharing clothing or bedding with an infected person can spread these tiny mites. Often an entire family, members of a child care group or school class will experience scabies.

Self-Care

Bathing and over-the-counter preparations will not eliminate scabies. Talk to your health care provider if you have symptoms or if you believe you had contact with someone who has scabies.

Medical Help

Your doctor may prescribe a medicated cream or lotion that you must apply all over your body and leave on overnight. All family members and sexual partners may require treatment. In addition, all clothing and bedding that you used before treatment must be washed with hot, soapy water and dried with high heat.

Psoriasis

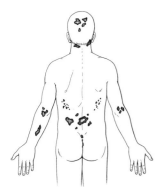

Some of the most common locations of psoriasis

For some people, **psoriasis** brings little more than recurrent bouts of mild itching, but for others, it's a lifetime of discomfort and unsightly skin changes.

Most often, psoriasis causes dry, red patches covered with thick, silvery scales. You may see a few spots of scaling or large areas of damaged skin. Knees, elbows, trunk and scalp are the most common locations. Patches on your scalp can shed large quantities of silvery-white scales resembling severe dandruff.

In more severe cases, pustules, cracked skin, itching, minor bleeding or aching joints also may develop. In addition, your fingernails and toenails may lose their normal luster and develop pits or ridges.

Many people inherit a tendency toward psoriasis. Dry skin, skin injuries, infections, certain drugs, obesity, stress and lack of sunlight can all aggravate your symptoms. This condition isn't contagious. You cannot spread it to other parts of your own body, or to other people, simply by touching it. Psoriasis typically goes through cycles. The symptoms can persist for weeks or months, followed by a break.

Self-Care

- Maintain good general health: a balanced diet, adequate rest and exercise.
- Maintain a normal weight. Psoriasis occurs often in skin creases or folds.
- Avoid scratching, rubbing or picking at the patches of psoriasis. Trauma worsens psoriasis.
- Bathe daily to soak off the scales. Avoid hot water or harsh soap.
- Keep your skin moist (see Dryness, page 121).
- Use soaps, shampoos, cleansers or ointments containing coal tar or salicylic acid.
- Expose your skin to moderate sunlight, but avoid sunburn.
- Apply over-the-counter cortisone creams, 0.5 percent or 1 percent, for a few weeks when symptoms are especially bad.

Medical Help

If self-care remedies don't help, stronger cortisone-type creams or various forms of phototherapy may be prescribed. Phototherapy involves a combination of medications and ultraviolet light. Skin ointments containing a form of vitamin D (Dovonex) also may offer some relief. In severe cases, the anti-inflammatory medication methotrexate, a medication that prevents rejection in organ transplant recipients, or other treatments may be prescribed.

Moles

Sometimes called beauty marks, **moles** are usually harmless collections of pigment cells. They may contain hairs, stay smooth, become raised or wrinkled and even fall off in old age.

In rare cases, a mole can become cancerous melanoma. Talk to your health care provider if pain, bleeding or inflammation occurs or if you notice a change in a mole (see Signs of Skin Cancer, page 129). Keep an eye on moles located around your nails, hands, feet or genitals, and those present since birth. Giant moles, present at birth, are a special problem, and may need to be removed to avoid the risk of cancer.

Self-Care

Healthy moles usually don't require special care unless they become cut or irritated. Normal skin care is sufficient.

■ Shingles

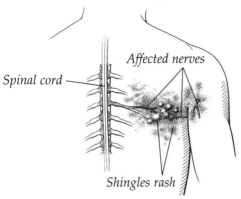

Spinal cord —

Affected nerves

Shingles rash

The shingles rash is associated with an inflammation of nerves beneath the skin.

Shingles (also known as herpes zoster) emerges when the virus that causes chickenpox (varicella zoster) reactivates after lying dormant within your nerve cells.

As this virus reactivates, you may notice pain or tingling in a limited area, usually on one side of your body or face. This pain occurs as the virus spreads along one of the nerves that extends outward on your face or from your spine. This pain or tingling can continue for several days or longer.

Subsequently, a rash with small blisters may appear. The rash may continue to spread over the next 3 to 5 days, often forming a band-like pattern on one side of your body. The blisters usually dry up in a few days, forming crusts that fall off over the next two to three weeks. The blisters contain a virus that is contagious, so avoid physical contact with others, especially pregnant women. Chickenpox in a newborn can be deadly.

Self-Care

You can relieve some of the discomfort by doing the following:
- Soak your blisters with cool, wet compresses (aluminum acetate solution).
- Wash blisters gently, and don't bandage them.
- Apply a lubricating cream or ointment.
- Take over-the-counter pain relievers to alleviate pain.
- Over-the-counter analgesic creams also may alleviate your pain.

Medical Help

Contact your doctor if you suspect shingles, especially in the following situations:
- The pain and rash occur near your eyes. If left untreated, this infection can lead to permanent eye damage.
- You or someone in your family has a weakened immune system (due to cancer, medications or a chronic medical condition).
- The rash is widespread and painful.
  Acyclovir (Zovirax), famciclovir (Famvir) and valacyclovir (Valtrex) may hasten healing and reduce the severity of some complications caused by shingles.

When the Pain Persists After Shingles

Pain persisting for months or even years after a bout with shingles is called postherpetic neuralgia (PHN). It occurs in 50 percent of people older than 60 who have had shingles.

PHN is as individual as you are, and effective treatment for you may be useless for someone else. But new treatments show promise, and new findings support the benefit of early treatment of the acute viral infection that precedes PHN.

Because the pain of PHN tends to lessen as time passes, it's difficult to tell whether a medication is effective or the pain is subsiding on its own.

Several treatments may provide relief. They include analgesic medications, electrical stimulation, antidepressants, certain anticonvulsant medications and neurosurgery in severe cases.

Most people are free of pain after five years.

■ Signs of Skin Cancer

Each year, <u>skin cancer</u> is diagnosed in more than 1 million people, and about 10,000 people die each year of the disease. More than 90 percent of skin cancers occur on areas regularly exposed to ultraviolet radiation (from sunlight or tanning lights), and this exposure is considered to be the chief cause. Other factors include a genetic tendency, chemical pollution and X-ray radiation.

Here are the signs of the three most common types of skin cancer:

Basal cell cancer, by far the most common skin cancer, usually appears as a smooth, waxy or pearly bump that grows slowly and rarely spreads or causes death.

Squamous cell cancer causes a firm, nodular or flat growth with a crusted, ulcerated or scaly surface on the face, ears, neck, hands or arms.

Melanoma is the most serious but least common skin cancer.

The ABCD rule (see below) can help you tell a normal mole from one that could be melanoma. Rapid growth, bleeding, nonhealing sores or any other change in a lesion could also be signs of cancer.

A

Asymmetry. Half of the lesion is unlike the other half.

B

Border irregular (ragged, notched or blurred).

C

Color varies from one area to another. Different shades of tan and brown, black, red, white or blue.

D

Dimension. The diameter is larger than the head of a pencil eraser.

Self-Care	• Avoid exposure to the sun to the point of a sunburn or a suntan. Both result in skin damage. Skin damage accumulates over time. Minimize your time in the sun and wear tightly woven clothing and a broad-brimmed hat. Remember, snow, water, ice and concrete all reflect the sun's harmful rays. • Use sunscreen regularly. Apply a broad-spectrum sunscreen with a sun protection factor (SPF) of at least 15. Broad-spectrum means it protects against ultraviolet A and B radiation. Fair-skinned individuals should use a sunscreen with an SPF of 35 or greater. Use sunscreen on all exposed skin, including your lips. Apply it 30 minutes before sun exposure and reapply every two hours. • Use 1 ounce of sunscreen per application — about 2 tablespoons. • Avoid tanning salons. • Check your skin at least every three months for the development of new skin growths or changes in existing moles, freckles, bumps and birthmarks.
Medical Help	If you notice a new growth, change in skin or sore that doesn't heal in two weeks, see your doctor. Don't wait for pain because skin cancers are usually not painful. The cure rate for skin cancer is high if you receive treatment early. If you have a family history of melanoma and many moles on your body — especially on the trunk — regular examination by a dermatologist may be appropriate.
Kids' Care	Getting severe, blistering sunburns as a child increases the risk of developing melanoma as an adult. Set time limits for your child when at the pool or beach. Remember, ultraviolet rays are strongest between 10 a.m. and 3 p.m. Clouds block only a small portion of ultraviolet rays. You can get sunburn on a cloudy day.

Common Problems

◾ Warts

<u>Warts</u> are skin growths caused by a common virus, but they can be painful and disfiguring and can spread to other individuals.

There are more than 200 types of warts. They can appear on any part of your body, but they are most common on the hands or feet. Warts found on the feet, called plantar warts, can be painful because they press inward as you stand on them.

You can acquire warts through direct contact with an infected person or surface, such as a shower floor. The virus that causes them stimulates the rapid growth of cells on the outer layer of your skin.

Each person's immune system responds to warts differently. Most warts aren't a serious health hazard and disappear without treatment. Warts are more common among children than adults, likely because many adults develop immunity to them. In adults, warts generally disappear within two years.

Certain warts trigger or signal more serious medical problems. Genital warts (see page 184) require treatment to avoid spreading them through sexual contact. Some strains of the papilloma virus increase a woman's risk of cervical cancer. Women also can pass this virus to their babies during birth, causing some complications.

Self-Care

- Over-the-counter topical medications may remove warts of the hands and feet. Look for products containing salicylic acid, which peels off the infected skin. They require daily use, often for a few weeks. **Caution:** The acid can irritate or damage normal skin.
- To avoid spreading warts to other parts of your body, avoid brushing, combing or shaving areas with warts.

Medical Help

You may want to see your health care provider if your warts are tender or a cosmetic nuisance or interfere with your activities. Common treatments for warts include freezing with liquid nitrogen or dry ice, electrical burning, laser surgery or minor surgery.

◾ Wrinkled Skin

Skin wrinkles

Wrinkles — sometimes called "character lines" — are an inevitable part of the aging process. As you grow older, your skin gets thinner, drier and less elastic. Sagging and wrinkling begin because connective tissue in your skin deteriorates. Some people don't seem to age as quickly as others. This difference is typically due to heredity and avoiding extensive sun exposure. Cosmetic products that promise youthful skin are often expensive and fail to deliver improvements.

Self-Care

There's no cure for wrinkled skin. These measures may help slow the process:
- Maintain good general health.
- Don't smoke cigarettes.
- Avoid prolonged exposure to the sun. Use sunscreen daily.
- Avoid harsh soaps and hot water when bathing.

Medical Help

Prescription medical treatments such as retinoic acid creams may be helpful for treating fine lines. Injection of botulinum toxin type A (Botox) is also used to reduce the appearance of wrinkles. Cosmetic procedures such as chemical peels, dermabrasion or lasers can alter your skin's appearance if it concerns you.

See back cover for online resource ⓘ

Hair Loss

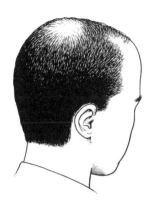

Male-pattern baldness typically appears first at the hairline or crown.

Healthy, lustrous hair has long been a symbol of youth and beauty. As a result, many people cringe at the first signs of hair thinning or baldness.

If your hair seems to be thinning, take comfort in the fact that it's normal to lose between 50 and 100 strands a day. Like your nails and skin, your hair goes through a cycle of growth and rest. Gradual thinning occurs as a normal part of the aging process.

Common **baldness**, which is largely hereditary, affects both men and women. Male-pattern baldness usually begins with thinning at the hairline, followed by moderate to extensive hair loss on the crown of the head. Bald patches rarely develop in women with common baldness. Instead, the hair thins all over the head, especially on top. Hormones and age also play roles in common baldness.

Gradual hair loss can also occur any time your hair's delicate growth cycle is upset. Diet, medications, hormones, pregnancy, improper hair care, poor nutrition, underlying diseases and other factors can cause too many follicles to rest at once, producing diffuse thinning.

Sudden patches of hair loss are usually due to a condition called alopecia areata. This fairly rare condition causes smooth, circular bald patches that may overlap. Stress and heredity may play a role in this disorder. Alopecia areata generally resolves without treatment over a period of weeks to years.

Self-Care

There's no magic bullet to prevent hair loss or encourage new growth, but the following tips can help keep your hair healthy:
- Eat a nutritionally balanced diet.
- Handle your hair gently. Whenever possible, allow your hair to air-dry naturally.
- Avoid tight hairstyles such as braids, buns or ponytails.
- Avoid compulsively twisting, rubbing or pulling your hair.
- Check with hair care experts about hairpieces or styling techniques that help minimize the effects of common baldness.
- An over-the-counter medication called minoxidil can promote new hair growth in a small percentage of people. Other over-the-counter hair growth products are of no proven benefit.

Medical Help

Although there's no cure for common baldness, you may want to ask your health care provider about medical treatments or hair replacement surgery. Because sudden hair loss can signal an underlying medical condition that may require treatment, contact your physician for evaluation.

Kids' Care

If your child has patches of broken hairs on the scalp or eyebrows, he or she may be rubbing or pulling out the hair. This signals a behavioral disorder called trichotillomania. Bald patches in children can also be a sign of a fungal infection or ringworm. Contact your health care provider for evaluation.

Common Problems

■ Nail Fungal Infections

Typical fungal infection

This stubborn, but harmless, problem often begins as a tiny white or yellow spot on your nail. Fungal infections can develop on your nails or under their outer edges if you continually expose them to a warm, moist environment. Depending on the type of fungus, your nails may discolor, thicken and develop crumbling edges or cracks.

Fungal infections usually affect your toenails more frequently than your fingernails and are more common among older adults. Your risk of a toenail fungal infection is greater if your feet perspire heavily, and if you wear socks and shoes that hinder ventilation and don't absorb perspiration. You can also contract this infection by walking barefoot in public places and as a complication of other infections.

Fingernail fungal infections often result from overexposure to water and detergents. Moisture caught under artificial nails also can encourage fungus growth.

Self-Care

To help prevent **nail fungal infections**, try the following:
- Keep your nails dry and clean. Dry your feet thoroughly after bathing.
- Change your socks often and wear leather-soled shoes.
- Use an antifungal spray or powder on your feet and inside your shoes.
- Don't pick at or trim the skin around your nails.
- Avoid walking barefoot around public pools, showers and locker rooms.

Medical Help

Self-care measures usually fail to prevent the infection. Oral antifungal medications such as griseofulvin, itraconazole, terbinafine and fluconazole are more effective than topical drugs, but they can cause side effects. Their use requires careful monitoring. In severe cases, surgical removal of the nail may be necessary.

■ Ingrown Toenails

Pain and tenderness in your toe often signal an **ingrown toenail**. This common condition occurs when the sharp end or side of your toenail grows into the flesh of your toe. It affects your big toe most often, especially if you have curved toenails, if your shoes fit poorly or if you cut your nails improperly.

Self-Care

- Trim your toenails straight across and not too short.
- Wear socks and shoes that fit properly, and don't place excessive pressure on your toes. Wear open-toe shoes, if necessary, or try sandals.
- Soak your feet in warm salt water (1 teaspoon salt per pint of water) for 15 to 20 minutes twice a day to reduce swelling and relieve tenderness.
- After soaking, put tiny bits of sterile cotton under the ingrown edge. This will help the nail eventually grow above the skin edge. Change the cotton daily until the pain and redness subside.
- Apply an antibiotic ointment to the tender area.
- If there's severe pain, take a nonprescription pain reliever and make an appointment to see your doctor.

Medical Help

If you experience severe discomfort or pus or redness that seems to be spreading, seek medical attention. Your doctor may need to remove the ingrown portion of the nail and prescribe antibiotics.

Throat and Mouth

■ Sore Throat

The tight, scratchy feeling in your throat may be a familiar sign that a <u>cold</u> or flu (<u>influenza</u>) is on the way. Most sore throats run their course in a few days, sometimes needing over-the-counter lozenges or gargles.

Most sore throats are caused by two types of infections — viral and bacterial — but they can also be caused by allergies and dry air. When a sore throat involves enlarged, tender tonsils, it's sometimes called tonsillitis.

Viral infections usually are the source of common colds and the flu and the sore throat that accompanies them. Colds usually go away on their own in about a week, once your system has built up antibodies that destroy the virus. Antibiotic medications are *not* effective in treating viral infections. The common symptoms are as follows:

- Sore or scratchy, dry feeling
- Coughing and sneezing
- Mild fever or no fever
- Hoarseness
- Runny nose and postnasal dripping

Bacterial infections aren't as common as viral infections, but they can be more serious. <u>Strep throat</u> is the most common bacterial infection. Often a person with strep was exposed to someone else with strep throat in the past two to seven days. Children ages 5 to 15 in a classroom or other group setting are most likely to get strep throat. It generally is spread by nose or throat secretions. Less commonly, infection may be transmitted through food, milk or water contaminated with streptococci bacteria. Strep throat requires medical treatment. Common symptoms are:

- Swollen tonsils and neck glands
- Back of throat is bright red with white patches
- Fever, often more than 101 F, and often accompanied by chills
- Pain when swallowing

Most sore throat germs are passed by direct contact. Mucus and saliva from one person's hands are transferred to objects, doorknobs and other surfaces, then to your hands and eventually to your mouth or nose.

Mononucleosis: A Tiresome Illness

Infectious <u>mononucleosis</u> is sometimes called the kissing disease. It's also known as mono, and it can be spread by kissing or, more commonly, through exposure resulting from coughing, sneezing or sharing a glass or cup.

Mono is caused by the Epstein-Barr virus. By some estimates, as many as 95 percent of adults between ages 35 and 40 have been exposed to the Epstein-Barr virus and have built up antibodies. They're immune and won't get it again. Full-blown mono is most common during adolescence and young adulthood. Children infected with the virus before age 15 may have only a mild flu-like illness.

Most people with mono experience fatigue and weakness. Other symptoms include a sore throat, fever, swollen lymph nodes in the neck and armpits, swollen tonsils, headache, rash and loss of appetite. Most symptoms abate within 10 days, but you shouldn't expect to return to your normal activities or contact sports for three weeks (your liver or spleen may be enlarged and at risk of injury). It may be two to three months before you feel completely normal. Rest and a healthy diet are the only treatments for mono.

If symptoms linger more than a week or two or if they recur, see your doctor.

Common Problems

Self-Care

- **Double your fluid intake.** Fluids help keep your mucus thin and easy to clear.
- **Gargle with warm salt water.** Mix about ½ teaspoon of salt with a glass of warm water to gargle and spit. This will soothe and help clear your throat of mucus.
- **Suck on a lozenge or hard candy, or chew sugarless gum.** Chewing and sucking stimulate saliva production, which bathes and cleanses your throat.
- **Take pain relievers.** Over-the-counter medications, such as acetaminophen, ibuprofen and aspirin, relieve sore throat pain for four to six hours. Don't give aspirin to children or teenagers (see page 258).
- **Rest your voice.** If your sore throat has affected your voice box (larynx), talking may lead to more irritation and temporary loss of your voice, called laryngitis.
- **Humidify the air.** Adding moisture to the air prevents your mucous membranes from drying out. This can reduce irritation and make it easier to sleep. Saline nasal sprays also are helpful.
- **Avoid smoke and other air pollutants.** Smoke irritates a sore throat. Stop smoking, and avoid all smoke and fumes from household cleaners or paint. Keep children away from secondhand smoke exposure.

Prevention

- Wash your hands frequently, especially during the cold and flu season.
- Keep your hands away from your face to avoid getting bacteria and viruses into your mouth or nose.

Medical Help

Serious throat infections, such as epiglottitis, can cause swelling that closes your airway. Seek emergency care if your sore throat is accompanied by any of the following symptoms:

- Drooling or difficulty swallowing or breathing
- A stiff, rigid neck and severe headache
- A temperature higher than 101 F in babies under age 6 months and 103 F in older children
- A rash
- Persistent hoarseness or mouth ulcers lasting two weeks or more
- Recent exposure to strep throat

If your doctor suspects strep throat, a throat swab may be ordered. For this test a cotton swab is rubbed against the back of your throat and secretions on the swab are analyzed in a laboratory. A rapid strep test can give an initial result within an hour. However, it misses up to 30 percent of strep cases. Therefore, it's often necessary to do a traditional throat culture, which takes one to two days for a confirmed result. There is a DNA strep test — developed at Mayo Clinic — that provides a final, confirmed result in about eight hours.

Generally only in cases of recurrent infection that cause serious problems will removal of the tonsils (tonsillectomy) be considered.

Caution

If your doctor does prescribe a medication, take it for the full time indicated. Stopping use of the medication early can allow some bacteria to remain in the throat, potentially leading to a recurrence and complications such as rheumatic fever or a blood infection.

If your child has been taking antibiotics for at least 24 hours, has no fever and feels better, it's usually OK for him or her to return to school or child care.

■ Bad Breath

Everyone would like to have breath that's always fresh. Because fresh breath is important to us, makers of mints and mouthwashes sell millions of dollars worth of products every year. These products are only temporarily helpful for controlling **bad breath**. They actually may be less effective than simply rinsing your mouth with water and brushing and flossing your teeth.

There are many causes of bad breath. First, your mouth itself may be the source. Bacterial breakdown of food particles and other debris in and around your teeth can cause a foul odor. A dry mouth, such as occurs during sleep or as the result of some drugs or smoking, enables dead cells to accumulate on your tongue, gums and cheeks. As a result, they decompose and cause odor.

Eating foods containing oils with a strong odor causes bad breath. Onions and garlic are the best examples, but other vegetables and spices also may cause bad breath.

Lung disease can cause bad breath. Chronic infections in the lungs can produce very foul-smelling breath. Usually, much of the mucus you cough up (sputum) is produced by these conditions. Several illnesses can cause a distinctive breath odor. Kidney failure can cause a urine-like odor, and liver failure may cause an odor described as fishy. People with diabetes often have a fruity breath odor. This smell is also common in ill children who have eaten poorly for a few days. Bad breath in these situations can be corrected by treatment of the underlying condition.

Self-Care

For most people, bad breath can be improved by following a few simple steps:
- Brush your teeth after every meal.
- Brush or scrape your tongue to remove dead cells.
- Floss once a day to remove food particles from between your teeth.
- Drink plenty of water (not coffee, pop or alcohol) to keep your mouth moist.
- Avoid strong foods that cause bad breath. Toothbrushing or use of mouthwashes only partially disguises odors of garlic or onion that come from your lungs.
- Change your toothbrush every two to three months.
- Rinse your mouth after using inhaler medications.
- If after trying these approaches your breath is still bad, talk to your dentist.

■ Hoarseness or Loss of Voice

Loss of voice (**laryngitis**) or hoarseness occurs when your vocal cords become swollen or inflamed and no longer vibrate normally. They produce an unnatural sound, or they may not produce any sound at all.

Your speaking voice is formed when the muscle above your stomach (diaphragm) pushes air from your lungs through your vocal cords. Air pressure forces your vocal cords to open and close, and the controlled escape of air vibrates the vocal cords, producing the sound that's your voice.

In addition to hoarseness, you may feel pain when speaking or have a raw and scratchy throat. Sometimes, your voice sounds higher or lower than normal.

Common causes of hoarseness or loss of voice are infections (as a result, you may lose your voice when you have a cold or flu), allergies, talking too loudly for too long or yelling (vocal strain), smoking and chronic esophageal reflux. Reflux, the backwash of acidic stomach contents into the food pipe, can sometimes spill into the voice box.

Common Problems

Self-Care	• Limit your talking and whispering. Whispering strains your vocal cords as much as talking.
	• Drink lots of warm, noncaffeinated fluids to keep your throat moist.
	• Avoid clearing your throat.
	• Stop smoking, and avoid exposure to smoke. Smoke dries your throat and irritates your vocal cords.
	• Stop drinking alcohol, which also dries your throat and irritates your vocal cords.
	• Use a humidifier to moisturize the air you breathe. Follow the manufacturer's instructions to clean the humidifier and prevent bacterial buildup.

Medical Help If hoarseness lasts for more than two weeks, seek medical help. Your doctor may prescribe medications for infection or allergy. Take them just as prescribed. Hoarseness is rarely caused by cancer.

■ Mouth Sores

Irritating, painful and repetitive. That's how many people describe canker sores and cold sores. But the terminology can be confusing. Cold sores have nothing to do with the common cold. What's more, the cause, appearance, symptoms and treatments of canker sores and cold sores are very different. Other mouth sores and conditions are often mistaken for canker sores and cold sores.

■ Canker Sores

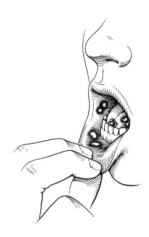

A canker sore is an ulcer on the soft tissue inside your mouth — on the tongue, soft palate, inside part of the lips and inside the cheeks. Typically, you notice a burning sensation and a round whitish spot with a red edge or halo. Pain usually lessens in a few days.

Despite a great deal of research into the problem, the cause of canker sores remains a mystery. Current thinking suggests that stress or tissue injury may cause the eruption of common **canker sores**. Some researchers believe certain nutritional deficiencies or food sensitivities may complicate the problem. In addition, some gastrointestinal and immunodeficiency disorders have been linked to canker sores, as well as some medications, including nonsteroidal anti-inflammatory drugs and beta blockers.

There are two types of canker sores: simple and complex. The simple type of canker sore may appear three or four times a year and last four to seven days. The first occurrence is usually between the ages of 10 and 40, but it can occur in younger children. As a person reaches adulthood, the sores occur less frequently and may stop developing altogether. Women seem to get them more often than men, and they seem to run in families.

Complex canker sores are less common but much more of a problem. As old sores heal, new ones appear.

See back cover for online resource ⓘ

| **Self-Care** | There's no cure for either simple or complex canker sores, and effective treatments are limited. The following practices may provide temporary relief:
- Avoid abrasive, acidic or spicy foods, which may increase the pain.
- Brush your teeth carefully to avoid irritating the sore.
- Use an over-the-counter topical ointment containing phenol.
- Rinse your mouth with over-the-counter preparations.
- Use an over-the-counter pain reliever. |

| **Medical Help** | For severe attacks of canker sores, your dentist or doctor may recommend a prescription mouthwash, a corticosteroid salve, an anti-inflammatory cream called amlexanox (Aphthasol) or an anesthetic solution called viscous lidocaine.
    Contact your doctor in any of the following situations:
- High fever with canker sores
- Spreading sores or signs of spreading infection
- Pain that's not controlled with the measures listed above
- Sores that don't heal completely within a week
    See your dentist if you have sharp tooth surfaces or dental appliances that are causing sores. |

◼ Cold Sores (Fever Blisters)

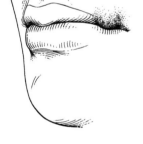

Also known as fever blisters, cold sores are very common. They may appear on your mouth, lips, nose, cheeks or fingers.

The herpes simplex virus causes <u>cold sores</u>. Herpes simplex virus type 1 usually causes cold sores. Herpes simplex virus type 2 is usually responsible for genital herpes. However, either form of the virus can cause sores in the facial area or on the genitals. You get cold sores from another person who has an active condition. Eating utensils, razors, towels or direct skin contact are common means of spreading this infection.

Symptoms may not start for as long as 20 days after you were exposed to the virus. Small, fluid-filled blisters develop on a raised, red, painful area of skin. Pain or tingling (prodromal stage) often precedes blisters by one to two days. Symptoms usually last seven to 10 days.

After the first infection, the virus periodically re-emerges at or near the original site. Fever, menstruation and exposure to the sun may trigger a recurrence.

The herpes simplex virus can be transmitted even when blisters aren't present. But the greatest risk of infection is from the time the blister appears until it has completely crusted over. Cold sores occur most often in adolescents and young adults, but they can occur at any age. Outbreaks decrease after age 35.

| **Self-Care** | Cold sores generally clear up without treatment. The following steps may provide relief:
- Rest, take over-the-counter pain relievers (if you have a fever) or use over-the-counter creams for comfort (they won't speed healing). Children should avoid aspirin use.
- Don't squeeze, pinch or pick at any blister.
- Avoid kissing and skin contact with people while blisters are present.
- Wash your hands carefully before touching another person.
- Use sunblock on your lips and face before prolonged exposure to the sun — during both the winter and the summer — to prevent cold sores. |

Medical Help	If you have frequent bouts of cold sores, an antiviral antibiotic may help. These medications inhibit the growth of the herpes virus. The topical antiviral medication penciclovir, available as a cream, also has shown some benefit in treating cold sores. Talk with your health care provider to learn more about treatment options if you have multiple episodes during a year.

You may feel a tingling sensation before the outbreak of a cold sore. Many doctors recommend using medication as soon as the tingling begins.

Caution

- If you have a cold sore, take special care to avoid contact with infants or anyone who has a skin condition known as eczema (see page 121). They're more susceptible to infection. Also, avoid people who are taking medications for cancer and organ transplantation because they have decreased immunity. The virus can cause a life-threatening condition in them.
- Pregnant women and nursing mothers should avoid using acyclovir for treatment of cold sores unless specifically advised by their doctor to use it.
- Herpes simplex virus infections have potentially serious complications. The virus can spread to your eye. This is the most frequent cause of corneal blindness in the United States. If you have a burning pain in the eye or a rash near the eye or on the tip of your nose, see your doctor immediately.

■ Other Oral Infections and Disorders

Trench mouth (**gingivostomatitis**). This is an oral infection that's common among children. It's caused by a virus and often accompanies a cold or flu. The infection generally lasts about two weeks and ranges from mild to severe. If your child has sores on the gums or on the inside of the cheeks, has bad breath, has a fever and feels generally unwell, consult your dentist or physician. Treatment of any under-lying infection will help clear the mouth infection. A medicated oral rinse may help relieve the pain and promote healing. Practice good oral hygiene and eat a nutritious diet of soft foods and drink plenty of fluids. Use a mouthwash made of half a teaspoon of salt dissolved in 8 ounces of water, or use an over-the-counter mouthwash. Avoid preparations with alcohol.

Oral thrush (Candidiasis). This infection is caused by a fungus. There will be creamy-white soft patches in the mouth or throat. It often occurs when your body has been weakened by illness or when your mouth's natural balance of microbes has been upset by medications. Many people will experience an outbreak of oral thrush at some point in their lives. It's most common among babies, young children and older adults. Although painful, oral thrush isn't a serious disorder. It can, however, interfere with eating and impair your nutrition. There's no self-care for this condition, but a dentist or physician can prescribe an oral medication that is taken for seven to 10 days. Thrush tends to recur.

Leukoplakia. Thickened, white patches on a cheek or the tongue are often signs of leukoplakia. Leukoplakia is the mouth's reaction to chronic irritation. It may be caused by ill-fitting dentures or a rough tooth rubbing against the cheek or gum. When white patches develop in the mouths of smokers, the condition is called smoker's keratosis. Snuff and chewing tobacco also produce chronic irritation. You can have leukoplakia at any time during your life, but it's most common among

See back cover for online resource ⓘ

older adults. Treatment involves removing the source of irritation. Once the source of irritation has been removed, the patch may clear up, usually within weeks or months. A doctor or dentist should evaluate white patches in the mouth. Tobacco use can lead to cancer of the lip, tongue or lungs.

Oral cancer. Cancer of the mouth usually occurs along the side or the bottom of the tongue or on the floor of the mouth. The tumors often are painless at first and frequently are visible or can be felt with a finger. Regular examination of the soft tissues of the mouth is essential for early diagnosis. If you notice any persistent change from the usual appearance or feel of the soft tissues in your mouth, consult a dentist or physician. Early detection is important for successful treatment. Unfortunately, about half of <u>oral cancers</u> are advanced at the time the cancer is diagnosed.

Routine self-examination of your mouth and tongue may enable you to see or feel an oral cancer when it's small and treatment may be most effective.

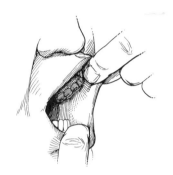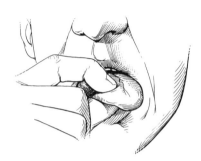

Men's Health

▌ Testicular Pain

Any sharp and sudden pain in your testicles should be treated carefully because it can be a symptom of a serious medical condition. Seek medical help if you have sudden pain in your testicles that doesn't go away in 10 or 15 minutes or if you have pain that recurs. Some causes of sudden testicular pain are discussed below.

Testicular torsion is caused when the spermatic cord, which carries blood to and from the testicle, gets twisted. This twisting cuts off the blood supply to the testicle, causing sharp and sudden pain. Testicular torsion sometimes occurs after strenuous physical activity, but it can happen with no apparent cause, even during sleep. This condition can occur at any age, but it usually occurs in boys. Symptoms include sudden and severe pain, which can cause fever, nausea and vomiting. You may also notice the elevation of one testicle within the scrotum. Testicular torsion is serious and requires immediate medical attention.

Epididymitis occurs when the epididymis, a coiled tube that carries sperm from the testicles to the spermatic cord, becomes inflamed, usually by a bacterial infection. Symptoms include aching to moderately severe pain in the scrotum, which develops over several hours or days. Fever and swelling may also occur. Epididymitis is occasionally caused by chlamydia, a sexually transmitted disease (see page 185). In these cases, your sexual partner may be infected and should also receive a medical exam.

Orchitis is an inflammation of the testicle, usually due to an infection. Orchitis frequently occurs with epididymitis (see above). Orchitis may occur when you have the mumps, or it may develop if you have a prostate infection. Orchitis is rare, but it may cause infertility if left untreated. Symptoms include pain in the scrotum, swelling (usually on one side of the scrotum) and a feeling of weight in the scrotum.

Screening for Cancer of the Testicle

Testicular cancer accounts for 1 percent of cancers in men, occurring most often in young men between the ages of 20 and 39. The major symptom is a lump, swelling or heavy feeling in a testicle.

A simple two-minute self-examination each month can help detect early signs of testicular cancer. Perform the examination after a shower or warm bath, when the skin of your scrotum is loose and relaxed. Examine one testicle at a time. Roll it gently between your thumbs and forefingers, feeling for any lump on the surface of the testicle. Also pay attention if the testicle is enlarged, hardened or otherwise in a different condition from the last examination. If you notice anything unusual, it may not necessarily mean cancer, but you should contact your doctor.

Don't be alarmed if you feel a small, firm area near the rear of the testicle and a tube leading up from the testicle. This is normal. These are the epididymis and the spermatic cord, which store and transport sperm.

■ Enlarged Prostate

The prostate is a walnut-sized gland that's located just below the bladder and is present only in males. The prostate produces most of the fluids in the semen. Testosterone, the male sex hormone, causes the prostate to slowly enlarge with age. As the prostate enlarges, it can restrict the flow of urine through the tube that passes urine from your bladder (urethra), causing slow or difficult urination. The symptoms can be mild and cause little difficulty with urinating, or they can be very painful if complete blockage occurs. Other symptoms may include more frequent nighttime voiding, a slow or dribbling urine stream, dribbling after voiding or voiding twice in a row within 10 to 15 minutes.

<u>Prostate gland enlargement</u> (benign prostatic hyperplasia, or BPH) rarely causes problems before age 40. More than half of men in their 60s and as many as 90 percent in their 70s and 80s experience symptoms of BPH. At some point, about 30 percent of men with BPH require some kind of treatment for the condition.

An enlarged prostate can produce difficulty with urination because the flow of urine is restricted.

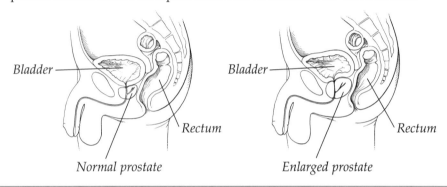

Bladder

Rectum

Normal prostate

Bladder

Rectum

Enlarged prostate

Medical Help

Your health care provider may ask you detailed questions about your symptoms and may do tests on urine and blood samples. Using a gloved, lubricated finger, your health care provider may examine your prostate for enlargement and lumps. Called the digital rectal examination, this procedure causes only mild discomfort.

Initial treatment for an enlarged prostate may be medications that reduce the size of the prostate gland or improve urine flow by relaxing the tissues in the area of the prostate gland. Various types of surgery can reduce the size of the prostate.

Screening for Prostate Cancer

Cancer of the prostate is the second-leading cause of cancer death in American men. <u>Prostate cancer</u> occurs most frequently in men older than age 65.

Screening for prostate cancer — which typically involves digital rectal examination and a blood test for prostate-specific antigen (PSA) — is controversial. Some doctors believe that many men will have unnecessary surgery or radiation because of screening. Others believe that screening is essential. In accordance with the American Cancer Society and the American Urological Association,

Mayo Clinic urologists recommend the PSA test and a digital rectal examination be offered to men yearly, beginning at age 50. If you're at high risk of prostate cancer — you're black or you have a family history of the disease — screening should begin earlier. Ultrasound examination is another way to detect cancer.

If detected early, prostate cancer often can be cured. When present, symptoms are similar to those for prostate enlargement, unless cancer has spread to the bone.

Common Problems

Painful Urination

Painful urination is usually caused by a <u>urinary tract infection</u> (UTI). UTIs are more common in women, but they also occur in men. Other symptoms include frequent or urgent urination, an inability to release more than a small amount of urine (followed by an urgent need to urinate again), blood in the urine and a burning sensation while urinating.

If your kidney also is infected, you may experience pain in your abdomen or back, chills, a fever or vomiting. A kidney infection is a serious condition that requires immediate medical attention.

Common Causes

***E. coli* bacteria.** *E. coli* bacteria are common in the bowel. If *E. coli* bacteria enter the tube through which urine passes (urethra) and then enter your urine or bladder, a UTI can result.

Chlamydia. It is one of several sexually transmitted organisms that can infect the urethra, causing penile drainage and painful urination.

Prostate problems. An enlarged prostate gland can restrict the flow of urine, causing urine retention and UTIs. In addition, if your prostate gland produces fewer proteins as you age, the absence of these proteins may make you more susceptible to UTIs.

Medical procedures. A urinary catheter or medical instruments can introduce bacteria into your urethra and bladder, causing a UTI.

Narrowed urethra. Injury to or frequent inflammation of the urethra can result in a narrowing (stricture) of the urethra. Strictures restrict urine flow and can cause UTIs.

Dehydration. Lack of fluids can lead to stagnant urine, which can cause a UTI.

Medical Help

See your health care provider, who will likely take a urine sample and perform tests to determine whether you have a UTI. Don't drink a lot of fluids just before you give a urine sample because your urine may be diluted and the results may be inaccurate. In most instances, UTIs can be treated with medications. Be sure to take all the medication, even if your symptoms go away after a few days. Failure to take all the medication can lead to a recurrence of the UTI.

Impotence

Occasional episodes of impotence are common in men. Impotence, also known as <u>erectile dysfunction</u>, is defined as an inability to achieve or maintain an erection adequate for sexual intercourse. When impotence is a recurring problem, it may affect self-image and relationships. Fortunately, impotence often can be treated successfully.

The causes of impotence can be psychological or physical. Stress, anxiety or depression can lead to impotence. Impotence can also be a side effect of alcohol use and some medications (such as some drugs used to treat high blood pressure). Impotence can be caused by diseases such as diabetes or multiple sclerosis or other chronic diseases. Impotence may be the result of a direct injury to the genitals or an injury that affects the spinal cord or nervous system. Radiation treatments or major pelvic surgeries, such as those performed for cancer of the prostate, bladder or rectum, also may result in impotence. If impotence is recurrent or persistent, discuss it with your doctor.

| Self-Care | If you can still get an erection at certain times of the day, such as the morning, you may benefit from the following advice:
- Limit alcohol consumption, especially before sexual activity.
- Quit smoking.
- Exercise regularly.
- Reduce stress.
- Work with your partner to create an atmosphere conducive to lovemaking. |

| Medical Help | **Psychological treatment.** If stress, anxiety or depression is the cause of impotence, you may want to seek counseling with a mental health professional or a sex therapist, either alone or with your partner.

Medications. Pills, such as sildenafil (Viagra), tadalafil (Cialis) or vardenafil (Levitra), or testosterone injections or topical cream may be prescribed by your doctor.

Penile injections. If impotence is caused by decreased blood supply to the penis, medications that increase blood flow may be prescribed. They're injected into the penis. The injections can be performed at home after training by your physician.

Intraurethral medication. A small suppository — half the size of a grain of rice — is slid into the opening of the penis to help achieve an erection.

Vacuum constriction device. A tube is placed over the penis, and air is withdrawn; as a result, blood flows to the penis and causes an erection. A rubber constricting band is placed around the base of the penis to prolong the erection. This low-cost device is available at most drugstores with a doctor's prescription.

Surgery. Surgery can be performed to increase blood flow to the penis or to implant devices to assist in achieving an erection. |

■ Male Birth Control

Vasectomy involves cutting and sealing the vas deferens, the tube that carries sperm. The procedure doesn't interfere with a man's ability to maintain an erection or reach orgasm, nor does it stop the production of male hormones or of sperm in the testicles. The only change is that the sperm's link to the outside is severed permanently. After a vasectomy, you continue to ejaculate about the same amount of semen because sperm account for only a small part of the ejaculate.

A vasectomy is done in an outpatient setting. Before the procedure, you'll be given an injection of anesthetic in the scrotum to numb the area so you won't feel pain. After your doctor has located the vas deferens, a pair of small cuts are made in the skin of the scrotum. Each vas deferens is then pulled through the opening until it forms a loop. Approximately a half-inch is cut out of each vas deferens and removed. The two ends of each vas deferens are closed by stitches or cauterization (or both) and are placed back in the scrotum. The incisions are closed with stitches.

The operation takes about 20 minutes. After a vasectomy, avoid strenuous activity, including intercourse, for at least two weeks. The stitches often are the type that dissolve in two to three weeks. You may notice swelling and minor discomfort in the scrotum for several weeks. If the pain is severe or if fever develops, call your doctor.

The failure rate for a vasectomy is less than 1 percent. Until your doctor has determined that your ejaculate doesn't contain sperm, continue to use alternative contraception. This typically takes several months and several ejaculations.

Women's Health

▧ Lump in Your Breast

Most breast lumps aren't cancerous. Even so, all lumps should be carefully assessed because of the risk of cancer. Many breast lumps are fluid-filled cysts that enlarge near the end of your monthly cycle. The lumps may or may not be painful. Perform a breast self-examination each month after your period to check for lumps and any other changes in your breasts (see below).

Self-Care

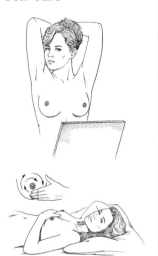

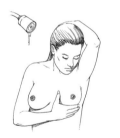

- Do a breast self-examination (BSE) routinely so that you'll know if a lump is new. Whether BSEs are beneficial is under debate, but many doctors still encourage them as one means of early cancer detection.
- If you're still menstruating, the best time to examine your breasts is seven to 10 days after your last period started. Breast cancer lumps usually aren't painful. Use your eyes and hands to search for lumps, thickened areas or swelling. If you take oral contraceptives, examine your breasts each time you open a new package of pills. Notify your health care provider of any changes.
- The illustrations at left provide one technique for BSE. The goal is to become familiar with the texture of your breasts and nodules within them, and to watch carefully for any changes.
  - Look into a mirror with your arms at your sides. Elevate your arms and examine the skin on your breasts for puckering, dimples or changes in their size or shape. Look for changes in the natural symmetry of both breasts. Check to see whether your nipples are pulled in (inverted). Also note any unusual discharge from your nipples. Check for the same signs while you rest your hands on your hips and again with your hands behind your head.
  - Examine your breasts while standing in the shower and while lying on your back. Hold one hand behind your head and use a circular massaging motion with the other hand to check the tissue over the entire opposite breast, including the nipple and the tissue under your armpit. Repeat the procedure on the other side.
  - Check for lumps that don't disappear or change. Abnormal lumps may seem to appear suddenly and remain. They vary in size and firmness and often feel hard with irregular edges. Sometimes they just feel like thickened areas without distinct outlines. Cancerous lumps usually aren't painful.
- If the lump causes discomfort, take a mild pain medication (see page 257) or eliminate caffeine from your diet.

Medical Help

See your doctor if a lump in your breast doesn't go away after your menstrual cycle. A fluid-filled cyst may be drained with a needle after an injection of a local anesthetic. If you have a breast infection, an antibiotic is typically prescribed. Lumps that aren't filled with fluid may require a needle biopsy or surgical removal to determine whether they're cancerous.

Women beyond menopause should see their doctor if a lump lasts more than a week or becomes reddened, painful or enlarged.

Mammograms: Who Should Have Them?

A mammogram is a breast X-ray that can detect very small tumors that your physician cannot feel. Mammography saves lives by identifying **breast cancer** at a stage when it's potentially curable. However, the test isn't perfect. Occasionally it fails to show a tumor, and at other times it indicates a problem when there isn't one. Mammography is best combined with regular breast examinations.

There's some controversy about what age you should begin to have regular mammograms. The breasts of young women are often too dense to X-ray well. Fortunately, young women are less likely to develop breast cancer. Because every woman's preferences, concerns and cancer risks are different, the final decision is up to you and your doctor. Here are some guidelines.

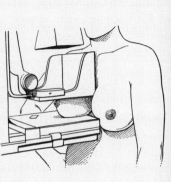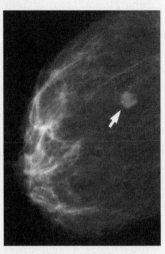

Mammograms are produced by a special X-ray device that can detect tumors before you or your doctor can feel them.

Age	Expert Opinion	What to Do
Younger than 40 not at high risk	General agreement	Monthly breast self-exam Physical exam every 3 years No mammogram
Younger than 40 at high risk (sister or mother with breast cancer at a young age)	Talk to your doctor for an individualized program	Monthly breast self-exam Annual physical exam Mammogram, often beginning 5-10 years before age at which mother or sister had cancer
40-49 not at high risk	Some disagreement	Monthly breast self-exam Physical exam every 1-2 years Mammogram every 1-2 years
40-49 at high risk	General agreement	Monthly breast self-exam Annual physical exam Annual mammogram and/or other imaging technologies
50-74 at normal or high risk	General agreement	Monthly breast self-exam Annual physical exam Annual mammogram and/or other imaging technologies
75 or older	Some disagreement	Monthly breast self-exam Annual physical exam Annual mammogram

Note: Risk factors for breast cancer include prior breast cancer, breast cancer in mother or sister, never pregnant or first pregnancy when older than 35, early onset of menses or late menopause. Your doctor may also consider other risk factors.

Common Problems

■ Pain in Your Breast

Generalized tenderness in both breasts is common, especially during the week before a menstrual period, and it's also a symptom of premenstrual syndrome (see page 147). Exercises, such as jogging and aerobics, can cause breast tenderness. Tenderness may also occur from an inflamed cyst. If fever and redness are present, infection is a concern. The most common cause of specifically located pain in the breast is mastitis, which is caused by an infection or inflammation. It usually occurs in only one breast. Infections can occur with breast-feeding.

Self-Care

- Wear a comfortable and supportive bra.
- Take an over-the-counter pain reliever (see page 258).
- Reduce the salt in your diet before your period.
- Avoid caffeine.
- If pain is due to high-impact exercises, switch to a low-impact workout such as biking, walking or swimming and use an athletic bra.
- See other tips in the section on premenstrual syndrome (page 147).

Medical Help

If you have fever or redness along with the pain, see your health care provider. You probably need an antibiotic. If pain is associated with a lump or a change in the texture of your breast, see your doctor.

■ Painful Menses

Most women are familiar with menstrual cramps. During menstruation, you may feel pain in the lower abdomen, possibly extending to the hips, lower back or thighs. Some women also have nausea, vomiting, diarrhea or general aching. It's normal to have mild abdominal cramps on the first day or two of your period (more than half of women do). About 10 percent to 15 percent of women experience pain so severe that they can't manage their normal routine unless they take medication.

If there's not an underlying gynecologic disorder, the pain is called primary dysmenorrhea. It's caused by high levels of a substance (prostaglandin) that makes the muscles of the uterus contract and shed its lining. Although painful, primary dysmenorrhea isn't harmful. It often disappears by your mid-20s or after you have a baby.

Pain that's caused by an underlying gynecologic disorder is called secondary dysmenorrhea. It may be due to a benign tumor in the wall of your uterus (fibroid tumor), a sexually transmitted disease, endometriosis, pelvic inflammatory disease or an ovarian cyst or tumor.

Self-Care

- Aspirin and other nonsteroidal anti-inflammatory drugs (see page 258) relieve pain in about 80 percent of women.
- Try soaking in a warm tub or exercising.

Medical Help

Treatment of the underlying cause should relieve the pain. If no cause for the pain is found, birth control pills may relieve the discomfort.

Talk to your health care provider if the menstrual pain is severe or is associated with fever; if you have unusual nausea, vomiting or abdominal pain, vaginal discharge or odor; or if the pain lasts beyond the third day of menstrual flow.

Irregular Periods

It's common for women to experience unexplained irregularities in their periods. Irregular periods are due to changes in hormone levels, which can be affected by stress or other emotional experiences, significant changes in the amount of aerobic exercise or dramatic changes in weight. Among women with excessively lean bodies who exercise extensively, their periods may stop altogether.

Self-Care

- Keep a menstrual calendar for at least three cycles. Record the first day of flow, the day of maximum flow, the day that flow stops and times of intercourse, to help evaluate menstrual changes.
- If your periods are irregular for more than three cycles, talk with your doctor.
- If you miss a period and have had intercourse, look for symptoms of pregnancy.

Bleeding Between Periods

Occasional bleeding between menstrual periods is common. It may occur spontaneously or with sexual intercourse. Usually it isn't serious, and is caused by a variation of your usual hormone cycles. Stress, new contraceptive pills, benign growths of tissue (polyps) and many other conditions can affect your menstruation. Because abnormal bleeding can also be the first warning sign of cancer, it needs prompt evaluation by your health care provider.

Premenstrual Syndrome

If you experience a predictable pattern of physical and emotional changes in the days before your period, you may have <u>premenstrual syndrome</u> (PMS). This condition is related to normal hormone cycles and occurs with normal hormone levels. One clue to its cause may lie in a woman's response to serotonin. Serotonin is a substance in the brain that has been associated with clinical depression and other emotional disorders. Sometimes an underlying psychological condition such as depression is aggravated by the hormonal changes before a period.

Symptoms of PMS

Physical Changes	**Emotional Changes**
• Fluid retention, bloating	• Depression and sadness
• Weight gain	• Irritability
• Breast soreness	• Anxiety
• Headache	• Tension
• Skin problems	• Mood swings
• Aches: head, back, stomach	• Difficulty in concentrating
• Aching, swollen hands and feet	• Lethargy
• Diarrhea, constipation	• Food cravings
• Fatigue, nausea and vomiting	• Forgetfulness

Common Problems

Self-Care

You can usually manage PMS with a combination of education and lifestyle changes.
- Maintain a healthy weight.
- Eat smaller, more frequent meals. Don't skip meals. Eat at the same time every day if possible.
- Limit salt and salty foods for one to two weeks before your period to reduce bloating and fluid retention.
- Avoid caffeine to reduce irritability, tension and breast soreness. See page 212 for information on caffeine.
- Avoid alcohol before your period to minimize depression and mood swings.
- Eat a well-balanced diet (see page 210).
- A diet that's adequate in calcium may help. Drink 2 to 3 cups of nonfat or low-fat milk daily and choose other calcium-rich foods (see page 149). If you cannot tolerate foods with calcium or you're unsure about the adequacy of calcium in your diet, a daily calcium supplement (1,200 milligrams) may help. Other supplements that may be helpful include magnesium and vitamin B-6. Talk with your doctor about recommended doses.
- Reduce stress (see page 225). Stress can aggravate PMS.
- Plan ahead for PMS. Don't overbook yourself the week you're expecting symptoms.
- Walk, jog, bike, swim or perform some other aerobic exercise at least three times a week.
- Record your symptoms for a few months. You may find that PMS is more tolerable if you see that your symptoms are predictable and short-lived.

Medical Help

There are no physical findings or lab tests for diagnosing PMS. Instead, doctors rely on careful evaluation of your medical history. As part of the diagnostic process, women are asked to record the onset, duration, nature and severity of symptoms for at least two menstrual cycles.

If your PMS symptoms seriously affect your life and the suggestions listed above don't help, your doctor may recommend the following medications:
- Nonsteroidal anti-inflammatory drugs (NSAIDs), including aspirin, can ease cramps and breast discomfort (see page 257).
- Birth control pills often relieve symptoms by stopping ovulation.
- Antidepressants are often effective in reducing severe emotional symptoms from PMS. Examples of these antidepressants are citalopram (Celexa), fluoxetine (Prozac), sertraline (Zoloft), paroxetine (Paxil), fluvoxamine (Luvox) and venlafaxine (Effexor). These drugs can be used in doses lower than those usually prescribed for depression and may be effective when taken only during the week or two before menstruation.
- An injection of medroxyprogesterone (Depo-Provera) can be used to temporarily stop ovulation and menstruation in severe cases.

■ Menopause

<u>Menopause</u> is a natural stage of life for women. Some women reach menopause during their 30s or 40s, and some not until their 60s. The average age for women to reach menopause in the United States is 51.

During menopause, the ovaries gradually stop producing estrogen. Your periods become irregular. The process may last several months to several years. Eventually, your menstrual periods stop, and you can no longer become pregnant.

As your ovaries produce fewer hormones, various changes occur, although they vary a great deal from person to person. Your uterus shrinks (atrophies), and the lining of your vagina becomes thin. Your vagina may also become dry, making intercourse painful. Hot flashes cause flushing or sweating that may last from several minutes to more than an hour and may interrupt sleep and produce night sweats.

During and after menopause, your body fat typically is redistributed as metabolism changes. Your bones lose density and strength. <u>Osteoporosis</u> may occur (see below).

Many women find that menopause can have a positive effect on their physical and emotional health. However, mood changes are not uncommon during menopause. They may be related to sleep disruption due to hot flashes, other hormonal changes or the normal midlife issues that affect both men and women.

Self-Care

- Accept the changes as normal and healthy.
- Eat a balanced diet, exercise regularly and dress in layers.
- Use a water-soluble lubricating jelly if intercourse is painful.

Medical Help

Your health care provider may prescribe hormone therapy (HT) to relieve postmenopausal symptoms, such as hot flashes. HT doesn't affect mood swings sometimes associated with menopause.

The disadvantages of HT are that it may slightly increase the risk of breast cancer, as well as vascular diseases, including blood clots and stroke. While HT is the most effective treatment for many menopausal symptoms, its risks lead many women to look for alternative treatments.

Alternative treatments include some dietary remedies, such as soy foods, and medications that may affect temperature regulation in the brain, including some antidepressants (such as SSRIs) or hormones (such as megestrol acetate).

How to Prevent Osteoporosis

Loss of estrogen after menopause increases the likelihood of osteoporosis, a disorder in which your bones become porous and brittle. The most effective way to manage osteoporosis is to prevent it by maximizing your bone density when you're young.

- Eat enough calcium (1,000 to 1,200 milligrams a day) during adulthood to help prevent osteoporosis. Foods rich in calcium include milk, yogurt, cheese, salmon and broccoli. One glass of milk has about 300 milligrams of calcium.

- If you're at an increased risk, your physician may suggest calcium supplements. Calcium, however, may be harmful for certain conditions. See your health care provider before taking a high-calcium supplement.
- Get adequate vitamin D — 15 minutes of sunshine three times a week or a daily supplement containing 400 international units (IU).
- Participate in weight-bearing exercises such as walking, jogging and dancing.

Common Problems

■ Urination Problems

Urinary tract infections (UTIs) are common among women. With the beginning of sexual activity, women have a marked increase in the number of infections. Sexual intercourse, pregnancy and urinary obstruction all contribute to the likelihood of such an infection. Symptoms of UTI include pain or a burning sensation during urination, increased frequency of urination and a feeling of urgency every time you need to urinate. If you have an infection, your doctor will prescribe an antibiotic.

Urinary incontinence is involuntary loss of urine. The condition is often divided into urge and stress incontinence. If leakage occurs when you feel the need to void, it's called urge incontinence. It's often caused by a mild UTI or by excessive use of bladder stimulants such as caffeine. Stress incontinence is loss of urine when pressure is put on your bladder by coughing, laughing, jumping or lifting something heavy. It usually is caused by weakening of the muscles that support your bladder. These muscles can weaken because of childbirth, being overweight or aging.

Self-Care for Urine Leakage

- Try Kegel exercises. Imagine that you're trying to stop the flow of urine. If you're using the right muscles, you'll feel a pulling sensation. Pull in your pelvic muscles and hold for a count of three. Relax for a count of three. Work up to 10 to 15 repetitions each time you exercise. Do Kegel exercises at least three times a day. It may take up to 12 weeks before you notice an improvement in bladder control.
- Empty your bladder more often.
- Lean forward when urinating to empty your bladder more completely.
- Decrease your intake of caffeine-containing foods and beverages (see page 212).
- Use tampons while exercising.

■ Vaginal Discharge

Vaginal discharge is one symptom of vaginitis. Vaginitis is an inflammation of your vagina. It usually is caused by an infection or an alteration in the normal vaginal bacteria. In addition to vaginal discharge, you may have itching, irritation, pain during intercourse, pain in your lower abdomen, vaginal bleeding and odor.

There are three common types of vaginitis: yeast infections, bacterial vaginosis and trichomoniasis. Yeast infections are caused by a fungus. You're more susceptible to a yeast infection if you're pregnant or have diabetes; if you're taking antibiotics, cortisone or birth control pills; or if you have an iron deficiency. The main symptom is itching; a white discharge also may be present. Bacterial vaginosis usually produces a gray, smelly discharge. This infection can be treated with metronidazole tablets or another antibiotic. Trichomoniasis is caused by a parasite. It may cause a smelly, greenish-yellow, sometimes frothy discharge. It usually develops as a result of sexual intercourse. Trichomonal vaginitis usually is treated with metronidazole tablets. Your partner also should be treated.

Self-Care for Yeast Infection

- Use a nonprescription antifungal cream or suppository for suspected yeast infections.
- Abstain from intercourse or have your partner use a condom for a week after beginning treatment.
- See your health care provider if symptoms persist still after one week.

■ Cancer Screening

See page 145 for breast cancer screening recommendations. Screening tests for <u>cervical cancer</u> include a Pap test and a pelvic examination. The Pap test can detect cervical cancer at an early and curable stage.

Cervical cancer is usually linked to forms of the human papillomavirus (HPV). This virus can be passed on through sexual contact. A condom — male or female — will usually prevent infection.

Most cervical cancers typically develop slowly. The cancer may begin with changes in cells on the surface of the cervix. Doctors refer to these abnormal cells as precancerous. They may become cancerous with time. Early precancerous changes in surface cells are called dysplasia or squamous intraepithelial lesions. Some of these abnormalities go away on their own, but others progress. Precancerous conditions generally don't cause any symptoms, including pain.

American Cancer Society guidelines recommend:
- An initial Pap test about three years after the start of sexual intercourse, but no later than age 21.
- Subsequent Pap tests every one to two years until age 30.
- Beyond age 30 and after three consecutive Pap tests with normal results, testing every two to three years.
- Following a complete hysterectomy (removal of uterus and cervix), Pap tests are unnecessary unless you've had surgery to treat cervical cancer or precancerous changes.
- Women age 70 or older with no abnormal test results in the last 10 years may discontinue the test.

Women at high risk should have more frequent testing. You're at high risk if:
- You began sexual activity as a teenager, especially if you had multiple sex partners
- You currently have more than one sex partner
- You've had or have a sexually transmitted disease
- You've had an abnormal Pap test or a prior cancer
- You have HIV or a weakened immune system
- You were exposed to diethylstilbestrol (DES) while in your mother's uterus
- You use tobacco

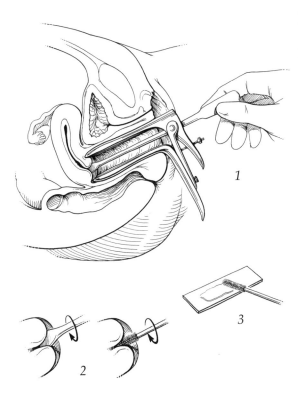

With speculum in place, your physician rotates a wooden spatula and then a brush to remove a sample of cells (1 and 2). The cells are smeared onto a glass slide (3) for examination under a microscope.

The Reliability of Pap Tests

The Pap test isn't perfect. It may miss abnormal cells, causing a false-negative result. That's why it's important to get regular Pap tests. A result could be inaccurate for these reasons:
- Abnormal cells are washed away during sexual activity or douching before examination.
- The health care provider doesn't collect cells from the entire cervical area, missing abnormal cells; doesn't smear the sample onto the slide properly; or doesn't process the cells immediately and correctly.
- There's a mistake in the laboratory by the equipment or technician.

Common Problems

Other Common Medical Conditions

Endometriosis

Endometriosis is a disorder of the reproductive system in which small pieces of the lining of the uterus (endometrium) are thought to migrate out of the uterus through the fallopian tubes. The pieces implant on the bowel, bladder, uterus, pelvic walls and the outside of the ovaries or fallopian tubes. During menstruation, blood from these patches is absorbed by the surrounding organs, causing inflammation. This process can create scar tissue that causes organs to stick together (adhesions), which can prevent pregnancy. Symptoms include painful periods, severe cramping during periods, pain deep in the pelvis during intercourse and pain during bowel movements or urination. Some women have severe pain, but others have no symptoms.

Treatment with hormones may relieve the symptoms, stop the progression and prevent infertility. Sometimes more extensive surgery is needed.

Uterine Fibroids

Uterine fibroids (myomas, fibromyomas or leiomyomas) are tumors of the uterus that occur in more than one out of five women under age 50. You may have a single uterine fibroid or several, and their growth is unpredictable. Fibroids aren't associated with an increased risk of uterine cancer, and they often go undetected because many women don't have any symptoms. When they occur, signs and symptoms may include abnormal menstrual bleeding, pelvic pressure, abdominal or lower back pain, pain during sexual intercourse, infertility or miscarriage, and difficulty with urination or bowel movements. Treatment generally includes drug therapy, surgery or focused ultrasound ablation, which uses heat to destroy fibroids.

Hysterectomy

Each year, approximately 600,000 women have a hysterectomy, a procedure in which all or a part of a woman's uterus is removed. After a hysterectomy, you no longer menstruate, and you can no longer become pregnant.

A **vaginal hysterectomy** is removal of the uterus through an incision in the vagina. An **abdominal hysterectomy** is removal of the uterus through an incision in your abdomen. Abdominal hysterectomy is performed if you have suspected or confirmed uterine or ovarian cancer, extensive endometriosis or scarring in the pelvis, a history of pelvic infection or a uterus that's too large to remove vaginally.

After a vaginal hysterectomy, you may feel pulling in your groin or have low back pain. You may have a discharge for about three weeks as the stitches at the top of the vagina dissolve. An abdominal hysterectomy may cause more discomfort because the incision goes through the abdominal wall. Both are major surgeries.

Toxic Shock Syndrome

Toxic shock syndrome (TSS) is a reaction to poisons produced by bacteria in the vagina. It typically occurs during menstruation and more frequently in tampon users. Symptoms develop suddenly, and the disease is serious. Your blood pressure can drop, and you may go into shock. Sometimes kidney failure results. TSS requires immediate medical attention. Symptoms include a fever of 102 F or higher, vomiting, diarrhea, weakness, dizziness, disorientation and a rash resembling a sunburn.

If you use tampons, avoid superabsorbent brands. Change tampons at least every eight hours. If you've ever had TSS, don't wear tampons at all.

Contraception

Method	How It Works	Effectiveness*	Cautions
Natural family planning	Intercourse determined by menstrual cycle.	78% to 98%	Works best in stable relationships. Requires special training.
Oral contraceptives (birth control pills)	Synthetic hormones prevent ovulation and impair implantation.	92% with typical use	Take pill at the same time every day. Don't smoke, especially after age 35.
Intrauterine devices (IUD)	Inserted into the uterus; inhibit sperm migration and fertilization.	98% to 99%	One may increase blood flow; one decreases blood flow; must check placement.
Diaphragm	Fitted rubber cap inserted into vagina to cover the cervix.	84% with typical use	May cause cervical irritation and increased risk of urinary tract infections. Inserted before intercourse; left in 8 hours afterward.
Cervical cap	Fitted plastic cervical cap placed on cervical opening.	86% in women who have not had a child	May cause cervical irritation and Pap test abnormalities. Must be inserted before intercourse.
Spermicidal sponge	Acts as barrier; can leave in up to 30 hours.	84% to 89%	Avoid with sulfa drugs.
Female condom	Polyurethane membrane inserted into vagina; extends outside vagina.	78% to 95%	Must be inserted before intercourse. Insertion difficult for some.
Depo-Provera shots	Hormone shot in the arm, buttock or under the skin every 3 months.	97% with typical use	May cause headache, menstrual irregularities, acne and weight gain. Prolonged use may increase risk of bone loss.
Implantable rod	Hormone released from rod placed under skin; up to 3 years.	99%	Acne, headache, weight gain, breast tenderness; scar on removal.
The patch	Skin patch that releases hormones into bloodstream.	99%	Less effective in women who weigh more than 198 pounds.
Hormonal vaginal contraceptive ring	Ring that releases hormones placed inside vagina.	92% with typical use	Need to remove ring after 3 weeks. Leave ring out 1 week for menstruation. Insert new ring.
Nonsurgical sterilization	Tiny devices inserted into fallopian tubes, causing them to scar and plug.	99%	Need to use another form of birth control for about 3 months.
Surgical sterilization**	Fallopian tubes are tied and cut or cauterized.	99%	Requires surgery, usually as an outpatient.
Male condom	Latex sheath placed over penis.	85% alone; 95% with spermicide	Avoid natural or lambskin; allergy to latex.
Emergency contraception	High-dose hormones in morning-after pill.	75%	Must be started within 72 hours of intercourse.

*Effectiveness is defined as preventing pregnancy during one year of typical use.
**For information about male sterilization (vasectomy), see page 143.

■ Pregnancy

Although **pregnancy** is a natural state, you want to take especially good care of your health to help ensure that your baby will have the best possible start in life. It's a good idea to see your health care provider for a complete physical examination before you become pregnant. You may be checked for several conditions that may not cause symptoms but can complicate pregnancy. These include diabetes, high blood pressure, pelvic tumors and anemia. If there's a health problem, your health care provider will want to control the condition, ideally before you become pregnant. Your health care provider will also review your immunizations to be sure you're immune to German measles (rubella), a viral infection.

Self-Care

To Prepare for Pregnancy

- If you're overweight, reduce your weight before you become pregnant. Don't begin a diet if you're pregnant.
- If you smoke, stop. And, if possible, avoid secondhand smoke (see page 195).
- Don't drink alcohol if you're trying to become pregnant.
- Take a multivitamin daily. Make sure it contains folic acid, which decreases the risk of birth defects of the spinal column (neural tube defects).
- Check with your health care provider about taking over-the-counter or prescription medicines.

During Pregnancy

Once you're pregnant, the best ways to ensure a healthy baby are to:
- Eat a healthy diet. Allow for appropriate weight gain.
- Make regular visits to your health care provider.
- Take a prenatal vitamin with folic acid, as prescribed by your physician.
- Obtain a book on pregnancy. Understand the changes your body is experiencing.
- Avoid harmful substances such as cigarettes, alcohol and some medications and chemicals.
- **Caution:** Bleeding from your vagina during pregnancy may indicate that something is wrong. Call your health care provider immediately. Although some harmless spotting and bleeding occur in many women during early pregnancy, your health care provider will want to rule out miscarriage, tubal (ectopic) pregnancy or other conditions such as a cervical lesion.

Home Pregnancy Tests

Home pregnancy tests provide a private way to find out whether you're pregnant. Most tests use a wand or stick placed into a urine stream or a collected urine specimen to detect the hormone human chorionic gonadotropin (HCG). The placenta begins to produce this hormone soon after conception. When performed correctly, the tests are up to 97 percent accurate one week after a missed period.

Home pregnancy tests can help you get your pregnancy off to a good nutritional start by using prenatal vitamin supplements early. They also help you avoid things that could harm the fetus such as alcohol, smoking, some medications or chemicals at home or work. Home pregnancy tests also provide early warning for women who've had a tubal pregnancy or early miscarriage so they can see their health care provider promptly.

■ Common Problems During Pregnancy

Common but bothersome concerns you may have during pregnancy are morning sickness, heartburn, backache and other problems. These may make you uncomfortable, but usually they don't threaten your health or the health of your developing baby. If they're severe or persist despite self-care measures, see your doctor.

Morning Sickness

During the first 12 weeks of pregnancy, approximately 80 percent of women experience nausea, and up to 50 percent experience vomiting. This condition is commonly referred to as morning sickness. Although it doesn't always happen during the morning, morning sickness is usually harmless. If you have problems with morning sickness:
- Munch a few crackers before arising in the morning.
- Eat several small meals a day so that your stomach is never empty.
- Avoid smelling or eating foods that trigger the nausea, and avoid spicy, rich and fried foods if you are nauseated.
- Drink plenty of liquids, especially if you're vomiting. Try crushed ice, fruit juice or frozen ice pops if water upsets your stomach.
- Try using acupressure or motion sickness bands to combat nausea.
- Take vitamin B-6 supplements, if recommended by your health care provider.

Anemia

Some pregnant women develop an inadequate level of hemoglobin in the blood (anemia) because of an iron deficiency or an inadequate supply of folic acid. Symptoms of anemia include fatigue, breathlessness, fainting, palpitations and pale skin. This condition can be risky for both you and your baby. It's easily diagnosed with a blood test. If you're anemic:
- Eat a diet rich in iron (including meat, liver, eggs, dried fruit, whole grains and iron-fortified cereals).
- Eat plenty of leafy green vegetables, liver, lentils, black-eyed peas, kidney beans and other cooked dried beans, oranges and grapefruit.
- Follow your health care provider's recommendations.

Edema (Swelling)

When you're pregnant, your body tissues accumulate more fluid, and swelling is common. Warm weather may aggravate the condition. If you have problems with edema:
- Use cold-water compresses to help relieve swelling.
- Eat a low-salt diet.
- Lie down; elevate your legs for an hour in the middle of the day.
- If your face becomes swollen, especially around the eyes, it may be a sign of a serious condition called preeclampsia. See your doctor right away.

Varicose Veins

Pregnancy increases the volume of blood in your body and may impair the flow of blood from your legs to your pelvis. Such impairment can cause the veins in your legs to become swollen and sometimes painful, a condition called varicose veins. If you have problems with varicose veins:
- Stay off your feet as much as possible, and elevate them as often as you can.
- Wear loose clothing around your legs and waist.
- Wear support stockings from the time you awaken until you go to bed.

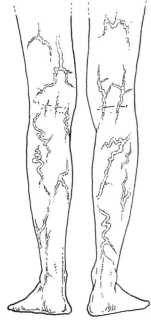

Varicose veins are enlarged veins that are easily seen beneath the surface of the skin.

Constipation

Constipation may worsen during pregnancy. Bowel activity may be slowed because of the increased pressure on the bowels from the growing baby inside the uterus.

- Drink plenty of liquids — at least eight to 10 glasses a day.
- Exercise moderately every day.
- Eat several servings of fresh fruits, vegetables and whole grains.
- Try a bulking agent that contains psyllium (available without a prescription).
- Don't take a laxative without discussing it with your health care provider.

Heartburn

Heartburn is a burning sensation in the middle of your chest, often with a bad taste in your mouth. It's caused by reflux — stomach acid flowing up into your food pipe (esophagus). It has nothing to do with your heart. During the later part of pregnancy, your expanding uterus pushes the stomach out of position, which slows the rate that food empties from the stomach.

- Eat smaller meals more often, but eat slowly.
- Avoid greasy foods.
- Don't drink coffee. Both regular and decaffeinated coffee may worsen heartburn.
- Don't eat for two to three hours before you go to bed, and raise the head of your bed 4 to 6 inches. Reflux is worse when you lie flat.
- If these steps don't work, consult your health care provider, who may recommend an antacid. (See page 64.)

Backache

Backache is common in pregnancy and may worsen if you bend, lift, walk too much or are fatigued. Pain may be in the lower back, or it may radiate down your legs. Your abdomen also may hurt because of the stretching of ligaments. During pregnancy your ligaments are more elastic, and so your joints are more prone to strain and injury. Your center of balance also changes during pregnancy. This puts more strain on your back.

- Don't gain more weight than your health care provider recommends.
- Eliminate as much strain as possible. Try wearing a maternity girdle.
- Your health care provider may recommend exercises to relieve the pain.

Hemorrhoids

Hemorrhoids are enlarged veins at the anal opening. They become enlarged from increased pressure. They're often worse during pregnancy and accompany constipation.

- Avoid becoming constipated.
- Don't strain during bowel movements.
- Take frequent warm-water baths.
- Apply a cotton pad soaked with cold witch hazel cream to the area.
- Lie down during pregnancy to help relieve pressure in the anal area.

Sleeping Problems

Your sleep may be disturbed during the later stages of pregnancy because of the frequent need to urinate, the movements of your baby or the many things on your mind.

- Avoid caffeine.
- Don't eat a large meal right before bedtime; take a warm bath before going to bed.
- Exercise more during the day.
- If you can't sleep, get out of bed and do something else.
- Don't take any medicines unless recommended by your health care provider.

Specific Conditions

- **Respiratory Allergies**
- **Arthritis**
- **Asthma**
- **Cancer**
- **Diabetes**
- **Heart Disease**
- **Hepatitis C**
- **High Blood Pressure**
- **Sexually Transmitted Diseases**

Asthma, arthritis, serious respiratory allergies, cancer, diabetes, high blood pressure, heart disease, hepatitis C and sexually transmitted diseases are common and costly medical conditions in which the normal rules of self-assessment and self-care may not apply. You should be examined by a doctor for correct diagnosis and treatment of these conditions.

In this section, you'll find general guidelines on the prevention and management of these diseases. In some cases, new treatments are included that may be helpful. Talk with your doctor about what's right for you.

Respiratory Allergies

Do you develop itchy, watery eyes or a stuffy, runny nose during the same season every year? Do you sneeze frequently when you're around animals or at work? If you answered yes to either of these questions, you may be one of approximately 50 million Americans with an allergy (see Allergic Reactions, page 12, and Hives, page 123).

Allergic Reactions and Immune Response

An allergy is an overreaction by your immune system to an otherwise harmless substance, such as pollen or pet dander. Contact with this substance, called an allergen, triggers production of the antibody immunoglobulin E (IgE). IgE causes immune cells in the lining of your eyes and airways to release inflammatory substances, including histamine.

When these chemicals are released, they produce the familiar symptoms of allergy — itchy, red and swollen eyes, a stuffy or runny nose, frequent sneezing and cough, hives or bumps on the skin. This allergic reaction causes or aggravates some forms of asthma (see page 165).

Substances found outdoors, indoors and in the foods you eat can cause allergic reactions. The most common allergens are inhaled:

- **Pollen.** Spring, summer and autumn are the pollen-producing seasons in many climates. During these seasons, exposure to airborne pollen from trees, grasses and weeds is inevitable.
- **Dust mites.** House dust harbors all kinds of potential allergens, including pollen and molds. But the main allergy trigger is the dust mite. Thousands of these microscopic spider-like insects are contained in a pinch of house dust. House dust is a cause of year-round allergy symptoms.
- **Pet dander.** Dogs and especially cats are the most common animals to cause allergic reactions. The animal's dander (skin flakes), saliva, urine and sometimes hair are the main culprits.
- **Molds.** Many people are sensitive to airborne mold spores. Outdoor molds produce spores mostly in the summer and early autumn in northern climates and year-round in subtropical and tropical climates. Indoor molds shed spores all year long.

Discovering Causes

It's not clear why some people become sensitive to allergens such as pollen. But doctors know the tendency to develop allergies is inherited. If you're bothered by allergies, chances are someone in your immediate family also copes with allergic reactions.

Yet, you and your relatives won't necessarily be sensitive to the same allergens. You're less likely to inherit a sensitivity to a specific substance than you are to inherit the general tendency to develop allergies. If your symptoms are mild, over-the-counter allergy medicines may be all the treatment you need. But if your symptoms are persistent or bothersome, a trip to the doctor may bring you relief.

To diagnose allergies accurately, your doctor will need to know about your:

- Symptoms
- Past medical problems
- Past and current living conditions
- Work environment
- Possible exposure to allergens
- Family's medical history
- Diet, lifestyle and recreational habits

The next steps are typically a physical examination and skin tests. During a skin test, tiny, dilute drops of suspected allergens are applied to your skin. Then small pricks or punctures are made through the droplets. If your response to an allergen is positive, a skin reaction like a mosquito bite or small hive — called a wheal and flare — appears at the test site within 20 minutes.

A positive result of a skin test means only that you might be allergic to a particular substance. To pinpoint the cause of your symptoms, your doctor considers the results of your skin test in addition to your history and physical examination.

The Difference Between Colds and Allergies

Because allergies often cause symptoms similar to those of a cold — congested head and chest, stuffy or runny nose, coughing and sneezing — many people mistake allergies for colds. With a cold, however, symptoms usually go away in a few days. If you have allergies, symptoms may flare under certain conditions or may seem never ending.

<u>Hay fever</u> (medically referred to as allergic rhinitis) is a common respiratory allergy. The symptoms often appear during pollen season — spring, summer or fall. Hay fever generally refers to seasonal allergic rhinitis due to pollen. It's not due to hay, and there's no fever.

Some people have allergy symptoms mainly in the winter. Others may experience symptoms when they enter a room with a cat. Still others find they have symptoms randomly all year long.

Signs and symptoms of hay fever include the following:

- Stuffy or runny nose
- Itchy eyes, nose, throat or roof of your mouth
- Frequent sneezing
- Cough

Myths About Allergy

Allergies often seem vague in origin and unpredictable in response. So it's not surprising that several misconceptions about their causes and cure exist. Three common myths about allergies are described below.

- **Allergies are psychosomatic.** Although hay fever affects your eyes and nose, allergies aren't "all in your head." An allergy is a real medical condition involving your immune system. Stress or emotions may bring on or worsen symptoms, but emotions don't cause allergies.
- **Moving to Arizona will cure allergies.** Some people who are bothered by allergies to pollens and molds believe moving to the Southwest, where the foliage and climate are different, will cause their allergies to disappear. The desert may lack maple trees and ragweed, but it does have other plants that produce pollen, such as sagebrush, cottonwood, ash and olive trees. People who are sensitive to some pollens and molds may become sensitive to the pollens and molds found in new environments.
- **Short-haired pets don't cause allergies.** An animal's fur (regardless of its length) isn't the culprit in allergies. The cause is the dander and sometimes saliva and urine. If you're allergic to furry pets, fish may be a better choice.

Specific Conditions

Self-Care

The best approach for managing allergies is to know and avoid your triggers:

Pollen
- Stay indoors when the pollen count is highest, between 5 a.m. and 10 a.m. Use an air conditioner with a good filter. Change it often.
- Wear a pollen mask when outdoors and for yardwork.
- Vacation out of the region during the height of the pollen season.

Dust or Molds
- Limit your exposure by cleaning your home at least once a week. Wear a mask while cleaning, or have someone else clean for you.
- Encase mattresses, pillows and box springs in dustproof covers.
- Consider replacing upholstered furniture with leather or vinyl, carpeting with wood, vinyl or tile (particularly in the bedroom).
- Maintain indoor humidity between 30 percent and 50 percent. Use kitchen and bathroom exhaust fans and a dehumidifier in the basement.
- Routinely change furnace filters according to the manufacturer's instructions. Also, consider installing a high-efficiency particulate air (HEPA) filter in your heating system.
- Clean humidifiers and dehumidifers often to prevent mold and bacteria growth.

Pets
- Avoid pets with fur or feathers. If you choose to keep a furry animal, keep it out of the bedroom and in an area of the home that's easily cleaned. Keep your animal outside as much as possible.

Medical Help

Antihistamines are widely used to control sneezing, runny nose and itchy eyes or throat. Antihistamines block the action of histamine, one of the irritating chemicals that are responsible for symptoms. **Caution:** Some antihistamines can cause drowsiness.

Decongestants relieve some allergy symptoms by reducing congestion or swelling in your nasal membranes. This allows you to breathe more easily. Many over-the-counter (OTC) medications for allergies and colds combine decongestants with antihistamines. Decongestants may cause heart palpitations, increase blood pressure and cause trouble sleeping.

Nasal sprays, available over-the-counter and by prescription, also can be part of your defense against allergies. The different forms are described here.
- *Corticosteroids.* Available by prescription, they relieve congestion when used daily but take at least a week to become fully effective.
- *Cromolyn sodium.* A nasal spray containing cromolyn sodium is available OTC and can prevent sneezing and an itchy, runny nose caused by mild to moderate allergies.
- *Saline.* Nonprescription nasal sprays containing a saltwater solution relieve mild congestion, loosen mucus and prevent crusting. You can use them safely as needed until symptoms improve.
- *Decongestants.* These sprays aren't intended for relief of chronic allergy symptoms. Avoid them or use sparingly for no more than three to four days.

Allergy shots (immunotherapy) involve injecting tiny amounts of known allergens into your system. After several injections, usually weekly, you may build up tolerance to the allergen. You then may need monthly injections for up to several years.

Arthritis

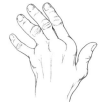

Arthritis is one of the most common medical problems in the United States. It affects one person in seven. There are more than 100 forms of arthritis, and they have varying causes, symptoms and treatments. Refer to the chart on page 162 for a summary of symptoms of the major forms of arthritis.

Rheumatoid arthritis can lead to soft swelling and deformities in the large and middle knuckles.

The warning signs of inflammatory arthritis include the following:

- Swelling in one or more joints
- Prolonged early-morning stiffness
- Recurring pain or tenderness in any joint
- Inability to move a joint normally
- Obvious redness and warmth in a joint
- Unexplained fevers, weight loss or weakness associated with joint pain

Any of these signs, when new, that last for more than two weeks require prompt medical evaluation. Distinguishing arthritis from simple aches and pains is important for treating the problem correctly.

Arthritis has many causes. It may result from degeneration of cartilage in your joints (osteoarthritis) or from genetic traits, injury, inflammation, infection or any number of unknown causes. Most joint ailments caused by inflammation are termed arthritis, from the Greek words *arthron,* for "joint," and *itis,* for "inflammation."

Heberden's nodes are lumps of bone and cartilage at the ends of fingers. They occur most often in women and are a sign of osteoarthritis.

The remainder of this section focuses on the management of **osteoarthritis**, which is the most common form of arthritis. Some of the self-care tips may apply to the other forms. Consult your health care provider regarding management of other forms of arthritis.

■ Exercise

Over time, exercise is probably the one therapy that will do the most good for managing your arthritis. Exercise must be done regularly to produce and sustain improvements. That's why you should check with your health care provider and begin a regular exercise program for your specific needs.

Overall, you want to be in good physical condition. This means maintaining flexibility, strength and endurance. Together, these will help protect your joints against further damage, keep them aligned, reduce stiffness and minimize pain.

Different types of exercise achieve different goals. For flexibility, range-of-motion exercises (gentle stretching) move the joint from one end position to the other. In severe osteoarthritis, range-of-motion exercises may cause pain. Don't continue an exercise beyond the point that's painful without the advice of your doctor or physical therapist.

Moving large muscle groups for 15 to 20 minutes is the primary way of exercising aerobically to strengthen muscles and build endurance. Walking, bicycling, swimming and dancing are good examples of aerobic-type exercises with low to moderate stress on the joint.

If you're carrying a lot of extra weight, moving around is more difficult. You're putting stress on your back, hips, knees and feet — all common places to have osteoarthritis. Obesity clearly worsens arthritis symptoms, as does deconditioning from lack of physical activity.

Common Forms of Arthritis

Cause and Frequency	Key Symptoms	How Serious Is It?

Osteoarthritis

Often associated with wear and tear on some joints. May be due to an imbalance of enzymes. Common in people older than 50; rare in young people unless a joint is injured or metabolic abnormality exists.

- Pain in a joint after use.
- Discomfort in a joint before or during a change in weather.
- Swelling and a loss of flexibility in a joint.
- Bony lumps at finger joints.
- Aching is common. Redness and warmth are less common.

Seriousness may depend on joint or joints affected and age. It doesn't go away, although the pain may come and go. The effects may be disabling in some cases. Joints such as the hip and knee may deteriorate to the point of needing surgical replacement.

Rheumatoid arthritis

Rheumatoid arthritis is the most common form of inflammatory arthritis.* Most often develops between ages 20 and 50. Probably caused by the body's immune system attacking joint-lining tissue, cartilage and bone.

- Pain and swelling in the small joints of hands and feet.
- Overall severe aching or stiffness, especially first thing in the morning or after periods of rest.
- Affected joints are swollen, painful and warm during initial attack and flare-ups.

It's one of the most debilitating forms of arthritis. Disease frequently causes deformed joints. Some people experience sweats and fever along with loss of strength in muscles attached to affected joints. Often chronic.

Infectious arthritis

Infectious agents include bacteria, fungi and viruses. Can be complication of sexually transmitted diseases. Can occur in anyone.

- Pain and stiffness in multiple joints, typically knee, shoulder, hip, ankle, elbow, finger or wrist.
- Surrounding tissues are warm and red.
- Chills, fever and weakness.
- May be associated with a rash.

In most cases, prompt diagnosis and treatment of a joint infection result in rapid and complete recovery.

Gout

Urate crystals form in joint. Most commonly affects men older than age 40.

- Gout causes severe pain that strikes suddenly in a single joint, often at the base of the big toe, but it can affect other joints, including knee and ankle.
- Swelling and redness.

An acute attack can be treated effectively. After an attack has run its course, the affected joint usually returns to normal. Attacks can recur and may require preventive treatment to lower uric acid levels in the blood.

*Other types of inflammatory arthritis include psoriatic arthritis, which occurs in people with psoriasis, especially in the finger and foot joints; post-infectious, which often is transmitted by sexual contact and is characterized by pain in the joints, penile discharge, painful inflammation of the eye and a rash; ankylosing spondylitis, which affects the joints of the spine and sometimes the limbs and, in advanced cases, causes a very stiff, inflexible backbone.

Medications Control Discomfort

The most common over-the-counter and prescription drugs used for osteoarthritis are described below. (See page 257 for more information on the use of these medications.)

- **Acetaminophen.** This nonprescription product relieves pain and is less likely to upset your stomach. It doesn't help inflammation, but because pain with osteoarthritis is often partly due to mechanical problems, it's often a good choice.
- **NSAIDs.** Nonsteroidal anti-inflammatory drugs (NSAIDs) include aspirin, ibuprofen, naproxen and ketoprofen. Dosage makes a difference. Your doctor should specify the amount that's right for you. Aspirin may relieve pain with two tablets every four hours. You might need to take this dosage for a week or two for temporary inflammation — longer for chronic inflammation. Other NSAIDs may work as well as aspirin and have fewer side effects, but they may cost more.
- **COX-2 inhibitors.** COX-2 inhibitors block the production of an enzyme that triggers inflammation and pain. These drugs were designed to provide pain relief without the side effects of gastrointestinal irritation and bleeding. They're best used under the care of an arthritis specialist.
- **Corticosteroids.** They decrease inflammation. About 30 types are available; the most common is prednisone. Doctors don't prescribe oral corticosteroids for osteoarthritis, but they may occasionally inject a cortisone drug into a painful joint. Because frequent use of this drug may accelerate joint damage, doctors are often cautious with its use.

Caution

Many over-the-counter pain relievers and anti-inflammatory drugs can irritate the lining of your stomach and intestines and cause ulcers and even severe bleeding with long-term use. Stomach and intestinal perforation can occur without bleeding. **Consult your doctor if you're using NSAIDs regularly for more than two weeks to treat joint pain.**

Other Methods to Relieve Pain

Ask your health care provider about the therapies described below:

- **Heat** is soothing. It helps relax muscles around a painful joint. You can apply heat superficially with warm water, a paraffin bath, electric pad, hot pack or heat lamp, but be careful to avoid a burn. For deep penetration, a physical therapist can use ultrasound or short-wave diathermy.
- **Cold** acts as a local anesthetic. It also decreases muscle spasms. Cold packs may help when you ache from holding muscles in the same position to avoid pain.
- **Splints** support and protect painful joints during activity and provide proper positioning at night, which promotes restful sleep. Constant splinting, however, can weaken muscles and decrease flexibility.
- **Relaxation** techniques, including hypnosis, visualization, deep breathing, muscle relaxation, yoga and other techniques may decrease pain.
- **Glucosamine supplements** are gaining in popularity. To date, there's little evidence that these nonprescription supplements are helpful. Use caution when selecting one. The products are not regulated by the Food and Drug Administration.
- **Other techniques,** such as low-impact exercise, orthotics (such as shoe inserts) and gait aids (canes and walking sticks), help strengthen muscles, reduce joint pressure and decrease pain. See a physical therapist for proper instruction.

■ Joint Protection

Correct "body mechanics" help you move with minimal strain. A physical or occupational therapist can suggest techniques and equipment that protect your joints by decreasing stress and conserving energy.

Modifications you can make include:

- Avoid grasping actions that strain your finger joints. For example, instead of a clutch-style purse or briefcase, select one with a shoulder strap. Use hot water to loosen a jar lid and pressure from your palm to open it, or use a jar opener. Don't twist or use your joints forcefully.
- Spread the weight of an object over several joints. Use both hands, for example, to lift a heavy pan or large book. Try using a walking stick or cane.
- Take a break periodically to relax and stretch and avoid muscle fatigue.
- Good posture helps promote even weight distribution and helps avoid strain on ligaments and muscles.
- Throughout the day, use your strongest muscles, and try to favor nonarthritic joints. Don't push open a heavy glass door. Lean into it. To pick up an object, bend your knees and squat while keeping your back straight.
- Special tools that make gripping easier are available for buttoning shirts and kitchen use. Look for them at grocery, hardware or discount stores, or contact your pharmacy or health care provider for information on ordering these items.

Don't Be Duped by Unproven Cures

Unproven arthritis remedies may cause harmful side effects. Here are some popular, but false, nutrition claims:

- **Cod liver oil 'lubricates' stiff joints.** It may sound logical, but your body treats cod liver oil like any other fat; it provides no special help for joints. Large amounts of cod liver oil can lead to vitamin A and D toxicity.
- **Some foods cause allergic arthritis.** There's no proof that food allergy causes arthritis. Nor do certain foods cure or improve arthritic symptoms. You can't relieve arthritis by avoiding tomatoes or other foods.
- **Fish oils reduce inflammation.** Research on rheumatoid arthritis suggests that omega-3 fatty acids in fish oils may give modest, temporary relief of inflammation. This finding is valid, but we don't advise fish oil supplements. You'd need about 15 capsules a day — doctors don't know whether that's a safe amount. A lower dose won't help.

FOR MORE INFORMATION

- Arthritis Foundation, P.O. Box 7669, Atlanta, GA 30357; (800) 568-4045; *www.arthritis.org.*
- National Institute of Arthritis and Musculoskeletal and Skin Diseases Information Clearinghouse, National Institutes of Health, 1 AMS Circle, Bethesda, MD 20892; (877) 226-4267; *www.niams.nih.gov.*
- American College of Rheumatology, 1800 Century Place, Suite 250, Atlanta, GA 30345; (404) 633-3777; *www.rheumatology.org.*

Asthma

Asthma occurs when the main air passages of your lungs, called bronchial tubes, become inflamed. The muscles of bronchial walls tighten, and extra mucus is produced. Airflow out of your lungs is diminished, often causing wheezing.

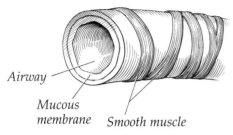

Airway
Mucous membrane
Smooth muscle

Normal airways in your lungs

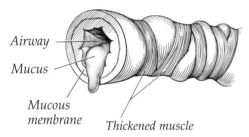

Airway
Mucus
Mucous membrane
Thickened muscle

In asthma, airways in your lungs are inflamed and swollen.

Common symptoms are wheezing, difficulty breathing, "tightness" in the chest and coughing. In emergencies, the person will have extreme difficulty in breathing, bluish lips and nails, severe breathlessness, increased pulse rate, sweating and severe coughing.

Asthma is a serious medical condition, but with proper care and treatment you usually can control your symptoms and lead a normal life.

Approximately 12 percent of children and 7 percent of adults in the United States have asthma. About half of the children who have asthma develop the condition before age 10. Asthma is usually an inherited condition, and it's not contagious.

There are many causes, or triggers, of asthma attacks. They can be triggered by an allergic reaction to dust mites, cockroaches, chemicals, pollen, mold or dead skin cells that fall off animals (animal dander). They can be triggered by exposure to substances in the home or workplace. Some people are more prone to suffer an asthma attack after exercise, especially if they exercise in cold air.

Respiratory infections caused by colds and the flu can aggravate the symptoms of asthma. Adults with chronic asthma should get a yearly flu shot. Pregnant women and children, however, should check with their health care provider before receiving flu shots. Some additional triggers of asthma include sulfites, which are sprayed on vegetables and fruits by restaurants and stores to keep them from turning brown. Other foods or beverages, such as wine, also may contain sulfites as a preservative. Aspirin and other nonsteroidal anti-inflammatory drugs (NSAIDs) may trigger an asthma attack in some people.

Asthma attacks can range from very mild to life-threatening (see below). Asthma attacks can last for just a few minutes, or they can go on for hours and even days. If you have asthma, you should be receiving treatment from a health care provider. Your health care provider will work with you to identify the triggers that cause your asthma attacks. Together, you will devise a strategy to limit your exposure to these triggers, help control your symptoms and make sure your breathing is not severely obstructed.

Recognizing a Life-Threatening Attack

Prevent fatal attacks by treating symptoms early. Don't wait for wheezing as a sign of severity. Wheezing may disappear when airflow is severely restricted. Get emergency care if:
- Breathing becomes difficult and your neck, chest or ribs pull in with each breath
- Nostrils flare
- Walking or talking becomes difficult
- Fingernails or lips turn blue
- Peak airflow (measured with a hand-held meter you can use at home) reading decreases 50 percent below your normal level or keeps decreasing even after you take your medication

Self-Care

The following tips help control symptoms by trigger-proofing your environment:

- Educate yourself about asthma. The more you know, the easier it is to control.
- Avoid allergens that might trigger your symptoms. If you're allergic to cats or dogs, remove these pets from your home and avoid contact with other people's pets. Avoid buying clothing, furniture or rugs made from animal hair.
- If you're allergic to airborne pollens and molds, use air conditioning at home, at work and in your car. Keep doors and windows closed to limit exposure to airborne pollens and molds.
- Avoid activities that might contribute to your symptoms. For example, home improvement projects might expose you to triggers that lead to an asthma attack, such as paint vapors, wood dust or similar irritants.
- Check your furnace. If you have a forced-air heating system and you're allergic to dust, use a filter for dust control. Change or clean filters on heating and cooling units frequently. The best filter is a high-efficiency particulate air filter, referred to as a HEPA filter. Wear a mask when you remove dirty filters.
- Use a vacuum cleaner with a small-particle filter.
- Avoid projects that raise dust. If you cannot, then use a dust mask, which is available at drugstores and hardware stores.
- Review exercise habits and consider adjusting your routine (see below). Consider exercising indoors, which may limit your exposure to asthma triggers.
- Avoid all types of smoke, even smoke from a fireplace or burning leaves. Smoke irritates the eyes, nose and bronchial tubes. If you have asthma, you shouldn't smoke and people should never smoke in your presence.
- Reduce stress and fatigue.
- Read labels carefully.
- If sensitive to aspirin, avoid other nonsteroidal anti-inflammatory agents, including ibuprofen (Motrin, Advil, others), naproxen (Naprosyn, Anaprox, others) and piroxicam (Feldene).

Staying Active With Well-Planned Workouts

Years ago if you had asthma, doctors told you not to exercise. Now they believe well-planned regular workouts are beneficial, especially if you have mild to moderate disease. If you're fit, your heart and lungs don't have to work as hard to expel air.

But, because vigorous exercise can trigger an attack, be sure to discuss an exercise program with your doctor. In addition, follow these guidelines:

- **Know when not to exercise.** Avoid exercise when you have a viral infection or in below-zero or extremely hot and humid conditions. In cold temperatures, wear a face mask to warm the air you breathe.

- **Medicate first.** Use your inhaled short-acting beta agonist 15 to 60 minutes before exercise.
- **Start slowly.** Five to 10 minutes of warm-up exercises may relax your chest muscles and widen your airways to ease breathing. Gradually work up to your desired pace.
- **Choose the type of exercise wisely.** Cold-weather activities such as skiing and long-distance, nonstop activities such as running most often cause wheezing. Exercise that requires short bursts of energy, such as walking, golf and leisure bicycling, may be better tolerated.

Medical Help

A peak flowmeter is a device used to evaluate lung function.

Testing for allergies. Your health care provider may perform some tests to try to determine the triggers of your asthma attacks. A skin test or blood test may be performed. The blood test is more expensive and is less sensitive than skin tests, but it's sometimes preferable when the person being tested has a skin disease or is taking medications that might affect the test results.

Medications. Your doctor may prescribe some of the medications listed below to prevent or treat your asthma attacks. Take all the medications as prescribed, even if you aren't experiencing any symptoms. Don't take more than the prescribed amount because excessive use of medications can be dangerous. These medications can be taken using an inhaler, or they may come in liquid, capsule or tablet form.

Controllers (anti-inflammatory medications) reduce the inflammation in your airways and also help reduce the production of mucus. The result is a reduction of the spasms in your breathing passages. Take the daily dose of these medications as prescribed to prevent asthma attacks from occurring. Controllers include inhaled corticosteroids, leukotriene modifiers, cromolyn and nedocromil. Long-acting bronchodilators (salmeterol, formoterol) can be used with inhaled corticosteroids.

Relievers (bronchodilators), unlike contollers, are taken once you're experiencing an asthma attack. Relievers help open narrow airways to allow you to breathe more easily during an attack. Relievers include short-acting beta agonists (albuterol, pirbuterol).

Self-monitoring with peak flow meter. You may be trained to use a peak flow meter, a device that measures how well you are breathing. The flow meter acts like a gauge for your lungs, giving you a number that helps evaluate lung function. A low reading means your air passages are narrow and is an early warning that you may experience an asthma attack.

Inhalers: Risks of Misuse

Inhaling a bronchodilator (see Medical Help above) helps you breathe better immediately during an attack. But the drug doesn't correct inflammation.

Maximal daily use of a bronchodilator is two puffs every four to six hours. If you use one more frequently to control symptoms, you need a more effective medication.

Fast relief may make it difficult to recognize worsening symptoms. Once the medication wears off, asthma returns with more severe wheezing.

You're then tempted to take another dose of the medication, delaying adequate treatment with anti-inflammatory medications.

Overuse also risks toxic drug levels that may lead to an irregular heartbeat, especially if you have a heart condition.

Over-the-counter inhalers also can relieve symptoms quickly — but temporarily. Relying on inhalers can mask a worsening attack and delay treatment with anti-inflammatory medications.

FOR MORE INFORMATION

- Asthma and Allergy Foundation of America, 1233 20th St. N.W., Suite 402, Washington, DC 20036; (800) 727-8462.; *www.aafa.org.*
- American Lung Association, 61 Broadway, 6th Floor, New York, NY 10006; (800) 548-8252; *www.lungusa.org.*
- National Institute of Allergy and Infectious Diseases (NIH), 6610 Rockledge Dr., MSC 6612, Bethesda, MD 20892-6612; (301) 496-5717; *www.niaid.nih.gov.*

Specific Conditions

Cancer

The day your cancer is diagnosed becomes a major event in your life. You may see everything that follows in the context of your cancer diagnosis and treatment. That's a normal reaction.

There are many different kinds of cancer. We're constantly finding new ways to detect and treat it. Recently, survival rates for some cancers have improved dramatically. Now, we talk of "living with cancer," rather than "dying of cancer" or becoming a "victim of cancer."

New cases of cancer by site and sex. The statistics are 2006 estimates by the American Cancer Society. Figures exclude basal and squamous cell skin cancers and superficial cancers (in situ carcinoma), except bladder. (By permission of the American Cancer Society.)

Male	Female
Prostate 234,460 (33%)	**Breast** 212,920 (31%)
Lung & bronchus 92,700 (13%)	**Lung & bronchus** 81,770 (12%)
Colon & rectum 72,800 (10%)	**Colon & rectum** 75,810 (11%)
Urinary bladder 44,690 (6%)	**Uterine corpus** 41,200 (6%)
Melanoma of the skin 34,260 (5%)	**Non-Hodgkin's lymphoma** 28,190 (4%)
Non-Hodgkin's lymphoma 30,680 (4%)	**Melanoma of the skin** 27,930 (4%)
Kidney & renal pelvis 24,650 (3%)	**Thyroid** 22,590 (3%)
Oral cavity & pharynx 20,180 (3%)	**Ovary** 20,180 (3%)
Leukemia 20,000 (3%)	**Urinary bladder** 16,730 (2%)
Pancreas 17,150 (2%)	**Pancreas** 16,580 (2%)
All sites 720,280 (100%)	**All sites** 679,510 (100%)

The diagram above shows the estimated number of new cases of various kinds of cancer in 2006, according to the affected body part. The remainder of this chapter includes some advice for you or a family member with cancer. To find specific information on various types of cancer, see "Cancer" on page 288 of the Index.

Responding to the Cancer Diagnosis

As with any crisis or difficult time in life, you need healthy and effective coping strategies. Here are some suggestions:

1. **Get the facts.** Try to obtain as much basic, useful information as possible. Consider bringing a family member or friend with you to doctor appointments. Write down your questions and concerns beforehand. This approach helps you organize your thoughts, obtain accurate information, understand your cancer and treatment and participate in decision making. But remember, the answers are frequently educated guesses or statistics. Everyone is different. Questions often include the following:
   - Is my cancer curable?
   - What are my treatment options?

- What can I expect during treatment?
- Will my treatments be painful?
- When do I need to call my doctor?
- What can I do to prevent cancer from recurring?
- What are the risk factors for my family members (especially children)?

2. **Develop your own coping strategy.** Just as each person's cancer treatment is individualized, so is the coping strategy that you must follow. Here are some ideas:
   - Learn relaxation techniques (see page 227).
   - Share feelings honestly with family, friends, a pastor or counselor.
   - Keep a journal to help organize your thoughts.
   - When faced with a difficult decision, list pros and cons for each choice.
   - Find a source of strength in your faith.
   - Find time to be alone.
   - Remain involved with work and leisure activities.

3. **Keep communication open** between you and your loved ones, health care providers and others. You may feel particularly isolated if people try to protect you by keeping disappointing news from you or trying to put up a strong front. If you and others feel free to express your emotions, you can gain strength from each other.

4. **Your self-image is important.** Although some people may not notice physical changes, you will. Insurance will often help pay for wigs, prostheses and special adaptive devices.

5. **A healthy lifestyle** can improve your energy level and promote healthy cell growth. This includes adequate rest, good nutrition, exercise and fun activities.

6. **Let friends and family help you.** Often they can run errands, drive the carpool, prepare meals and help with household chores. Learn to accept help. Accepting help also gives those who care about you a sense of purpose at a difficult time.

7. **Review your goals and priorities.** Consider what's really important in your life. Reduce unnecessary activities. Find a new openness with loved ones. Share your thoughts and feelings with them. Cancer can affect all of your relationships. Communication can help reduce the anxiety and fear that cancer can cause.

8. **Try to maintain your normal lifestyle.** Take each day one at a time. It's easy to overlook this simple strategy during stressful times. When the future is uncertain, organizing and planning for it can suddenly become overwhelming.

9. **Maintain a positive attitude.** Celebrate each day. If a day is difficult, let go of it and move on. Don't let cancer control your life.

10. **Fight stigmas.** Many of the old stigmas associated with cancer still exist. Your friends may wonder if cancer is contagious. Co-workers may doubt you're healthy enough to do your job and think you'll drain their health benefits. Reassure others that research shows cancer survivors are just as productive as other workers and don't miss work any more often. Remind friends that even if cancer has been a frightening part of your life, it shouldn't scare them to be near you.

11. **Look into insurance options.** If you're employed, you may feel "trapped," unable to change jobs for fear of not being eligible for new insurance. If you're retired, you may have difficulty purchasing supplemental insurance. Find out whether your state provides health insurance for people who are difficult to insure. Look into group insurance options through professional, fraternal or political organizations.

Nutrition: A Big Plus

There's no conclusive evidence that avoiding or overeating any specific food helps treat cancer. But good nutrition is important to living with cancer. Your cancer treatment may reduce your appetite and change the flavor of foods. It may also interfere with absorption of nutrients in foods. Studies show that good nutrition can:

- Improve your chances of tolerating your treatment successfully
- Improve your sense of well-being
- Enhance your tissue and immune system functions
- Help meet demands for calories and proteins to rebuild damaged tissues

The medicine megestrol acetate (available in pill or liquid form) taken several times a day may help maintain or increase your weight.

Self-Care

Here are some nutrition tips if you're losing weight and need more calories:

- If the taste of meat bothers you, mild-tasting dairy products such as cottage cheese and yogurt are good alternative sources of protein. Try eating a peanut butter sandwich or peanut butter spread on fruit. Legumes, such as kidney beans, chickpeas and black-eyed peas, are good sources of protein, especially when combined with grains such as rice, corn or bread.
- Pack as many calories as possible into the foods you eat. Warm your bread, and spread it with butter, margarine, jam or honey. Sprinkle foods with chopped nuts.
- Lightly seasoned dishes made with milk products, eggs, poultry, fish and pasta often are well tolerated.
- If you have trouble eating an adequate amount of food at a single sitting, eat smaller amounts more frequently. Chew your food slowly.
- If the aroma of food being prepared makes you ill, use a microwave or choose foods that need little cooking or that can be warmed at a low temperature.
- Nourishing liquids can boost protein and calories. Cream soups, milk, cocoa, milk shakes or malts or commercially prepared nutritional beverages may help. Your physician or dietitian can help determine whether you need a supplement.

What About Pain?

Pain is a major concern among people with cancer, but it need not be. Only about one-third of people who have cancer have pain. In fact, people with cancer often experience less pain than people with arthritis or nerve disorders. Pain is almost always controllable. Pain control medications include the following:

- **Non-narcotic drugs.** Aspirin is highly effective, and it often provides relief equivalent to more powerful painkillers. Other nonsteroidal anti-inflammatory drugs (NSAIDs) and acetaminophen are equally effective and may require fewer doses a day than aspirin (see page 257). Antidepressants also are helpful pain relievers.
- **Narcotics** (morphine and codeine), used for severe pain, may be given by mouth (pills or liquid), injections, implantable pumps or a slow-release skin patch.
- **Anticonvulsants and some antidepressants** may help with nerve pain.

Nondrug pain control measures include radiation to shrink a tumor and lessen pain; injection or surgery to block pathways of nerves carrying pain messages to your brain; biofeedback; behavior modification; breathing and relaxation exercises; massage; transcutaneous electrical nerve stimulation (TENS); and hot and cold packs.

Self-Care

- Don't wait for the pain to become severe before taking a pain medication. Take pain medicines on a schedule.
- Don't be concerned about addiction. When used properly, the chance for addiction to narcotics is very small. Besides, if a narcotic is needed for a long time to relieve severe pain, the comfort it provides is often more important than any possibility of addiction.
- Develop a strategy for dealing with emotions such as anxiety and depression. They can make the pain seem worse.

Cancer in Children

Cancer in children is uncommon, but when it happens parents face special issues and problems. Researchers have made great strides in finding effective treatments for childhood cancers. Today, nearly 80 percent of American children with cancer survive for more than five years.

Self-Care

If your child has cancer, it's important to:

- Carefully choose the person who will treat your child. Look for a medical center with the latest treatments for childhood cancers. Staff there should provide emotional support for your family.
- Try to maintain as normal a lifestyle as possible. Keeping schedules, rules and previous expectations in place will help your child cope and plant the idea of a long future.
- Talk to your child's teachers to establish behavioral and academic expectations.
- Do your best to deal with the possibility of death in an honest, straightforward manner. Children need to be told as much as they can understand. There is no single right way to tell children about death. Encourage them to ask questions. Give them simple answers. Their fears may keep them from asking questions, so start by asking how they feel. Never lie, make promises you may not be able to keep or be afraid to say, "I don't know."
- Promote activities that reduce anxiety (such as drawing) and express feelings (role-playing or puppets).
- Don't ignore the needs of your other children. Siblings can be very supportive to their ill brother or sister, but they must know that their special place in the family is secure.
- Read "When Someone in Your Family Has Cancer," from the National Institutes of Health (pamphlet No. P619), available from the National Cancer Institute (see below).

FOR MORE INFORMATION

- National Cancer Institute Public Inquiries Office, Suite 3036A, 6116 Executive Blvd., MSC8322, Bethesda, MD 20892; (800) 422-6237; *www.cancer.gov.*
- American Cancer Society, 1599 Clifton Road N.E., Atlanta, GA 30329; (800) 227-2345; *www.cancer.org.*

Specific Conditions

Diabetes

Diabetes is a disorder of your metabolism — the way your body uses digested food for energy and growth. Normally, your digestive system converts the food you eat into a sugar called glucose. That sugar then enters your bloodstream, ready to fuel your cells.

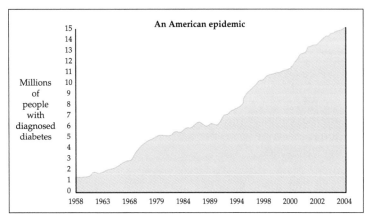

The number of people in the United States who have diabetes has been climbing steadily since 1958.

In order for your cells to receive the sugar, insulin, a hormone produced by your pancreas, must "escort" it in. Normally, your pancreas produces enough insulin to handle all the sugar present in your blood. There are two types of diabetes, both of which disrupt this process.

In type 1 diabetes, your pancreas produces reduced amounts of insulin. In type 2 diabetes, your body doesn't respond normally to the insulin that is made. In both types of diabetes, blood sugar enters body cells only in limited amounts. Some of the sugar then builds up in your blood, overflows into your urine and passes from your body unused.

Both types of diabetes can cause long-term complications such as heart disease, kidney failure, nerve damage, blindness and deterioration of blood vessels and nerves. Damage to your body's small and large blood vessels is at the root of most of these complications.

Type 1 and Type 2: What's the Difference?

Type 1 diabetes accounts for 5 percent to 10 percent of all cases of diabetes. It's also known as juvenile-onset diabetes and usually develops before age 30. If you have type 1 diabetes, you must receive insulin daily for the rest of your life. The symptoms can develop abruptly and include the following:

- Excessive thirst
- Frequent urination
- Extreme hunger
- Unexplained weight loss
- Weakness and fatigue

Type 2 diabetes is the most common form of diabetes. It used to be called adult-onset diabetes. Type 2 diabetes most often occurs after age 45 in overweight people. A balanced diet, moderate weight loss and exercise often can control it. If diet and exercise aren't effective, you may need oral or injected medication. Many people with type 2 diabetes have few or no symptoms. Symptoms can develop slowly and include the following:

- Excessive thirst
- Frequent urination
- Blurred vision
- Recurring bladder, vaginal and skin infections
- Slow-healing sores
- Irritability
- Tingling or loss of feeling in your hands or feet

How Does Family History Affect Your Risk of Diabetes?

Type 1		Type 2*	
Relative With Diabetes	**Your Estimated Risk**	**Relative With Diabetes**	**Your Estimated Risk**
Mother	1% to 5%	Mother	5% to 20%
Father	5% to 15%	Father	5% to 20%
Both parents	10% to 25%	Both parents	25% to 50%
Brother or sister	5% to 10%	Brother or sister	25% to 50%
Identical twin	25% to 50%	Identical twin	60% to 75%

*Having a healthy diet, maintaining a healthy weight and exercising regularly can substantially lower your overall risk of type 2 diabetes.
Source: Based on a review of recent medical journal articles and textbooks

Self-Care

Managing diabetes is a balancing act. Illness, eating too much or too little, a change in exercise, travel and stress all affect your blood sugar level. Here are some tips to help you gain tighter control of your blood sugar level.

Diet

A well-balanced diet is the cornerstone of diabetes management. Remember to:

- **Stick to a schedule.** Eat three meals a day. Be consistent in the amount of food you eat and the timing of eating. If you're hungry after dinner, choose a food low in calories or carbohydrates before going to bed, such as raw vegetables.
- **Focus on fiber.** Eat a variety of fresh fruits, vegetables, legumes and whole-grain foods. These are low-fat and rich sources of vitamins and minerals.
- **Limit foods that are high in fat** to less than 30 percent of your total calorie intake. Choose lean cuts of meats and use low-fat dairy products.
- **Don't push proteins.** Too much protein can take its toll on your kidneys. Limit meat to about 6 ounces a day. This will also help you limit cholesterol.
- **Avoid 'empty' calories.** Candy, cookies and other sweets aren't forbidden. But because they have little nutritional value, eat them in moderation and count them in your total carbohydrate intake.
- **Use alcohol in moderation.** If your doctor says it's safe, choose drinks that are low in sugar and alcohol, such as light beer and dry wines. Count alcoholic drinks in your total carbohydrate intake and don't drink on an empty stomach.
- **Watch your weight.** If you're overweight, losing even a few pounds can improve your blood sugar levels.

Exercise

Regular exercise helps maintain overall health, benefits your heart and blood vessels, and may improve circulation. It helps control your blood sugar level and may help prevent type 2 diabetes. If you have type 2 diabetes, regular exercise and a healthy diet may reduce or even eliminate your need for injected insulin or an oral medication.

Exercise alone isn't enough to achieve good control of your blood sugar level if you have type 1 diabetes, but it may enhance the effects of insulin that you take. You may need to eat additional food just before or during exercise to prevent sudden changes in your blood sugar level. Follow your doctor's advice on exercise.

Monitoring Your Blood Sugar

Checking your blood sugar level regularly is essential for managing your diabetes. How often you need to perform this test depends on your treatment regimen. Your health care team can help you determine reasonable goals for your blood sugar level. In addition to maintaining a proper diet and exercise routine, you may also need to learn how to adjust your medications, especially insulin, to keep your blood sugar level near normal.

Today, blood tests are the most accurate way to check your blood sugar level. To do so, put a drop of fingertip blood onto a chemically treated test strip. The test strip reacts to the amount of glucose in your blood by changing color. You can read the blood glucose level by holding the test strip next to a color guide chart or by having an electronic glucose monitor read it. Reliable monitors cost between $40 and $120.

Understanding Your Fasting Glucose Testing Results

If you have symptoms that suggest diabetes, ask your doctor for a fasting blood glucose test. Have a baseline test by age 45. If your results are normal, get tested every three years. If you have prediabetes, have this test at least once a year. If you're overweight with one or more additional risk factors for diabetes, get tested at a younger age and more frequently.

Glucose Level	Indicates
Under 100 mg/dL	Normal
100 to 125 mg/dL	Prediabetes*
126 mg/dL or higher on two separate tests	Diabetes

mg/dL = milligrams of glucose per deciliter of blood
*Prediabetes means that you're at high risk of developing diabetes.

Medications

You may need medication to control your blood sugar level. But even with medication, exercise and diet are integral to managing your diabetes.

If you have type 1 diabetes, you must take insulin. Insulin can't be taken by mouth because it breaks down in your digestive tract. It's often given by injection. The number of daily injections and type of insulin prescribed (short-, intermediate- or long-lasting) depend on your individual needs. If your blood sugar level is hard to control, you may need frequent injections or benefit from an insulin pump. Recently, the Food and Drug Administration approved an inhaled form of insulin — a short-acting version that can be taken before meals.

If you have type 2 diabetes and have trouble controlling your blood sugar with diet and exercise alone, your doctor may prescribe one of several oral medications. These medications help your pancreas produce more insulin or help insulin to work better in your body. If oral medications don't work well, the next step is often medication that you inject under the skin of your thigh, abdomen or upper arm. This may include insulin or one of the new noninsulin medications. The new medications are exenatide (Byetta), which helps prevent the need for insulin in people with type 2 diabetes, and pramlintide (Symlin), which is used with insulin for better glucose control in both type 1 and type 2 diabetes.

Diabetes can cause one or more of the following emergencies:

Insulin reaction. This is also called low blood sugar (hypoglycemia). It can occur when excess insulin, excess exercise or too little food causes a decreased blood sugar level. Symptoms usually appear several hours after eating and include trembling, weakness and drowsiness followed by confusion, dizziness and double vision. If untreated, a low blood sugar level may cause seizures or loss of consciousness.

If you're concerned that you're having an insulin reaction, check your blood sugar level. If it's low, eat something containing sugar, such as fruit juices, candy or soft drinks containing sugar. If you're helping someone in this condition, seek emergency medical care if the person vomits, is unable to cooperate, is unconscious, or if symptoms persist beyond 30 minutes after treatment. Remain with the person for an hour after recovery to ensure that he or she is thinking clearly.

Diabetic coma. Also called diabetic ketoacidosis or DKA, this complication develops more slowly than an insulin reaction, often over hours or days. DKA occurs when insulin levels are low and the body is unable to utilize glucose, resulting in high blood sugar (hyperglycemia). Nausea, vomiting, abdominal pain, weakness, thirst, sweet-smelling breath, and deeper and more rapid breathing all can precede gradual confusion and loss of consciousness. This reaction is most likely to occur in people with type 1 diabetes who are ill or skip an insulin dose. It can be the first symptom of previously undiagnosed diabetes.

Metabolic Syndrome Increases Your Risk of Disease

Although not all experts agree, metabolic syndrome (also called insulin resistance syndrome) is a group of risk factors that make you more likely to develop type 2 diabetes, heart disease and stroke. If you have three or more of the risk factors below, you may be diagnosed with metabolic syndrome.

- Abdominal obesity: More than a 35-inch waist for women and more than a 40-inch waist for men; for Asian Americans, more than a 31-inch waist for women and more than a 35-inch waist for men

- Triglycerides: 150 mg/dL or above, or drug treatment for high triglycerides
- HDL cholesterol (high-density lipoprotein, the "good" kind): Lower than 50 mg/dL for women and lower than 40 mg/dL for men, or drug treatment for low HDL
- Blood pressure: Systolic (top number) of 130 millimeters of mercury (mm Hg) or above or diastolic (bottom number) of 85 mm Hg or above, or drug treatment for high blood pressure
- Fasting blood glucose: 100 mg/dL or higher, or drug treatment for high blood glucose

If you think that you have metabolic syndrome, talk with your doctor about tests that can help determine this. Healthy eating, achieving a healthy weight and increasing your level of physical activity can help combat metabolic syndrome and play a role in preventing diabetes and other serious diseases.

Foot Care Reduces the Risk of Injury and Infection

Diabetes can impair the circulation and nerve supply to your feet. Foot care is essential:

- Inspect your feet daily. Look for sores, color changes or altered sensation. Get help or a mirror to view all surfaces.
- Wash your feet daily. Use warm (not hot) soapy water. Dry them thoroughly and gently.
- Trim nails straight across, file rough edges.
- Don't use wart removers or trim calluses and corns yourself. See your doctor or a podiatrist.
- Wear cushioned, well-fitted shoes. Check inside shoes daily for fabric wear or rough edges. Don't walk barefoot.
- Avoid tight clothing around your legs or ankles. Don't smoke; smoking can make bad circulation worse.
- Avoid exposing your feet to temperature extremes. If your feet are cold, wear socks.

FOR MORE INFORMATION
- American Diabetes Association, 1701 N. Beauregard St., Alexandria, VA 22311; (800) 342-2383; *www.diabetes.org.*

Heart Disease

Your heart pumps blood to every tissue in your body through a 60,000-mile network of blood vessels. Blood supplies the tissues with oxygen and nutrients that are essential for good health.

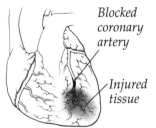

Problems can arise in the heart muscle, the heart valves, the electrical conduction system, the sac that surrounds the heart (pericardium) or the arteries that supply blood to the heart muscle itself (coronary arteries). This section focuses on problems in the coronary arteries. Coronary artery problems cause **heart attacks**, which cause the deaths of approximately 225,000 Americans annually.

As you age, fatty deposits may form in the coronary arteries in your heart, creating a condition called coronary artery disease. "Hardening of the arteries" (atherosclerosis) can occur in arteries in other areas of your body as well. As the coronary arteries become narrowed or blocked, blood flow to your heart muscle is reduced or stopped.

Blocked coronary artery

Injured tissue

A heart attack occurs when arteries supplying your heart with blood and oxygen become blocked.

When your heart muscle doesn't receive enough blood, you may feel chest pain or pressure (angina). If blood flow is blocked long enough in a coronary artery (about 30 minutes to four hours), the portion of the heart muscle that's supplied by that artery will die. Heart muscle death is known as a myocardial infarction (MI) or heart attack.

A heart attack usually is caused by sudden blockage of a heart artery by a blood clot. The clot usually forms in an artery that has been narrowed by fatty deposits.

Heart Attack: Reacting Promptly May Save a Life

A heart attack generally causes chest pain for more than 15 minutes. But a heart attack also can be "silent" and have no symptoms. About half of heart attack victims have warning symptoms hours, days or weeks in advance.

The American Heart Association lists the following warning signs of a heart attack. Be aware that you may not have them at all and that symptoms may come and go.

- Uncomfortable pressure, fullness or squeezing pain in the center of your chest, lasting more than a few minutes
- Pain spreading to your shoulders, neck, back, jaw or arms

The pain of heart attack varies. Symptoms may be nonspecific, especially in women. Or you may experience a squeezing sensation in the chest, accompanied by profuse sweating. Pain may radiate to the left, right, or both shoulders and arms, to the back neck and to the jaw.

- Lightheadedness, fainting, sweating or nausea
- After age 65, most common symptom is shortness of breath

The more of these symptoms you have, the more likely it is that you're having a heart attack. Whether you suspect a heart attack or think it's just indigestion, act immediately:

- Call emergency medical assistance — phone 911.
- Sit quietly or lie down if you feel faint. Breathe slowly and deeply.
- Chew an aspirin, unless you're allergic to it. Aspirin thins the blood and can decrease death rates significantly. If you have nitroglycerin tablets, place one under your tongue.

If you observe someone with chest pain, follow the steps above. If the person faints or loses consciousness, evaluate for CPR (see page 2).

When the heart attack patient arrives at a hospital, he or she may be given clot-dissolving drugs or undergo a procedure called angioplasty, which involves widening blocked arteries to let blood flow more freely to the heart. If the use of clot-dissolving drugs or angioplasty is delayed beyond four hours, benefits are substantially reduced.

Specific Conditions

What Is Your Risk of Heart Disease?

High blood cholesterol, cigarette smoking and high blood pressure are some of the major risk factors for coronary artery disease. Your chances of having a heart attack or dying of heart disease within the next 10 years increase with each risk factor you have. Estimate your risk by adding up the points shown in the various categories below.

Framingham Global Points

If you're a man:

Age	Points
20-34	-9
35-39	-4
40-44	0
45-49	3
50-54	6
55-59	8
60-64	10
65-69	11
70-74	12
75-79	13

Total Cholesterol	Points				
	Age 20-39	Age 40-49	Age 50-59	Age 60-69	Age 70-79
<160	0	0	0	0	0
160-199	4	3	2	1	0
200-239	7	5	3	1	0
240-279	9	6	4	2	1
≥280	11	8	5	3	1

	Points				
	Age 20-39	Age 40-49	Age 50-59	Age 60-69	Age 70-79
Nonsmoker	0	0	0	0	0
Smoker	8	5	3	1	1

HDL (mg/dL)	Points
≥60	-1
50-59	0
40-49	1
<40	2

Systolic BP (mmHg)	If Untreated	If Treated
<120	0	0
120-129	0	1
130-139	1	2
140-159	1	2
≥160	2	3

Point Total	10-Year Risk %
<0	<1
0	1
1	1
2	1
3	1
4	1
5	2
6	2
7	3
8	4
9	5
10	6
11	8
12	10
13	12
14	16
15	20
16	25
≥17	≥30

Tables are based on data from the Framingham Heart Study.

10-Year Risk_____ %

If you're a woman:

Age	Points
20-34	-7
35-39	-3
40-44	0
45-49	3
50-54	6
55-59	8
60-64	10
65-69	12
70-74	14
75-79	16

Total Cholesterol	Points				
	Age 20-39	Age 40-49	Age 50-59	Age 60-69	Age 70-79
<160	0	0	0	0	0
160-199	4	3	2	1	1
200-239	8	6	4	2	1
240-279	11	8	5	3	2
≥280	13	10	7	4	2

	Points				
	Age 20-39	Age 40-49	Age 50-59	Age 60-69	Age 70-79
Nonsmoker	0	0	0	0	0
Smoker	9	7	4	2	1

HDL (mg/dL)	Points
≥60	-1
50-59	0
40-49	1
<40	2

Systolic BP (mmHg)	If Untreated	If Treated
<120	0	0
120-129	1	3
130-139	2	4
140-159	3	5
≥160	4	6

Point Total	10-Year Risk %
<9	<1
9	1
10	1
11	1
12	1
13	2
14	2
15	3
16	4
17	5
18	6
19	8
20	11
21	14
22	17
23	22
24	27
≥25	≥30

10-Year Risk_____ %

■ Lowering Your Risk of Heart Disease

Several risk factors for coronary artery disease can be modified through lifestyle changes or medications. Here's what you can do to reduce your risk:

- Stop smoking. If you smoke a pack of cigarettes a day, your risk of heart attack is more than twice that of a person who doesn't smoke. For more information on smoking and ways to stop, see page 192.
- Reduce high blood pressure. See page 183.
- Reduce your cholesterol level. See pages 213-216.
- Control diabetes. See pages 172-176.
- Maintain proper weight. See page 206.
- Exercise. See page 217.
- Reduce stress. See page 225.

The risk factors listed above may interact with one another to affect your total risk of developing coronary artery disease. The more risk factors you have, the greater your risk of a heart attack. The Framingham risk calculator on page 178 can help you determine your risk factors.

Controlling these risk factors often involves using medications. But you can usually lower your risk significantly through a balanced diet, loss of excess weight and regular exercise. These efforts sometimes prevent the need for medications.

In addition to a good diet and regular exercise, studies have shown that the following also may lower your risk of heart attack. Discuss with your doctor how each of these factors fits into lowering your risk.

Aspirin is often recommended to prevent heart attacks. It reduces the tendency of blood to clot by weakening the activity of small cell fragments in the blood that stick to each other to form a clot (platelets). Aspirin may help reduce a clot or prevent a clot from causing a heart attack. It's inexpensive, generally safe and easy to take. One baby aspirin (which equals one-fourth of a regular-strength adult aspirin) is enough to reduce the risk of a heart attack substantially. An analysis of data from five studies showed that aspirin reduced the risk of heart disease by about 25 percent. However, a more recent study found aspirin didn't affect heart attack risk in women. Ask your doctor whether you should take an aspirin regularly.

Vitamins. In the past, vitamin E was recommended for possible heart benefit. However, recent studies haven't found any benefit and vitamin E isn't recommended to prevent heart attacks. Vitamin C also hasn't been clearly shown to have a cardiovascular benefit, and isn't recommended for heart attack prevention. Folic acid, another vitamin, may be of benefit for some individuals with increased risk of heart disease. It's important to discuss vitamin use with your doctor to make sure that you're taking the right vitamins at the appropriate doses.

Fish oil. Omega 3 fatty acids in fish oil have been shown to lower the chance of sudden cardiac death. Fish oil supplements may be recommended by your doctor if you're at risk. The recommended amount is generally 1,000 milligrams (1 gram) daily.

Risk-lowering prescription medications. If you've had a heart attack or you've been told by your doctor that you have coronary artery disease, other medicines may lower your risk of heart disease or heart attack. Talk with your doctor about cholesterol-lowering medicines, beta blockers and angiotensin-converting enzyme (ACE) inhibitors. These medicines, like aspirin, have been shown to lower your risk of heart attack, and their use may be appropriate.

Hepatitis C

Experts call it the silent disease. That's because nearly 4 million Americans have the virus, but many of them don't know it. Its symptoms can be very subtle.

Could you have the virus and not know it? Or should you be worried that you can catch the disease?

If you're in an at-risk group, you should be tested. Treatments are limited, but there are things you can do to manage your lifestyle and live with the virus. If you don't have <u>hepatitis C</u>, there's little concern about acquiring it through casual contact. The main risk is through contact with contaminated blood.

What Is Hepatitis C?

Hepatitis C is a virus that, like <u>hepatitis A</u> and <u>hepatitis B</u>, causes inflammation of your liver. It ranks with alcoholic liver disease as the leading causes of chronic liver disease and cirrhosis in the United States, and is a leading reason for liver transplantation.

Your liver is one of your body's largest organs. It's a virtual chemical factory, manufacturing vital nutrients and neutralizing toxins.

Generally, hepatitis C is spread through contact with blood contaminated with the virus. Rarely is it transmitted sexually. Many people with the virus became infected from blood transfusions received before 1992 — before improved blood-screening tests were available. Today, contaminated needles associated with illicit drug use cause most infections. The virus may also be passed from mother to infant during pregnancy or labor. Unlike hepatitis A and B, there's no vaccine to prevent hepatitis C.

If you have hepatitis C, you may not have noticed any symptoms. Most people don't for years, even decades. And if you did have early symptoms, you may have passed them off as a harmless case of the flu. Many people discover that the virus is present purely by accident during a routine blood test.

Attacking Your Liver

Up to 40 percent of people infected with hepatitis C fight off the virus on their own without liver damage. For the rest, the disease settles in and slowly attacks the liver. Between 5 percent and 25 percent of people with chronic hepatitis develop scarring (cirrhosis) of the liver, usually within the first two decades after infection. Cirrhosis can lead to the development of liver failure or liver cancer.

Should You Be Tested?

Because you can be infected with hepatitis C for years before symptoms appear, you should be tested if you:
- Received a blood transfusion before 1992.
- Used illicit intravenous or intranasal drugs (even once).
- Received an organ transplant before 1992.
- Were exposed to others' blood.
- Had dialysis for kidney failure.

- Received clotting factor concentrates before 1987.
- Had body or ear piercing, tattoos or acupuncture using unsterile equipment.
- Experienced an accidental needle-stick while delivering health care.
- Have abnormal liver function test results.
   If you think you may be at risk of hepatitis C, talk to your doctor.

See back cover for online resource

Self-Care

If you're diagnosed with hepatitis C, you may be referred to a liver specialist. Recommended lifestyle changes may include:

- **Eliminating alcohol consumption.** Alcohol use appears to speed progression of liver disease.
- **Avoiding medications that may carry a risk of liver damage.** Your doctor can advise you on what that list might include.
- **Maintaining a healthy lifestyle.** This includes a healthy diet, exercise and appropriate rest.
- **Getting vaccinated against hepatitis A and B.** This can reduce your risk of liver damage from these diseases.

   You'll also want to prevent others from coming in contact with your blood. Cover wounds, don't share your toothbrush or razors, and advise health care workers that you have the virus. In addition, don't donate blood, body organs, tissues or semen. Following safe sex practices is also advised.

Medical Help

Early treatment with a combination of medications seems to be the best approach. Physicians often pair alpha-interferon, a medication that inhibits duplication of the virus, with another antiviral drug, such as ribavirin.

   Researchers are exploring other forms of interferon and other antiviral drugs to enhance the effectiveness of these drugs in treating hepatitis C.

Specific Conditions

High Blood Pressure

High blood pressure (hypertension) is called the silent killer. Most people with high blood pressure have no symptoms. In fact, about 30 percent of the 65 million Americans with the condition don't know they have it and, therefore, are unaware of its damaging effects on the arteries, heart, brain, kidneys and eyes.

High blood pressure is more common in blacks than in whites. It also becomes more common with age. Until age 55, a higher percentage of men than women have high blood pressure. From age 55 on, the percentage of women with the condition is higher than that of men.

What Is Blood Pressure?

Have you ever had your blood pressure taken, then wondered what the numbers mean? Knowing and understanding your numbers, then taking steps to control your blood pressure, are critical. Being informed and taking the proper steps can mean the difference between good health and hypertensive heart disease, stroke and kidney disease.

Blood pressure is determined by the amount of blood your heart pumps and the resistance to blood flow in the arteries. Small or stiff arteries limit blood flow. The more blood the heart pumps and the smaller or stiffer the arteries, the higher the blood pressure (your heart has to work harder to pump the same amount of blood).

A blood pressure reading below 120/80 millimeters of mercury (mm Hg) is normal. The top number (120), called systolic pressure, is the amount of pressure your heart generates when pumping blood out through your arteries. The bottom number (80), known as diastolic pressure, is the amount of pressure in the arteries when the heart is at rest between beats. Your blood pressure normally varies during the day. It rises during activity. It decreases with rest.

High blood pressure is defined as a systolic pressure of 140 mm Hg or higher, or a diastolic pressure of 90 mm Hg or higher. **Prehypertension** is the term for blood pressure that's above normal but not elevated enough to meet the definition of high blood pressure. Why blood pressure rises isn't always known. In fact, in only about 10 percent of cases is the cause of high blood pressure identified. When a cause cannot be determined, high blood pressure is called **essential** or **primary hypertension.**

When a cause is determined, the term **secondary hypertension** is used because the increased pressure is the result of another condition. These specific causes may include medications such as oral contraceptives and kidney disorders such as renal failure, glomerulonephritis and certain adrenal gland problems.

Hypotension (Low Blood Pressure)

Hypotension is low blood pressure. If blood pressure falls to dangerously low levels (shock), the situation can be life-threatening. Shock may result from significant loss of fluid or blood and, in rare instances, from serious infections.

Postural hypotension is one potentially dangerous manifestation of low blood pressure. Dizziness or faintness that occurs on standing up quickly from a seated position is the key symptom. (See Dizziness and Fainting, page 34.) It can be caused by medications, pregnancy or illnesses.

Classifying Blood Pressure

Condition	Systolic (Top Number)		Diastolic (Bottom Number)	What to Do
Normal	119 or lower	and	79 or lower	Maintain healthy lifestyle.
Prehypertension	120-139	or	80-89	Adopt a healthy lifestyle.
Hypertension				
Stage 1	140-159	or	90-99	Lifestyle changes plus a medication.
Stage 2	≥160	or	≥100	Lifestyle changes plus more than one medication.

Note: Normal blood pressures above apply to all people 18 and older. Blood pressure conditions are diagnosed based on the average of two or more readings taken at two different visits to your doctor, in addition to the original screening visit.

Source: National Institutes of Health

Self-Care

Electronic blood pressure monitors require that you do just two things — put the cuff on your upper arm and push a button to inflate the cuff and get a reading. It's a good way to monitor your blood pressure at home.

The best strategy is to begin with lifestyle changes such as weight control, dietary changes and exercise. If, after three to six months, your blood pressure hasn't decreased, your doctor may prescribe medication. Here's what you can do to help:

- **Diet.** Eat a nutritionally balanced diet emphasizing fruits and vegetables and low-fat dairy foods.
- **Salt restriction.** Salt causes the body to retain fluids and so, in many people, can cause high blood pressure. Don't add salt to food. Avoid salty foods such as cured meats, snack foods and canned or prepared foods.
- **Weight reduction.** If your body mass index (BMI) is 25 or more, lose weight. A loss of as few as 10 pounds (4.5 kilograms) may lower your blood pressure. In some people, weight loss alone is sufficient to avoid the need to take blood pressure medications. (See Body Mass Index, page 207.)
- **Exercise.** Regular aerobic exercise alone seems to lower blood pressure in some people, even without weight loss.
- **Stop smoking.** Tobacco use can accelerate the process of narrowing of blood vessels (atherosclerosis) in people with high blood pressure. Smoking in combination with high blood pressure greatly increases your risk of artery damage.
- **Limit alcohol consumption.** Too much alcohol — more than two drinks a day for men and one for women and lighter weight men — can increase blood pressure.

The Use of Medications

Your doctor will determine which drug or combination of drugs may be best for you. Some drugs work better than others at different ages or in certain races. Your doctor may consider the cost, side effects, the interaction between multiple drugs and how the drugs affect other illnesses. There may be several steps in the process to select medication because the first drug may not lower your blood pressure. A second, third or even fourth drug may be prescribed either as a substitute or as an additional drug.

Specific Conditions

Sexually Transmitted Diseases

Sexually transmitted disease (STD) is increasing in the United States. Most STDs are treatable, but human immunodeficiency virus (<u>HIV</u>), the cause of acquired immunodeficiency syndrome (<u>AIDS</u>), currently has no cure, and death eventually occurs in most cases.

Although HIV can be spread through use of contaminated needles or, rarely, through blood transfusion, it usually is transmitted by sexual contact. The virus is present in semen and vaginal secretions and enters a person's body through small tears that can develop in the vaginal or rectal tissues during sexual activity. Transmission of the virus occurs only after intimate contact with infected blood, semen or vaginal secretions. There have been cases of HIV being passed to health care workers through needlesticks.

STDs such as <u>chlamydia</u> infections, <u>gonorrhea</u>, hepatitis B and C, <u>genital herpes</u>, <u>genital warts</u> and <u>syphilis</u> are highly contagious. Many can be spread through only one sexual contact. The microorganisms that cause STDs, including HIV, all die within hours once they're outside the body. However, none of these infections are spread through casual contact such as handshaking or sitting on a toilet seat.

The only sure way of preventing STDs and AIDS is through sexual abstinence or a relationship exclusively between two uninfected people. If you have several sexual partners or an infected partner, you place yourself at higher risk of contracting an STD.

The Use of Condoms

Correct and consistent use of a latex condom and avoidance of certain sexual practices can decrease the risk of contracting AIDS and other STDs, although condoms don't completely eliminate the risk. Condoms sometimes are made of animal membrane, and the pores in such natural skin condoms may allow the AIDS virus to pass through. The use of latex condoms is recommended.

To be effective, a condom must be undamaged, applied before genital contact and remain intact until removed on completion of sexual activity. Extra lubrication (even with lubricated condoms) can help prevent the condom from breaking. Use only water-based lubricants. Oil-based lubricants can cause a condom to break down.

A new condom for females can help reduce the risk of contracting an STD. Other forms of female-directed contraception — for example, the pill — don't provide protection against STDs.

Risky Behaviors

HIV is commonly transmitted sexually by penile-anal intercourse. The receptive (passive) partner is at much higher risk of contracting HIV than is the active partner, although gonorrhea and syphilis can be acquired from the passive partner's rectum. The likelihood of HIV transmission is also affected by the stage of the infected person's infection.

Heterosexual vaginal intercourse, particularly with multiple partners, carries a risk of contracting HIV. The virus is believed to be transmitted more easily from the man to the woman than vice versa.

Oral-genital sex is also a possible means of transmission of HIV, gonorrhea, herpes, syphilis and other STDs.

Sharing needles to self-inject drugs also increases your risk of acquiring HIV and hepatitis C virus.

Sexually Transmitted Diseases

If you think you have a sexually transmitted disease (STD), see a doctor immediately. If an STD is diagnosed, it's important that you share the information with your sexual partner(s). In all cases of STD, abstain from sexual contact until the infection is eliminated completely. Some STDs do not cause signs or symptoms, and you may not know you're infected.

Signs and Symptoms	About the Disease	How Serious Is it?	Medical Treatment

AIDS

Signs and Symptoms	About the Disease	How Serious Is it?	Medical Treatment
<ul><li>Persistent, unexplained fatigue and flu-like illness</li><li>Soaking night sweats</li><li>Shaking chills and fever (above 100 F) for several weeks</li><li>Lymph node swelling for more than 3 months</li><li>Chronic diarrhea</li><li>Persistent headaches</li><li>Dry cough and shortness of breath</li></ul>	AIDS, caused by HIV. Unfortunately, an HIV test isn't accurate immediately after exposure because it takes time for your body to develop or make antibodies. It can take up to 6 months to detect this antibody response.	HIV weakens the immune system to the point that opportunistic diseases (ones that your body would normally fight off) begin to affect you. AIDS is a fatal illness, although there have been significant recent advances in the treatment of AIDS.	There's no vaccine for AIDS. Treatment includes use of antiviral drugs, immune system boosters and medications to help prevent or treat opportunistic infections. A new class of drugs, called protease inhibitors, has shown promise.

Chlamydia infection

Signs and Symptoms	About the Disease	How Serious Is it?	Medical Treatment
<ul><li>Painful urination</li><li>Vaginal discharge in women</li><li>Discharge from penis in men</li><li>Lower abdominal pain</li></ul>	Can cause scarring of fallopian tubes in women and prostatitis or epididymitis in men.	Touching your eye with infectious secretions can cause eye infection. A mother can pass the infection to her child during delivery, causing pneumonia or eye infection.	Antibiotics are prescribed. The infection should disappear within 1 to 2 weeks. All sexual partners must be treated, even though they may not have symptoms. Otherwise, they may pass the disease back and forth between them.

Genital herpes

Signs and Symptoms	About the Disease	How Serious Is it?	Medical Treatment
<ul><li>Pain or itching in the genital area</li><li>Water blisters or open sores</li><li>Genital sores present but invisible inside the vagina (women) or urethra (men)</li><li>Recurrent outbreaks</li></ul>	**Genital herpes** is caused by the herpes simplex virus, usually type 2. Symptoms begin 2 to 7 days after exposure. Itching or burning is followed by blisters and sores. They erupt in the vagina or on the labia, buttocks and anus. In men, on the penis, scrotum, buttocks, anus and thighs. Virus remains dormant in the infected areas and periodically reactivates, causing symptoms.	There's no cure or vaccine. The disease is very contagious whenever sores are present. Newborn infants can become infected as they pass through the birth canal of mothers with open sores.	Self-care consists of keeping sores clean and dry. The prescription oral antiviral drug acyclovir helps speed healing. If recurrences are frequent, an oral antiviral medication can be taken daily to suppress the virus.

Specific Conditions

Signs and Symptoms	About the Disease	How Serious Is it?	Medical Treatment

Genital warts

Signs and Symptoms	About the Disease	How Serious Is it?	Medical Treatment
• Warty growths on the genitals, anus, groin, urethra	Venereal warts or genital warts are caused by the human papillomavirus (HPV). They affect men and women. People with impaired immune systems and pregnant women are more susceptible.	Generally not serious, but contagious. Women with a history of genital warts have a higher risk of cervical cancer and should get yearly Pap test.	Warts are removed with medication, cryosurgery (freezing), lasers or electrical current. These procedures may require local or general anesthesia.

Gonorrhea

Signs and Symptoms	About the Disease	How Serious Is it?	Medical Treatment

• Thick, pus-like discharge from urethra
• Burning, frequent urination
• Slight increase in vaginal discharge and inflammation in women
• Anal discharge or irritation
• Occasionally fever and abdominal pain
	Gonorrhea is caused by bacteria.
	   In men, symptoms first appear 2 days to 2 weeks after exposure.
	   In women, symptoms may not appear for 1 to 3 weeks. Infection usually affects the cervix and sometimes the fallopian tubes.
		Highly contagious, acute infection that may become chronic. In men, it may lead to epididymitis. In women, it can spread to fallopian tubes and cause pelvic inflammatory disease. May result in scarring of the tubes and infertility. Rarely causes joint or throat infection.	Many antibiotics are safe and effective for treating gonorrhea. Although treatable, gonorrhea is becoming resistant to some antibiotics. It may be cured with a single injection of ceftriaxone. Oral antibiotics, such as ciprofloxacin, also are effective.

Hepatitis B

Signs and Symptoms	About the Disease	How Serious Is it?	Medical Treatment
• Skin and eyes are yellowish • Urine is tea-colored • Flu-like illness • Fatigue and achiness • Fever	Hepatitis B is caused by a virus. Some carriers never have symptoms but are capable of passing the virus to others.	A pregnant woman may pass the virus to her developing fetus. Rarely causes liver failure and death.	No antiviral treatment. Bed rest isn't essential, although it may help you feel better. Maintain good nutrition. Abstain from alcohol use because of damage to the liver. Preventable by vaccination.

Syphilis

Signs and Symptoms	About the Disease	How Serious Is it?	Medical Treatment
• Painless sores on the genitals, rectum, tongue or lips • Enlarged lymph nodes in the groin • Rash over any area of the body, especially on palms and soles • Fever • Headache • Soreness and aching in bones or joints	Syphilis is a complex disease caused by a bacterium. Primary stage: Painless sores appear in the genital area, rectum, or tongue or lips 10 days to 6 weeks after exposure. Second stage, 1 week to 6 months later: Red rash may appear anywhere on skin. Third stage, often after years-long latent period: heart disease, mental deterioration.	It can be completely cured if the diagnosis is made early and the infection is treated. Left untreated, the disease can lead to death. In pregnant women, it can be transmitted to the fetus, causing deformities and death.	Usually treated with penicillin. Other antibiotics can be used for patients allergic to penicillin. A person usually can no longer transmit syphilis 24 hours after beginning therapy. Some people don't respond to the usual doses of penicillin. They must get periodic blood tests to make sure the infectious agent has been destroyed.

Mental Health

- Addictive Behavior
- Anxiety and Panic Disorders
- Depression and the Blues
- Domestic Abuse
- Memory Loss

This section examines a range of issues that affect the mental health of millions of Americans and their families. Helpful information is offered on how to deal with addictive behavior, anxiety and panic disorders, depression, domestic abuse and memory loss.

Addictive Behavior

You can become addicted to many substances and practices. The main traits of addictive behavior include a compelling need to use the addictive substance or engage in the activity, impaired control as a result of the use or activity, and continued use or activity despite adverse consequences. In this section, alcohol, tobacco, drug dependency and compulsive gambling are discussed.

Alcohol Abuse and Alcoholism

Alcohol abuse and **alcoholism** (alcohol dependence) cause major social, economic and public health problems. Each year, about 80,000 people die of alcohol-related causes. The annual cost of lost productivity and health expenses related to alcoholism is more than $180 billion. According to the National Institute on Alcohol Abuse and Alcoholism, nearly 14 million Americans abuse alcohol or are alcoholic.

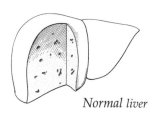

Normal liver

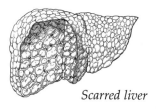

Scarred liver

Excessive alcohol intake can damage body tissues, particularly the liver. Excess use can cause scarring, called cirrhosis.

How Alcohol Works in Your Body

The form of alcohol in the beverages we drink is ethanol (ethyl alcohol), a colorless liquid that in its pure form has a burning taste. Ethanol is produced by the fermentation of sugars, which occur naturally in grains and fruits such as barley and grapes.

When you drink alcohol, it depresses your central nervous system by acting as a sedative. In some people, the initial reaction may be stimulation, but as drinking continues, sedating or calming effects occur. By depressing the control centers of your brain, it relaxes you and reduces your inhibitions. The more you drink, the more you're sedated. Initially, alcohol affects areas of thought, emotion and judgment. In sufficient amounts, alcohol impairs speech and muscle coordination and produces sleep. Taken in large enough quantities, alcohol is a lethal poison — it can cause life-threatening coma by severely depressing the vital centers of your brain.

Excessive use of alcohol can produce several harmful effects on your brain and nervous system. It can also severely damage your liver, pancreas and cardiovascular system. Alcohol use in pregnant women can damage the fetus.

Alcohol Intoxication

The intoxicating effects of alcohol relate to the concentration of alcohol in the blood. For example, if you're not a regular drinker and your blood alcohol concentration is more than 100 milligrams of alcohol per deciliter of blood (mg/dL), you may be quite intoxicated and have difficulty speaking, thinking and moving around. As your blood alcohol concentration increases, mild confusion may give way to stupor and, ultimately, coma. Alcoholics and regular drinkers develop a tolerance for alcohol.

How much food you have eaten and how recently you ate before drinking affect how you respond to alcohol. Size, body fat and tolerance to the effects of alcohol also play significant roles. Drinking equal amounts of alcohol may have a greater effect on a woman than on a man. Women generally have a higher blood alcohol concentration per drink because of their smaller size and less dilution of the alcohol. They may also metabolize alcohol more slowly than men.

Many states now define legal intoxication as a blood alcohol concentration of at least 0.08 percent. In others it's 0.1 percent. Even at concentrations much lower than the legal limit, some people lose coordination and reaction time.

See back cover for online resource (i)

What Is Alcohol Abuse?

Drinking problems in people who don't have all the characteristics of alcoholism are often referred to as alcohol abuse or problem drinking. These individuals engage in excessive drinking that results in health or social problems, but they're not dependent on alcohol and have not fully lost control over the use of alcohol.

What Is Alcoholism?

Alcoholism is a chronic disease. It's often progressive and fatal. It's characterized by periods of preoccupation with alcohol and impaired control over alcohol intake. There's continued use despite adverse consequences and distortion in thinking. Most alcoholics deny there's a problem. Other signs include:

- Drinking alone or in secret
- Not remembering conversations or commitments
- Making a ritual of having drinks before, with or after dinner and becoming annoyed when this ritual is disturbed or questioned
- Losing interest in activities and hobbies that used to bring pleasure
- Irritability as usual drinking time nears, especially if alcohol isn't available
- Keeping alcohol in unlikely places at home, at work or in the car
- Gulping drinks, ordering doubles, becoming intoxicated to feel good or "normal"
- Having problems with relationships, employment, finances or legal matters
- Having a morning "eye opener" to "steady your nerves"

■ Treating Alcohol Abuse and Alcoholism

Most alcoholics, and alcohol abusers, enter treatment reluctantly because they deny the problem. They often must be pressured, such as required treatment following a DWI. Health problems also may prompt treatment. Intervention helps an alcoholic recognize and accept the need for treatment. If you're concerned about a friend or family member, discuss intervention with a professional.

Self-Administered Alcoholism Screening Test

To screen for alcoholism, Mayo Clinic developed the Self-Administered Alcoholism Screening Test (SAAST). It consists of 37 questions.

The SAAST tries to identify behaviors, medical symptoms and consequences of drinking in the alcoholic. Here is a sample of questions from the test:

1. Do you feel you are a normal drinker (that is, drink no more than average)?
2. Do close relatives ever worry or complain about your drinking?
3. Are you always able to stop drinking when you want to?
4. Has your drinking ever created problems between you and your wife, husband, parent or other near relative?
5. Do you ever drink in the morning?
6. Have you ever felt the need to cut down on your drinking?
7. Have you ever been told by a doctor to stop drinking?
8. Have you been a patient in a psychiatric facility because of problems related to your drinking?
9. Have you been arrested for driving while intoxicated (DWI)?

These responses suggest you're at risk of alcoholism: 1. No 2. Yes 3. No 4. Yes 5. Yes 6. Yes 7. Yes 8. Yes 9. Yes

If you answered three or four of the questions with the responses listed, you likely have a drinking problem and need professional evaluation.

Individualized Treatment

A wide range of treatments are available to help people with alcohol problems. Treatment should be tailored to the individual. Treatment may involve an evaluation, a brief intervention, an outpatient program or counseling, or a residential inpatient stay.

It's important to first determine whether you are alcohol-dependent. If you haven't lost control over your use of alcohol, your treatment may involve reducing your drinking. If you're an alcohol abuser, you may be able to modify your drinking. If you have alcoholism, cutting back is ineffective and inappropriate. Abstinence must be a part of the alcoholic's treatment goal.

For people who aren't dependent on alcohol but are experiencing the adverse effects of drinking, the goal of treatment is reduction of alcohol-related problems, often by counseling or a brief intervention. A brief intervention usually involves alcohol-abuse specialists who can establish a specific treatment plan. Interventions may include goal setting, behavioral modification techniques, use of self-help manuals, counseling and follow-up care at a treatment center.

Many residential alcoholism treatment programs in the United States are based on the "Minnesota Model." This includes abstinence, individual and group therapy, participation in Alcoholics Anonymous, educational lectures, family involvement, work assignments, activity therapy and use of counselors (many of whom are recovering alcoholics) and multiprofessional staff. Contact your insurance provider to determine whether residential treatment is included in your coverage.

In addition to residential treatment, there are many other approaches, including acupuncture, biofeedback, motivational enhancement therapy, cognitive behavior therapy and aversion therapy. Aversion therapy involves pairing the drinking of alcohol with a strong aversive response such as nausea or vomiting induced by a medication. After repeated pairing, the alcohol itself causes the aversive response, and that decreases the likelihood of relapse. For obvious reasons, aversion therapy tends to be unappealing, although it's often effective.

Coping With Teenage Drinking

Although it may take years for many adults to develop alcohol dependence, teenagers can become addicted in months. Alcohol use among teens generally increases with increasing age. However, recent reports suggest alcohol use among teenagers is declining. Each year in the United States, more than 3,000 young people between the ages of 15 and 20 die in alcohol-related automobile accidents, and many more are left disabled. Alcohol is also often implicated in other teenage deaths, including drownings, suicides and fires.

For young people, the likelihood of addiction depends on the influence of parents, peers and other role models, the age they begin using alcohol, susceptibility to advertising, their psychological need for alcohol and genetic factors (family alcoholism) that may predispose them to addiction. Look for these signs:

- Loss of interest in activities and hobbies
- Anxious and irritable
- Difficulties with or changes in relationships with friends — joins a new crowd
- Dropping grades

To prevent teenage alcohol use:

- Set a good example regarding alcohol use.
- Communicate with your children.
- Discuss the legal and medical consequences of drinking.

The Minnesota Model

Here's what you might expect from a typical residential treatment program based in part on the Minnesota Model.

- **Detoxification and withdrawal.** Treatment may begin with a program of detoxification. This usually takes about four to seven days. Medications may be necessary to prevent delirium tremens (DTs) or other withdrawal seizures.
- **Medical assessment and treatment.** Common medical problems related to alcoholism are high blood pressure, increased blood sugar, and liver and heart disease.
- **Psychological support and psychiatric treatment.** Group and individual counseling and therapy support recovery from the psychological aspects of alcoholism. Sometimes, emotional symptoms of the disease may mimic psychiatric disorders.
- **Recovery programs.** Detoxification and medical treatment are only the first steps for most people in a residential treatment program.
- **Acceptance and abstinence are emphasized.** Effective treatment is impossible unless you can accept that you're addicted and unable to control your drinking.
- **Drug treatments.** An alcohol-sensitizing drug called disulfiram (Antabuse) may be useful. If you drink alcohol, the drug produces a severe physical reaction that includes flushing, nausea, vomiting and headaches. Disulfiram won't cure alcoholism nor can it remove the compulsion to drink. But it can be a strong deterrent. Naltrexone, a drug long known to block the narcotic high, recently has been found to reduce the urge to drink in recovering alcoholics. Unlike disulfiram, however, naltrexone doesn't cause a reaction within a few minutes of taking a drink. Naltrexone can produce side effects, particularly liver damage.
- **Continuing support.** Aftercare programs and Alcoholics Anonymous help recovering alcoholics maintain abstinence from alcohol, help to manage any relapses and help with needed lifestyle changes.

FOR MORE INFORMATION

- Alcoholics Anonymous, 475 Riverside Drive, New York, NY 10115. (Check phone book for nearest group.); *www.alcoholics-anonymous.org*.
- Al-Anon Family Group Headquarters, 1600 Corporate Landing Parkway, Virginia Beach, VA 23454; (888) 425-2666.
- National Council on Alcoholism and Drug Dependence, 22 Cortlandt St., Suite 801, New York, NY 10010; 24-hour referral (800) NCA-CALL or (800) 622-2255.

Treatment for Hangover: Avoid Alcohol Altogether

Even small amounts of alcohol can cause unpleasant side effects. Some people develop a flushed feeling, whereas others are sensitive to the chemical tyramine found in red wines, brandy and cognac.

The classic hangover, although well-studied, isn't fully understood. It's probably due to dehydration, byproducts from the breakdown of alcohol, liver injury, overeating and disturbed sleep.

The best treatment for a hangover is prevention and avoiding drinking alcohol. The next best thing is to drink in moderation.

If you have a hangover, it's too late to do much to improve your health and function. A lot of hangover remedies have been tried, but there isn't much evidence that they help — and they may hurt.

If you have a hangover, follow this advice:

- Rest and rehydrate. Drink bland liquids (water, soda, some fruit juices or broth). Avoid acidic, caffeinated or alcohol-containing beverages.
- Use over-the-counter pain medication with care (see page 258).

■ Smoking and Tobacco Use

When you inhale the smoke of a cigarette, you're letting loose a chemical parade that will march through some of your body's vital organs — brain, lungs, heart and blood vessels. Cigarette smoke delivers to your body at least 75 known cancer-causing chemicals — tiny amounts of poisons such as arsenic and cyanide, and more than 4,000 other substances. About 440,000 Americans die annually from smoking cigarettes. One-fifth of all deaths in the United States are smoking-related.

Nicotine, one of the key ingredients in tobacco, is a powerfully addictive substance. It's the nicotine that keeps you smoking. It increases the amount of a brain chemical called dopamine, which produces feelings of pleasure and satisfaction. Getting that "dopamine boost" is part of the addiction process, making you want to keep smoking to re-experience the pleasure. It also triggers your adrenal glands to produce hormones that stress your heart by increasing blood pressure and heart rate.

Another reason people continue to smoke is because they've become accustomed to smoking in certain situations, and they find it very difficult to break these ingrained habits. This includes having a cigarette: with the first cup of coffee in the morning, while driving, after meals, to relieve a stressful situation, and as a reward for making it through a difficult event.

■ How to Stop Smoking

Many smokers want to stop, but find it hard because of nicotine's powerful addictive hold. In fact, most people need more than one attempt before they successfully stop. Here are some suggestions to help you stop smoking:

Do your homework. Talk to ex-smokers. Find out how they stopped and what they found helpful. Find a smoking cessation program. Group programs sponsored by the American Cancer Society and the American Lung Association are available in many communities. Your health care provider, a specialist trained in treatment of tobacco dependence, and your state's tobacco quitline (800) QUIT-NOW or (800) 748-8669, or *www.naquitline.com* on the Internet, may be of help.

Make small changes. Limit places where you smoke. Smoke in only one room in your home or even outside. Don't smoke in the car. Buy cigarettes by the pack instead of the carton. Change to a brand that's less satisfying.

Pay attention to your smoking. As you prepare to stop smoking, pay attention to your behavior. When do you smoke? Where? With whom do you smoke? List your key triggers to smoking. Plan to cope with them when you stop. Practice coping with these situations without smoking.

Seek help. Participate in a formal program. The more help you get, the better your chance of success. Studies show that people who participate in formal programs are up to eight times more likely to succeed than those who try on their own.

Be motivated. The key to stopping is commitment. When Mayo Clinic studied the results of its own programs, it found that smokers who were more motivated to stop were twice as likely to be successful in stopping as those who were less motivated. List your reasons for stopping. To increase your motivation, add to the list regularly.

Set a stop date. Make it a day with low stress. Tell your friends, spouse and co-workers your intention. Let them know how they can support your efforts.

■ Nicotine Replacement Therapy

The best-tested treatments currently available to help people stop smoking are based on delivering nicotine to the brain by means other than smoking, or with medications that modify brain chemistry to reduce withdrawal symptoms and other effects that nicotine has on the brain.

Over-the-Counter Medications

Nicotine patch. The patch delivers nicotine through your skin and into your bloodstream. Studies show people who properly use the patch are twice as likely to stop smoking. Place the patch on the least hairy areas of your body (your chest, upper arms or abdomen) in the morning. Rotate locations. Remove the old patch before putting on a new one. Strengths vary by brand. Heavier smokers may need to use more than one patch at a time — under the direction of a doctor. Length of use varies with individual needs. Usually six to eight weeks is necessary to establish the required behavior changes. **Caution:** Up to 50 percent of people get an itchy rash at the site of the patch. If it's a minor redness, use a small amount of hydrocortisone cream on the area after the patch is removed. If it's irritated, you'll need to stop using the patch or switch to another brand. Don't smoke while wearing a patch.

Nicotine gum. This is a gum-like resin that delivers nicotine to the blood through the lining of your mouth. Studies show that people who properly use the gum are more successful than those who try to stop smoking without it. Two strengths are available: 2 and 4 milligrams (mg). Heavier smokers may need the higher dose. Put a piece of gum in your mouth and bite it gently a few times until you experience a tingling or peppery taste. Then park the gum between your cheek and gum. Repeat the process every few minutes. A piece should last about 30 minutes. Use the gum when you feel the urge to smoke or in situations when you know the urge will be present. Initially, you may use up to 10 to 12 pieces a day. Gradually decrease the number over a period of weeks. **Caution:** Rapid chewing and swallowing the saliva inactivates the nicotine and may cause nausea. Read labels carefully.

Nicotine lozenge. The lozenge is like a cough drop that delivers nicotine to your body through the lining of your mouth. It has a mild mint flavor and you move it around in your mouth as it slowly dissolves. It's available without prescription in 2 and 4 mg. doses. You can use a lozenge to control withdrawal symptoms or cravings. When starting, use a minimum of eight to nine lozenges a day but no more than 20 without consulting with your health care provider. Taper use after six to eight weeks.

Prescription Medications

Nicotine nasal spray. The nicotine in the nasal spray is sprayed directly into each nostril where the nicotine is absorbed through nasal membranes into veins, transported to the heart and then sent to the brain. It's a somewhat quicker delivery system than the gum or patch, although it's not nearly as quick as a cigarette. The usual dose is one spray into each nostril. People typically are directed to start with one to two doses an hour; the minimum is eight doses a day and the maximum is 40 doses a day. For most people, use of the spray should be reduced six to eight weeks into the treatment. During the early days of treatment, the spray can be irritating to the nose, causing a hot, peppery feeling along with coughing and sneezing. These symptoms subside in five to seven days.

The nicotine inhaler. It looks like a short cigarette with a plastic mouthpiece into which a cartridge of nicotine is inserted. You puff on it, and it gives off small amounts of nicotine vapors in your mouth. The nicotine is absorbed slowly through the lining of the mouth — not through the lungs as smoke does — and into your bloodstream and then to the brain, relieving withdrawal symptoms.

Bupropion. Bupropion is an antidepressant that is effective in helping people stop smoking. For treatment of depression, it's sold as Wellbutrin. For smoking cessation, it's sold as Zyban. Bupropion increases the level of dopamine, a brain chemical boosted by smoking. Side effects include insomnia and dry mouth. If you have a history of seizures, it may make you more prone to them. Two other prescription medications can be effective alternatives but are considered secondline medications. One is clonidine, a blood pressure medication, and the other is nortriptyline, an antidepressant. Your doctor may recommend one of them if other medications don't work, or if you experience significant side effects. New medications for tobacco cessation are being tested.

Of smokers who would like to quit but are having difficulty, those who combine medication with visits to a health care provider for support and counseling are often more successful than those who try to do it alone. U. S. Public Health Service guidelines recommend use of combination treatments — for example, two nicotine medications or a nicotine medication and bupropion along with professional help.

■ Coping With Nicotine Withdrawal

Below is a list of common withdrawal symptoms and some suggestions for coping.

Problem	Solutions
Craving	• Distract yourself. • Do deep-breathing exercises (see page 227). • Realize that the craving will pass.
Irritability	• Take a few slow, deep breaths. • Image an enjoyable outdoor scene and take a minivacation. • Soak in a hot bath.
Insomnia	• Take a walk several hours before going to bed. • Unwind by reading. • Take a warm bath. • Eat a banana or drink warm milk. • Avoid beverages with caffeine after noon. • See sleep disorders, page 44.
Increased appetite	• Make a personal survival kit that include straws, cinnamon sticks, sugar-free candy, licorice, toothpicks, gum or fresh vegetables. • Drink lots of water or low-calorie liquids.
Inability to concentrate	• Take a brisk walk — outside if possible. • Simplify your schedule for a few days. • Take a break.
Fatigue	• Get more exercise. • Get an adequate amount of sleep. • Take a nap. • Try not to push yourself for two to four weeks.
Constipation, gas, stomach pain	• Drink plenty of fluids. • Add fiber to your diet: fruit, raw vegetables, whole-grain cereals. • Gradually change your diet. • See constipation, page 58; gas, page 60.

Source: Mayo Nicotine Dependence Center

■ Teenage Smoking: What Can Be Done?

What's the harm in children and teens experimenting with cigarettes? Cigarette smoking is rapidly addictive. Most teenagers overestimate their ability to stop once they start. Many teenagers believe that they can stop smoking anytime they choose. The reality is that among high-school seniors who smoke from one to five cigarettes a day, about 60 percent will still be smoking five years later. About three-fourths of those who smoke in high school have unsuccessfully tried to stop.

Here are some strategies parents might try to help keep children from smoking:

- **Learn what your children think about smoking.**
- **Help your child explore personal feelings about peer pressure and smoking.**
- **Encourage your teenager to stay physically active.**
- **Note the social repercussions of smoking.**
- **Set a personal example of not smoking.**
- **Help your child find alternatives to smoking.**

Chewing tobacco

Call it what you want — smokeless tobacco, spit tobacco, chew, snuff, pinch, plug or dip — but don't call it harmless. If you're considering making the switch from cigarettes to chewing tobacco because you think the smokeless version of tobacco won't hurt you, be warned — chewing tobacco can also cause serious health problems.

- **Addiction.** Chewing tobacco gets you hooked on nicotine, similar to the way cigarettes get you hooked. And once you're addicted, it becomes difficult to stop using chewing tobacco.
- **Cavities and gum disease.** Chewing tobacco and other forms of smokeless tobacco cause tooth decay. That's because chewing tobacco contains high amounts of sugar, which contributes to cavities, and coarse particles that can irritate your gums, scratch away at the enamel on your teeth and cause gum disease (gingivitis).

- **Heart problems.** Smokeless tobacco increases your heart rate and blood pressure. Some evidence suggests that it may put you at an increased risk of heart attack. People who use smokeless tobacco also have higher cholesterol levels than those of people who don't use tobacco.
- **Precancerous mouth sores.** People who use smokeless tobacco are more likely to develop small white patches called leukoplakia (loo-ko-PLA-ke-uh) inside their mouths. These mouth sores are considered precancerous — meaning that the sores could one day develop into cancer.
- **Oral cancer.** Your risk of oral cancer is increased if you use smokeless tobacco. Oral cancer includes cancers of the mouth, throat, cheek, gums, lips and tongue. Surgery to remove cancer from any of these areas can leave your jaw, chin, neck or face disfigured.

The Dangers of Secondhand Smoke

The health threat to the nonsmoker from exposure to tobacco smoke is well documented. Secondhand smoke exposure is associated with lung cancer and heart disease in nonsmokers. Most states have enacted laws limiting smoking in public places.

People with respiratory or heart conditions and the very young and very old in general are at special health risk when exposed to secondhand smoke. Infants are three times more likely to die of sudden infant death syndrome if their mothers smoke during and after pregnancy.

Children younger than 1 year who are exposed to smoke have a higher frequency of admissions to hospitals for respiratory illness than do children of parents who don't smoke. Secondhand smoke increases a child's risk of getting ear infections, pneumonia, bronchitis and tonsillitis.

■ Drug Dependency

Dependency on drugs (<u>drug addiction</u>), whether prescription or illegal, is dangerous because of its long-term physical effects, its disruptive effect on family and work, and the potential risks of sudden withdrawal. Medical help is often essential to quitting.

Common Drugs of Abuse

Glue. Children may sniff glue, which is a central nervous system depressant. At first, a few sniffs may give a high, but the child develops a tolerance in a matter of weeks. The initial symptoms mimic alcoholic inebriation, including slurred speech, dizziness, breakdown of inhibitions, drowsiness and amnesia. The child may have hallucinations, lose weight and lose consciousness.

Central nervous system stimulants (amphetamines and cocaine). Known as uppers, amphetamines produce an extraordinarily strong psychological dependence that amounts to a compulsion. Abusers develop a high degree of tolerance to the euphoric effects, which last for several hours. Methamphetamines ("meth") are produced as pills, powder or chunky crystals. Most of the chemicals used to make meth are found in household products or nonprescription medicines, adding to the popularity of meth use. Signs of meth use include excited speech, agitation, irritability, false sense of confidence, violent behavior, intense paranoia and hallucinations. Cocaine triggers the release of chemicals in your body that stimulate your heart to pump faster and harder. These reactions result in the rush of euphoria, the illusion of control and heightened sexual drive. Injecting or smoking cocaine ("crack") can be more dangerous because a greater amount of it goes into your bloodstream.

Opioids. Opium is produced from the milky discharge from seeds of the poppy plant. Opioids include substances naturally produced from opium, such as heroin and morphine (opiates) and synthetic substances that have morphine-like action. Physicians may prescribe them as pain relievers, anesthetics or cough suppressants (such as codeine and methadone). Signs of abuse include depression, anxiety, impulsiveness, low frustration tolerance and the need for immediate gratification.

Marijuana and hashish. Marijuana is made from the leaves and flowers of the hemp plant, *Cannabis sativa*. Hashish comes from the resin of the same plant. Your body absorbs the psychoactive substances in these drugs. These compounds affect your concentration and perceptual and motor functions. Chronic users have an increased heart rate, redness of the eyes and a decrease in lung function. Withdrawal symptoms include aggression, irritability, stomach discomfort and anxiety.

Hallucinogens. Lysergic acid diethylamide (LSD) produces profound changes in mood and thought processes, resulting in hallucinations and a state resembling acute psychosis. Acute panic reactions may occur, as may rapid heart rate, hypertension and tremors. The most common street preparation of PCP (phencyclidine) is called angel dust, a white granular powder. In low doses (5 mg), PCP produces excitement, incoordination and absence of sensation (analgesic). In high doses, it can cause drooling, vomiting, stupor or coma. When there's acute psychosis associated with PCP, the person is at high risk of suicide or violence toward others.

Designer drugs. These drugs became popular in the 1990s. They're formulated to achieve specific effects and to chemically modify existing drugs to avoid criminal prosecution under current laws. Names include Ecstasy, Adam, Eve and China White. Use of these drugs produces intoxication and has caused serious medical conditions, including movement disorders and death.

Medical Help	Drug users may require intervention on the part of family and friends, and may require hospitalization for detoxification. Follow-up outpatient programs lasting weeks, months or even years may be necessary to prevent a relapse.

FOR MORE INFORMATION
- National Institute on Drug Abuse, NIH, 6001 Executive Blvd., Rockville, MD 20852; *www.drugabuse.gov.*
- Narcotics Anonymous (NA), World Services Office, P.O. Box 9999, Van Nuys, CA 91409; 818-773-9999; *www.na.org.*

How to Identify Drug Use Among Teenagers

These clues are only possible indications that your teenager is using drugs:

- **School.** The child suddenly shows an active dislike of school and looks for excuses to stay home. Contact school officials to see if your child's attendance record matches what you know about his or her absent days. An A or B student who suddenly begins to fail courses or receives only minimally passing grades may be using drugs.
- **Physical health.** Listlessness and apathy are possible indications of drug use.
- **Appearance.** Appearance is extremely important to adolescents. A significant warning sign can be a sudden lack of interest in clothing or looks.
- **Personal behavior.** Teenagers enjoy their privacy. However, be wary of exaggerated efforts to bar you from going into their bedrooms or knowing where they go with their friends.
- **Money.** Sudden requests for more money without a reasonable explanation for its use may be an indication of drug use.

What can you do?

Adolescents need to feel that there's an open line of communication with their parents. Even in the face of your child's reluctance to share feelings, continue to express an interest in listening to your child talk about his or her experiences.

■ Compulsive Gambling

Gambling odds, as the saying goes, are stacked in favor of the house. But that doesn't stop people from trying. The amount gambled yearly in the United States is estimated at more than $50 billion. Since 1975, the gambling industry in the United States has grown tenfold.

Most people who wager don't have a problem. But a minority — an estimated 1 percent to 3 percent of the general population — become compulsive gamblers. People in this group lose control of their betting, often with serious and sometimes fatal consequences.

What Is Compulsive Gambling?
The American Psychiatric Association (APA) classifies compulsive gambling as an impulse-control disorder. To meet the APA's diagnostic criteria for compulsive gambling, a person must show persistent gambling behavior as indicated by at least five of the following criteria:

---

1. Being preoccupied with gambling (for example, being preoccupied with reliving past gambling experiences, handicapping or planning the next venture, thinking of ways to get money with which to gamble)
2. Needing to gamble with increasing amounts of money to achieve desired excitement
3. Having repeated unsuccessful efforts to cut back or stop gambling
4. Being restless or irritable when attempting to cut down or stop gambling
5. Gambling as a way of escaping problems or of relieving a dysphoric mood (feelings of helplessness, guilt, anxiety, depression)
6. After losing money gambling, often returning another day to get even — chasing one's losses
7. Lying to family members, therapist or others to conceal extent of involvement with gambling
8. Having committed illegal acts such as forgery, fraud, theft or embezzlement to finance gambling
9. Having jeopardized or lost a significant relationship, job or educational or career opportunity because of gambling
10. Relying on others to provide money to relieve a desperate financial situation caused by gambling

Medical Help

The best therapy probably resembles the best therapy for other forms of addiction. That involves education and development of a therapeutic relationship with another person or group of people with the intent to stop gambling.

- **Group therapy** provides support and encouragement and helps reduce the use of defense mechanisms. People who have "been there" can see through a person's denial and help confront the problem.
- **Medications** to ease the process of recovery are being investigated. Some of the drugs being considered are those that have been helpful in treating diseases such as alcoholism, obsessive-compulsive disorders and depression.
- **Gamblers Anonymous** provides a 12-step program patterned after that of Alcoholics Anonymous. For people who wonder whether they may have a gambling problem, Gamblers Anonymous publishes a list of 20 questions as a screening tool and provides a list of local chapters. You may also find state-sponsored help groups in your local telephone directory. Gamblers Anonymous has more than 1,200 U.S. locations and 20 international chapters.

Signs of an Uncontrollable Urge to Gamble

You may have a gambling addiction if:
- You take time from work and family life to gamble.
- You gamble in secret.
- You feel remorse after gambling and repeatedly vow to quit. You may even quit for a while and then start again.
- You don't plan to gamble. You just "end up" gambling. And you gamble until your last dollar is gone.

- You gamble with money you need to pay bills or solve financial problems. You lie, steal, borrow or sell things to get gambling money.
- When you lose, you gamble to win back your losses. When you win, you gamble to win more. You dream of the "big win" and what it will buy.
- You gamble when you feel down or when you feel like celebrating.

Anxiety and Panic Disorders

It can happen at any time. Suddenly, your heart begins to race, your face flushes and you have trouble breathing. You feel dizzy, nauseated, out of control — some people even feel like they are dying. Each year, thousands of Americans have an experience like this. Many, thinking they're having a heart attack, go to an emergency room. Others try to ignore it, not realizing that they've experienced a panic attack.

Panic attacks are sudden episodes of intense fear that prompt physical reactions in your body. Approximately 2 percent of the population is affected by such attacks. Once dismissed as "nerves" or stress, a panic attack is now recognized as a potentially disabling but treatable condition.

Tripping an Alarm System

Panic attacks typically begin in young adulthood and can happen throughout your life. An episode usually begins abruptly, peaks within 10 minutes and lasts about half an hour. Symptoms can include a rapid heart rate, sweating, trembling and shortness of breath. You may have chills, hot flashes, nausea, abdominal cramping, chest pain and dizziness. Tightness in your throat or trouble swallowing is common.

If panic attacks are frequent, or if fear of having them affects your activities, you may have a condition called panic disorder. Women are more likely than men to have panic attacks. Researchers aren't sure why or what causes panic attacks. Heredity may play a role — your chance of having panic attacks increases if you have a close family member who has had them.

Many researchers believe your body's natural fight-or-flight response to danger is involved. For example, if a grizzly bear came after you, your body would react instinctively. Your heart and breathing would speed up as your body readied itself for a life-threatening situation. Many of the same reactions occur in a panic attack. No obvious stressor is present, but something trips your body's alarm system.

Other health problems — such as an impending heart attack, hyperthyroidism or drug withdrawal — can cause symptoms similar to panic attacks. If you have symptoms of a panic attack, seek medical care.

Treatment Options

Fortunately, treatment for panic attacks and panic disorder is very effective. Most people are able to resume everyday activities. Treatment may involve:

- **Education.** Knowing what you experienced is the first step in learning to manage it. Your doctor may give you information and teach you coping techniques.
- **Medication.** Your doctor may prescribe an antidepressant, even though you aren't depressed. Antidepressants usually are effective for preventing future attacks. In some cases, a tranquilizer may be given alone or with other medications. Effectiveness varies. The duration of treatment depends on the severity of your disorder and your response to treatment.
- **Therapy.** During sessions with a psychiatrist or psychologist, coping skills and management of anxiety triggers are taught. Most people need only eight to 10 sessions. Long-term psychotherapy usually isn't necessary.
- **Relaxation techniques.** See page 227.

FOR MORE INFORMATION

- National Mental Health Association, 2001 N. Beauregard St., 12th Floor, Alexandria, VA 22311; (800) 969-6642; *www.nmha.org*.

Depression and the Blues

Almost everyone has the blues from time to time — a period of several days or a week in which you seem to be in a funk. This condition usually goes away, and you resume your normal patterns. Nevertheless, having the blues is troublesome, and there are steps you can take to avoid them.

Having the blues isn't the same as having clinical depression. The blues are temporary and usually go away after a short time.

Depression is a persistent medical illness, but one that can be treated. It may improve eventually, but leaving it untreated typically means it will persist for many months or longer. If you're depressed, you may find little, if any, joy in life. You may have no energy, feel unworthy or guilty for no reason, find it difficult to concentrate or be irritable. You might wake up after only a few hours of sleep or experience changes in appetite — eating less than usual or eating too much. You may experience a sense of hopelessness or even consider suicide (see page 202). A person with depression may have some, most or all of these symptoms. The following list shows the different signs for depression and the blues:

Signs of depression
- Persistent lack of energy
- Lasting sadness
- Irritability and mood swings
- Recurring sense of hopelessness
- Continual negative view of the world and others
- Overeating or loss of appetite
- Feelings of unworthiness or guilt
- Inability to concentrate
- Recurrent early morning awakening or other changes in sleep patterns
- Inability to enjoy pleasurable activities
- Feeling as though you'd be better off dead

Signs of the blues
- Feeling down for a few days but still able to function normally in daily activities
- Occasional lack of energy, or a mild change in sleeping patterns
- Ability to enjoy some recreational activities
- Stable weight
- A quickly passing feeling of hopelessness

Self-Care for the Blues

If your mood falls into the blues column, try these things:
- Share your feelings. Talk to a trusted friend, spouse, family member or your spiritual counselor. They can offer you support, guidance and perspective.
- Spend time with other people.
- Engage in activities that have interested you in the past, particularly activities that you have enjoyed.
- Regular moderate exercise may lift your mood.
- Get adequate rest and eat balanced meals.
- Don't undertake too much at one time. If you have large tasks to do, break them into smaller ones. Set goals you can accomplish.
- Look for small opportunities to be helpful to someone less fortunate.
- Avoid alcohol and sedative drugs.

See back cover for online resource

Causes of Depression

Every year in the United States, approximately 19 million adults have a depressive illness. Occasionally, it's a side effect of a prescription drug, illness or poor diet. Imbalances of certain brain chemicals may be a factor. But often the cause is unclear.

You're at a higher risk of depression if a blood relative has had it. Depression also may recur. If you've had it once, you're at a higher risk of developing it again. Don't let these factors control your life. But be aware of them in assessing your mood. And don't delay seeking medical attention if you notice recurrent depressive symptoms. In addition, if you're being treated for depression by one clinician, let your other health care providers know so that confusion and medication interactions can be avoided.

Depression may also be preceded by a severe shock or stress in life, such as the death of a loved one (see below) or the loss of a job, or it can arise when things are going very well. Certainly it's normal to feel sad after losses or setbacks. But if that sadness doesn't stop fairly quickly, a serious depression likely has developed.

Depression may not go away by itself. Don't expect to snap out of it all of a sudden or expect to be able to beat your depression through sheer determination. If depressive symptoms last more than a few weeks, or if you're feeling hopeless or suicidal, it's time to seek help. Don't blame yourself for feeling depressed. It's not your fault, and it's not a sign of weakness.

Contact your family doctor or ask for a referral to a psychiatrist. A psychiatrist, just as your family physician, is trained as a medical doctor and can help you exclude significant medical illnesses that might be contributing to your symptoms.

If your symptoms have been mild — but persistent — a psychologist may be helpful. A psychologist is trained in various types of psychotherapy but doesn't have a medical degree. Discussing feelings with a family member or close friend is helpful, but it's no substitute for seeking professional help.

If you know someone who's depressed, invite him or her to take part in normal social activities. Gently but firmly encourage participation. But don't overdo it. Friends and family should encourage and support professional care. The problem shouldn't be trivialized, but rather it should be viewed as an opportunity to help, because depression can be treated successfully in most cases. Offer reassurance that things will get better, but don't expect a depressed person to improve suddenly. Don't minimize a depressed person's feelings. Instead, listen carefully to what he or she says.

Seasonal affective disorder, another form of depression, seems to be related to light exposure. It occurs in northern and southern hemispheres but is rare in people living near the equator, where daylight hours are long. The disorder is more common in women than men and sometimes is treated with increased light exposure during the day, obtained with a light box containing a source of bright broad-spectrum light.

Coping With Loss: Practical Suggestions

- **Express your feelings.** Write a book of memories, or even a letter to the person who died.
- **Ask for help.** When we experience sudden loss, our friends may not know how to respond. We can relieve others and help ourselves by asking for specific kinds of help.
- **Stay involved.** People who grieve may need to remind themselves about exercise, diet and rest.
- **Evaluate yourself for depression.** If the grief is extremely severe in the short run or persistent over the long run (six months or more), consider depression as a possible cause.

■ Treatment Options

Most people who have depression improve a great deal when treated with anti-depressant medicines. There are more than a dozen such medicines, some of which work in different ways. A doctor will select a medicine likely to be helpful. Discuss potential side effects with your doctor. If you experience symptoms that concern you, call the doctor who prescribed the medication. Common side effects may include nausea, fatigue and drowsiness, **dry mouth**, insomnia, **constipation**, blurred vision, dizziness, jitteriness, weight gain and sexual side effects. Among children, antidepressants have been linked to suicidal behavior. Talk to your child's doctor about the benefits and risks of antidepressant use.

Other treatment methods include talking about your feelings (psychotherapy) and other programs with a psychiatrist, psychologist or other qualified professional. There are various kinds of psychotherapy, some involving just the patient and the therapist, others involving a group of people with the same general problem who meet to discuss their situation under the guidance of a therapist.

Treatment takes time. Some signs of change may be evident in as little as two weeks, but full benefit may require six weeks or more. That process can be discouraging, so it's important for friends and family to give support and encouragement during this time when medications may need adjustment. In addition, you may need to stay on medication for six to nine months after you're feeling well again.

Someone who is being treated shouldn't expect a sudden dramatic change in mood and activity. Look for gradual improvement in sleep and mood and a slow improvement in appetite and level of energy.

Aside from making sure that the person providing the treatment is qualified, it's important to feel comfortable with your clinician. He or she should listen to you describe your problem, ask questions, discuss findings and recommendations and explain possible risks and alternatives to the treatments being recommended.

Warning Signs of Potential Suicide

It's important to keep in mind that these warning signs are only guidelines. There's no one type of suicidal person. If you're concerned, seek help immediately.

- **Withdrawal.** Unwilling to communicate and appears to have an overwhelming urge to be alone.
- **Moodiness.** An emotional high one day followed by being down in the dumps. Sudden, inexplicable calm.
- **Life crisis or trauma.** Divorce, death, an accident or the loss of self-esteem that may occur after loss of a job or a financial setback may produce suicidal thinking.

- **Personality change.** A change in attitude, personal appearance or activities. An introvert suddenly becomes an extrovert.
- **Threats.** The popular assumption that people who threaten suicide don't do it isn't true.
- **Gift giving.** The person bequeaths cherished belongings to friends and loved ones.
- **Depression.** The person appears to be physically depressed and may be unable to function socially or in the workplace.
- **Risk taking.** The suicidal urge may be manifested in sudden participation in high-speed driving or unsafe sex.

FOR MORE INFORMATION

- National Mental Health Association, 2001 N. Beauregard St., 12th Floor, Alexandria, VA 22311; (800) 969-6642; *www.nmha.org*.

Domestic Abuse

Beatings, forced sex, being afraid of violence from a spouse or partner or living in fear that your spouse or partner will harm or abuse your children: All of these situations are examples of domestic abuse.

Women predominantly, but not exclusively, suffer domestic abuse. Every year, between 2 million and 4 million women are battered and about 1,200 women are murdered by a husband, ex-husband or partner. Domestic violence can happen among people of all races, ages, income levels and religious groups.

Battering is the use of physical force to control and maintain power over another person. Domestic abuse may also involve intimidation, psychological abuse, harassment, humiliation and threats.

Symptoms of Abusive Behavior

You may be in an abusive relationship if you:

- Have ever been hit, kicked, shoved or threatened with violence
- Feel that you have no choice about how you spend your time, where you go or what you wear
- Have been accused by your partner of things you've never done
- Must ask your partner for permission to make everyday decisions
- Go along with your partner's decisions because you're afraid of his or her anger

Self-Care

How to Respond

- If you're concerned about the potential for physical abuse, talk to someone as soon as possible. Local crisis hot lines are one option. Social service agencies are another. Confide in a friend, physician or member of the clergy.
- If you're in an abusive relationship, have a flight plan. Be prepared to take your children, house keys and important papers. It's important to be alert. Be ready to leave at a moment's notice.
- Keep cash on hand in case of an emergency.
- Keep a list of phone numbers of friends who may be able to help you.
- Know the number of a women's shelter.

Professional Help

Some people are reluctant to discuss these issues because it's embarrassing to talk openly about such matters with strangers. But by calling a social service agency or confiding in a counselor, feelings of embarrassment or shame can be discussed.

If police are called, request a timely and serious response. Some jurisdictions have a mandatory arrest law, which means that an abuser will be removed from the home while the case is adjudicated.

If you go to a shelter, expect to be safe and to receive counseling. You should also inquire about legal assistance (for instance, the possibility of obtaining a restraining order that would legally bar the abuser from having contact with you).

Counseling should also be available as a means to provide support and discussion of your feelings. Counselors should discuss with you the decision as to whether to pursue legal action.

FOR MORE INFORMATION

- National Domestic Violence Hotline, (800) 799-7233
- National Organization for Victim Assistance, (800) 879-6682

Memory Loss

All of us experience recent memory loss. We can't remember where we put the car keys, or we forget the name of a person we just met. This is normal. But if memory loss is persistent, you need to see a health care professional.

An infant is born with billions of brain cells. With age, some of these brain cells die and aren't replaced. As we grow older, our bodies also produce less of the chemicals that our brain cells need to work. Although short-term and long-term memory aren't usually affected, recent memory can deteriorate with age.

The three types of memory are described below:

- **Short-term memory.** This is your temporary memory. You may look up a number in the phone book, but after you dial the number you forget it. Once you've finished using the information, it vanishes.
- **Recent memory.** This is memory that preserves the recent past, such as what you ate for breakfast today or what you wore yesterday.
- **Long-term memory.** This is memory that preserves the distant past, such as recollections from childhood.

Memory loss can be caused by many things: a side effect of medications, a head injury, alcoholism or a stroke. Hearing and vision problems can affect memory. Pregnant women sometimes have short-term or recent memory problems.

<u>Alzheimer's disease</u> is the most common form of dementia. Symptoms include gradual loss of memory for recent events and inability to learn new information; a growing tendency to repeat oneself, misplace objects, become confused and get lost; a slow disintegration of personality, judgment and social graces; and increasing irritability, anxiety, depression, confusion and restlessness.

Self-Care to Improve Your Memory	<ul><li>**Establish a routine.** Managing your daily activities is easier when you follow a routine. Choose a set time to do household chores — clean the bathroom on Saturday, water the plants on Sunday.</li><li>**Exercise your 'mental muscles.'** Play word games, crossword puzzles or other activities that challenge your mental abilities.</li><li>**Practice.** When you walk into a room, make a mental inventory of people you recognize. When you meet someone, repeat his or her name in conversation.</li><li>**Nudge the numbers.** For example, if your wife's birthday is October 3, do something to remind you, such as hum the song "Three Coins in a Fountain."</li><li>**Make associations.** When driving, look for landmarks to associate with your route and name them out loud to imprint them on your memory. Example: "Turn left at the high school to get to Bob's house."</li><li>**Try not to worry.** Fretting about memory loss can make it worse.</li><li>**Write lists.** Keep track of important tasks and appointments. For example, pay the water bill on a certain day each month.</li></ul>
Medical Help	Consult a health care provider if you're concerned about memory loss.

FOR MORE INFORMATION

- Alzheimer's Association, 225 N. Michigan Ave., 17th Floor, Chicago IL 60601; (800) 272-3900; *www.alz.org*.

Staying Healthy

- **Weight: What's Healthy for You?**
- **Eating Well**
- **Lowering Your Cholesterol**
- **Physical Activity and Fitness**
- **Screening and Immunizations**
- **Keeping Stress Under Control**
- **Protecting Yourself**
- **Hand Washing**
- **Aging and Your Health**

This section is filled with practical information about how you can improve your health by establishing and maintaining a healthy lifestyle.

Weight: What's Healthy for You?

It seems almost everywhere you turn these days, you're bombarded by diets and weight-loss schemes. Weight loss sells! However, as anyone who has tried to lose weight knows, doing so isn't easy. Success at losing weight requires the key ingredients of knowledge, commitment, healthy eating and regular physical activity.

For most overweight Americans, <u>**weight loss**</u> is a healthy goal. Losing weight often means a reduced risk of heart disease, diabetes and high blood pressure. However, some people, often women, who aren't fat are trying to lose pounds. For them, losing weight offers no healthful benefits and may even be detrimental.

The Risks of Being Overweight

Your desirable weight is the weight at which you're as healthy as possible. And your weight is only one part of the lifestyle picture that contributes to your long-term health.

Being overweight may place you at risk of:

- Increased blood pressure
- Heart disease
- Type 2 diabetes
- Deteriorating joints
- Abnormal blood fats
- Certain cancers
- Chronic low back pain
- Gallstones
- Respiratory problems

Losing weight can be a challenge. Of people who lose weight, especially those who lose it rapidly, a majority regain the weight within one to five years. So, what should you do? First, determine how much you're overweight, and then develop a safe and healthy weight management program.

Your body has a nearly unlimited capacity to store fat. Losing weight reduces crowding of your organs and the strain on your lower back, hips and knees.

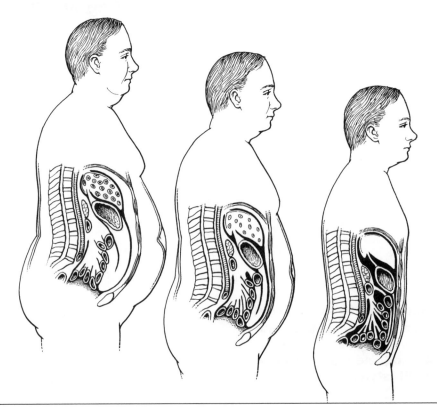

See back cover for online resource ⓘ

■ Determining Your Body Mass Index

What is a healthy weight? If you have high blood pressure or if you're at risk of high blood pressure, it's not critical that you become "thin." But you should try to achieve or maintain a weight that improves control of your blood pressure and also lessens your risks of other health problems.

Two do-it-yourself evaluations can tell you whether your weight is healthy or whether you could benefit from losing a few pounds.

Body Mass Index

The first step in determining your healthy weight is to figure out your body mass index (BMI). You can do that by using the chart below.

A BMI of 19 to 24.9 is desirable. If your BMI is 25 to 29.9, you're overweight. You're considered obese if you have a BMI of 30 or more. Extreme **obesity** is a BMI of more than 40.

You're at increased risk for development of a weight-related disease, such as high blood pressure, if your BMI is 25 or greater.

Body Mass Index (BMI)

BMI	Healthy		Overweight					Obese				
	19	**24**	25	26	27	28	29	30	35	40	45	50
Height					Weight in Pounds							
4'10"	91	115	119	124	129	134	138	143	167	191	215	239
4'11"	94	119	124	128	133	138	143	148	173	198	222	247
5'0"	97	123	128	133	138	143	148	153	179	204	230	255
5'1"	100	127	132	137	143	148	153	158	185	211	238	264
5'2"	104	131	136	142	147	153	158	164	191	218	246	273
5'3"	107	135	141	146	152	158	163	169	197	225	254	282
5'4"	110	140	145	151	157	163	169	174	204	232	262	291
5'5"	114	144	150	156	162	168	174	180	210	240	270	300
5'6"	118	148	155	161	167	173	179	186	216	247	278	309
5'7"	121	153	159	166	172	178	185	191	223	255	287	319
5'8"	125	158	164	171	177	184	190	197	230	262	295	328
5'9"	128	162	169	176	182	189	196	203	236	270	304	338
5'10"	132	167	174	181	188	195	202	209	243	278	313	348
5'11"	136	172	179	186	193	200	208	215	250	286	322	358
6'0"	140	177	184	191	199	206	213	221	258	294	331	368
6'1"	144	182	189	197	204	212	219	227	265	302	340	378
6'2"	148	186	194	202	210	218	225	233	272	311	350	389
6'3"	152	192	200	208	216	224	232	240	279	319	359	399
6'4"	156	197	205	213	221	230	238	246	287	328	369	410

Note: Asians with a BMI of 23 or higher may have an increased risk of health problems.
Source: National Institutes of Health, 1998

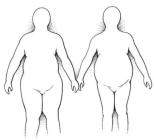

Pear shape   Apple shape

It's not only how much you weigh that's important but also where your body stores extra fat. People with an apple shape tend to have a higher risk of health problems than do people with a pear shape.

Waist Circumference

This measurement is second to your BMI in importance. It indicates where most of your fat is located. People who carry most of their weight around their waists are referred to as having an apple shape. Those who carry most of their weight below their waist, around their hips and thighs, are said to have a pear shape.

Generally, it's better to have a pear shape than an apple shape. Fat accumulation around your waist is associated with an increased risk of high blood pressure, diabetes, abnormal blood fats, such as high triglycerides, and coronary artery disease. That's because fat in your abdomen is more harmful. The exact mechanism for why this is hasn't been proved, although resistance to the effects of insulin is a key feature.

To determine whether you're carrying too much weight around your abdomen, measure your waist circumference. Find the highest point on each of your hipbones and measure across your abdomen just above those points. A measurement of more than 40 inches (102 centimeters) in men and 35 inches (88 centimeters) in women signifies increased health risks, especially if you have a BMI of 25 or more. In general, the greater the waist measurement the greater the health risks.

■ Tips on Losing Weight

To lose weight, you need to modify your lifestyle. This often means making changes in your diet and physical activity level. Commit to losing weight and work to gradually change your eating and exercise habits. It's long-term changes that spell success.

Self-Care

Getting started:
- **Determine a good time to begin your weight-loss program.** It's best to start when you can devote some time and attention to making changes in your life. A hectic schedule, stress or depression can be barriers to a successful start.
- **Set reasonable weight-loss goals** (long- and short-term). If you want to lose 40 pounds, start with a short-term goal of losing 5 pounds the first month.
- **Check your food intake carefully.** Most adults underestimate how many calories they are eating. It's usually reasonable to cut 500 to 1,000 calories a day from what you're currently eating to produce a weight loss of 1 to 2 pounds a week. On average, women should aim for 1,200 calories a day and men 1,400 calories a day. Diets that restrict you to fewer than 1,200 calories a day may not meet your daily nutritional needs. (Refer to Eating Well, page 210.)
- **Keep a food journal.** People who write down everything they eat are more successful at long-term weight maintenance. In addition, record factors that influence your eating behaviors, such as stress or skipping meals.

Improve food selections:
- **Enjoy more healthy foods.** See the Mayo Clinic Healthy Weight Pyramid on page 211 for healthy diet recommendations. Keep healthy foods on hand, both for meals and snacking. Plan snacks.
- **Eat more vegetables and fruits.** They help you feel full and don't contain a lot of calories. Eat at least three fruit and four vegetable servings daily.
- **Limit fat in your diet.** You can lower your fat intake dramatically by eating less meat and, eating skim or low-fat dairy products and avoiding fried foods, fat-laden desserts and fatty add-ons such as margarine, mayonnaise and salad dressing.

- **Limit sugar and sweets.** Both are high in calories and low in other nutrients. Sweets such as candy and desserts also can be high in fat.
- **Consider what you drink.** Limit regular soft drinks. Alcohol, also high in calories, can increase your appetite and decrease your willpower. Low-fat milk and juices should be within limits — they have calories too. Drink water. Occasional diet soft drinks are OK.

Change eating behaviors:
- **Don't skip meals.** Eat at regular times to keep your appetite and food selections under better control.
- **Serve yourself and other family members,** rather than placing the entire dish of food on the table. This helps prevent taking second helpings.
- **Use a smaller plate.** Doing so encourages you to take smaller portions, while still appearing as though your plate is "full."
- **Focus on eating.** Don't reading or watch television while you're eating.
- **Stop eating when you're full.** Contrary to what your mother may have taught you, you don't have to clean your plate.
- **Try to ride out food cravings** when they hit. They usually pass in minutes. If not, eat something healthy and low in calories.

Other suggestions:
- **Don't weigh yourself too often.** Once a week is often enough.
- **Use a daily multiple vitamin/mineral supplement** if you're limiting your calories to 1,200 a day and feel you're not getting adequate vitamins and minerals.
  Being excessively overweight (medically complicated obesity) can greatly affect some people's health. For these people, medications to suppress appetite, or surgery may be necessary to improve their health. Any of these approaches must be done under the careful supervision of a physician. However, without a change in eating habits, even these more radical steps may fail.

■ Physical Activity: The Key to Burning Calories

Physical activity and exercise are important to any weight-loss program. Make changes gradually, especially if you are out of shape. If you're older than 40, you're a smoker, you've had a heart attack or you have diabetes, consult your doctor before you start an exercise program. An exercise stress test can assess your risks and limitations.

Self-Care

- **Try to find one or more activities that you enjoy** and can do regularly. Begin slowly, and increase gradually to your goal. Your goal is to maintain moderate activity for at least 30 minutes or more every day — preferably 60 minutes.
- **Your activity doesn't need to be overly strenuous** to produce positive results. You can achieve your goal through moderate, regular exercise like walking.
- **Vary your exercises** to improve overall fitness and to keep it interesting.
- **Break up your activity into 5- to 10-minute increments.** Every activity counts.
- **Find an exercise partner.** It may help you stick to your schedule.
- **Little things can add up.** Park at the far end of the parking lot. Take the stairs rather than the elevator. Get off the bus a stop or two early and walk.
- **Keep a log of your activity.**
- **Stick with your exercise schedule.** Don't use lack of time as an excuse.

Eating Well

The food you eat is the source of energy and nutrition for your body. And, of course, eating is a pleasurable experience for most people. Getting enough food is rarely a problem, but getting good nutrition can be a challenge. To feel well, ward off disease and perform at a peak level, you need balanced nutrition.

Many chronic diseases (heart disease, cancer and stroke) are, in part, caused by eating too much of the wrong kinds of food. For most people, the best approach to good nutrition is to follow the principles of the Mayo Clinic Healthy Weight Pyramid, which advises that you do the following:

- Aim for a healthy weight.
- Be physically active every day.
- Make vegetables and fruits the foundation of your diet. They're low in fat and calories and contain many disease-fighting nutrients.
- Eat grain products, such as bread and pasta, made from whole grains.
- Consume low-fat or fat-free dairy products.
- Eat more plant sources of protein, such as beans, lentils and peas, and less meat.
- Try to eat fish — which contains healthy omega-3 fatty acids — twice a week.
- Limit fats, and select monounsaturated sources found in olive and canola oils, avocados and nuts.
- Limit sweets to 75 calories a day.
- If you drink alcoholic beverages, do so in moderation.

Eat More Fruits and Vegetables for a Healthy Diet

Fruits and vegetables contain many nutrients known to protect health.

Practically all fruits are desirable, but some fruits are better than others. Whole fresh and frozen fruits are best because they're higher in fiber and lower in calories than canned fruits, fruit juices and dried fruits. Dried fruits are relatively high in calories because their water content has been removed in the drying process. With the water gone, the volume the fruit occupies is much smaller. A quarter-cup of raisins contains the same calories — about 100, as almost 2 cups of grapes. The grapes are more filling because they occupy a greater volume. Choosing the grapes allows you to consume almost eight times more volume than choosing the raisins would allow. In addition to grapes, other excellent choices include apples, bananas, blueberries, cantaloupes, cherries, grapefruits, honeydew melon, kiwi and mangos.

Vegetables are also highly desirable options, including salad greens, asparagus, green beans, broccoli, cauliflower, zucchini, summer squash, carrots, eggplant, mushrooms, onions, tomatoes and many more.

Some vegetables can be considered carbohydrates because they are starchy, containing more calories than typical vegetables, and they function more like a carbohydrate in your body. Starchy vegetables include corn, potatoes, sweet potatoes and winter squash. Other healthy carbohydrates include whole grains, such as brown rice, whole-wheat pasta and whole-grain breads and cereals.

The Mayo Clinic Healthy Weight Pyramid

If weight is an issue for you, the Mayo Clinic Healthy Weight Pyramid can show you what foods to buy and eat when choosing foods that promote healthy weight. You'll also reduce your risk of weight-related diseases. What's more, you'll feel fuller and less hungry if you follow this approach.

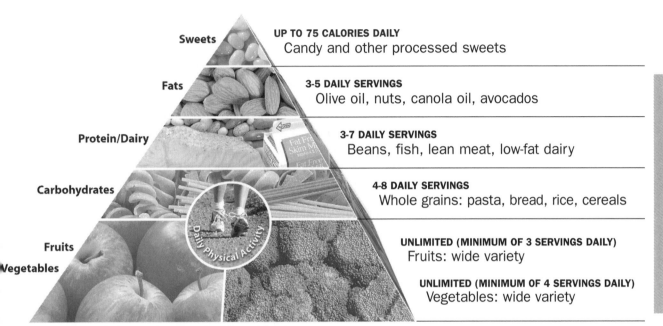

Sweets
UP TO 75 CALORIES DAILY
Candy and other processed sweets

Fats
3-5 DAILY SERVINGS
Olive oil, nuts, canola oil, avocados

Protein/Dairy
3-7 DAILY SERVINGS
Beans, fish, lean meat, low-fat dairy

Carbohydrates
4-8 DAILY SERVINGS
Whole grains: pasta, bread, rice, cereals

Fruits
UNLIMITED (MINIMUM OF 3 SERVINGS DAILY)
Fruits: wide variety

Vegetables
UNLIMITED (MINIMUM OF 4 SERVINGS DAILY)
Vegetables: wide variety

Daily Physical Activity

See your doctor before you begin any healthy-weight plan.

Recommended Servings*

	Weight Loss, Average Woman	Weight Loss, Average Man	Weight Maintenance, Average Adult	Weight Maintenance, Active Adults and Teenagers
Calorie level**	About 1,200	About 1,400	About 2,000	About 2,600
Carbohydrates	4	5	8	12
Vegetables	4 or more	4 or more	5 or more	5 or more
Fruits	3 or more	4 or more	5 or more	5 or more
Protein/Dairy	3	4	7	8
Fats	3	3	5	8

*Based on the Mayo Clinic Healthy Weight Pyramid.
**These are the recommended calorie levels if you choose low-fat, lean foods from the major food groups and use foods from the fats, oils and sweets group sparingly.

■ Caffeine

Caffeine occurs naturally in coffee, tea and chocolate. Caffeine is frequently added to soft drinks and over-the-counter drugs, including headache and cold tablets, stay-awake medications and allergy remedies.

Although relying on caffeine isn't recognized medically as a drug addiction, you may come to depend on caffeine as a pick-me-up. You may feel somewhat drowsy or have a mild headache until you have your caffeinated beverage. Indications that you may be using too much caffeine include difficulty sleeping, headaches, tiredness, irritability, nervousness, vague depression or frequent yawning.

Self-Care

If caffeine is bothering you, try to decrease your intake gradually (by one serving a day) as you switch to decaffeinated beverages:

- When you're thirsty, drink decaffeinated beverages or water.
- Mix decaffeinated coffee in with your regular coffee before brewing.
- Substitute regular instant coffee, which contains less caffeine than brewed coffee.
- Switch to tea or other beverages. Be careful when switching to herbal teas, however. Some types, particularly homemade varieties, can have the same effects as coffee, or worse.
- Symptoms should begin clearing in four to 10 days.

Lowering Your Cholesterol

Cardiovascular disease remains the leading cause of death in this country. Many of the more than 600,000 annual deaths occur because of narrowed or blocked arteries (atherosclerosis). Cholesterol plays a major role in this largely preventable condition.

Atherosclerosis is a silent, painless process in which cholesterol-containing fatty deposits (plaques) accumulate in the walls of your arteries over many years, beginning in childhood. As plaques build up, the interior of your artery narrows and the flow of blood is reduced.

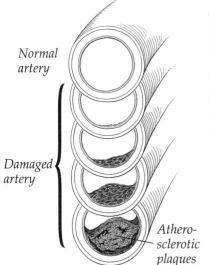

Normal artery

Damaged artery

Athero-sclerotic plaques

An excess of LDL cholesterol particles in your blood increases your risk of a buildup of cholesterol within your artery walls. Eventually, bumps called plaques may form, narrowing or even blocking one or more arteries.

What Is Cholesterol?

Cholesterol is in every cell of your body, and every cell needs it. But your risk of cardiovascular disease goes up considerably if you have too much of this waxy, fatty substance in your blood.

Weight loss, a low-fat diet and other lifestyle changes can help bring your cholesterol down. But sometimes, they aren't enough. Your cholesterol level may still put you at risk of heart attack or stroke.

Fortunately, there's now an array of powerful drugs available that can rapidly reduce your cholesterol and, ultimately, the health risks it poses.

Why You Need Cholesterol

Cholesterol is just one kind of fat (lipid) in your blood. It's often talked about as if it were a poison, but you can't live without it. It's essential to your body's cell membranes, to the insulation of your nerves and to the production of certain hormones. It also helps you digest food.

Your liver manufactures about two-thirds of the cholesterol in your body. You take in the rest when you eat animal products.

Like nutrients from digested food, cholesterol is transported throughout your body by your bloodstream. For this to happen, your body coats cholesterol with a protein. The cholesterol-protein package is called a lipoprotein (lip-oh-PRO-teen). Low-density lipoprotein (LDL) cholesterol is often referred to as "bad" cholesterol. Over time, it can build up in your blood vessels with other substances to form plaques. That can cause a blockage, resulting in heart attack or stroke. In contrast, high-density lipoprotein (HDL) cholesterol is often called "good" cholesterol because it helps "clean" cholesterol from your blood vessels.

Drug Therapy

If, despite dietary changes and exercise, you still have too much bad cholesterol (**high blood cholesterol**) or not enough good (see page 215), your physician may consider drug therapy. Medications can change your blood levels of cholesterol or triglycerides, another type of lipid in your blood.

Coronary artery angiograms taken five years apart show the kind of results that can be achieved with cholesterol-lowering medications.

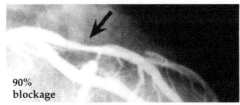

90% blockage

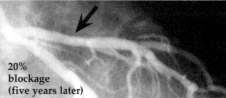

20% blockage (five years later)

See back cover for online resource (i)

By reducing LDL cholesterol or other lipids, the drugs can help prevent buildup of plaques or even reduce them. They also help stabilize plaques within your blood vessels, preventing them from rupturing, which can cause an obstruction or blood clot. Types of drugs available include:

- **Bile acid-binding resins (sequestrants).** Cholestyramine (Questran), colesevelam (WelChol), colestipol (Colestid). They bind with bile acids in your intestinal tract, prompting your liver to make more bile acids. Because your liver uses cholesterol to make the acids, less cholesterol is available to reach your bloodstream.
- **Fibrates.** Gemfibrozil (Lopid), fenofibrate (Antara, TriCor, others) reduce triglyceride production and remove triglycerides from circulation.
- **Statins.** These drugs work directly in your liver to block a substance your liver needs to manufacture cholesterol. This depletes cholesterol in your liver cells and causes the cells to remove cholesterol from circulating blood. Statins include atorvastatin (Lipitor), fluvastatin (Lescol), lovastatin (Altoprev, Mevacor), pravastatin (Pravachol), rosuvastatin (Crestor) and simvastatin (Zocor).
- **Niacin.** Niacin comes in a variety of prescription and nonprescription formulas. It helps increase HDL cholesterol and reduce LDL cholesterol and triglycerides.
- **Cholesterol absorption inhibitor.** This includes the drug ezetimibe (Zetia), which selectively inhibits absorption of cholesterol and related substances in the intestine.
- **Combination cholesterol absorption inhibitor and statin.** The drug Vytorin is a combination of ezetimibe and simvastatin. It works in two different ways to help reduce LDL cholesterol and triglycerides and increase HDL cholesterol.

Do You Need Medication?

To determine whether you need medication, your doctor looks at your cholesterol and other blood fat levels and considers these alongside your heart disease risk factors. You may need medication if:

- Your LDL level is 190 mg/dL or higher with none or one heart disease risk factor
- Your LDL level is 160 mg/dL or higher with two or more risk factors and less than a 10 percent risk of having a heart attack in the next 10 years
- Your LDL level is 130 mg/dL or higher with two or more risk factors and you have a 10 percent to 20 percent risk of having a heart attack in the next 10 years
  You're considered at high to very high risk if:
- Your LDL level is 100 mg/dL or higher, you have heart disease or diabetes, you have two or more risk factors and your heart attack risk is greater than 20 percent
- Your LDL level is 70 mg/dL or higher, you have heart disease with multiple and poorly controlled risk factors and your heart attack risk is greater than 20 percent

Why Do You Have High Cholesterol?

Your genes and your lifestyle influence how much and what kind of cholesterol you have. Your liver may make too much LDL cholesterol or may not "clean" enough of it from your blood. Or it may not make enough HDL cholesterol.

Smoking, a high-fat diet and inactivity also can increase LDL levels and reduce HDL levels. They also affect levels of other blood lipids.

The best way to find out how much and what kind of cholesterol you have is to have your doctor check your blood lipids. Home tests can't tell you how much good or bad cholesterol you have.

Nonprescription Products to Help Lower Cholesterol

There are a number of ways to lower your bad cholesterol (LDL) in addition to taking the standard medications called statins. Here's a list of some of them.

Agent	Where Found	Effect	Dose
Plant sterols and stanols	Take Control or Benecol margarine	Blocks cholesterol absorption.	1.6–3.4 grams a day; use equivalent of two pads of margarine twice a day
Soluble fiber	Metamucil, (contains psyllium) or oat beta-glucan (such as in oatmeal)	Increases bile acid loss of cholesterol into intestine.	One scoop a day
Policosanol	One-A-Day Cholesterol Plus vitamins	Stimulates degradation of LDL cholesterol, similar to statins	10 milligrams (mg) a day
Soy protein	Soybeans, soy milk, tofu	Reduces cholesterol production in the liver.	25 grams a day in four servings
Nuts	Almonds	Good source of monounsaturated fats.	42 grams a day (1.5 ounces)
Fish oil	Fish oil capsules (provide omega-3 fatty acids)	Beneficial for endothelium (the lining of the arteries in the heart) and reduces the chance of irregular, lethal heartbeats. Doesn't lower cholesterol but will lower triglycerides at doses of 6 to 7 grams a day.	1,000 mg a day

What Do Your Cholesterol and Triglyceride Levels Mean?*

Total cholesterol	What the numbers mean	HDL ('good') cholesterol	What the numbers mean**
Below 200	Desirable	Below 40	Low
200 to 239	Borderline high	40 to 59	Better, but not optimal
240 or higher	High	60 and above	Optimal

LDL ('bad') cholesterol	What the numbers mean	Triglycerides	What the numbers mean
Below 100	Optimal***	Below 150	Desirable
100 to 129	Near optimal	150 to 199	Borderline high
130 to 159	Borderline high	200 to 499	High
160 to 189	High	500 or higher	Very high
190 or higher	Very high		

Source: National Cholesterol Education Program, Adult Treatment Panel III, 2001

*Levels are in milligrams of cholesterol per deciliter (mg/dL) of blood and apply to adults age 20 and older. LDL means low-density lipoprotein, and HDL means high-density lipoprotein. Desirable ranges may vary, depending on individual health conditions. Check with your doctor.

**HDL cholesterol helps keep bad cholesterol from building up in your arteries. So for HDL, higher numbers are better. But high numbers for total cholesterol, LDL cholesterol or triglycerides may increase your risk of cardiovascular disease.

***If you have coronary artery disease, the goal is less than 70.

Weighing Your Options

Which lipid-lowering drug your doctor recommends for you depends on many factors. These include how much good or bad cholesterol you have and whether other lipids in your blood are high. Your age may also be a factor. Sometimes your doctor may recommend a combination of drugs.

The effectiveness of lipid-lowering drugs varies from person to person. There isn't one drug that's best for everyone. Nor is it necessary to take the newest drug if your current medication is effective.

A Long-Term Program

The decision to take any kind of lipid-lowering drug is a serious matter. Once you start, you must typically take the drug the rest of your life. That can be expensive. Lipid-lowering drugs can cost $200 or more a month. You may also need to have your liver checked after starting these drugs. Rarely, the drugs can cause liver damage, which is why they're not recommended if you have liver disease.

Other side effects for most lipid-lowering drugs usually aren't serious, but may be bothersome enough to keep you from taking the medication. The statins, for example, can cause muscle pain when taken alone or in combination with other drugs, such as gemfibrozil, antifungal medications or the popular antibiotic erythromycin. However, this side effect is rare.

The resins can cause constipation and bloating, or decrease the effectiveness of other medications taken at the same time. Niacin sometimes causes irritating skin flushing and can increase your blood sugar level, aggravate a stomach ulcer or trigger an attack of gout. And gemfibrozil can cause gallstones.

In addition, because lipid-lowering drugs have been available for only about 20 years, doctors haven't been able to study their safety when used over a lifetime.

Physical Activity and Fitness

Regular physical activity — at least 30 minutes a day most days of the week — can reduce your risk of a number of serious health problems including heart disease, high blood pressure, stroke, diabetes, certain cancers and osteoporosis.

The benefits of exercise include the following:

- **Heart.** Exercise increases your heart's ability to pump blood and decreases your resting heart rate. Your heart can pump more blood with less effort.
- **Cholesterol and triglycerides.** Exercise improves blood fat levels.
- **Blood pressure.** Exercise can lower blood pressure and is especially helpful if you have mild hypertension. Regular exercise can also help prevent as well as reduce high blood pressure.
- **Diabetes.** If you have diabetes, exercise can lower your blood sugar. Exercise can help prevent type 2 (adult-onset) diabetes.
- **Bones.** Women who exercise have a better chance of avoiding osteoporosis, provided that they do not become so active that menstruation stops.
- **Weight.** Exercise lowers body fat stores.
- **General.** Regular physical activity can also relieve stress, improve your overall sense of well-being, help you sleep better and improve concentration.

Aerobic vs. Anaerobic Exercise

Aerobic exercise (meaning "to exercise with oxygen") occurs when you continuously move large muscle groups such as your leg muscles. This type of exercise places increased demands on the heart, lungs and muscle cells. It's not so intense, however, that it causes pain (from lactic acid buildup). If you're exercising in a good aerobic range, you should be breaking a sweat and breathing faster but still be able to exercise comfortably for 30 to 60 minutes. Aerobic exercise improves your overall endurance. Walking, biking, jogging and swimming are familiar aerobic exercises.

Anaerobic exercise ("to exercise without oxygen") occurs when the demands made on a muscle are great enough that it uses up all of the available oxygen and starts to burn stored energy without oxygen. This path for burning energy produces lactic acid, which causes pain as it builds up in muscles. That's one reason why you can't carry on anaerobic exercises very long. Lifting very heavy weights or sprinting are classic examples. Anaerobic exercise builds strength and speed more than endurance. When starting an exercise program, work with light weights or set machines at light resistance to avoid injuries, and supplement your anaerobic exercises with aerobic exercises.

What It Means to Be Fit

You're fit if you can:

- Carry out daily tasks without fatigue and have ample energy to enjoy leisure pursuits
- Walk a mile or climb a few flights of stairs without becoming winded or feeling heaviness or fatigue in your legs
- Carry on a conversation during light to moderate exercise such as brisk walking

If you sit most of the day, you're probably not fit. Signs of deconditioning include feeling tired most of the time, being unable to keep up with others your age, avoiding physical activity because you know you'll quickly tire and becoming short of breath or fatigued when walking a short distance.

Starting a Fitness Program

Consult your health care provider before you begin a **fitness program** if you smoke, are overweight, are older than 40 years and have never exercised or have a chronic condition such as heart disease or a family history of heart disease, diabetes, high blood pressure, lung disease or kidney disease. The risks of exercise stem from doing too much, too vigorously, with too little previous activity.

If you are medically able to begin a program, here are some helpful hints:

- **Begin gradually.** Don't overdo it. If you have trouble talking to a companion during your workout, you probably are pushing too hard.
- **Select the exercise that's right for you.** It should be something you enjoy — or at least find tolerable. Otherwise, in time you will avoid it.
- **Do it regularly but moderately** and never exercise to the point of nausea, dizziness or extreme shortness of breath. Your goals should be:
  - *Frequency.* Try to exercise or be physically active most days of the week.
  - *Intensity.* Aim for about 60 percent of your maximal aerobic capacity. For most people, 60 percent capacity means moderate exertion with deep breathing, but short of panting or becoming overheated. Use the talk test (see No. 1 near the bottom of page 219) to gauge intensity.
  - *Time.* Try to accumulate 30 to 60 minutes of exercise or physical activity each day. If time is a factor, three 10-minute sessions can be as beneficial as one 30-minute workout. If you're not used to exercise, start at a comfortable length of time and gradually work up to your goal.
- **Always warm up and cool down.** Warm up and stretch to help loosen muscles; stretch in cool-down to increase flexibility.

How Many Calories Does It Use Up?

Exercise that's equivalent to burning about 1,000 calories a week significantly lowers your overall risk of a heart attack. The chart shows the estimated calories used while performing various activities for 1 hour. The more you weigh, the more calories you use. Note that the figures are estimates — actual calories used vary from person to person.

Activity (1-hour duration)	Calories Used 120- to 130-lb person	Calories Used 170- to 180-lb person	Activity (1-hour duration)	Calories Used 120- to 130-lb person	Calories Used 170- to 180-lb person
Aerobics class	290-575	400-800	Racquetball	345-690	480-960
Backpacking	290-630	400-880	Rope skipping	345-690	480-960
Badminton	230-515	320-720	Running (8 mph)	745	1,040
Bicycling (outdoor)	170-800	240-1,120	Skating, ice- or roller-	230-460	320-640
Bicycling (stationary)	85-800	120-1,120	Skiing (cross-country)	290-800	400-1,120
Bowling	115-170	160-240	Skiing (downhill)	170-460	240-640
Canoeing	170-460	240-640	Stair climbing	230-460	320-640
Dancing	115-400	160-560	Swimming	230-690	320-900
Golfing (walking, no cart)	115-400	160-560	Tennis	230-515	320-720
Hiking	170-690	240-960	Volleyball	170-400	240-560
Jogging (5 mph)	460	640	Walking (2 mph)	150	210
Jogging (6 mph)	575	800	Walking (3 mph)	200	275

For other body weights, you can calculate approximate calories used by selecting the number of calories used from the column for a 170- to 180-pound person. Multiply it by your weight and divide by 175. For example, if you weigh 220 lb, jogging at 5 mph uses $\frac{640 \times 220}{175} = 805$ calories/hour.

See back cover for online resource

Walk Your Way to Fitness

Less than half of American adults exercise regularly. Yet a brisk walk, 30 to 60 minutes each day, can help you attain the fitness level associated with a longer, more healthy life. Exercise doesn't have to be intense. Even walking slowly can lower your risk of heart disease. Faster, farther or more frequent walking offers greater health benefits.

First Things First

The best walking program takes advantage of your fitness goals while being safe, convenient and fun. Here are tips to get the most out of walking:

- **Set realistic goals.** What do you want to gain from regular exercise? Be specific. Are you 45 and concerned about warding off a heart attack? Are you 75 and wanting to enjoy more recreational activities and prolong your independence? Do you want to lose weight? Lower your blood pressure? Relieve stress? Maybe you just want to feel better.

    Walking can help you achieve these goals. Decide what's most important to you. Then be specific about how you can reach that goal. Don't say, "I'm going to walk more." Say, "I'm going to walk from 7 to 7:30 on Tuesday, Thursday and Saturday mornings."

- **Buy good shoes.** You don't need to spend a lot of money on shoes designed specifically for walking. You do need to wear shoes that provide protection and stability.

- **Dress right.** Dress in loosefitting, comfortable clothes. Choose materials appropriate for the weather — a windbreaker for cool and windy days, layers of clothing in cold weather. Wear bright colors trimmed with reflective fabric or tape. Avoid rubberized material; it doesn't allow perspiration to escape. Protect yourself from the sun with sunscreen, sunglasses or a hat.

- **Drink water.** When you exercise, you need extra water to maintain your normal body temperature and cool working muscles. To help replenish the fluids you lose during exercise, drink water before and after activity. If you walk for more than 20 minutes, drink $\frac{1}{2}$ to 1 cup of water every 20 minutes, especially in hot weather.

- **See your doctor.** If you're age 40 or older or have a chronic health problem, review your exercise goals with your doctor before starting.

Planning Your Program

If you put out a little more physical effort than usual, your body responds by improving its capacity for exercise. By gradually increasing the amount of exercise you do, and allowing the adaptive processes to occur, you can improve your fitness level in eight to 12 weeks. To condition your heart and lungs safely, plan these aspects of your program:

- **Intensity.** Remember, exercise doesn't have to be strenuous to be healthful. But what is a desirable range of exercise intensity for you? Here are two simple tools to help you find out:
    1. Talk test. While you walk, you should be able to carry on a conversation with a companion. If you can't, you're probably pushing too hard. Slow your pace.
    2. Perceived exertion. This refers to the total amount of physical effort you experience. The perceived exertion scale accounts for all sensations of exertion, physical stress and fatigue.

Borg Ratings of Perceived Exertion (RPE) Scale

On this scale, a rating of 6 indicates no exertion, such as sitting comfortably in a chair. A rating of 20 corresponds to maximal exertion, such as jogging up a steep hill.

Aim for a rating of 12 to 14. In general, it corresponds to 70 percent of the maximal exercise capacity. This is considered to be nearly ideal for most people. When you use the scale, don't become preoccupied with any one factor such as leg discomfort or labored breathing. Instead, try to concentrate on your overall feeling of exertion.

© 1998 Gunnar Borg

6	No exertion at all
7	Extremely light
8	
9	Very light
10	
11	Light
12	
13	Somewhat hard
14	
15	Hard (heavy)
16	
17	Very hard
18	
19	Extremely hard
20	Maximal exertion

- **Frequency.** Walk at least three times a week. For conditioning and health benefits, your goal is eventually to walk three to four hours a week.
- **Duration.** Walk for at least 15 to 30 minutes. If you've never exercised regularly or you haven't exercised for a long time, start at a level that's comfortable for you. It may be no more than five minutes.

A 10-Week Schedule

Use this schedule to enhance what walking you're already doing or to start a regular program.

Week	Time (min)*	Days	Total minutes
1	15	2	30
2	15	3	45
3	20	3	60
4	25	3	75
5-6	30	3	90
7-8	30	4	120
9-10	30	5	150

*This does not include warm-up and cool-down time.

■ Stretching Exercises for Walkers

Calf stretches.
1. Lean against a wall as shown. While maintaining a straight right knee, bend your left knee as if moving it toward the wall. Hold for 30 to 45 seconds. Feel the stretch in your right calf. Repeat with your other leg.

2. Position yourself similar to the previous exercise, but with your right knee bent instead of straight. Bend your left knee as if to move it toward the wall. Hold for 30 to 45 seconds. Feel the stretch in the deep calf muscle. Repeat with your other leg.

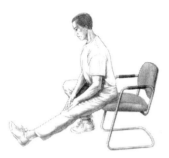

Hamstring stretch.
1. Position yourself as shown above. Slowly straighten your left knee until you feel a stretch. Hold for 30 to 45 seconds. Don't stretch to the point of experiencing pain. You may apply gentle downward pressure with your hands. Repeat with your right leg.

Chest stretch.
1. Position yourself in a neutral posture as shown above.

2. Move your arms backward while rotating your palms forward. Squeeze shoulder blades together, breathe deeply, and lift your chest upward. Hold for 30 to 45 seconds. Return to starting position.

Hip stretch.
1. Lie on a sturdy table or bed. Hold both your knees to your chest. Release your left leg and slowly straighten, allowing it to hang off the table or bed. Hold for 30 to 45 seconds. Feel the stretch in your left hip. Repeat with your other leg.

Back stretches.
1. Position yourself as shown above. Slowly pull your right knee up toward your chest. Keep your left leg relaxed. Hold for 30 to 45 seconds. Feel the stretch in your low back and hip. Repeat with your left leg.

2. Position yourself as shown above. Pull both knees up toward your chest. Hold for 30 to 45 seconds. This variation usually provides a more intense low back stretch.

In addition to the time you spend walking, be sure to warm up and cool down. Use the stretching and flexibility exercises that are illustrated on the previous page.

A good exercise program includes three phases:

- **Warm-up.** Before each walk, spend about five minutes preparing your body for walking. For the first three to five minutes, walk at a slower pace to gradually increase your heart rate, body temperature and blood flow to the exercising muscles. Stretching also develops and maintains adequate muscle and joint flexibility.
- **Conditioning.** Walking develops your aerobic capacity by increasing your heart rate, depth of breathing and muscle endurance. You'll also burn calories. Calories burned depend on how fast and how long you walk and how much you weigh (see How Many Calories Does It Use Up?, page 218).
- **Cool-down.** At the end of your walk, slow your walking pace for three to five minutes to gradually reduce your heart rate and blood pressure. Then, repeat the same stretching exercises you used for warm-up to help improve your flexibility.

Stepping Out Safely

Congratulations. You've committed to a regular walking program. You're confident of the benefits you'll gain. But as you prepare, beware of the terrible toos — doing

- Too much
- Too hard
- With too little preparation

Foot or heel pain is a common result. Problems such as these can derail your walking program and sap your motivation. Here's how to walk without wearing yourself out:

- **Progress gradually.** If you haven't been physically active in the past two months, start conservatively. In the first two to three weeks, choose an intensity at the lower end of the Borg Ratings of Perceived Exertion Scale. Gradually increase intensity only after you're walking comfortably for your desired length of time.
- **Listen to your body.** Expect to feel some mild muscle soreness after adding time to your schedule. However, gasping for breath and feeling sore joints are signals to slow down. Muscle stiffness lasting several days means you went too far.

See your doctor immediately if you notice any symptoms suggesting heart or lung disease, such as chest pain, chest pressure, unusual fatigue lasting several hours, heart irregularity, dizziness, or unusual shortness of breath during or immediately after exercise.

- **Replace worn-out shoes.** Shoes begin to lose their cushioning after 300 to 500 miles of use and should be replaced, even though they may still look good. In addition, invest in a new pair when soles start to separate from uppers. Check for loss of stability by lining up your shoes side by side. Then look to see if either shoe tilts to the right or left.
- **Choose your course carefully.** Check out the route you plan to walk. Avoid paths with cracked sidewalks, potholes, low-hanging limbs or uneven turf. Don't walk at night along a road. When possible, walk with a companion, and always carry personal identification.
- **Don't overdo it.** If exercise begins to feel like an obligation, take a day off each week. Use the time to do some other recreational activity that you enjoy.

Screening and Immunizations

Adult Screening Tests and Procedures

Test or Procedure	Purpose	Recommendation
Blood cholesterol test	Detect people at high risk of coronary artery disease	• Baseline test in your 20s. If values are within desirable ranges, every 5 years. See page 215.
Blood pressure measurement	Early detection of high blood pressure	• Every 2 years or as your health care provider recommends.
Colon cancer screening (several tests are available)	Detect cancers and growths (polyps) on the inside wall of the colon that may become cancerous	• Flexible sigmoidoscopy, every 5 years after age 50. • Colon X-ray, every 5 years after age 50, in combination with proctoscopy or sigmoidoscopy. • Colonoscopy, every 5 to 10 years after age 50. Replaces the need for other tests and is the best method, but it also has more risk and is the most expensive.
Complete physical examination*	Detect conditions before symptoms develop; preventive care, counseling, symptom evaluation and review of medications	• Twice in your 20s. • Three times in your 30s. • Four times in your 40s. • Five times in your 50s. • Annually after 60. • More frequently if you have a chronic medical condition or take medications.
Dental checkup	Detect cavities of teeth and problems of the gums, tongue and mouth	• Once a year or as your dentist recommends.
Chest X-ray	Detect lung abnormalities	• Not a routine test. As needed for symptoms or conditions.
Electrocardiogram (ECG)	Identify injury to heart or irregular rhythms	• Not a routine test. As needed for symptoms or conditions.
Eye examination	Detect vision problems	• Every 4 to 5 years, or as recommended by your doctor.
Mammogram (breast X-ray)	Early detection of breast cancer	• Yearly in women older than 50. Yearly in women in their 40s may be appropriate. See page 145.
Pap test	Detect abnormal cells that could develop into cancer	• Every 3 years, or more often based on your age, risk and as recommended by your health care provider. See page 151 for details.
Prostate-specific antigen (PSA)	Measure amount of a protein secreted by the prostate gland; high levels can indicate prostate cancer	• Consider the test if you have a strong family history of prostate cancer or as recommended by your health care provider. An enlarged or inflamed prostate also may increase the PSA level.

*Screening recommendations apply to those in good health and without symptoms of illness. Symptoms or previous diagnosis may change screening recommendations. Talk with your doctor. Components of a complete physical depend on your age, sex, past illnesses, current medical conditions, health risks based on your behavior and your family history of diseases. How often you have a physical will vary according to your personal health needs.

Staying Healthy

Adult Immunization Schedule

Vaccine	Recommendation
Tetanus/diphtheria, pertussis booster (Td, Tdap)	Every 10 years. After a deep or dirty wound if the most recent booster was more than five years ago. Boosters should be given as soon as possible after the injury. A new tetanus/diphtheria booster (Tdap) also contains the pertussis (whooping cough) vaccine. Ask your doctor if it's right for you.
Hepatitis A (2-shot series)	Travelers and people in high-risk groups (chronic liver disease, men with male sex partners, intravenous drug users, people who have had contact with someone who has hepatitis A).
Hepatitis B (3-shot series)	Health care workers, high-risk groups (people with multiple sexual partners or a sexual partner who's a carrier) and others who might be exposed to infected blood or body fluids. The vaccine is now routinely given to infants and teenagers not previously vaccinated.
Flu (influenza)	Every year for people 50 or older and others at high risk (health care workers and people with chronic illnesses or those living with people at high risk).
Measles, mumps, rubella (MMR)	Two shots for adults born after 1956 without proof of previous immunization or immunity. Not to be given during pregnancy or to women planning pregnancy within four weeks.
Pneumococcal vaccination (pneumonia vaccine)	Age 65 or older or any adult with a medical condition that increases the risk of infection. People who are generally healthy may need only one shot. Those less healthy and people who received their first shot before age 65 may need shots more often.
Chickenpox (varicella) (2-shot series)	Susceptible adults (health care workers without immunity or adults without known disease who are exposed to chickenpox).
Meningococcal vaccination	Not routinely given. Consider for travel or young adults living in close quarters.

Pediatric and Adolescent Immunization Schedule

The following chart includes the recommended schedule of vaccines used at Mayo Clinic. It's a modification of recommendations endorsed by the American Academy of Pediatrics and the Centers for Disease Control and Prevention. Check with your doctor regarding the timing of immunizations for your child.

Age	Vaccine	Age	Vaccine
2 months	PCV, HBV-Hib, DTaP, IPV	15 months	PCV, DTaP, Hib
4 months	PCV, HBV-Hib, DTaP, IPV	4 years	MMR, DTaP
6 months	PCV, DTaP, Hib	5 years	IPV
9 months	HBV, IPV	11 years	Tdap, (HBV, MMR, Varivax if not previously given)
12 months	MMR, Varivax	17 years	Meningococcal vaccine

Abbreviations

PCV — Pneumococcal conjugate vaccine
HBV-Hib — Hepatitis B-*Haemophilus influenzae* type b vaccine
DTaP — Diphtheria-tetanus-acellular pertussis vaccine
Tdap — Tetanus-reduced diphtheria-acellular pertussis vaccine
IPV — Poliovirus vaccine inactivated (Salk)

HBV — Hepatitis B vaccine
MMR — Measles-mumps-rubella vaccine
Varivax — Chickenpox vaccine
Td — Tetanus-diphtheria vaccine

Keeping Stress Under Control

Stress is something that most people know well and experience often. It's that feeling of pressure, often resulting from having too much to do and too little time to do it. In today's busy world, stress is unavoidable. Stress may be caused by positive events — a job promotion, vacation or marriage — as well as negative events — the loss of a job, a divorce or the death of a loved one. It's your personal response to situations and circumstances that cause you to experience stress.

When you experience stress — especially severe stress — a physical response occurs to meet the perceived energy demands of the situation. Your heart beats faster, your breathing quickens, and your blood pressure rises. In addition, your blood sugar rises, and blood flow to your brain and large muscles increases. After the threat passes, your body slowly relaxes again.

Stress may be short-term (acute) or long-term (chronic). Chronic stress is often related to situations that aren't easily solved, such as relationship problems, loneliness, financial worries or long workdays. You may be able to handle an occasional stressful event, but when stress occurs regularly, the effects multiply and compound over time.

Stress produces a variety of physical, psychological and behavioral symptoms. And it can lead to illness — aggravating an existing health problem, or possibly triggering a new one, if you're already at risk of that condition. Stress may produce the following health effects:

Suppresses Immune System

The hormone cortisol produced during the stress response may suppress your immune system, increasing your susceptibility to infections. Studies suggest the risk of bacterial infections such as tuberculosis and group A streptococcal disease increases during stress. Stress may also make you more prone to upper respiratory viral infections such as a cold or the flu (influenza).

Increases Risk of Cardiovascular Disease

During acute stress your heart beats quickly, which makes you more susceptible to heart rhythm irregularities and a type of chest pain called angina. What's more, if you're a "hot reactor," acute stress may add to your risk of a heart attack. Hot reactors exhibit extreme increases in heart rate and blood pressure in response to daily stress. These surges may gradually injure your coronary arteries and heart. Increased blood clotting from persistent stress also can put you at risk of a heart attack or stroke.

Worsens Other Illnesses

Other relationships between illness and stress aren't as clear-cut. However, stress may worsen your symptoms if you have any of the following conditions:

- **Asthma.** A stressful situation may make your airways overreactive, precipitating an asthma attack.
- **Gastrointestinal problems.** Stress may trigger or worsen symptoms associated with some gastrointestinal conditions, such as irritable bowel syndrome or non-ulcer dyspepsia.
- **Chronic pain.** Stress can heighten your body's pain response, making chronic pain associated with conditions such as arthritis, fibromyalgia or a back injury more difficult to manage.
- **Mental health disorders.** Stress may trigger depression in people who are prone to the disorder. It may also worsen symptoms of other mental health disorders, such as anxiety.

Signs and Symptoms of Stress

Your first indications that your body and brain are feeling pressured may be associated symptoms of stress — headache, insomnia, upset stomach and digestive changes. An old nervous habit such as nail biting may reappear. Another common symptom is irritability with people close to you. Occasionally, these changes are so gradual that you or those around you don't recognize them until your health or relationships change.

Physical	Psychological	Behavioral
Headaches	Anxiety	Overeating or loss of appetite
Grinding teeth	Irritability	Impatience
Tight, dry throat	Feeling of impending danger or doom	Argumentativeness
Clenched jaws	Depression	Procrastination
Chest pain	Slowed thinking	Increased use of alcohol or drugs
Shortness of breath	Racing thoughts	Increased smoking
Pounding heart	Feeling of helplessness	Withdrawal or isolation
High blood pressure	Feeling of hopelessness	Avoiding or neglecting
Muscle aches	Feeling of worthlessness	responsibilities
Indigestion	Feeling of lack of direction	Poor job performance
Constipation or diarrhea	Feeling of insecurity	Burnout
Increased perspiration	Sadness	Poor personal hygiene
Cold, sweaty hands	Defensiveness	Change in religious practices
Fatigue	Anger	Change in family or close relationships
Insomnia	Hypersensitivity	
Frequent illness	Apathy	

Relaxation Techniques to Manage Stress

Relaxed Breathing

With practice, you can breathe in a deep and relaxing way. At first, practice lying on your back while wearing clothing that is loose around your waist and abdomen. Once you've learned this position, practice while sitting and then while standing.

- Lie on your back on a bed or padded surface.
- Place your feet slightly apart. Rest one hand comfortably on your abdomen near your navel. Place your other hand on your chest.
- Inhale through your nose while pushing your abdomen out. Then slowly exhale through your nose while pushing your abdomen in.
- Concentrate on your breathing for a few minutes and become aware of the hand on your abdomen rising and falling with each breath. Make each breath a smooth, wave-like motion.
- Gently exhale most of the air in your lungs.
- Inhale while slowly counting to four, about 1 second per count.
- As you breathe in, imagine the warmed air flowing to all parts of your body.
- Pause 1 second after inhaling.
- Slowly exhale to a count of four. While you're exhaling, your abdomen will slowly fall.
- As air flows out, imagine that tension also is flowing out.
- Pause 1 second after exhaling.
- If it's difficult to inhale and exhale to a count of four, shorten the count slightly and later work up to four. If you feel lightheaded, slow your breathing or breathe less deeply.

- Repeat the slow inhaling, pausing, slow exhaling and pausing five to 10 times. Inhale slowly: 1, 2, 3, 4. Pause. Exhale slowly: 1, 2, 3, 4. Pause. Inhale: 1, 2, 3, 4. Pause. Exhale: 1, 2, 3, 4. Pause.

If it's difficult to make your breathing regular, take a slightly deeper breath, hold it for a second or two and then let it out slowly through pursed lips for about 10 seconds. Repeat this once or twice and return to the other procedure.

Progressive Muscle Relaxation

- Sit or lie in a comfortable position and close your eyes. Allow your jaw to drop and your eyelids to be relaxed but not tightly closed.
- Mentally scan your body, starting with your toes and working slowly to your head. Focus on each part individually; imagine tension melting away.
- Tighten the muscles in one area of your body and hold them for a count of five, relax and move on to the next area.

Visual Imagery

- Allow thoughts to flow through your mind but do not focus on any of them. Suggest to yourself that you are relaxed and calm, that your hands are warm (or cool if you are hot) and heavy, that your heart is beating calmly.
- Breathe slowly, regularly and deeply.
- Once you are relaxed, imagine you are in a favorite place or in a spot of great beauty.
- After five or 10 minutes, rouse yourself from the state gradually.

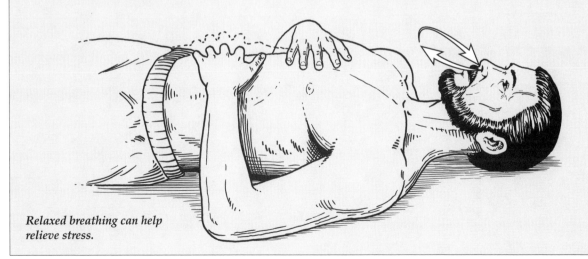

Relaxed breathing can help relieve stress.

- **Learn to relax.** Techniques such as guided imagery, meditation, muscle relaxation and relaxed breathing can help you relax (see page 227). Your goal is to lower your heart rate and blood pressure while reducing muscle tension.
- **Discuss your concerns** with a trusted friend. Talking helps to relieve strains and put things in perspective, and it may lead to a healthy plan of action.
- **Plan your work** in a step-by-step manner. Accomplish small tasks.
- **Deal with your anger.** Anger needs to be expressed, but carefully. Count to 10, compose yourself and respond to the anger in a more effective manner.
- **Get away.** A change of pace can help develop a new outlook.
- **Be realistic.** Set realistic goals. Prioritize. Concentrate on what's important. Unrealistically high goals invite failure.
- **Avoid self-medication.** At times we may seek to use medication or alcohol for a feeling of relief. Such substances only mask the problem.
- **Get plenty of sleep.** A healthy body promotes good mental health. Sleep helps us tackle problems in a refreshed state.
- **Keep physically active.** Exercise is good for your body and it helps burn off the excess energy that stress can produce.
- **Eat well.** Junk food only increases your stress level. Enjoy healthy meals and snacks.
- **Limit caffeine.** Too much coffee, tea or soda will only increase your stress level.
- **Make time for activities you enjoy.** This may include going to the movies, joining a book club, going golfing with friends or getting together for a game of cards.
- **Nuture your inner spirituality.** This can be done through nature, art, music, meditation, prayer or attending religious services.
- **Develop a support network.** Family members, friends and co-workers whom you can turn to for emotional and practical support can be very important when coping with stress.
- **Seek help.** Contact your physician or a mental health professional if stress is building or you're not functioning well.

Protecting Yourself

Nearly 100,000 deaths in the United States each year result from accidents (unintentional injuries). Accidents are the most common cause of death in people ages 1 to 34. In the following pages, you'll find a variety of safety tips. This information isn't comprehensive, but it may help you prepare for some potentially dangerous circumstances. For information about workplace safety, see page 237.

■ Emergency Preparedness

Many people face emergencies at one time or another, from a car breakdown to a kitchen fire. Major emergencies from a natural disaster, toxic spill, pandemic or act of terrorism are rare but affect more people at once. A major emergency potentially involves death or injury, lack of food and water, and the loss of public utilities, transportation and services. Your survival in these circumstances may depend on your level of preparedness.

Need for Action

An emergency requires quick decisions: Should you stay where you are? Or is your best choice to evacuate? How will you connect with your family and friends?
In chaotic, fast-changing conditions, your decisions will depend on common sense and your knowledge of the immediate danger. Steps you may take to be better prepared include:

- **Being informed.** Determine the likely disaster scenarios that could take place in your area, for example, floods, wildfires, infectious disease or hazardous spills. Learn how you'll be notified of emergencies. There may be special sirens, radio or television broadcasts, or emergency workers going door to door.
- **Staying in touch.** Choose a common "emergency contact" phone number — the home of a friend or relative, for example — that all family members can use to stay in touch during emergencies. Note that when there are major disruptions, it's often easier to contact someone far away than nearby. It's advisable to have a backup contact at a different location.
- **Planning for evacuation.** If you must evacuate, determine locations where you and your family can meet, both within and outside the community. Know how to turn off the home utilities — water, electricity and gas. Plan to take pets with you, if possible. Always keep your vehicles' gas tanks at least half-full.
- **Maintaining your calm.** Major emergencies are generally unexpected, unfamiliar and uncontrollable. Stress from these events causes panic and confusion. Your ability to make sound decisions may depend on:
  - Practicing your emergency plan
  - Knowing your community's resources
  - Including your children in preparations and practice

Disaster Supplies Kit

Emergency preparations include gathering supplies that are ready to use in the event of a disaster. Keep in mind that water, food and clean air are your highest priorities. You may customize the kit to fit your needs and preferences, and to handle the most likely disasters.

There should be enough supplies to last everyone for at least three days. Store the kit in a dry, cool place, preferably out of the sun. Pack items in easy-to-carry, easily accessible containers for use in your home or if you need to evacuate.

Basic items include:

- **Water.** Plan on 1 gallon per person per day, for drinking and for sanitation. Store water tightly sealed in clean plastic containers.
- **Food.** Select foods that require no refrigeration or preparation, that have a long shelf life, and that require little or no water.
- **Hygiene and sanitation items.** Dust mask, moist towelettes, hand sanitizer, toothpaste and toothbrush, toilet paper, heavy-duty garbage bags and ties.
- **Tools.** Manual can opener, eating utensils, flashlight, battery-powered radio, extra batteries, matches (in waterproof container), plastic sheeting and duct tape, knife, wrench or pliers, scissors, whistle.
- **First-aid kit.** Adhesive bandages, cleansing agent (soap or towelette), antibiotic ointment, thermometer, tweezers, burn ointment, eyewash solution, sterile dressing, tape, elastic wrap, and aspirin or other pain reliever.
- **Family items.** Cash and coins, supply of regularly used medications, copies of credit cards, bank numbers, important documents, medical prescriptions, driver's licenses and passports, extra sets of keys.

Additional items include:

Cooking and eating accessories, blankets or sleeping bags, change of clothing and footwear, bathing supplies, items for infants (if necessary), compass, tent, camp shovel, fire extinguisher, paper towels, disinfectant or household chlorine bleach, pet supplies, special needs items, inhalers, contact lenses, extra eyeglasses, hearing aid batteries and feminine supplies

Facing Infectious Disease Threats

If you live in or must travel to a region with an outbreak of an infectious disease — for example, hantavirus, SARS, monkeypox or avian influenza, commonly called bird flu — try to do the following:

- Avoid crowded areas.
- Wear a mask in public.
- Keep hands washed and away from your face.
- Eat only well-cooked foods in clean restaurants or eat canned foods.
- Carry antiseptic wipes and a first-aid kit with rubber gloves and submicron masks.
- Speak with your doctor about whether getting special vaccinations or carrying special medications is advisable.
- If you're traveling abroad, check the Centers for

Disease Control and Prevention (CDC) Web site prior to travel for precautions, and know the U.S. Embassy contact numbers in the host countries.

A kit with the following items also may help you deal with infectious threats:

- Insect repellent containing DEET
- Antibacterial hand wipes or alcohol-based hand sanitizer
- Water purification tablets
- Oral rehydration solution packets (to manage diarrheal dehydration)

See pages 280-286 for more travel-related recommendations.

FOR MORE INFORMATION

- U.S. Department of Homeland Security; *www.ready.gov*
- CDC Emergency Preparedness & Response; *www.bt.cdc.gov*

■ Reduce Your Risk on the Road

Approximately 50,000 people die on roads and highways in the United States every year. Many more are severely injured. To reduce your risk, follow these suggestions:

- **Always wear a seat belt,** even when you are traveling a short distance.
- **Place children in car seats and secure the seat properly.** (See sidebar below.)
- **Drive defensively.** Be aware of other traffic at all times.
- **Consider the weather** and adjust your speed according to conditions.
- **Don't drive while impaired.** Don't drive after consuming alcohol.
- **Avoid distractions.** Don't let the radio, talking on your cellular phone or a roadside attraction distract you.
- **Keep your car properly serviced** to reduce the risk of breakdowns.
- **Carry an emergency kit.** A kit may include a cellular phone (or change for a pay phone), flashlight, first-aid supplies, jumper cables, flares, a candle and matches.

Air Bags and Infant Car Safety Seats Don't Mix

The force of an air bag's deployment can kill or severely injure an infant or small child. Here's some advice for safely transporting your children:

- For infants who weigh less than 20 pounds or are younger than age 1, use infant car safety seats — or convertible infant-toddler safety seats. In a collision, the rigid seat supports your baby's back, neck and head. Secure the safety seat properly in the back seat of your car.

- For children who weigh 20 to 40 pounds or are younger than 4 years, use a child safety seat, anchored correctly, in the back seat. The safety seat's straps should hold the upper third of your child's chest securely.

  For children who weigh more than 40 pounds but who are too small to wear a lap and shoulder belt properly, use a car booster seat to obtain correct positioning of the lap and shoulder belt.

■ Reduce Your Risk at Home

Use this safety checklist to make your home a safer place.

- ❑ Household emergency preparedness plan and kit (see pages 229-230).
- ❑ Fire escape plan reviewed with all occupants.
- ❑ Smoke detectors installed on each floor and working.
- ❑ Carbon monoxide detectors installed on each floor and working.
- ❑ Fire hazards removed — flammable items away from open flame or heat source.
- ❑ Poisonous or dangerous substances locked up or out of the reach of children.
- ❑ Poison control, other emergency numbers and home address posted near phone.
- ❑ Dangerous objects away from children — tools, firearms, electrical or hot objects.
- ❑ Electrical equipment away from water; cords and equipment in good condition.
- ❑ Walkways and stairs well lighted, free of slippery surfaces, foreign objects.
- ❑ Night lights and visual aids in place for use at night.
- ❑ Handrails and nonslip surfaces in bathrooms, showers and on stairs.
- ❑ Allergen sources removed — gutters cleaned, drains in good working order, damp areas cleaned of mold and mildew and dehumidifier installed inside. Dusty spots, carpets and rugs vacuumed.
- ❑ Emergency shut-off valves for water and gas and master switch for electricity location and function known and accessible.
- ❑ Protective gear easily accessible — eye goggles, hearing protection, gloves, masks.

Preventing Falls

Trips and falls pose a danger to young children and older adults. Falls are a common cause of injury among older adults — sometimes resulting in death. Falls may be caused by faulty balance, poor vision, illness, medications and other factors. The best self-care is to develop a plan that reduces risk and prevents injury in the first place.

Self-Care

Here are some tips to prevent falls:

- **Have your vision and hearing checked regularly.** If vision and hearing are impaired, you lose important cues that help you maintain balance.
- **Exercise regularly.** Exercise improves your strength, muscle tone and coordination. This not only helps prevent falls but also reduces the severity of injury if you do fall.
- **Be wary of drugs.** Ask your doctor about the drugs you take. Some drugs may affect balance and coordination.
- **Avoid alcohol.** Even a little alcohol can cause falls, especially if your balance and reflexes are already impaired.
- **Get up slowly.** A momentary decrease in blood pressure, due to drugs or aging, can cause dizziness if you stand up too quickly.
- **Maintain balance and footing.** If you feel dizzy, use a cane or walker. Wear sturdy, low-heeled shoes with wide, nonslip soles.
- **Eliminate loose rugs or mats.**
- **Install adequate lighting,** especially night lighting.
- **Block steps** for infants and toddlers — install handrails for older people.

Lead Exposure

Approximately 310,000 children in the United States ages 1 to 5 have potentially dangerous levels of lead in their bloodstream, according to the Centers for Disease Control and Prevention. Lead poisoning can affect nearly every system in the body. Children are more sensitive to lead poisoning than are adults. The U.S. Environmental Protection Agency (EPA) recommends having your child tested for lead poisoning at age 6 months if you think that your home has high levels of lead, and after that as recommended by your doctor.

Here are some potential sources of lead poisoning:

- **Soil.** Lead particles that settle on the soil from paint or gasoline used years ago can stay there for many years. High concentrations of lead in soil can be found around old homes and in some urban settings.
- **Household dust.** This can contain lead from paint chips or soil brought in from outside.
- **Water.** Lead pipes, brass plumbing fixtures and copper pipes soldered with lead can release lead particles into tap water. If you have such plumbing, let cold water run 30 to 60 seconds before drinking it. Hot water absorbs more lead than does cold water. The EPA warns against making baby formula with hot tap water from old plumbing systems.
- **Lead paint.** Although now outlawed, lead paint is still on walls and woodwork in many older homes. When sanding or stripping in an older home, wear a mask and keep children away from dust and chips.

Carbon Monoxide Poisoning

Carbon monoxide is a poisonous gas produced by incomplete burning of fuel. It has no color, taste or odor. Carbon monoxide builds up in red blood cells, preventing oxygen from being carried and starving your body of oxygen.

Each year, approximately 500 Americans die of unintentional carbon monoxide poisoning. A few simple measures can help prevent poisoning:

- **Know the signs and symptoms.** They include headache, fever, red-appearing skin, dizziness, weakness, fatigue, nausea, vomiting, shortness of breath, chest pain and trouble thinking. Symptoms of carbon monoxide poisoning often come on slowly and may be mistaken for a cold or the flu. Clues include similar symptoms being experienced by everyone in the same building or improvement of symptoms when you leave the building for a day or more and then a return of the symptoms when you come back to the building.
- **Be aware of possible sources.** The most common sources are gas and oil furnaces, wood stoves, gas appliances, pool heaters and engine exhaust fumes. Cracked heat exchangers on furnaces, blocked chimneys, flues or appliance vents can allow carbon monoxide to reach living areas. An inadequate supply of fresh air to a furnace also can allow carbon monoxide to build up in living spaces. Tight home construction also may increase your risk because less fresh air gets in.
- **Get a detector.** It sounds a warning when carbon monoxide builds up. Look for UL 2034 on the package, an indication the detector meets industry standards.
- **Know when to take action.** If the alarm sounds, ventilate the area by opening doors and windows. If anyone is experiencing poisoning symptoms, evacuate immediately and call for emergency medical assistance from a nearby phone. If no one is experiencing symptoms, continue to ventilate, turn off all fuel-burning appliances and have a qualified technician inspect your home.

Indoor Air Pollution

The U.S. Environmental Protection Agency (EPA) rates indoor air pollution among the top environmental health risks. Others are outdoor air pollution, toxic chemicals in the workplace and contaminated drinking water.

The most dangerous pollutants found in indoor air include:

- **Tobacco smoke.** Smoking causes lung cancer. Even if you don't smoke but live with someone who does, you have a 20 percent higher risk of lung cancer than someone who lives in a smoke-free home. Air-filtering devices help, but remove mainly smoke's solid particles, not the gases.
- **Radon.** This naturally occurring gas is made by the radioactive decay of uranium in rocks and soil. You can easily overlook radon because you can't see, taste or smell it. Yet, radon can seep into your home and other buildings through basement cracks, sewer openings and joints between walls and floors. After chronic exposure at high levels, radon may lead to lung cancer. To check your home's radon level, buy a radon detector. If your radon level is high, call the EPA radon hot line: (800) 767-7236.
- **Household chemicals.** When using chemical compounds indoors such as glues, paints, cleaners, solvents and drain openers, be sure to ventilate the area.

Hand Washing

Americans spend billions of dollars annually to fight infections. With today's high-tech approach to health care, it's easy to forget the simplest way to avoid infection — wash your hands. Simple soap and water and careful washing is a proven ounce of prevention.

Why Is It Important?
Most cases of the common cold, flu (influenza), diarrhea, vomiting and hepatitis are caused by inadequate hand washing. Germs accumulate on your hands as you perform daily activities. By not washing your hands, you can acquire or pass on a host of ailments.

Overall, infections claim more lives than any other diseases except for heart disease and cancer. Pneumonia and flu are leading causes of death in the United States.

What's Proper Hand Washing?
Follow these steps:
- Place your hands under running water. Water temperature isn't essential. Water that's warm enough (about 110 F) to cut through grease is best. Water that's hot enough to kill germs can harm your hands.
- Apply soap or detergent to your hands.
- Rub vigorously for at least 10 seconds to suspend the germs (microorganisms).
- Clean around your cuticles, beneath your fingernails and in the creases of your hands.
- Rinse all soap from your hands to remove as many microorganisms as possible.

If you don't have time to wash with soap and water, there are a number of waterless hand-cleaners available. Alcohol-based hand rubs significantly reduce the number of microorganisms on your skin and are fast acting.

When Should You Wash?
It's impossible to keep your hands germ-free, but there are times when it's critical to wash your hands. Always wash:
- Before you handle or eat food
- After you use the toilet
- After changing a diaper
- After playing with a pet or handling pet equipment, such as brushes, aquariums or litter-boxes
- After handling garbage
- After handling money
- After blowing your nose, sneezing or coughing into your hand
- After handling uncooked food (especially meat)
- Before entering a hospital room and after leaving it

Aging and Your Health

■ How Age Can Affect Your Health

If you're older than age 40, you've undoubtedly confronted some realities of aging. You've probably peeked into a mirror at a face that has developed a few more wrinkles. You may have noticed that aches and pains linger a little longer after you exercise or spend time doing yardwork. Until adults reach the fourth or fifth decade of life, aging rarely means much to them — even though it's a lifelong process that begins at birth.

Most adults experience common physical changes as they get older. These examples come from the Baltimore Longitudinal Study of Aging, published by the Department of Health and Human Services:

- Your systolic blood pressure increases as artery walls thicken and become less flexible.
- Your body redistributes fat and your muscle mass declines.
- Your ability to hear high frequency sounds decreases, starting around age 20, and low frequency sounds become more difficult to hear during your 60s.
- Your maximum breathing capacity declines.
- Your brain sustains loss and damage of nerve cells.
- Your bladder loses capacity, leading to more frequent urination and, sometimes, leakage.
- Your kidneys become less efficient in removing waste from your bloodstream.

This list describes what happens on average to groups of people. It doesn't predict how aging will affect you in particular. By taking care of your health, you may be able to delay or avoid at least some of these occurrences.

How Long Can You Expect to Live?

This chart shows how many more years, on average, a person can expect to live, based on current age, sex and race. Of course, these are just general estimates. If you smoke or drive without a seat belt, you lower your odds. If you have a healthy lifestyle, you might increase the odds.

Average Number of Years Remaining

Current Age	All Races Male	All Races Female	White Male	White Female	Black Male	Black Female
50	28.5	32.5	28.8	32.6	24.9	30.0
55	24.4	28.0	24.6	28.1	21.3	25.9
60	20.5	23.8	20.6	23.8	18.0	22.1
65	16.8	19.8	16.9	19.8	15.0	18.5
70	13.5	16.1	13.5	16.0	12.2	15.3
75	10.6	12.7	10.5	12.6	9.9	12.3
80	8.1	9.7	8.0	9.6	8.0	9.8
85	6.1	7.2	6.0	7.1	6.5	7.7

Source: National Vital Statistics Reports, 2003

■ Maintaining Your Health as You Age

Successful aging involves many factors that are within your control. Begin with strategies to maintain your overall health.

Adopt a positive attitude. Remember that attitudes color the quality of your life. You're old only when you think you are. True, your body will age. Yet your mind, for the most part, will stay as young as you feel. If you expect to live a long life filled with physical vitality, humor and social connections, then that attitude shapes your future to a large degree.

In all of life, stay focused on what's important and shrug off what isn't. A sense of humor and ability to adapt to change are golden assets. Also see the suggestions for stress management on page 227.

Eat well. Numerous studies indicate that a healthy diet, when combined with regular physical and mental activity, can help you live longer and better. As you age, however, you may need to make certain adjustments in your approach to eating. In addition to the guidelines for eating well, beginning on page 210, keep the following suggestions in mind:

- To allow for the fact that your metabolism slows down, consider limiting serving sizes and calories to maintain a healthy weight.
- Increase your fiber intake, which can help prevent constipation and may decrease your risk of colon diseases, including colon cancer.
- To prevent cardiovascular disease, decrease the amount of fat, cholesterol and sodium you consume.
- If you drink alcohol, do so in moderation — in general, a maximum of one drink a day for women and two drinks a day for men.
- Remember that as you get older, your thirst mechanism declines. Make it a habit to drink at least six glasses a day of nonalcoholic liquids.

Avoid nicotine. Smoking has been linked to gum disease, high blood pressure, heart disease, stroke, lung cancer and a variety of other cancers. If you smoke or chew tobacco, make a plan to quit. For ideas, see page 192.

Keep physically active. Regular exercise can help prevent coronary artery disease, high blood pressure, stroke, diabetes, depression, falls and some cancers. Fitness also reduces the lifestyle-limiting effects of osteoporosis and arthritis.

It's never too late to become more active. You'll find many suggestions for doing so on page 217. But before you begin an exercise program that's more vigorous than walking, get a medical evaluation from your doctor.

Stay mentally sharp. Your brain is like a muscle. To keep it strong, use it. Participate in community activities such as tutoring, serving on boards or volunteering.

Stay socially connected. Having strong ties with family and friends is always important. With age, those connections become even more crucial. Studies indicate that if you have few social ties, your risk of premature death is two to four times greater than that of people who cultivate many caring relationships.

Seek out spirituality. Research supports the wisdom of believing in something larger than yourself as a way to cope with whatever life hands you. People who attend religious services are more likely to enjoy better health, live longer and recover from illness sooner and with fewer complications.

Everyone defines spirituality differently. For some people, it's organized religion. For others, spirituality is expressed through meditation, music or art — any source of meaning and purpose that allows you to withstand suffering and experience serenity in daily life.

Your Health and the Workplace

- Health, Safety and Injury Prevention
- Stress Relievers
- Coping With Technology

This section focuses on ways to improve your success and well-being in the work environment. You'll find practical information on a variety of basic health and safety issues. There also are tips on managing stress and strategies to deal with computer-related pains and strains.

Health, Safety and Injury Prevention

■ Protect Your Back

Your back moves in several directions and is used in weight-bearing activities. Back pain, especially low back pain, is one of the most common problems reported, both in the workplace and at home. The good news is that with as little as five to 10 minutes of exercises a day — along with following some simple guidelines when lifting — you can **prevent** many back problems.

Self-Care

Take care of your back:
- **Exercise regularly.** See page 55 for exercises designed to strengthen your back.
- **Lift properly.** For help in using proper lifting technique, see page 54.
- **Avoid back injury at work.** See Back Injuries in the Workplace on page 53 for more things you can do to reduce the risk of back injury and pain.
- **If you do have back pain.** The good news is there are several things you can do to feel better without going to the doctor or chiropractor. See Self-Care on page 51 for a list of things you can do on your own.

■ Hand and Wrist Care

What Causes Carpal Tunnel Syndrome?
The <u>carpal tunnel</u> is a passageway between your wrist and hand that contains and protects nerves and tendons. When the tissues in the carpal tunnel become swollen or inflamed, they put pressure on a nerve that provides sensation to your thumb and index, middle and ring fingers. Excess pressure on this nerve may cause you to experience any of the above-mentioned symptoms. If the condition is left untreated, nerve and muscle damage can occur.

Warning Signs of Carpal Tunnel Syndrome
- Numbness, or a tingling sensation in your hands or thumb, index and middle fingers (but not your little finger)
- Discomfort in the forearm or hand after forceful or repetitive use
- Awakening with these same symptoms during the night

Avoiding the Problem
Quick breaks, massage and ibuprofen, aspirin or other over-the-counter anti-inflammatory medications can relieve your symptoms temporarily. Take these precautions:
- **Take a five-minute break every hour.** Stop your activity and gently stretch your hands and fingers back. Alternate tasks when possible.
- **Watch your form.** Avoid bending your wrist all the way up or down. A relaxed middle position is best.
- **Relax your grip.** Avoid using a hard grip when driving your car, painting or writing. Oversized grips on pens, pencils and tools may allow a softer grasp.

Medical Help   Try the measures listed above, but if pain, numbness or weakness persists for more than a couple of weeks, see your doctor. Splints, therapy, injection or prescription medications may be recommended. Occasionally, surgery is necessary.

For more information on hand problems, see page 96.

■ Coping With Arthritis at Work

Here are tips on dealing with arthritis at work:

- Know and accept your limitations; sometimes long-term changes are necessary.
- Communicate special needs to your employer. Minor adaptations of your work environment or a different routine may take care of your problem.
- Check on a flexible work schedule; allow time to warm up and loosen joints before starting work.
- Try to organize your work activities to minimize significant repetitive motion; alternate heavy lifting with standing or sitting.
- Consider special equipment, such as pencil grippers, arm supports and floor mats for prolonged standing.

See pages 161-164 for more on managing arthritis.

■ Exercises for Office Workers

Sitting at work for eight hours a day can cause office workers syndrome — fatigue, stress, back pain, even blood clots. These stretches will help — and may even improve — your job performance.

Three five-minute stretch breaks a day will perk you up, relax your muscles and enhance your flexibility. Below and on the following page are exercises you can do without leaving your desk. Hold each stretch for 10 to 20 seconds. Repeat each exercise once or twice on both sides.

1. *Stretch your fingers out as far as you can. Hold for 10 seconds. Relax. Now bend your fingers at the knuckles and squeeze.*

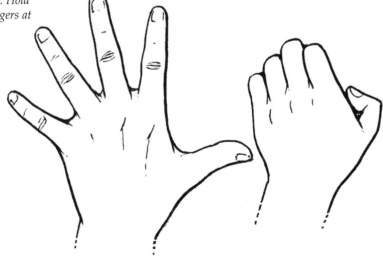

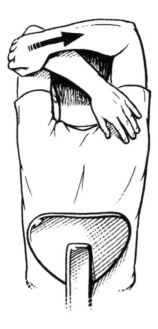

2. Slowly tilt your head to the left until you feel a stretch on the side of your neck. Repeat to the right and forward.

3. Hold your left arm just above the elbow with your right hand. Gently pull your elbow across your chest toward the right shoulder while turning your head to look over the left shoulder. Repeat with other arm.

4. Raise your left elbow above your head and put your left palm on the back of your neck. Now grasp your left elbow with your right hand. Gently pull your elbow behind your head and toward your right shoulder until you feel a nice stretch in your shoulder or upper arms. Repeat with other arm.

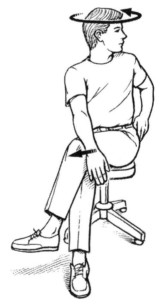

5. Hold your left leg just below the knee. Gently pull your bent leg toward your chest. Hold it with your right arm and pull it toward your right shoulder. Repeat with right leg.

6. Cross your left leg over your right leg. Cross your right elbow over your left thigh. Gently press your leg with your elbow to twist your hip and lower and middle parts of your back. Look over your left shoulder to complete the stretch. Repeat to other side.

Safety in the Workplace

Protect yourself and others by following these safety rules and common-sense guidelines:

- **Protective eye wear.** If your job carries a risk of eye injury, your employer is required by law to provide you with protective glasses, and you are required to wear them. If they interfere with your efficiency, try another design.
- **Protection from noise.** In conditions of excessively loud noise, your employer should regularly measure noise levels or provide protective devices. Specially designed earmuffs are available. Some types close out the outside world; others are fitted with earphones and a microphone that enable you to communicate with other workers. Commercially available earplugs made of foam, plastic or rubber or custom-molded plugs also effectively decrease your exposure to excessive noise. Don't use cotton balls. They can get stuck deep in your ear canal.
- **Fumes, smoke, dust and gas hazards.** Many respiratory symptoms can result from exposure to toxic fumes, gases, particles and smoke in the workplace. The exposure may be long-term with low levels of chemicals, or it may be accidental, in which high levels of industrial toxic chemicals are inhaled for a short time. Wear proper clothing, air-filtration masks, eye gear and other appropriate protection. Be sure ventilation is adequate.

If you're pregnant or are trying to become pregnant, avoid any exposure to hazardous chemicals.

If you suspect that you're being exposed to dangerous smoke, fumes, dust or chemicals in your workplace, discuss the matter with your health care provider. Many permanent respiratory ailments develop slowly as a result of industrial exposure over a period of years. Small exposures that may seem harmless can result in chronic disease. If you think that you or your co-workers are at unnecessary risk, consult with your company safety office, or contact the Occupational Safety and Health Administration (OSHA) or your union.

Medication and alcohol use. Don't consume alcohol before or during working hours. Do not operate machinery when you are taking medications that might make you drowsy. If taking medications, ask your health care provider or pharmacist how these substances might affect your job.

Emergency preparedness. Make sure you understand the steps you need to take in case of an emergency at your place of employment. Many companies have plans that outline what to do in various types of emergencies. If your company doesn't have such a plan, talk to someone about preparing one.

Sleeping Tips for Shift Workers

Changing your normal rhythm of waking and sleeping, as a result of switching shifts, requires a period of adjustment. If your job requires constant changing of shifts, your body will have more difficulty adjusting and readjusting as you get older.

Here are some things to try:

- Work a shift for three weeks rather than rotating to a different schedule every week.

- Change the sequence. A more normal sleep pattern results when the shift sequence is day-evening-night rather than day-night-evening.
- Tolerance to shift rotation varies among people. If you have difficulty making the adjustment, consider changing your job. If you experience severe insomnia, ask your doctor about a short-acting sleeping pill.

For more information, see page 44.

■ Drugs, Alcohol and Work

Illicit street drugs and alcohol can affect your health and safety in the workplace, as well as the safety of your co-workers. The problem is extensive.

Consider the following statistics:
- Approximately 75 percent of illegal drug users are employed.
- Alcoholism causes 500 million lost workdays a year.
- Alcohol and drug abuse has been estimated to cost American businesses roughly $81 billion in lost productivity in just one year.
- Individuals who are illicit drug users or heavy alcohol users are twice as likely to skip one or more days of work a month than do those who are not.
- Up to 40 percent of industrial fatalities and 47 percent of industrial injuries can be linked to alcohol consumption and alcoholism.
- Drug users, as a group, use medical benefits at a rate two to three times higher than nonusers.

Self-Assessment

To determine if you have a problem with alcohol or drugs, ask yourself the following questions:
- Have I used an illicit drug in the past six months?
- Have I misused a prescription drug because of its effect (to sleep or calm myself, or for pleasure)?
- Have I done something unsafe or taken risks while under the influence of alcohol or drugs, such as driving a car, operating heavy equipment or making decisions that affect the safety of others?
- Have I used alcohol within 12 hours of going to work?
- Has my drug or alcohol use negatively affected my relationships, my health or my ability to work?

If you answered yes to any of these questions, you're showing signs of substance abuse and should take action.

Self-Care

- If you or a family member is dependent on alcohol, refer to Alcohol Abuse and Alcoholism on page 188.
- If you or a family member has problems with drug addiction, refer to Drug Dependency on page 196.
- Many large corporations offer confidential employee assistance programs to help workers deal with drug and alcohol abuse. Inquire about their availability through your personnel or human resources department.
- If your company doesn't offer an alcohol or drug rehabilitation program, contact your health care provider or a mental health professional for a confidential referral.

Stress Relievers

■ Burned Out? Get a Tuneup

If you dread going to work or feel burned out or stressed over a period of weeks, you are facing a situation that could affect your professional and personal relationships and even your livelihood. Overwhelming frustration or indifference toward your job, persistent irritability, anger, sarcasm and a quickness to argue are indicators of a condition that needs to be dealt with. Here are strategies you can use:

- **Take care of yourself.** Eat regular, balanced meals, including breakfast. Get adequate sleep and exercise.
- **Develop friendships at work and outside the office.** Sharing unsettling feelings with people you trust is the first step toward resolving them. Limit activities with "negative" friends who reinforce bad feelings.
- **Take time off.** Take a vacation or a long weekend. Plan private time each week when you do not answer calls or pages. During the workday, take short breaks.
- **Set limits.** When necessary, learn to say no in a friendly but firm manner.
- **Choose battles wisely.** Don't rush to argue every time someone disagrees with you. Keep a cool head, and save your argument for things that really matter. Better yet, try not to argue at all.
- **Have an outlet.** Read, do a hobby, exercise or get involved in some other activity that gets your mind off work and is relaxing.
- **Seek help.** If none of these steps relieves your feelings of stress or burnout, ask a health care professional for advice.

■ Co-worker Conflict: 5 Steps to Make the Peace

The best way to deal with differences is directly, that is, talking with the person with whom you have a conflict. However, the mood of that discussion is crucial. Here are some helpful tips:

- **Discuss the matter privately.** Choose neutral territory, at a specific time that each can agree on. Approach the other person in a nonthreatening manner, such as "I would like to talk something over with you. I'm feeling..." Another opening line is, "I would like to check something out with you when you have a chance to talk."
- **Don't blame the other person.** Use "I" statements. It will make the other person feel less defensive or angry.
- **Listen closely to the other person.** Understanding the other person's point of view may help you feel less stressed or angry.
- **Focus on ways to resolve the problem.** Don't get sidetracked in an argument.
- **Seek help.** Talk with an employee assistance counselor who can help develop ground rules for such discussions and promote respectful communication.

Workplace Health

■ 5 Tips for Managing Time

- Create realistic deadlines for yourself, and set regular progress reviews.
- Throw away all but the important papers on your desk. Prepare a master list of tasks. Pitch files older than six months.
- Throughout the day, scan your master list and work on tasks in priority order.
- Use a planner. Store addresses and telephone numbers there. Copy master list items onto the page for the day on which you expect to do them. Evaluate and prioritize daily.
- For especially important or difficult projects, reserve an interruption-free block of time behind closed doors.

■ Get to Know Your Boss and Get Along Better

If you and your boss mix like oil and water, don't despair. To revive your relationship, work on getting to know him or her better. Here's how:

- Ask yourself, "What does my boss really need?" Is it more important to him or her that you stay on schedule while producing fair-to-good results, or is sacrificing a deadline OK if it means making a project perfect? Does your boss like to know your every move, or does he or she feel taxed with information overload when you provide updates? Learn your boss's preferences and use the information to make your boss's life and yours easier.
- Know what your boss expects. If the person you report to isn't forthcoming about expectations, be direct in asking what they are.
- Determine your boss's personal style. Formal or informal? Big picture or details? Without becoming a clone, try to adapt your behavior.

■ Halt Hostility: Talk It Out

To head off hostility, the most important thing to do is to talk with someone to release tension and possibly gain a new perspective.

When a conflict is already brewing:

- Talk about *solutions* as well as problems. Work with others to rectify the situation.
- Try to put off your anger until you've heard all the facts.
- If you feel an outburst coming on, take a break. Count to 10, breathe deeply, go for a walk — whatever it takes to cool off and avoid doing something you might regret later.
- Use active-listening skills and calmly repeat back what you've heard. ("Let me make sure I understand you. ...")
- When an angry confrontation seems inevitable, seek a neutral third party to help talk it through.

Coping With Technology

■ Computer Screens and Eyestrain

There you sit, peering at your video display terminal (VDT). If you're one of a growing number of people for whom using a computer is integral to their work, you may be peering for the umpteenth hour today. And like many computer users, you may be experiencing eyestrain as a result.

Symptoms may include:
- Sore, tired, burning, itchy or dry eyes
- Blurred or double vision
- Distance vision blurred after prolonged staring at monitor
- Headache, sore neck
- Difficulty shifting focus between monitor and source documents
- Difficulty focusing on the screen image
- Color fringes or afterimages when you look away from the monitor
- Increased sensitivity to light

Eyestrain associated with VDTs isn't thought to have serious or long-term consequences, but it is disruptive and unpleasant. Although you probably can't change every factor that may cause eyestrain, here are some things you can try to ease the strain:
- Change your work habits.
- Take eye breaks. Look away from the screen and into the distance or at an object several feet away for 10 seconds every 10 minutes.
- Change of pace. Try to move around at least once every two hours, giving both your eyes and your body a needed rest. Arrange noncomputer work as breaks from the screen. Consider standing while doing such work.
- Wink 'em, blink 'em. Dry eyes can result from prolonged computer use, especially for contact lens wearers. Some people blink only once a minute when doing computer work (once every five seconds is normal). Less blinking means less lubrication from tears, resulting in dry, itchy or burning eyes. So blink more often. If that doesn't help, you may want to consider using an eyedrop form of artificial tears available over-the-counter.
- Close 'em. If possible, lean back and close your eyes for a few moments once in a while. You may not want to do this at your desk and risk being accused of sleeping on the job.

Everything in Its Place

Monitor. Position your monitor 18 to 30 inches from your eyes. Many people find that putting the screen at arm's length works well. If you have to get too close to read small type, consider using larger font sizes for characters on your screen.

The top of the screen should be at eye level or below so that you look down slightly at your work. Place the monitor too high and you'll have to tilt your head back to look up at it, a recipe for a sore neck, and for dry eyes because you may not close your eyes completely when you blink. If you have your monitor on top of your central processing unit (CPU), consider placing the CPU to one side or on the floor.

Dust on the screen cuts down contrast and may contribute to glare and reflection problems. Keep it clean.

Keyboard. Put your keyboard directly in front of the monitor. If you place it at an angle or to the side, your eyes will be forced to focus separately, a tiring activity.

Source documents. Put reading and reference material on a copy stand beside the monitor and at the same level, angle and distance away. That way, your eyes aren't constantly readjusting as they go back and forth.

Surrounding (ambient) light and glare. To check glare, sit at your computer with the monitor off. You will be able to see the reflected light and images you don't normally see — including yourself. Note any intense glare. The worst problems likely will be from sources above or behind you, including fluorescent lighting and sunlight.

If possible, place your monitor so that the brightest light sources are off to the side, parallel with your line of sight to the monitor. Consider turning off some or all overhead lights. If you can't do that, tilting the monitor downward a little may reduce glare. Closing blinds or shades also may help. A hood or glare-reducing screen is an option, but be sure you aren't sacrificing the intensity of whites on your screen. Adjustable task lighting that doesn't shine into your eyes as you look at the screen can reduce eyestrain. Overall, the surrounding light should be darker than the whitest white on your screen.

Glasses. The correct correction can help. If you wear glasses or contacts, make sure the correction is right for computer work. Most lenses are fitted for reading print and may not be optimal for computer work. For example, many bifocal wearers are constantly craning their necks to look through the bottom half of the lenses, bringing on a backache or neck ache. Glasses or contact lenses designed to focus correctly for computer work may be worth the investment.

See an eye care professional if you have:
- Prolonged eye discomfort
- A noticeable change in vision
- Double vision

The Healthy Consumer

- **You and Your Health Care Provider**
- **Home Medical Testing Kits**
- **Your Family Medical Tree**
- **Medications and You**
- **Dietary Supplements**
- **Alternative Medicine and Your Health**
- **The Healthy Traveler**

In this section, you'll find information about being a savvy health care consumer. You'll learn how to best communicate and work with your doctor, what you can learn from your family's medical history, and about the effectiveness of home medical testing kits. The proper use of medications is also covered, along with easy-to-understand descriptions of cold remedies and over-the-counter pain medications. What to include in your family's home medicine chest and first-aid kit is also covered, as well as the potential health risks associated with travel.

You and Your Health Care Provider

Medical care is becoming increasingly complex. And finding the right health care provider for you and your family can be a challenge. You may be in good health and not need a doctor immediately. But when you do, it's good to have someone who knows you and who can quickly and efficiently coordinate your care. In this section, you'll find tips on selecting the health care team that's right for you.

■ Start With Primary Care

You'll likely begin by looking for a doctor who is a generalist — a primary care doctor who often leads a team that includes medical assistants, physician assistants, nurses and nurse practitioners. A primary care doctor and his or her team can do the following:

- Be the point of first contact for urgent and acute care.
- Provide preventive care, such as blood pressure monitoring, cancer screening and vaccinations.
- Provide telephone and e-mail consultation when advice is needed but an office visit isn't required.
- Provide continuity of care. This is especially important if you or someone in your family has a chronic condition.
   Here are examples of primary care specialties:
- **Family practitioner.** Provides care to people of all ages and may also provide obstetric care.
- **Internal medicine specialist.** Provides care focused on the general needs of adults, including older adults.
- **Geriatrician.** Provides care focused on the general needs of older adults.
- **Pediatrician.** Provides care for children and adolescents.
- **Gynecologist.** A provider of specialty care, but many gynecologists provide primary care for adult females.

■ How to Find a Doctor

Once you have an idea about what kind of primary care provider you want, identify several candidates. Talk with friends and co-workers about their experiences with doctors in your community. In addition, consider whether you want one primary care doctor for all family members or more focused care from a pediatrician or gynecologist.

If you're on a managed care insurance plan, you'll probably be limited to the doctors on the insurance plan's list. If so, make sure you have the current list.

Verify Credentials
Before you visit a doctor, make a phone call or visit a Web site to confirm the doctor's credentials. If your doctor is board certified in a specialty, such as family practice, internal medicine or geriatrics, you can confirm this by checking with the

American Board of Medical Specialties. You can call this organization toll-free at (866) 275-2267 or log on to the Web site *www.abms.org*. The American Medical Association also has a Web site that identifies specialists. It's called AMA DoctorFinder, *www.ama-assn.org/aps/amahg.htm*.

To determine if any disciplinary action has been taken or may be pending against a doctor, call your state medical licensing board. For the number, look under state government listings in your phone book or call directory assistance. Keep in mind, however, that even the best doctors occasionally have legal problems. So don't let this be the only factor in your decision.

Visit the Doctor's Office

Once you've selected two or three doctors, set up get-acquainted visits. Tell the receptionist you're looking for a doctor and you'd like to speak with someone who could answer a few questions about the doctor and office procedures.

A good place to start is to find out if the doctor is accepting new patients. Next, ask if the doctor accepts your medical insurance plan.

Here are some additional questions you might ask:
- What's the doctor's training and special field of practice?
- What are your office hours?
- How many days a week does the doctor see patients?
- Are evening or weekend appointments possible?
- If I call the office with a medical question, can I speak with the doctor?
- How does the doctor arrange to answer medical questions after hours?
- How far in advance do people have to make an appointment? (If longer than a month, the doctor is probably overloaded. You might want to look elsewhere.)
- How long do people generally have to wait in the office?
- How willing is the doctor to refer people to a specialist?
- How long will you be able to visit with the doctor? (Some HMOs restrict total time to less than 30 minutes.)

Trust Your Instincts

If you don't feel compatible with the doctor, try the next one on your list. You're more likely to follow the advice of a doctor with whom you feel comfortable. Doctors know it. So don't worry about offending them. Concentrate on your needs.

■ Specialists You May Need

How do you know when you need a specialist or other health care provider, such as a physical therapist, a physician extender or a nurse practitioner? Generally, your primary care doctor will refer you to a specialist when you have a problem that warrants it. If you're concerned that you have medical problems not being adequately cared for by your primary care doctor, you might want to seek a specialist whose training and experience matches the problem.

If you visit a specialist, ask that the records of your diagnosis and treatment be sent to your primary care doctor, who needs to keep track of your overall health care. Ask for a copy of the records for yourself. Also, next time you visit your primary care doctor, be sure to give a report of what the specialist did for you.

Specialists

Here's a list of specialists you might need along with the systems, diseases, conditions or therapies that they can help you with:

Allergist, immunologist. Treats allergies and diseases of the immune system

Anesthesiologist. Administers and monitors anesthetics

Audiologist. Tests hearing and treats hearing disorders

Cardiologist. Treats disorders of the heart, blood vessels and circulation

Dermatologist. Treats skin diseases

Emergency medicine specialist. Evaluates and treats trauma, emergencies

Endocrinologist. Treats problems with the glands, including diabetes

Family physician. Treats all family members and conditions

Gastroenterologist. Treats digestive diseases

Geneticist. Specializes in inherited diseases

Gynecologist. Specializes in care of women

Hematologist. Treats diseases of the blood

Infectious diseases specialist. Treats infectious diseases, immunization

Internist. Involved in diagnosis and nonsurgical treatment of disease in adults

Nephrologist. Treats kidney problems

Neurologist. Specializes in nervous system disorders

Neurosurgeon. Treats nerve diseases surgically

Obstetrician. Specializes in pregnancy, delivery and infant care

Oncologist. Specializes in cancer

Ophthalmologist. Treats eye disorders

Orthopedist. Treats bone disorders and injuries with surgery

Otorhinolaryngologist. Treats ear, nose and throat disorders

Pathologist. Studies bodily fluids and tissues

Pediatrician. Treats childhood diseases

Physiatrist. Treats disorders of the nervous and musculoskeletal systems

Preventive medicine specialist. Focuses on preventing disease and injury

Psychiatrist. Treats mental health conditions

Psychologist. Specializes in psychological assessment and counseling therapy

Pulmonologist. Treats respiratory disorders and also sleep disorders

Radiologist. Uses imaging techniques to diagnose and treat disease

Rheumatologist. Treats problems of the joints, muscles and connective tissue

Surgeon. Treats various conditions with surgery; many subspecialties

Urologist. Specializes in disorders of the urinary and urogenital tracts

Other Health Care Providers

Nurse. If you're in the hospital, you'll probably see nurses more frequently than doctors because nurses provide most of the care. The nurses observe symptoms and listen to you describe them, help carry out the treatment plan and evaluate the results.

The initials *R.N.* after a nurse's name mean registered nurse. To be an R.N., a person must complete a bachelor's degree in nursing or a similar program, and then pass a licensing examination. Some registered nurses have postgraduate degrees.

The initials *L.P.N.* mean licensed practical nurse. The L.P.N. course of study is shorter, and the L.P.N. generally works under the supervision of an R.N.

Some nurses specialize. They might focus on pediatrics or cardiology. Some not only specialize but also become a nurse practitioner (N.P.). A nurse practitioner usually has at least a master's degree and performs many of the same basic tasks as a doctor — examining and treating people as well as writing prescriptions.

Occupational therapist. If you're injured or disabled, an occupational therapist helps you regain your ability to carry out everyday tasks, such as the activities required to make a living. The word *occupational* is misleading because the therapy isn't aimed solely at helping you get back to work, but at regaining the ability to do daily tasks wherever you are, at home or on the job: eating, dressing, bathing, home-making and recreational skills. This therapist may recommend physical changes to your home or workplace — such as rearranging furniture or adding ramps and railings — to make it easier for you to get around and carry out your tasks.

Pharmacist. Your pharmacist is a good source of information about your medicine, whether it's prescription or nonprescription drugs. Since the pharmacist keeps a record of all prescriptions you buy at his or her pharmacy, it's helpful to use the same pharmacy for all your prescription drugs. This provides a double-check, to make sure you don't take a medication that reacts with something else you're taking. The pharmacist can also help you select nonprescription drugs that are best for you.

Physical therapist. Like an occupational therapist, a physical therapist also helps injured and disabled people regain lost physical functions, using techniques such as exercise, massage and ultrasound. The focus here is to maximize physical ability and compensate for physical functions that have been lost.

Physician assistant. Like a nurse practitioner, a physician assistant (P.A.) often works with a doctor by diagnosing and treating people with some of the more common health care problems. Most P.A.s have at least a bachelor's degree. They generally work under the supervision of a doctor, performing work assigned by the doctor. Working as part of the health care team, they take medical histories, treat minor injuries that may require stitches or casting, order and interpret lab tests and X-rays, and make diagnoses. In most states they can also write prescriptions.

In some clinics, most of the routine care is given by P.A.s. You may not see the doctor unless you have a major problem.

Selecting a Surgeon

Your primary doctor will help you find a good surgeon should you ever need an operation. If you need a joint replacement, for example, you'll probably be recommended to an orthopedic surgeon, who specializes in operations involving joints, muscles and bones. When choosing a surgeon, try to select one who has performed a lot of the kind of surgery you'll be having.

Given the potential risks and costs of many surgeries, it often makes good sense to get a second opinion. Either you or your primary doctor can make the decision to get that second opinion. So don't feel you need to be secretive about visiting a second surgeon. Keep your primary doctor informed.

Questions to Ask Before Surgery

Whether your regular doctor or a surgeon recommends surgery, you'll want to ask several questions:

What is done during the operation? Ask for a clear description of the operation. If necessary, perhaps you could ask the doctor to draw a picture to help explain exactly what the surgery involves.

Are there alternatives to surgery? Sometimes surgery is the only way to correct the problem. But one option might be watchful waiting, to see if the problem gets better or worse.

How will surgery help? A hip replacement, for example, may mean you'll be able to walk comfortably again. To what extent will the surgery help, and how long will the benefits last? You'll want realistic expectations.

What are the risks? All operations carry some risk. Weigh the benefits against the risks. Ask also about the side effects of the operation, such as the degree of pain you might expect and how long that pain will last.

What kind of experience have you had with this surgery? How many times has the doctor performed this surgery, and what percentage of the patients had successful results? To reduce your risks, you want a doctor who is thoroughly trained in the surgery and who has plenty of experience doing it.

Where will the surgery be done? Many surgeries today are done on an outpatient basis. You go to a hospital or a clinic for the surgery and return home the same day.

Will I be put to sleep for the surgery? Your surgery may require only local anesthesia, which means that just part of your body is numbed for a short time. In case of general anesthesia, you are put to sleep.

How long will recovery take? You'll want to know when most people are able to resume their normal activities, such as doing chores around the house and returning to work. You may think there would be no harm in lifting a sack of groceries after a week or two. But there might be. Follow your doctor's advice as carefully as possible.

What will it cost me? Health insurance coverage varies. You may not have to pay anything. You might have a deductible to meet. Or perhaps you'll have to pay a percentage of the cost. The doctor's office can usually give you information about this, but also check with your insurance company.

Be certain to know if you are responsible for a flat copay — a set amount for the surgery — or if you have to pay a percentage of the bill. There's a big, and expensive, difference.

Home Medical Testing Kits

Your pharmacy or drugstore has kits that can be used to perform medical tests at home, without the involvement of a physician or other health care provider.

Like most tests in a laboratory, home tests use urine, blood or stool. Some of them are relatively inexpensive and can be performed more than once.

Types of Kits

- **Pregnancy tests** to determine whether you are pregnant.
- **Ovulation prediction tests** to help determine the best time for intercourse that may lead to conception.
- **Sugar tests,** of either urine or blood, to determine whether diabetes is present or well controlled.
- **Cholesterol tests** to determine your total cholesterol level.
- **Other urine tests**, such as for excess protein, which may signal a kidney problem.
- **Tests to detect blood** in the stool, which may indicate a tumor in the colon.
- **Human immunodeficiency virus (HIV) tests** check for antibodies to HIV, the virus that causes AIDS. The test involves placing a drop of blood on a test card with an identification number. You mail the card to the designated certified laboratory, then call for results in about one week.

Disadvantages of Home Tests

- **There's the risk of simply doing the test wrong** and, therefore, getting a misleading result. You must follow the instructions exactly, or the test won't work properly. Professionals in a medical laboratory are less likely to make a mistake because they have more experience and better equipment.
- **Medical tests don't always work correctly.** This is true for tests done at home and for tests performed in a medical laboratory. A certain percentage of test results suggest that something is present when it's not (false-positive). For example, a false-positive test result would indicate that you have hidden blood in the stool when in fact you don't, or that you are pregnant when you aren't.
- **False-negative results** can be found. A certain percentage of test results indicate that something isn't present when it is, which is called a false-negative. For example, a false-negative test result would indicate that your blood glucose concentration is normal when it is not, or that you are not pregnant when you are. A physician is in a better position to judge false-negative and false-positive test results on the basis of other medical evidence, training and experience.
- **You may interpret the result incorrectly.** Changes in the appearance of the test result, such as the color, may be confusing. And oftentimes, you need to see your physician or have the test repeated by a medical laboratory no matter what the result.
- **Indecision** is a factor. After performing the test, it's often difficult to decide what to do next. For example, if you're certain there is blood in your stool but the test indicates otherwise, should you still see your physician?

Caution

When used appropriately, many home testing kits can be accurate. Nevertheless, use them carefully. They're not a substitute for appropriate medical care, especially when you think you may be at risk of a serious medical condition. Follow up worrisome, unexpected test results with your health care provider.

Healthy Consumer

Your Family Medical Tree

Family gatherings are an ideal time to catch up on family news. They're also an opportunity to learn more about your family health history.

Approximately 5 percent of people with colon cancer have an inherited form. Children of alcoholics are three to four times more likely to become addicted to alcohol or other drugs than children whose parents aren't alcoholics. And a family history of high blood pressure, diabetes, some cancers and certain psychiatric disorders significantly increases all family members' odds of developing the condition.

If blood relatives have had a particular disease or condition, are you destined to get it? Usually not. But it may mean that you're at an increased risk.

Many major diseases have a hereditary component. Medical trees reveal patterns of inherited illness. With the information that a medical tree provides, your doctor may prescribe tests to determine if you have a particular condition, or use the tree as a basis for recommending lifestyle changes to reduce your risk.

When you know that you're at increased risk of a disease, you may be able to take steps to prevent it — or at least detect it early, when the odds for a cure may be in your favor.

Creating a Family Medical Tree

- **Learn who's who.** Research your parents, siblings and children. Then add information about grandparents, aunts and uncles, cousins and nieces and nephews. The more relatives you include, the better.

- **Dig for details.** Interview relatives by phone, or mail them questionnaires.

- **Look into the past.** Information about any ailment — from allergies to limps — could prove helpful. Pay special attention to serious but potentially preventable conditions, such as cancer, high blood pressure, heart disease, diabetes, depression and alcoholism. Note the age of the relative when the illness was diagnosed. What kind of lifestyle did the person lead — tobacco use, activity level, diet?

- **Put it all together.** Organize your chart so you can view the health histories of several relatives at once (see the illustration). Assign each medical condition a letter, and then write this letter next to the person's name or figure. Note the person's age when he or she died.

- **Talk it over.** Ask your physician to review your medical tree.

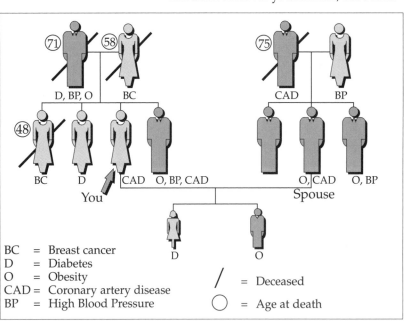

BC = Breast cancer
D = Diabetes
O = Obesity
CAD = Coronary artery disease
BP = High Blood Pressure

/ = Deceased

◯ = Age at death

A family tree showing how you can chart a family medical history.

Medications and You

No matter what your age or condition, there are fundamental rules to follow when taking medications:

- **Advise your health care provider about any over-the-counter products** you're taking, including laxatives or antacids; aspirin or acetaminophen; cough, cold or allergy medicines; weight-loss or weight-gain products; mineral and vitamin supplements; or herbal preparations. Nonprescription products can be potent, and some can cause serious reactions when mixed with prescription drugs.
- **Be informed.** Know what medications you take and why you're taking them.
- **Read labels and provided information carefully.** Ask your health care provider and pharmacist about potential side effects, about any dietary restrictions you should follow, whether you should avoid alcohol while taking the drug or about other concerns you have. If you get a prescription refilled and it appears different from what you had been taking, ask your pharmacist why.
- **Follow instructions.** Anyone who uses more than the recommended dosage is in danger of an overdose. The "more is better" theory doesn't apply to drugs.
- **Don't stop taking a prescribed drug** just because your symptoms seem to lessen. Take your medication for the entire length of time prescribed, even if symptoms have disappeared, unless instructed otherwise by your physician.
- **Keep a list** of what you take if you're taking several medications on a daily basis. Carry it in your purse or wallet. In addition, list allergies and drug intolerances.
- **Inform your health care provider of side effects.** Be alert to headache, dizziness, blurred vision, ringing in your ears, shortness of breath, hives and other unexpected effects.
- **Inform your health care provider if you're pregnant, trying to become pregnant or are breast-feeding.** Some medications can be harmful to a fetus or may be excreted in breast milk, which could harm your baby.
- **Have prescriptions filled at one pharmacy.** Using one pharmacy can help you avoid problems with drug interactions. Your pharmacist can help monitor the mix of medications, even if they're prescribed by different physicians. Let your pharmacist know if you have any chronic conditions, to make sure your medications won't worsen your condition or become toxic in your body.
- **Properly store medications.** Most require a dry, secure place at room temperature and out of direct sunlight. Some drugs need refrigeration. A bathroom cabinet is a poor place to store medications because of temperature and moisture variations.
- **Discard outdated drugs.** Medicine deteriorates over time and can sometimes become toxic. Never take leftover medicine.
- **Be concerned for children.** Keep prescription and nonprescription drugs safely away from the reach of children. Buy child-resistant packages, especially if you have young children, grandchildren or very young guests.
- **Keep medicines in their original containers.** Prescription containers are designed to protect medications from light and provide vital information. If the label gets separated from a medicine container and there's any doubt as to its contents, discard the medicine immediately.
- **Don't lend or share prescription drugs.** What helps you might harm others.
- **Don't mix medications and alcohol.** The two can produce a harmful interaction.
- **Don't let cost discourage you.** If the cost of a drug is more than you can pay, ask your doctor or pharmacist if there's a less expensive alternative medication.

Healthy Consumer

Ordering Medications on the Internet

Ordering prescription drugs online can save you time and sometimes money. Many online pharmacies provide information about drug interactions. Some even e-mail alerts when a drug is recalled or a generic equivalent becomes available.

But you must be careful. Questionable online pharmacies may ship expired drugs or those that haven't been stored properly. Others don't require a prescription or check for drug interactions. Some sites skirt the edge of legality.

To safeguard your health and finances, here are some things to remember:

- **Consult your doctor.** Your doctor can determine if a particular drug is safe for you or if another treatment would be better. Make sure your doctor knows all the medications you're taking, including over-the-counter and prescription drugs.
- **Use a licensed pharmacy.** The National Association of Boards of Pharmacy can tell you whether a particular online pharmacy is licensed and in good standing. Some sites carry a seal of approval from Verified Internet Pharmacy Practice Sites, or VIPPS. To gain this approval, sites must maintain state licenses and allow inspections by the National Association of Boards of Pharmacy.
- **Insist on access to a registered pharmacist.** Reputable sites offer toll-free access to registered pharmacists for help answering your medication questions. Some online pharmacies have traditional physical locations as well. If you have questions about a medication after you begin taking it or you're concerned about drug reactions, it may be especially valuable to speak with a pharmacist in person.
- **Read the privacy and security policies.** Before placing an order, be confident that your credit card number, personal health information and other personally identifiable information will be protected.
- **Compare prices.** You may find great deals online. But there aren't any guarantees. Your local drugstore might beat the online price.
- **Be cautious of sites based in foreign countries.** Legitimate international sites exist. But there are risks. The product label or instructions may be in a language you don't understand. The medication may not be held to the same rigorous safety standards. A medication sold in the United States may be a different product with the same name in another country. Some foreign sites sell drugs that are illegal in the United States.
- **Avoid sites that bypass prescriptions.** Only your doctor can safely prescribe medication for you and safely monitor side effects.
- **Get an address and telephone number.** Steer clear of sites that don't provide a street address and phone number or list only foreign information. An e-mail address isn't enough.
- **Be wary of false claims.** Don't buy medication from sites that advertise "miracle cures" or those that use impressive terminology to disguise a lack of good science.
- **Report problems.** If your order doesn't arrive, you find unauthorized charges on your credit card or you have another problem with an online pharmacy, report it to the Food and Drug Administration. Speaking up can help promote a safer marketplace for everyone.

■ Pain Relievers: Matching the Pill to the Pain

All nonprescription oral pain relievers contain one of five ingredients — salicylates (including aspirin), acetaminophen, ibuprofen, naproxen sodium and, most recently, ketoprofen. For pain relief, the differences among products are generally more subtle than significant.

Pain relievers are called analgesics (from the Greek words *an*, meaning "without," and *algos*, meaning "pain"). Over-the-counter (OTC) oral analgesics often relieve mild to moderate pain associated with headache, colds, toothache, muscle ache, backache, arthritis and menstrual cramps. They also reduce fever. OTC analgesics fall into two main categories: those products that also decrease inflammation and those that don't.

- **NSAIDs.** Aspirin, ibuprofen, naproxen sodium and ketoprofen reduce inflammation and are called nonsteroidal anti-inflammatory drugs (NSAIDs). They're most helpful for pain associated with conditions such as arthritis and tendinitis. Common side effects include stomach upset, ulcer and bleeding.
- **Acetaminophen** doesn't relieve inflammation. Because it's relatively free of side effects at recommended doses, it may be an alternative for long-term use or when taking NSAIDs presents a risk.

All regular-strength doses of OTC pain relievers provide comparable relief for everyday pain such as headache or sore muscles. For menstrual pain, ibuprofen, naproxen sodium and ketoprofen may offer better relief.

Separating Help From Hype

OTC pain medications come in a great variety of forms. Sometimes a less expensive generic form is all you need. If you have questions, ask a pharmacist or your doctor.

Here's a guide for sorting through different forms of drug delivery:

- **Buffered.** A buffered analgesic contains an antacid to reduce acidity. It's controversial whether these products actually protect your stomach.
- **Enteric-coated.** A special coating allows pills to pass through your stomach and dissolve in the small intestine. This helps reduce stomach irritation. Consider an enteric-coated product if you need daily relief for chronic pain. Because the coating delays absorption, it's not the best choice for quick relief (such as for a headache).
- **Timed-release.** Also called extended-release and sustained-release, these products dissolve slowly. They prolong relief by maintaining a constant level of analgesic in your blood. Use them if you need lasting, not immediate, relief.
- **Extra-strength.** A single dose of these preparations contains more pain-relieving medicine than regular-strength products — typically 500 milligrams of aspirin or acetaminophen vs. 325 milligrams. They're more convenient when it takes more than one regular-strength dose to improve your symptoms, but you should take them less often.
- **Combination formulas.** Some products are paired with caffeine or an antihistamine to boost their effect. Studies show that the addition of caffeine to aspirin or acetaminophen does improve pain relief.
- **Tablet, caplet, gelcap, gum or liquid.** If you have trouble swallowing a round tablet or oval caplet, a smooth gelcap might work better. Other options include taking aspirin in liquid or chewable form, as an effervescing pain reliever plus antacid (Alka-Seltzer) or chewing aspirin as a gum (Aspergum).
- **Generic.** Generic pain relievers almost always cost less than brand-name drugs, but they're just as effective.

Healthy Consumer

Self-Care

- **Know your special risks.** In general, don't take NSAIDs if you also take a blood thinner or if you have kidney disease, ulcers, a bleeding disorder or an allergy to aspirin.
- **Avoid drug interactions.** If you take other OTC or prescription medications, talk with your doctor or pharmacist about which pain reliever is best.
- **Don't exceed the recommended dose,** unless your doctor advises it.
- **Avoid alcohol.** Mixing alcohol with aspirin, ibuprofen or naproxen sodium increases the chance of stomach upset and bleeding. In combination with higher than recommended doses of acetaminophen, alcohol increases the risk of serious damage to your liver.
- **Take NSAIDs with milk and food** to help minimize stomach upset.
- **Don't take longer than necessary.** Periodically re-evaluate your need for pain relievers.
- **Always read and follow label instructions.**

Over-the-Counter Oral Pain Relievers

	Aspirin	Acetaminophen	Ibuprofen	Naproxen Sodium	Ketoprofen
Sampling of brand names	Ascriptin, Bayer, Bufferin, Ecotrin	Tylenol	Advil, Motrin IB	Aleve	Orudis KT
Reduces pain and fever	Yes	Yes	Yes	Yes	Yes
Reduces inflammation	Yes	No	Yes	Yes	Yes
Side effects	Stomach pain, heartburn, gastrointestinal (GI) bleeding	Rare when taken as directed for short periods (days to weeks)	Stomach pain, heartburn, GI bleeding, dizziness	Stomach pain, heartburn, GI bleeding, dizziness	Stomach pain, heartburn, GI bleeding, dizziness
Special cautions	Don't take if you have asthma, bleeding disorder, gout, ulcers or allergy to aspirin.	Overdoses can be toxic to the liver. Alcohol enhances toxic effects of high doses.	Don't take if you have liver, heart or kidney disease, bleeding disorder, or stomach problems.	Don't take if you have liver, heart, or kidney disease, bleeding disorder, or stomach problems.	Don't take if you have liver, heart, or kidney disease, bleeding disorder, or stomach problems.
Children's use	Can cause Reye's syndrome* in children with chickenpox, the flu or other viral illness.	Available for children. Dosages based on age and weight. Consult your doctor.	Available for children. Dosages based on age and weight. Consult your doctor.	Don't give to children younger than 12 except on advice of a doctor.	Don't give to children younger than 16 except on advice of a doctor.

*Reye's syndrome is a potentially fatal swelling of brain tissues. *Note:* This list is not comprehensive and is not an endorsement. We have not tested these products but rely on data supplied by the manufacturers.

Cold Remedies: What They Can and Cannot Do

There's no cure for the common cold. Yet drugs used to treat the effects of the common cold — runny nose, fever, congestion and cough — are the largest segment of the over-the-counter market for America's pharmaceutical industry. Some of these medications are also formulated as allergy medicines to treat itchy eyes and sneezing.

Most people don't need any medication for a cold. However, if your cold is particularly bothersome, certain medications may help. Regarding a cough, newly released guidelines developed by the American College of Chest Physicians state that nonprescription cough expectorants and suppressants often don't help relieve symptoms. If your cough is persistent, severe or accompanied by a fever, see your health care provider.

Nonprescription Cold Remedies

	Antihistamines	Decongestants	Cough/Cold Combinations
Sampling of brand names	Benadryl Chlor-Trimeton Allergy Tavist Allergy Claritin	Afrin Neo-Synephrine Sudafed	Actifed Contac Dimetapp Drixoral Sudafed Cold & Cough Tavist
Symptoms relieved	Sneezing, runny nose, itchy eyes, congestion due to allergies	Congestion, stuffiness	Depends on ingredients: sneezing, runny nose, congestion, stuffiness, cough, general discomfort
Side effects and cautions	Drowsiness, dry mouth, may dry secretions making mucus harder to clear. Alcohol may enhance drowsiness.	Insomnia, jitters, palpitations, may raise blood pressure. Don't use nasal decongestants more than three days.	May contain three or more ingredients. Side effects depend on ingredients.
Time of maximal benefit	Early in a cold when sneezing and watery, runny nose are common.	When nose is stuffed up.	When variety of symptoms are prominent. For limited symptoms, consider using individual products.

Self-Care

Here's some helpful advice on the use of cold medicines:

- **Always read the labels** to determine the active ingredients and side effects.
- **A single-symptom medicine may be better** than a combination medication.
- **Most combination cold medications contain some form of analgesic** such as aspirin, ibuprofen or acetaminophen (see page 258). Therefore, you don't need to take a separate analgesic.
- **Don't mix** various cold medications or take with other medications without consulting your health care provider or pharmacist.
- **Avoid alcohol** when taking cold medications.
- **Consult your physician** before giving any cold medicine to a child.
- **If you have high blood pressure, glaucoma or an enlarged prostate,** avoid cough and cold medications, unless directed by your health care provider. Some ingredients can make these conditions worse.

■ Home Medical Supplies

When an emergency or medical problem occurs in the home, you often don't have time to search for supplies. Keep your medical supplies in a place that's easily accessible to adults but out of the reach of children. And remember to replace items after their use to make sure the kit is always complete.

Here's what you need to be properly prepared for accidents and common illnesses that are mentioned in this book. Check your supplies yearly for outdated items that may need replacing. Also make sure to include a first-aid manual.

- **For cuts.** Bandages of various sizes, gauze, adhesive tape, an antiseptic solution to clean wounds and an antiseptic cream to prevent infection.
- **For burns.** Cold packs, gauze, burn spray and an antiseptic cream.
- **For aches, pain and fever.** Thermometer, aspirin (for adults only) or another non-steroidal anti-inflammatory drug, and acetaminophen for children or adults.
- **For eye injuries.** Sterile eyewash (such as a saline solution), an eyewash cup, eye patches and eye goggles.
- **For sprains, strains and fractures.** Cold packs, elastic wraps for wrapping injuries, finger splints and a triangular bandage for making an arm sling.
- **For insect bites and stings.** Cold packs to reduce pain and swelling. Hydrocortisone cream (0.5 percent or 1 percent), calamine lotion or baking soda (combine with water to form a paste) to apply to site until symptoms subside. Antihistamines (Benadryl, Chlor-Trimeton, others). If a family member is allergic to insect stings, include a kit containing an EpiPen — a syringe containing epinephrine (adrenaline). Your doctor can prescribe one.
- **For ingestion of poisons.** Keep the number of your local poison control center or the poison information hotline number — (800) 222-1222 — on a sticker on your telephone.
- **For general care.** Sharp scissors, tweezers, cotton balls and cotton-tipped swabs, plastic bags, safety pins, tissues, soap, cleansing pads or instant hand sanitizer, latex or synthetic gloves for use if blood or body fluids are present, anti-diarrheal medication and a medicine cup or spoon.

Dietary Supplements

Your body needs many nutrients to stay healthy. These include protein, carbohydrates and fat (macronutrients), and vitamins and minerals (micronutrients).

To improve your health and help prevent disease, it's important to eat a well-balanced diet — one rich in fruits, vegetables and whole grains and low in saturated fat. But what about dietary supplements — pills, capsules and other products — that claim to fight off illness or improve disease symptoms? In some instances, supplements may be beneficial. In other cases, there's no clear proof that the product is of any benefit.

Here's an overview of what's known about some of the more popular dietary supplements.

Antioxidants

Antioxidants are certain vitamins, minerals and enzymes that protect your body by neutralizing free radicals, byproducts of your cell's normal metabolism. Free radicals are believed to contribute to age-related changes and certain diseases. Antioxidant supplements touted to fight diseases of aging include:

- **Vitamin E.** Vitamin E has been touted to help counter oxidation, a process that damages cells and can accelerate aging and lead to cardiovascular disease and cancer. But a 2004 report suggests that taking megadoses of vitamin E may do more harm than good. Researchers reviewed 19 studies and found that people who took more than 400 international units (IU) of vitamin E daily died at a higher rate than those who didn't take the supplements. The cause isn't clear. Until more is known, don't take more than 400 IU of vitamin E daily. The best approach is to get the vitamin from dietary sources (nuts, vegetable oils, whole grains).
- **Vitamin A and beta carotene.** Several studies have found that supplements of beta carotene — which is converted into vitamin A in your body — offer no protection against cardiovascular disease. Two studies found an increased risk of lung cancer among smokers who took beta carotene supplements. You're better off eating red and yellow vegetables than taking supplements.
- **Vitamin C.** Studies have shown that people whose diets are high in vitamin C, found mainly in citrus fruits, have lower rates of cancer and heart disease. But it's unclear whether taking vitamin C supplements has similar benefits. Eating more citrus fruits and drinking more citrus juices may be a more reasonable approach than taking supplements.
- **Selenium.** This antioxidant mineral is found primarily in seafood and liver. It may help prevent cancer. An excessive amount may cause hair and nail loss. More research is needed.
- **Coenzyme Q-10.** This antioxidant has many dietary sources, including meat and seafood. Claims that it can slow aging and stop cancer spread are unproved. Some evidence suggests that it may help treat congestive heart failure.
- **Folic acid and B complex vitamins.** Vitamins B-6, B-12 and especially folic acid have been shown to work together to reduce blood levels of homocysteine, an amino acid that, in increased levels, has been linked to increased risk of cardiovascular disease. Studies are under way to determine if lowering homocysteine levels through vitamins lowers risk of heart attack, stroke and related diseases. The American Heart Association doesn't recommend widespread use of folic acid and other B vitamin supplements to reduce the risk of heart disease and stroke. Instead, eat a healthy diet that includes at least five servings of fruits and vegetables daily.

Fish Oils

Increasing your consumption of fish oils — omega-3 fatty acids or long-chain n-3 polyunsaturated fatty acids — decreases your risk of sudden cardiac death. Eating fish — especially fatty fish, such as mackerel, lake trout, herring, sardines, albacore tuna and salmon — is safe in moderate amounts and a worthwhile investment, even if you haven't experienced heart disease. Women still capable of having children should limit their intake of fish with high mercury content, such as shark, swordfish and king mackerel, or fish containing traces of industrial pollutants. According to the American Heart Association, fish oil supplements may be appropriate for people with cardiovascular disease. Make sure the supplements are high quality and free of contaminants.

Herbs

People take herbs for a host of reasons. Here's a look at some of the most popular ones, what they claim to do and what research says about them:

- **Black cohosh.** With some effects similar to the female hormone estrogen, black cohosh is used to relieve menstrual cramps, painful periods and menopausal symptoms, such as hot flashes. A number of clinical studies indicate that black cohosh may be effective, but more long-term studies are needed.
- **Echinacea.** Derived from the purple coneflower, echinacea is typically used to prevent colds and flu. Some studies show that it may shorten the duration of colds and flu. But it probably doesn't keep you from getting them. Some researchers have raised concerns about the potential of this herb to be toxic to the liver. Don't take it for more than eight weeks at a time. Echinacea affects your immune system, so some medical professionals advise against its use if you have diabetes, an autoimmune disease such as multiple sclerosis or rheumatoid arthritis, or impaired immunity from cancer or human immunodeficiency virus (HIV).
- **Ephedra (ma-huang).** This potent herb should be avoided. It was found in many products designed to suppress appetite or to boost energy. Because ephedra may increase your risk of heart attack, seizure, stroke and sudden death, it has been taken off the market by the Food and Drug Administration (FDA).
- **Feverfew.** The leaves of this plant are used to prevent migraines. Studies indicate that the herb's active ingredient, parthenolide, may reduce the frequency and severity of migraines. Don't take feverfew if you're pregnant because it can cause miscarriage.
- **Garlic.** The jury is still out on garlic. Some studies have suggested that garlic and garlic supplements may be useful in lowering "bad" (LDL) cholesterol. Garlic may also help prevent certain cancers and heart problems. But the positive effects seem modest and research, though ongoing, is limited.
- **Ginger.** The root of the ginger plant is used to relieve nausea and indigestion. Studies show it may be effective for preventing nausea associated with motion sickness and anesthesia. Ginger isn't recommended for treatment of morning sickness. In addition, if you have gallstones, check with your doctor before using ginger because it increases the production of digestive juices.
- **Ginkgo.** Ginkgo is used to increase blood flow to the brain in an effort to ease symptoms such as short-term memory loss, dizziness, ringing in the ears and headache. It's also taken to treat activity-related leg pain due to poor circulation in the legs (claudication). However, ginkgo's supposed memory and circulation benefits haven't been supported by more recent research. Don't take it if you're taking anti-clotting medication or a thiazide diuretic.

- **Ginseng.** Some people use ginseng to boost energy, increase sexual stamina, reduce stress and counter the effects of aging. No scientific evidence indicates that it does any of these things. Don't use it for more than three months or exceed the recommended dose. Don't use ginseng if you have an estrogen-related disease, such as breast cancer, or if you have uncontrolled high blood pressure.
- **Kava.** Also known as kava kava, this herb looked promising as a treatment for anxiety, insomnia and other problems. However, kava has been linked to serious liver problems even with short-term use at a normal dose. It's been banned in several countries.
- **St. John's wort.** St. John's wort is used to treat mild depression. Some studies suggest that it may work as well as some antidepressant drugs for mild depression, and with fewer side effects. It hasn't been shown effective in treating major depression. A concern is that the herb can dangerously alter the effects of a number of prescription drugs. Until more is known, don't mix St. John's wort with any medication without discussing it in advance with your doctor.
- **Saw palmetto.** Some research indicates that saw palmetto may improve urine flow and bladder emptying in men with noncancerous enlargement of the prostate gland. Studies are inconclusive as to whether the herb can affect results of the prostate-specific antigen (PSA) test used to screen for prostate cancer. For information on prostate cancer screening, see page 141.

Hormones

Hormones are chemicals made by your body to regulate the activities of vital organs. Because hormone levels decline with age, some scientists speculate that hormones may play a role in the aging process. Proponents of hormone products tout that these products can set back your body's clock.
- **DHEA.** Dehydroepiandrosterone (DHEA) is converted by your body into the sex hormones estrogen and testosterone. Proponents of DHEA supplements claim the products can slow aging, increase muscle and bone strength, burn fat and improve cognition. There's no proof that the supplements do any of these. DHEA was banned in 1985 by the FDA before it reappeared as an unregulated dietary supplement.
- **Melatonin.** This hormone helps regulate sleep and may help overcome jet lag. But claims that it can slow or reverse aging, fight cancer and enhance sexuality are far from proved. Supplements sold in stores typically contain many times the melatonin produced by your body. If taken improperly, they can actually disrupt your sleep cycle.

Others

Dietary supplements that have gained considerable attention as possible treatments for arthritis include:
- **Glucosamine and chondroitin.** Glucosamine is found naturally in your body. It helps give cartilage its strength and rigidity. The supplements sold in stores are a synthetic version of this substance. Chondroitin is part of a large protein molecule that gives cartilage elasticity. If you have an allergy to shellfish, you shouldn't take glucosamine. If you take blood thinners (anticoagulants), chondroitin may affect the levels. To date, there's little evidence that these supplements are helpful.

Healthy Consumer

- **SAM-e.** S-adenosyl-methionine (SAM-e) occurs naturally in all human tissue and organs. It helps produce and regulate hormones and cell membranes. Europeans have used SAM-e for years as a prescription medication for arthritis and depression. It became available in the United States as an over-the-counter supplement in 1999. Researchers have studied SAM-e in numerous clinical trials. The studies indicate SAM-e may relieve osteoarthritic pain as well as can nonsteroidal anti-inflammatory drugs (NSAIDs), but with fewer side effects.

Whole Foods Are Your Best Source

Benefits of Whole Foods

Whole foods — fruits, vegetables, grains, lean meats and dairy products — have three main benefits you can't find in a pill:

- **Whole foods are complex.** They contain a variety of the nutrients your body needs — not just one — giving you more bang for your nutrition buck. An orange, for example, provides vitamin C but also beta carotene, calcium and other nutrients. A vitamin C supplement lacks these other nutrients.
- **Whole foods provide dietary fiber.** Fiber is important for digestion and in preventing certain diseases. Soluble fiber — found in certain beans and grains and in some fruits and vegetables — and insoluble fiber — found in whole-grain breakfast cereals and in some vegetables and fruits — may help prevent heart disease, diabetes and constipation.
- **Whole foods contain other substances that may be important for good health.** Fruits and vegetables, for example, contain naturally occurring food substances called phytochemicals, which may help protect you against cancer, heart disease, osteoporosis and diabetes. It's not yet known precisely what role phytochemicals play in nutrition. If you depend on supplements rather than eating a variety of whole foods, you miss the potential health benefits of phytochemicals.

The Bottom Line

Concentrate on getting your nutrients from food, not supplements, as much as possible. Whole foods provide an ideal mix of nutrients, fiber and other food substances. It's likely that all these work in combination to keep you healthy.

Should You Take Supplements?

The American Dietetic Association and other major medical organizations all agree that the best way to get the vitamins and minerals you need is through a nutritionally balanced diet. But sometimes a supplement may be appropriate.

If you're going to take supplements, a multivitamin and calcium supplement are probably your best bet. Other supplements may be appropriate if:

- **You're a female beyond menopause.** It can be difficult to get the recommended amounts of calcium and vitamin D without supplementation. Both calcium and vitamin D supplements have been shown to protect against osteoporosis. Even if you're a younger woman or you're a male, you may benefit from calcium and vitamin D supplementation.

- **You don't eat well.** If you don't eat the recommended five servings a day of fruits and vegetables, taking a multivitamin supplement may be reasonable. Your best course of action would be to adopt better eating habits.
- **You're on a very low-calorie diet.** If you eat fewer than 1,200 calories a day, you may benefit from a vitamin-mineral supplement. Remember: A very low-calorie diet limits the types and amounts of foods you eat and, in turn, the types and amounts of nutrients you get. Very low-calorie diets should be undertaken only with guidance from your doctor.
- **You smoke.** Tobacco decreases absorption of many vitamins and minerals, including vitamin B-6, vitamin C, folic acid and niacin.
- **You drink alcohol excessively.** Alcoholics have impaired digestion and absorption of thiamin, folic acid and vitamins A, D and B-12. Altered metabolism also affects minerals such as zinc, selenium, magnesium and phosphorus. If you drink excessively, you may also substitute alcohol for food, resulting in a diet lacking in essential nutrients. Excessive drinking is defined as more than one drink a day if you're a nonpregnant woman and more than two drinks a day if you're a man.
- **You're pregnant or breast-feeding.** During these times, you need more of certain nutrients, especially folic acid and iron. Folic acid helps prevent neural tube defects in your baby, such as spina bifida. Iron helps prevent fatigue by helping you make the red blood cells you need to deliver oxygen to your baby. Your doctor can recommend a supplement — usually a prenatal vitamin. It's important to start taking a supplement before becoming pregnant.
- **You eat a special diet.** If your diet has limited variety because of intolerance or food allergy, you may benefit from a vitamin-mineral supplement. If you're a vegetarian who eliminates all animal products from your diet, you may need additional vitamin B-12. In addition, if you don't eat dairy products and don't get 15 minutes of sun each day on your hands and face, you may need to supplement your diet with calcium and vitamin D.
- **You're age 65 or older.** As you get older, health problems can contribute to a poor diet, making it difficult for you to get the vitamins and minerals you need. You may lose your appetite, as well as some of your ability to taste and smell. Depression or problems with dentures also can inhibit eating. If you eat alone, you may not eat enough to get all the nutrients you need from food. In addition, as you get older, your body may not be able to absorb vitamins B-6, B-12 and D like it used to, making supplementation more necessary. There's also evidence that a multivitamin may improve your immune function and decrease your risk of some infections if you're older.

◼ Vitamins and Minerals: How Much Do You Need?

You may be confused about how much of a specific vitamin or mineral you need. Here's how to figure out what you need:
- **Recommended Dietary Allowances (RDAs)** describe the average amount of each vitamin and mineral needed each day to meet the needs of nearly all healthy people. They're determined by the Food and Nutrition Board of the Institute of Medicine, part of the National Academy of Sciences. RDAs for some vitamins and minerals vary according to your sex or age, or both.

- **Daily Values (DV)** are used on food and supplement labels. They have their origin in the Recommended Dietary Allowances (RDAs), but they're set by the Food and Drug Administration (FDA). The FDA bases DVs on a 2,000-calorie-per-day diet. Of course, the 2,000-calorie-a-day standard is just a guideline. Individual needs may vary. Many women and older adults may actually need only about 1,600 calories a day. Active women and most men need about 2,200 calories a day. Active men may need about 2,800 calories a day. If your calorie needs are greater or less than 2,000 a day, your DVs for various nutrients generally rise or fall accordingly.
- **Percent Daily Value (% DV)** tells you what percentage of the DV one serving of a food or supplement supplies — that is, how it measures up as a percentage of the daily recommendation. For example, if the label on your multivitamin bottle says that your multivitamin provides 30 percent of the DV for vitamin E, you have 70 percent still needed to meet the recommended goal. The higher the % DV, the greater its contribution to meeting nutrient goals.

■ Choosing and Using Supplements

Supplements aren't substitutes. They can't replace the hundreds of nutrients in whole foods that you need for a nutritionally balanced diet. If you do decide to take a vitamin or mineral supplement, here are some factors to consider:

- **Avoid supplements that provide 'megadoses.'** In general, choose a multi-vitamin-mineral supplement that provides about 100 percent DV of all the vitamins and minerals instead of one that supplies, for example, 500 percent DV of one vitamin and only 20 percent DV of another. The exception to this is calcium. You may notice that calcium-containing supplements don't provide 100 percent DV. If they did, the tablets would be too large to swallow. Doses above 100 percent DV don't give extra protection in most cases, but they do increase your risk of encountering toxic side effects. Most cases of nutrient toxicity stem from high-dose supplements. Some specific conditions are treated with large doses, such as Hartnup disease, a genetic condition treated with large doses of niacin. Such conditions are uncommon.
- **Consider buying generic.** Generic brands are generally less expensive and equally effective as name brands. Compare the list of ingredients and the % DV to make sure the brands are comparable.
- **Look for 'USP' on the label.** This ensures that the supplement meets the standards for strength, purity, disintegration and dissolution established by the testing organization, U.S. Pharmacopeia (USP).
- **Beware of gimmicks.** Synthetic vitamins are the same as so-called natural vitamins. Don't give in to the temptation of added herbs, enzymes or amino acids — they add nothing but cost.
- **Look for expiration dates.** Supplements can lose potency over time, especially in hot and humid climates. If a supplement doesn't have an expiration date, don't buy it.
- **Store all vitamin and mineral supplements out of the sight and reach of children.** Put them in a locked cabinet or other secured location. Don't leave them sitting out on the counter or rely on child-resistant packaging. Be especially careful with any supplements containing iron. Iron overdose is a leading cause of poisoning deaths among children.

- **Explore your options.** If you have difficulty swallowing, ask your doctor whether liquid or children's chewable vitamin and mineral supplements might be right for you.
- **Play it safe.** Before taking anything other than a standard multivitamin-mineral supplement of 100 percent DV or less, check with your doctor or a registered dietitian. This is especially important if you have a health problem or are taking medication. High doses of niacin, for example, can aggravate a stomach ulcer. In addition, supplements may interfere with medications. Vitamin E, for example, isn't recommended if you're taking blood-thinning medications (anticoagulants) because it can complicate the proper control of blood thinning. If you're already taking an individual vitamin or mineral supplement and haven't told your doctor, discuss it at your next checkup.

Supplements and Digestive Health Problems: What You Need to Know

If you have a digestive health problem, such as a disease of your liver, gallbladder, intestine or pancreas, or you've had surgery on your digestive tract, you may not be able to digest and absorb nutrients properly. Therefore, your doctor may recommend that you take a vitamin or mineral supplement. Some conditions that may require you to take supplements include:

- **Crohn's disease.** A chronic inflammation of the intestine. It mainly involves the lower part of the small intestine (ileum). It can also affect your colon or any other part of your digestive tract. Your ability to absorb adequate nutrients often is limited with Crohn's disease, particularly if the disease affects large portions of your small intestine or if you've had portions of your small intestine removed surgically. If you have Crohn's disease, doctors often advise that you take a standard multivitamin that provides 100 percent DV. Your doctor may also advise specific replacement of certain vitamins or minerals, if there's evidence of deficiency. If you have Crohn's disease, you may not be able to absorb vitamin B-12. Left untreated, a deficiency of this vitamin can lead to pernicious anemia. If this occurs, you can get the vitamin B-12 you need with monthly injections.
- **Primary biliary cirrhosis.** A condition characterized by chronic inflammation and scarring of the microscopic bile ducts within the liver. This

inflammation and scarring can cause bile flow to become blocked, which can interfere with your body's absorption of fat-soluble vitamins (A, D, E and K). If you have primary biliary cirrhosis, your doctor may prescribe supplements for these vitamins in a special form that's easier to absorb.
- **Pancreatitis.** An inflammation of the pancreas. The inflammation may be acute or chronic. With chronic pancreatitis, your pancreas gradually becomes less able to secrete the enzymes you need to properly digest dietary fats. This pancreatic insufficiency therefore also affects your ability to absorb fat-soluble vitamins. If you have chronic pancreatitis, your doctor may prescribe pancreatic enzyme supplements to help improve digestion and absorption. In addition, a multivitamin or specific vitamins or mineral supplements may be recommended, if there's evidence of deficiency.
- **Gastric bypass surgery.** Gastric bypass is weight-loss surgery that limits your ability to absorb calories. It also limits the amount of nutrients you can absorb. As a result, your doctor may recommend that you take calcium supplements, vitamin D, vitamin B-12 shots or nasal or oral spray, and a multivitamin. If you're a premenopausal woman, you may also be advised to take additional iron.

Alternative Medicine and Your Health

Complementary and alternative treatments have become more popular as Americans seek greater control of their own health. A study in the *Journal of the American Medical Association* found that Americans visited complementary and alternative practitioners more frequently than they did primary care doctors, even though many of the complementary and alternative services weren't covered by medical insurance.

What Is Complementary and Alternative Medicine?

Most of what we call complementary and alternative treatments aren't new. Many have been practiced for thousands of years. They include a broad range of healing philosophies, approaches and therapies. Often, though not always, the practices are used in conjunction with traditional medical treatment. Examples might be using yoga, in addition to medication, to relieve anxiety. Or integrating acupuncture into your physical therapy regimen to help manage chronic pain. Sometimes, alternative treatments are used in place of traditional medicine. An example might be using an herbal or dietary preparation instead of conventional chemotherapy to treat cancer.

The Promise — and Peril — of New Treatment Options

The option to pick and choose among nontraditional treatments makes the complicated world of health care even more so. You have many treatment options — conventional, complementary and alternative — available to you. But you also face greater risk of confusion and harm.

You can't always accept the claims of complementary and alternative medicine practitioners at face value. True, the vast majority of these practitioners are well-intentioned, and many have specialized training. Yet quack treatments have always existed, and some unscrupulous people may falsely claim to be experts in complementary and alternative medicine. Even practitioners with the best of intentions may be undertrained, uninformed or both.

Arm Yourself With Two Strategies

If you decide to use complementary and alternative treatments, take steps to protect your health, and your wallet. When deciding on any unconventional treatment — or conventional, for that matter — consider its safety and effectiveness. Safety means its benefits outweigh its risks. Effectiveness is the likelihood the treatment will be of benefit when used appropriately.

Research various treatments. Learn about the five major forms of complementary and alternative medicine. Find out what they are and what benefits their practitioners claim to provide.

- Herbal preparations
- Manipulation and touch
- Mind-body interventions
- Natural energy restoration
- Alternative systems

Take responsibility for your own care. See 5 Steps in Considering Any Treatment on pages 278-279.

Check Out Claims of Treatment Success

Ask your doctor for information on research results to help you make an informed decision about using a particular treatment. You can also find information on your own, but it's important to understand the quality of research. If you dig into the medical literature for studies about complementary and alternative treatments, you'll see several terms that describe different types of research. For example:

- *Clinical studies* are those that involve human beings as subjects — not animals. They're usually preceded by studies that demonstrate safety and effectiveness of the treatment in animals.
- In *randomized, controlled trials,* participants are usually divided into two groups. The first group receives the treatment under investigation. The second is a control group — they receive standard treatment, no treatment or an inactive substance called a placebo. Participants are assigned to these groups on a random basis. This helps to ensure that the groups will be similar.
- In *double-blind studies,* neither the researchers nor the human subjects know who will receive the active treatment and who will receive the placebo.
- *Prospective studies* are forward-looking. Researchers establish criteria for study participants to follow and then measure or describe the results. Information from these studies is usually more reliable than that of retrospective studies. Retrospective studies involve looking at past data (for example, asking participants to recall information), which leaves more room for errors in interpretation.
- *Peer-reviewed journals* only publish articles that have been reviewed by an independent panel of medical experts.

Identify the Best Research

Prospective double-blind studies that have been carefully controlled, randomized and published in scientific (peer-reviewed) journals provide the best information. When these involve large numbers of people (several hundred or more) studied over several years, they gain even more credibility. Doctors also like to see studies that are replicated — repeated by different investigators with generally the same results.

To date, few complementary and alternative treatments have been researched according to rigorous standards. For the majority of unconventional treatments, the jury is still out on whether they're helpful.

Why People Seek Alternative Medicine

(Survey of more than 31,000 adults)

5 Leading Reasons	5 Most Common Therapies
1. Back pain	1. Prayer (self)
2. Head cold	2. Prayer (others)
3. Neck pain	3. Natural products
4. Joint pain	4. Deep breathing
5. Arthritis	5. Prayer group

Source: *Use of Complementary and Alternative Medicine in the United States,* National Center for Complementary and Alternative Medicine, September, 2004

Healthy Consumer

■ Herbal Treatments

Although popularly thought of as "natural" and less risky than prescription drugs, herbal supplements aren't subject to the same rigorous quality control as drugs. There has been careful study of some of these treatments, but it's a good idea to be cautious when considering a supplement.

Limited FDA Regulation

Herbs, vitamins and minerals are all considered dietary supplements by the Food and Drug Administration (FDA). These substances aren't considered either a food or a drug, and as such, aren't subject to usual regulatory and safety guidelines.

In 1994, Congress passed the Dietary Supplement Health and Education Act (DSHEA). This law limits the FDA's control over dietary supplements. The DSHEA states that manufacturers don't have to prove a product is safe or effective before it goes on the market. As a result, in the United States, herbs can be marketed with limited regulation. Vendors can make health claims about products based on their own review and interpretation of studies — without FDA authorization. The FDA can pull a product off the market if it's proved dangerous.

Use Herbs Safely

If you're considering taking an herbal treatment, keep these points in mind:

- **Discuss with your doctor what you're taking.** Some herbs may interfere with the effectiveness of prescription or nonprescription drugs or have other harmful effects. (See Choosing and Using Supplements on pages 266-267.) Make sure you don't have an underlying medical condition that calls for treatment by your doctor.
- **Follow directions.** Like over-the-counter (OTC) and prescription drugs, herbal products have active ingredients that can affect how your body functions. Don't exceed the recommended dosages. Some herbs can be harmful if taken for too long. Get advice from your doctor and other reputable resources.
- **Keep track of what you take.** Take one type of supplement at a time to try to determine its effect. Make a note of what you take, how much and how it affects you. Does it do what it claims to do? Do you experience any side effects, such as drowsiness, sleeplessness, headache or nausea?
- **Read the label for content.** Quality and strength can vary greatly by brand. Look for the letters USP (United States Pharmacopeia) or NF (National Formulary), which indicate the supplements meet certain standards of quality.
- **Avoid herbs if you're pregnant or breast-feeding.** Unless your doctor approves, don't take any medications — prescription, OTC or herbal — when you're pregnant or breast-feeding. They can harm your baby.
- **Be cautious about herbal products manufactured or purchased outside the United States.** In general, European herbs are well regulated and standardized. Toxic ingredients (including lead, mercury and arsenic) and prescription drugs (such as prednisone) have been found in some herbal supplements manufactured in other countries, particularly China and India.

- **Avoid dangerous herbs.** According to the FDA, these include belladonna, broom, coltsfoot, comfrey, life root, lobelia and pennyroyal. Goldenseal and licorice root are other controversial herbs that can cause serious health problems.

    Ephedra, also known as ma-huang, is found in a number of "natural" weight-loss and energy-boosting products. It's supposed to suppress your appetite and stimulate your metabolism. Ephedra may increase risk of heart attack, seizure, stroke and sudden death. Another popular herb, called kava, used to treat insomnia and anxiety, reportedly has been associated with liver damage in some people. There may be other harmful herbs. Overdoses of any of these herbs can be fatal.

    The effectiveness of many herbs still hasn't been established. And few studies have investigated the risks of taking several different herbs at the same time. Of all the unconventional treatments, herbal therapies may present the greatest potential for harm. This is especially true when people self-prescribe herbs, or products are mislabeled or contaminated.

What the Research Shows

If you're thinking about using **herbal supplements,** read information on clinical studies about safety and effectiveness. From the examples below, you'll see why it's important to tell your doctor if you're using herbal products so that you can work out an effective treatment plan.

- A review of 37 randomized, controlled trials published in the *British Journal of Psychiatry* on **St. John's wort** concluded that the herb seemed to be useful for mild to moderate depression and that it produced results similar to some prescription antidepressants. However, the journal reported that six recent, large, more precise trials found St. John's wort produced only minimal benefits among individuals with major depression. If your depression is serious, don't treat it yourself. The analysis also found that St. John's wort caused fewer side effects than older antidepressants and that it may cause slightly fewer side effects than newer antidepressants.

- Multiple studies have shown that the herb **saw palmetto** improves urinary symptoms such as frequent urination, painful urination, hesitancy and urgency in men with noncancerous enlargement of the prostate gland (benign prostatic hyperplasia, or BPH). Some studies suggest the herb might not be helpful in men with only mild symptoms. Saw palmetto does not appear to interfere with the results of the prostate-specific antigen (PSA) test, a tool that helps detect prostate cancer. However, if you take saw palmetto, mention it to your doctor before the test.

- Some studies indicate that **feverfew** may reduce the frequency and severity of migraines because of an active ingredient called parthenolide. Other studies show no benefit. Feverfew products vary widely in the amount of parthenolide they contain. Avoid feverfew if you're using aspirin or warfarin (Coumadin). Don't take feverfew or any other herbs if you're pregnant.

Avoid Herb-Drug Interactions

Although "natural" and therefore popularly considered harmless, herbal supplements contain ingredients that may not mix safely with prescription or over-the-counter (OTC) drugs. In addition, some medical problems may increase your risk of adverse effects if you take herbal products.

Talk to your doctor before taking any herbal products if you're pregnant or nursing. Also see your doctor before you take herbs if you have any of the following conditions:
- High blood pressure
- History of stroke
- Blood-clotting problems
- Thyroid problems
- Diabetes
- Heart disease

- Epilepsy
- Parkinson's disease
- Glaucoma
- Enlarged prostate gland
- HIV, AIDS or other diseases of the immune system
- Depression or other psychiatric problems

In addition, herbal supplements can be just as dangerous as prescription and OTC drugs when used with anesthesia. If you're anticipating surgery, tell your doctor about any drugs you're taking — including herbal supplements.

Stop taking herbal supplements at least two to three weeks before surgery to allow them to clear from your body. If this isn't possible, bring the herbal product in its original container to the hospital so the anesthesiologist knows exactly what you're taking.

■ Healing Through Manipulation and Touch

One attraction of many complementary and alternative treatments is that they involve human touch. Examples are chiropractic treatment, osteopathy, massage, therapeutic touch and acupuncture.

Chiropractic Treatment

Chiropractic care has come a long way since the days of its founders, who pointed to misaligned vertebrae as the source of all disease. Today, chiropractors sometimes even work with medical doctors. Although they can't prescribe drugs or perform surgery, chiropractors use many standard medical procedures. And the services of chiropractors are increasingly covered by medical insurance.

5 Tips If You Seek Chiropractic Care

To get the most out of chiropractic care or other treatments that rely on spinal manipulation, here are some tips:
1. Ask your primary doctor to refer you to an appropriate provider. This could be a chiropractor or an osteopath, a doctor specifically trained in manipulation to treat joint and spinal problems.
2. If you seek chiropractic care without a referral, do so carefully. Find someone who's licensed and who completed the training program at a school accredited by the Council on Chiropractic Education.
3. See chiropractors who are willing to send a report to your doctor and give you a written treatment plan.
4. Avoid chiropractors who order frequent X-rays or ask to extend your treatment indefinitely.
5. Avoid chiropractors who view spinal manipulation as a cure for "whatever ails you." There's no evidence to support this idea.

Most chiropractors use a hands-on type of adjustment called spinal manipulative therapy or spinal manipulation. According to chiropractic theory, misaligned vertebrae can restrict your spine's range of motion and affect nerves that radiate out from your spine. In turn, the organs that depend on those nerves may function improperly or become diseased. Chiropractic adjustments aim to realign your vertebrae, restore range of motion and free up nerve pathways.

People other than chiropractors do spinal manipulation. Many osteopathic doctors and physical therapists are trained in this treatment. And there's no evidence that chiropractors do better spinal manipulation than other health care providers. Some chiropractors hold tightly to the theory that spinal manipulation can treat disease other than back pain, but no scientific evidence supports this.

What the Research Shows

Chiropractic treatment. Although research results sometimes conflict, studies indicate that spinal manipulation can effectively treat *uncomplicated* low back pain, especially if the pain has been present for less than four weeks.

After reviewing many studies, the Agency for Healthcare Research and Quality concluded that spinal manipulation may provide temporary relief from acute low back pain. The agency limited its conclusions to short-term treatment. There was little evidence that long-term treatment was effective. And most acute low back pain improves without treatment in four to six weeks.

In another review of medical studies, Dutch researchers found evidence that spinal manipulation can effectively treat low back pain. The low quality of many of the studies prevented the researchers from making strong conclusions about spinal manipulation.

Osteopathic Manipulation

Osteopathy is a recognized medical discipline that has much in common with conventional medicine and chiropractic treatment. Like traditional physicians, doctors of osteopathy go through long training in academic and clinical settings. Osteopaths are licensed to perform many of the same therapies and procedures as traditional doctors. They can perform surgery and prescribe medications. Osteopaths may also specialize in various areas of medicine, such as gynecology or cardiology.

Osteopathy does differ from conventional medicine in one area: manipulation to address joint and spinal problems. Similar in this respect to a chiropractor, an osteopath may perform manipulations to release pressure in your joints, align your muscles and joints, and improve the flow of body fluids. Interestingly, a 1995 survey of osteopath family physicians found that they used spinal manipulation only occasionally.

Massage

Massage is often used as part of physical therapy, sports medicine and nursing care. It may be used, for example, to relieve muscle tension or promote relaxation, helping people as they undergo other types of medical treatment. It's also accepted as a simple means for healthy people to relieve stress and just feel good.

Massage is the kneading, stroking and manipulation of your body's soft tissues — your skin, muscles and tendons. Your massage will vary depending on the rhythm, rate, pressure and direction of these movements.

You shouldn't get massage over an open wound, skin infection, phlebitis or areas of weakened bones. In addition, don't get a massage if any of your joints are inflamed. And if you've been injured, consult your doctor first. Don't rely exclusively on massage to repair damaged tissues.

Generally, a massage should feel good or cause very little discomfort. If this isn't the case, speak up promptly.

Therapeutic Touch

Therapeutic touch resembles the religious concept of "laying on of the hands," where healing power is believed to flow from a minister's hands to a patient. However, therapeutic touch is not necessarily based on a religious concept. Instead, it comes from the idea that your body is surrounded by a field of energy. Illness results from disturbances in that field.

Some practitioners of therapeutic touch attempt to get rid of these disturbances by moving their hands back and forth across your body. Practitioners believe that by transferring healing energy through their hands to your body, they can reduce pain, stress and anxiety. Many conventional health care providers are skeptical of therapeutic touch, which isn't supported by solid research.

Acupuncture

Acupuncture is a part of Chinese traditional medicine that has been around for at least 2,500 years. According to this Eastern philosophy:

- Health depends on the free circulation of blood and a subtle energy called chi (pronounced CHEE and sometimes written *qi*).
- Chi flows through your body along pathways called meridians.
- Inserting needles into points along the meridians promotes the free flow of chi.

Medical researchers are skeptical about these claims. Even so, acupuncture is one of the most well-researched and accepted practices in complementary and alternative medicine. Pain specialists at Mayo Clinic have used acupuncture since 1974 as part of their pain treatment program.

Depending on your reasons for seeking acupuncture, you'll have one or several hair-thin needles inserted under your skin. Some may go in as deep as three inches, depending on where they're placed in your body and what the treatment is for. Others will be placed superficially. The needles usually are left in for 15 to 30 minutes. Once inserted, needles are sometimes stimulated with an electrical current.

Expect to have several sessions. If you experience no relief after six to eight sessions, acupuncture probably isn't for you.

To find a qualified practitioner, ask for a referral from your doctor or contact the American Academy of Medical Acupuncture (AAMA). Visit the AAMA Web site at *www.medicalacupuncture.org* or call (323) 937-5514. AAMA's members are all licensed physicians with more than 200 hours of training in acupuncture.

Getting Safe Acupuncture Treatment

Adverse side effects from acupuncture are rare, but they do occur. Hepatitis B has been transmitted from needles that aren't properly sterilized. Make sure your acupuncturist uses disposable needles.

You should feel little or no pain from the needles. You might even find their insertion to be relaxing. Significant pain from the needles is a sign that the procedure is being done improperly.

◼ Mind-Body Connection

These treatments are based on the idea that mind and body function as a unified field. Practitioners who take this approach may hold that negative thoughts and feelings can produce symptoms in your body. Treatment often aims to help you detach from these thoughts and feelings, or to actively change them.

Biofeedback

This practice uses technology to teach you how to control certain body responses. During a biofeedback session, a trained therapist applies electrodes and other sensors to various parts of your body. The electrodes are attached to devices that monitor your responses and give you visual or auditory feedback. For example, you might see patterns on a monitor that display your levels of muscle tension, brain wave activity, heart rate, blood pressure, breathing rate or skin temperature.

With this feedback, you can learn how to produce positive changes in body functions, such as lowering your blood pressure or raising your skin temperature. These are signs of relaxation. The biofeedback therapist may use relaxation techniques to further calm you, reducing muscle tension or slowing your heart rate and breathing even more.

You can get biofeedback treatments in several settings — physical therapy clinics, medical centers and hospitals.

Hypnosis

Hypnosis produces a state of deep relaxation, but your mind stays alert. During hypnosis, you can receive suggestions designed to decrease your perception of pain or to help you stop habits such as smoking. No one knows exactly how hypnosis works, but experts believe it alters your brain wave patterns in much the same way as other relaxation techniques.

The success of hypnosis depends on the expertise of the practitioner, your understanding of the procedure and your willingness to try it. You need to be strongly motivated to change. Some people eventually develop the skills to hypnotize themselves.

Psychiatrists and psychologists occasionally practice hypnosis. There are also professional hypnotists, but beware, because this field is poorly regulated.

Yoga

People do yoga for many reasons. For some, yoga is a spiritual path. For others, yoga is a way to promote physical flexibility, strength and endurance. In either case, you may find that yoga helps you to relax and manage stress.

Americans generally associate the term *yoga* with one particular school of this ancient discipline — hatha yoga. In most cases, hatha yoga combines gentle breathing exercises with movement through a series of postures called asanas.

Yoga teachers commonly offer instruction in meditation. According to one of the most ancient yoga texts, the purpose of yoga is to calm the mind in preparation for meditation.

One principle of meditation is that stress comes with a racing mind. Meditators observe the flow of thoughts without judging them, a process that helps the mind to slow down naturally.

Tai Chi

One sophisticated and enjoyable method to improve physical and emotional balance is an ancient form of exercise called tai chi (TIE-chee). Originally developed in China, tai chi involves slow, gentle, dance-like movements that relax and strengthen muscles and joints. Many people who practice tai chi view it as a form of meditation in motion.

You'll find tai chi classes offered in cities throughout the United States. To locate a class in your community, contact your local YMCA, fitness club or senior center.

Research indicates that tai chi can prevent falls in older adults by improving strength and balance. In one large study, those who practiced tai chi reduced their risk of multiple falls by about 47 percent.

What the Research Shows

Biofeedback. According to a consensus statement from the National Institutes of Health (NIH), there is evidence that biofeedback may help to relieve some types of chronic pain, including tension and migraine headaches. The American Academy of Family Physicians recommends biofeedback as a possible treatment option for preventing migraines.

Hypnosis. The NIH consensus statement cited evidence that hypnosis may reduce chronic pain associated with cancer and other conditions, such as irritable bowel syndrome and tension headaches. According to another analysis of several studies, hypnosis may enhance the effects of therapy for phobia, obesity and anxiety.

Yoga. The National Center for Complementary and Alternative Medicine (NCCAM) has acknowledged that the practice of yoga can help people control body functions including heart rate, blood pressure, respiration and body temperature. In one study, people who used yoga and relaxation techniques in addition to a wrist splint experienced more relief from carpal tunnel syndrome than did people who used the splint alone. Yoga has also been shown to help in reducing stress and anxiety.

■ Systems That Combine Treatments

Homeopathy

Homeopathy (ho-me-OP-uh-thee) is a controversial treatment. It's based on two basic beliefs:

- *The law of similars.* When given to a healthy person in large quantities, some plant, animal and mineral substances produce symptoms of disease. But when given to a sick person, much smaller doses of the same substances can (theoretically) relieve the same symptoms.
- *The law of infinitesimals.* Literally, infinitesimal means too small to be measured. According to this belief, substances treat disease most effectively when they are highly diluted, often in distilled water or alcohol.

The law of similars is sometimes stated as "like cures like" — a capsule summary of homeopathy. Vaccination, a conventional practice, is based on a similar idea: Injecting a small dose of a modified infectious agent stimulates the body's immune system to fight diseases caused by that agent.

Homeopathy in general departs widely from conventional medicine. Modern drug therapy primarily uses substances to reverse symptoms, not produce them. In addition, medical doctors find it difficult to accept the law of infinitesimals — especially when homeopathic treatments are so diluted that no trace of the original substance remains. Although highly diluted substances may not help you, they probably won't harm you either.

People who practice homeopathy (homeopaths) may also recommend changes in diet, exercise and other health-related behaviors. But avoid practitioners who encourage you to use homeopathic remedies instead of the medications that your doctor prescribed.

Many studies of homeopathy examine whether the benefits claimed for this treatment result from a placebo effect — that is, from the belief of patients in the treatment rather than the treatment itself. One analysis of 89 controlled studies concluded that homeopathy appeared to have results that went beyond the placebo effect. However, there's little published evidence that homeopathy can effectively treat specific diseases or conditions.

Ayurveda

One of the oldest systems of health care comes from Hindu medicine practiced in India since ancient times. It's called ayurveda (i-YUR-ved-uh), a Sanskrit word that means "the science of life."

Ayurveda begins with the premise that people differ both physically and psychologically. So treatments take these differences into account.

According to ayurvedic practitioners, there are three main types of energy (doshas) that create differences between people and govern health:

- Vata is the energy of movement. People dominated by vata are alert, creative and physically active.
- Pitta is the energy of digestion and metabolism. People with this primary dosha have larger appetites, warmer bodies and more stable temperaments than vata-dominated people.
- Kapha is the energy of lubrication. People dominated by kapha generally have oily skin. They easily gain weight and tend to be less physically active. In addition, kapha types are usually calm, patient and forgiving.

It's believed that one of these energies can go to extremes, creating a lack of balance. For example, kapha types can become lethargic. Treatment in this case might include recommendations to exercise regularly, avoid naps and stay away from fatty, oily foods.

Naturopathy

Based on their belief in the healing power of nature, early naturopaths prescribed hydrotherapy — literally, water treatment — to treat illness. They recommended soaks in hot springs, walking barefoot on grass or through cold streams, and other water-related treatments.

Today, naturopaths employ a combination of therapies, including nutrition, herbs, acupuncture and massage. They also use techniques from homeopathy, ayurveda, Chinese medicine and conventional treatments. The main emphasis of naturopathy is on prevention of illness through a healthy lifestyle, including fresh air, clean water and exercise.

■ 5 Steps in Considering Any Treatment

1. Gather Information About the Treatment

The Internet offers a good way to keep up with the latest on complementary and alternative treatments. Begin with Web sites created by national organizations, government agencies, major medical centers or universities. U.S. government Web sites that provide information on complementary and alternative medicine include:

National Center for Complementary and Alternative Medicine
http://nccam.nih.gov

Office of Dietary Supplements
http://dietary-supplements.info.nih.gov

National Institutes of Health
http://www.nih.gov

National Library of Medicine MEDLINEplus Health Information
http://www.nlm.nih.gov/medlineplus

U.S. Department of Health and Human Services
http://www.healthfinder.gov

For the latest health information from Mayo Clinic, visit:
Mayo Clinic Health Information
http://www.MayoClinic.com

Steer Clear of Misinformation on the Internet — Apply the Three D's

You can find thousands of Web sites devoted to health. But, be careful. The material you'll find ranges from solid research to outright quackery.

Remember to look for these three features:

- *Dates.* Search for the most recent information you can find. Reputable Web sites include a date for each article they post.
- *Documentation.* Check for the source of information and whether articles refer to published medical research. Look for a board of qualified professionals who review content before it's published. Be wary of commercial sites or personal testimonials that push a single point of view or sell miracle cures.
- *Double-checking.* Visit several health sites and compare the information they offer. And before you follow any medical advice, ask your doctor for guidance.

Some Web sites post a logo from the Health on the Net (HON) Foundation. Sites that display this logo have agreed to abide by the HON Code of Conduct.

2. Find and Evaluate Treatment Providers

After gathering information about a treatment, you may decide to find a practitioner who offers it. Choosing a name from the classified section of the phone book is risky if you have no other information about the provider. Check your state government listings for agencies that regulate and license health care providers. These agencies may list names of practitioners in your area and offer a way to check credentials.

Talk to people who've received the treatment you're considering and ask about their experience with specific providers. Start by asking friends and family members.

There are risks and side effects with many types of treatment, both conventional and unconventional. With any treatment you consider, find out if the benefits outweigh the risks.

3. Consider Treatment Cost

Many complementary and alternative approaches are not covered by health insurance. Find out exactly how much the treatment will cost you.

4. Check Your Attitude

When it comes to complementary and alternative medicine, steer a middle course between uncritical acceptance and outright rejection. Learn to be both open-minded and skeptical at the same time. Stay open to various treatments but evaluate them carefully. Also remember that the field is changing: What's alternative today may be well accepted — or discredited — tomorrow.

5. Opt for Complementary Over Alternative Medicine

Research indicates that the most popular use of unconventional medical treatments is to *complement* rather than *replace* conventional medical care. Ideally, the various forms of treatment should work together.

You can use complementary treatments to maintain good health and to relieve some symptoms. But continue to rely on conventional medicine to diagnose a problem and treat the sources of disease. And tell your medical doctor about all the treatments you get — both conventional and unconventional.

Be sure to seek conventional treatment if you have a sudden, severe or life-threatening health problem. If you break a bone, get injured in a car accident or develop food poisoning, then make the emergency room your first stop.

Also, remember that your lifestyle choices make a difference. Most practitioners — conventional, complementary and alternative — will tell you that nutrition, exercise, not smoking, stress management and safety practices are your keys to a longer life and better health.

Too Good to Be True — Signs of Medical Fraud

The Food and Drug Administration and the National Council Against Health Fraud recommend that you watch for the following claims or practices. These are often warning signs of potentially fraudulent herbal products or other "natural" treatments:

- The advertisements or promotional materials include words such as *breakthrough, magical* or *new discovery.* If the product were in fact a cure, it would be widely reported in the media, and your doctor would recommend it.
- Promotional materials include pseudo-medical jargon such as *detoxify, purify* and *energize.* Such claims are difficult to define and to measure.
- The manufacturer claims that the product can treat a wide range of symptoms, or cure or prevent a number of diseases. No single product can do this.
- The product is supposedly backed by scientific studies, but references aren't provided, are limited or are out-of-date.
- The product promotion mentions no negative side effects, only benefits.
- The manufacturer of the product accuses the government or medical profession of suppressing important information about the product's benefits. There is no reason for the government or medical profession to withhold information that could help people.

Healthy Consumer

The Healthy Traveler

Getting sick away from home can pose a special set of problems. This section suggests ways to deal with common conditions that plague travelers. For people with chronic health problems, it's always a good idea to talk with your doctor before you leave home.

Traveler's Diarrhea

Diarrhea affects up to 50 percent of people who travel to developing countries. To reduce your risk:
- Don't drink the water. Drink bottled water, sodas, beer or wine served in their original containers. Avoid ice cubes. Beverages from boiled water, such as coffee and tea, are usually safe.
- Use bottled water to brush your teeth. Keep your mouth closed while showering.
- Don't buy food from street vendors.
- Avoid salads, buffet foods, undercooked meats, raw vegetables, grapes, berries, fruits that have been peeled or cut, and unpasteurized milk and dairy products.
- Ask your doctor whether you should take along diarrhea medication or antibiotics.

Heat Exhaustion

In hot climates, a day of sightseeing can leave you weak, dizzy, nauseated and perspiring faster than you can replenish lost fluids. To prevent heat exhaustion:
- Pace yourself. Go slow the first few days after arriving in a warm climate.
- Plan regular breaks in the shade. Carry water if you're unsure of sources along the way.
- Don't overeat.
- Drink liquids before you feel thirsty. Avoid alcoholic beverages.
- Wear lightweight, light-colored clothing and a broad-brimmed hat.
- At the first sign of heat exhaustion, get out of the sun and rest in the shade or an air-conditioned building.

Blisters

Blisters can be an unwelcome reminder to slow down. To avoid them:
- Wear comfortable shoes. Break in new shoes before leaving.
- Wear cotton or wool socks dusted inside with talcum powder.
- Use moleskin as a cushion and to protect hot spots.

Altitude Sickness

Decreased oxygen at higher altitudes can cause altitude sickness. Symptoms are usually mild but can be severe enough to require immediate medical help. They include headache, breathlessness, fatigue, nausea and disturbed sleep. To reduce the risk:

- **Start slowly.** Begin at an altitude below 9,000 feet.
- **Allow time to adjust.** Rest a day after arriving to adjust to the altitude.
- **Take it easy.** Slow down if you're out of breath or tired.
- **Limit ascent.** Once you reach 8,000 feet, don't climb more than 1,000 feet a day.
- **Sleep at a lower altitude.** If you're above 11,000 feet during the day, spend your nights at 9,000 feet or lower.
- **Avoid cigarettes, alcohol and too much caffeine.**
- **Consider medication.** Ask your doctor about acetazolamide (Diamox) or other prescription medications that may help prevent or lessen symptoms.
- **Talk with your doctor.** If you've had altitude sickness before, or if you have a chronic lung or heart problem, get your doctor's advice before departing.

■ Motion Sickness

Any type of transportation can cause motion sickness. It can progress from a feeling of restlessness to a cold sweat, dizziness and then vomiting and diarrhea. Motion sickness usually quiets down as soon as the motion stops. You may escape motion sickness by planning ahead.

- If you're traveling by ship, request a cabin in the forward or middle part of the ship, near the waterline. If you're on a plane, ask for a seat over the front edge of a wing. Once aboard, direct the air vent at your face. On a train, take a seat near the front and next to a window, and face forward. In an automobile, drive or sit in the front passenger's seat.
- If you begin to feel sick, focus on the horizon or a stationary object. Don't read. Keep your head still, resting against a seat back. Eat dry crackers or a carbonated beverage to help settle your stomach. Avoid spicy food and alcohol.
- If you know you'll be sick, take an over-the-counter antihistamine such as meclizine (Antivert, Bonine), or one with dimenhydrinate (Dramamine). Talk to your doctor about prescription medication such as scopolamine.

■ Traveling Abroad

Before traveling overseas, especially if you have a health condition or take medications, review your plans with your doctor. If your plans include travel to a relatively remote location, consider consulting a specialist in travel medicine.

- **Get a head start on immunization updates.** Immunizations you may need depend on your destination, the length of your visit and your medical history. See your doctor at least four to six weeks — and preferably six months — before your departure to schedule the immunizations you'll need. Some vaccinations require several injections spaced days, weeks or even months apart.

   Information on immunizations and health precautions for travelers is available from your local health department, your doctor and the Centers for Disease Control and Prevention (see Travel Information Sources, page 286).
- **Get medical clearance.** Depending on your circumstances, your doctor may clear you for travel even if you have an unstable health condition. Have this in writing.
- **Take your medical history summary.** Make multiple copies. In case of an emergency, you may need copies for the medical professionals caring for you. If you have a history of heart problems or wear a pacemaker, ask for a copy of a recent electrocardiogram (ECG).

Healthy Consumer

- **Know where medical care will be available.** Take with you a list of the names, addresses and telephone numbers of the recommended English-speaking physicians and hospitals at your destination. Your doctor, local or state medical society, the International Association for Medical Assistance to Travellers (IAMAT) or the U. S. Department of State's Office of Overseas Citizens Services (see Travel Information Sources, page 286) can help you make your list.
- **Take copies of your prescriptions.** Request typewritten prescriptions (they're easier to read). Take your eyeglasses prescription too.
- **Pack medication carefully.** Keep your prescription medications in their original containers, with typed labels, in your carry-on luggage. Always fill your prescriptions before you leave home and bring more than you think you'll need. If you're taking a prescription narcotic, obtain a letter of authorization on your physician's letterhead stationery. Know the laws of the countries you'll be in.
- **Double-check your health insurance.** Find out ahead of time how your health insurance plan handles medical care abroad.
- **Learn about the countries you plan to visit.** Before you go, read up on the culture, people and history. For up-to-date information, obtain a consular information sheet from the U. S. Department of State's Office of Overseas Citizens Services. This provides information on health and security conditions.

■ Vaccines for International Travel

In addition to making sure you've had your primary vaccine series (measles-mumps-rubella, diphtheria, pertussis, tetanus, polio), the Centers for Disease Control and Prevention (*www.cdc.gov/travel*) recommends that you consider these additional vaccines:

Booster Vaccines or Additional Doses
- **Tetanus, diphtheria and whooping cough (pertussis).** A new vaccine is available that protects adolescents and adults against tetanus, diphtheria and pertussis. Ask your doctor about the Tdap vaccine.
- **Polio.** Unless you've had a polio booster as an adult, you may need an additional single dose if you're traveling to Africa, Asia, the Middle East, India and neighboring countries, and most of the former republics of the Soviet Union.
- **Measles.** If you were born in 1957 or after, consider a measles vaccine booster.
- **Pneumonia (pneumococcal).** Consider if you're over age 65 or have a chronic health problem.
- **Influenza.** Recommended for everyone over age 50, but may be for others depending on destination and time of year for travel.

Additional Vaccines
- **Yellow fever.** Recommended if you're traveling to certain parts of Africa and South America.
- **Hepatitis B vaccine.** Consider if you'll be staying more than one month in areas with high rates of hepatitis B (Southeast Asia, Africa, the Middle East, islands of the South and Western Pacific and the Amazon region of South America).
- **Hepatitis A vaccine (or immune globulin).** Recommended for travelers to all areas except Japan, Australia, New Zealand, Northern and Western Europe, Canada and the United States.

- **Typhoid.** Recommended if you'll be staying six weeks or longer in areas where food and water precautions are recommended (such as many developing countries).
- **Meningococcal vaccine.** Recommended if you'll be traveling to sub-Saharan Africa.
- **Japanese encephalitis.** Consider if you'll be staying long-term in Southeast Asia where this disease is common.
- **Rabies vaccine.** Recommended if you'll be staying one to two months or longer (or in a rural region) in a developing country.

◼ Air Travel Hazards

The fastest way to travel — by airplane — is also one of the safest. Yet by placing you thousands of feet in the air, moving at a speed of hundreds of miles per hour, air travel does subject your body to special challenges. Here are common problems that you might experience during air travel:

Dehydration

The pressurized cabin of an airplane has extremely low humidity, only 5 percent to 10 percent. This can cause dehydration. To prevent dehydration, drink liquids such as water and fruit juices during your flight. Limit alcohol and caffeine.

Blood Clots and Leg Swelling

Sitting during a long flight causes fluid to accumulate in the soft tissues in your legs. This increases your risk of a blood clot (thrombophlebitis). To improve circulation back to your heart:

- Stand up and stretch periodically after the "wear your seat belt" sign is turned off. Take a walk through the cabin once an hour or so.
- Flex your ankles or press your feet against the floor or seat mountings in front of you.
- If you're prone to swollen ankles or have varicose veins, consider wearing support hose.

Ear Pain

To avoid ear pain during ascent or descent, try this exercise to equalize the pressure in your ears:

- Take a deep breath; hold it for two seconds.
- Slowly exhale about 20 percent of the air while gradually pursing your lips.
- With your lips tightly closed, try to gently blow air as though you were playing a trumpet. Don't blow too hard.
- After about two seconds, exhale normally.
- To avoid lightheadedness, limit your pressure breaths to no more than 10.
- Yawning, chewing gum and swallowing also help during ascent or descent (see page 68 for more information).

Jet Lag

If you've traveled by air to a different time zone, you're probably familiar with what it's like to get jet lag — that dragged-out, out-of-sync feeling. Not all jet lag is the same. Flying eastward — and therefore resetting your body clock forward — is often more difficult than flying westward and adding hours to your day. Most peoples' bodies adjust at the rate of about an hour a day. Thus, after a change of four time zones, your body will require about four days to resynchronize its usual rhythms.

- Reset your body's clock. Begin resetting your body's clock several days in advance of your departure by adopting a sleep-wake pattern similar to the day-night cycle at your destination.
- Drink plenty of fluids and eat lightly. Drink extra liquids during your flight to avoid dehydration, but limit beverages with alcohol and caffeine. They increase dehydration and may disrupt your sleep.

■ Questions and Answers

Flying When You Have a Cold

QUESTION: Can flying make a head cold worse?

Answer: Air travel probably won't make your cold worse. But landing with a cold can cause severe ear pain. The problem is air pressure. At high altitudes, air pressure is low. But as you descend, it increases.

When you have a cold, the tiny tube (eustachian tube) that connects your throat and middle ear is often blocked. Normally, the eustachian tube equalizes air pressure in your middle ear with the increasing outside pressure. Blockage in the tube leaves a vacuum in your middle ear, leading to a buildup of painful pressure on your eardrum. Your body's attempt to fill the vacuum causes fluid and sometimes blood to enter the middle ear.

To prevent ear pain when you fly with a cold, take a decongestant at least an hour before landing. You might also use a decongestant nasal spray before descent. These over-the-counter medicines help keep your eustachian tubes open. Sipping a nonalcoholic drink on takeoff and landing also helps keep these tubes open.

Drink plenty of nonalcoholic fluids when you fly, but especially when you have a cold. Liquids keep your throat and sinus membranes from drying and keep sinus secretions thin and easy to clear.

Melatonin and Jet Lag

QUESTION: A friend suggested that I take melatonin supplements to prevent jet lag. Do they work?

Answer: Melatonin is sometimes called the "hormone of darkness" because it's produced naturally in your brain at night. It helps control your body's schedule for sleeping and waking. For that reason, it's been explored as a way to prevent or reduce jet lag. Some research suggests that taking a small amount of melatonin may help. You may try taking 1 to 3 milligrams of melatonin at bedtime for several days once you arrive at your destination. However, the benefits of melatonin are often exaggerated.

Despite numerous books and articles about melatonin, much remains unknown about this hormone and its effects on the body, particularly when it's used long term or with other medications. There are also concerns about the quality and purity of the supplements. Because melatonin isn't considered a drug, the Food and Drug

Administration doesn't regulate the safety of supplements before they go on the market. A prescription medication may be helpful. Talk to your doctor.

Travel After a Heart Attack

QUESTION: My husband has had a heart attack. Are there any special precautions we should take when traveling?

Answer: If you have cardiovascular disease, chest pain (angina) or a history of a heart attack or stroke:

- Be alert to the symptoms of a heart attack or stroke. At the first warning, seek emergency care. Know in advance where this medical care is available.
- Check the expiration date of nitroglycerin tablets. Get a new supply if they're older than six months.
- Don't drive for more than four hours without a rest.
- Stay out of the midday sun if you're traveling in a hot, humid climate.
- Limit or avoid alcohol. It reduces your heart's pumping action.
- If you wear a pacemaker, have your doctor check the battery before you go.

Traveler's First-Aid Kit

Accidents and minor injuries can happen away from home. Be prepared to treat yourself and any companions for minor medical mishaps. Include these basic supplies:

Adhesive tape	Insect repellent with DEET (30 percent to 35 percent)
Aloe gel for sunburn	Laxative
Antacid	Moist towelettes
Antibacterial cream	Moleskin (for blisters)
Antibacterial handwipes	Oral rehydration solution packets
Anti-diarrheal tablets	Over-the-counter heartburn medicine
Antihistamine	Over-the-counter pain relievers
Anti-motion sickness medication	Scissors
Bandages (including elastic type)	Skin cream or moisturizing lotion
Cotton swabs	Sunscreen with a sun protection factor (SPF) of at least 15
Cough suppressant	Digital thermometer
Decongestant	Throat lozenges
Eyedrops	Tweezers
Hydrocortisone cream (1 percent)	

■ Travel Information Sources

Centers for Disease Control and Prevention (CDC)
1600 Clifton Road
Atlanta, GA 30333
(800) 311-3435
www.cdc.gov
    The CDC offers 24-hour phone recordings on specific countries, detailing diseases and how to prevent them. In addition, its Web site also offers this information, along with immunization recommendations for regions of the world. The CDC book *Health Information for International Travel* also is available for purchase.

Bureau of Consular Affairs
2201 C St. N.W., Room 4811
U.S. Department of State
Washington, D.C. 20520
Travelers' hot line: (877) 394-8747
www.travel.state.gov

International Association for Medical Assistance to Travellers (IAMAT)
1623 Military Rd., #279
Niagara Falls, NY 14304-1745
716-754-4883
www.iamat.org
    This organization offers a free list of English-speaking doctors outside of the United States.

Index

Italic page numbers indicate illustrations.

Italic page numbers indicate illustrations.

Italic page numbers indicate illustrations.

Protonix, 67
Prozac (fluoxetine), 148
PSA (prostate-specific antigen) test, 141, 223
Psoriasis, 127
Psychological problems. *See* Mental health
Psyllium, 156
Pubic lice, 126
"Pulled" muscle, 87
Puncture wounds, 23
Pupil (of the eye), *76*
Pyloric stenosis, 66

Q

Questran (cholestyramine), 214

R

Rabies, 14, 283
Radon, 233
Rashes, 124–125
Raw eggs, 27
Raw oysters, 27
Rectal bleeding, 62
Rectal itching, 62
Rectal pain, 62
Rectal temperature, 39
Rectum, *56*
Refresh Plus, 77
Registered nurse (R.N.), 251
Relaxation techniques, 227
REM (rapid eye movement) sleep, 44
Respiratory allergies, 158–160
Respiratory problems, 107–110
Restless legs syndrome, 45
Retinal detachment, 77
Retinoic acid, 130
Reye's syndrome, 38
Rheumatoid arthritis, 162
Ribavirin, 181
Ringing in ears, 72
Ringworm, 122
Riopan Plus, 60
Rocky Mountain spotted fever, 16
Roseola, 125
Rosuvastatin, 214
Rotator cuff injury, 93
Rubella
    and pregnant women, 154
    vaccine, 224

Runner's knee, 100
Runny nose, 115
Rupture. *See* Hernias
Ruptured disk, 53
Ruptured eardrum, 69

S

Sacral vertebrae, *50*
Safety
    back injury at work, 53
    cold weather, 20–21
    driving, 231
    driving and vision problems, 80
    eye protection, 25
    food handling, 26
    at home, 231–233
    hot weather, 28
    sports, 88
    workplace, 241–242
Salicylic acid, 118, 120, 127, 130
Salmonella, 27
SAM-e (S-adenosyl-methionine), 264
SARS (severe acute respiratory syndrome), 230
Saw palmetto, 263, 271
Scabies, 126
Scars, 23
Sciatica, 53
Sclera, *76*
Scrapes and cuts, 22–23
Screening tests, 223
Seasonal affective disorder, 201
Seborrheic dermatitis, 121
Second-degree burns, 17
Secondhand smoke, 195, 233
Selenium, 261
Selenium sulfide, 120
Senility. *See* Dementia
Septum, nasal, 114
Sertraline, 148
Sexually transmitted diseases, 184–186
Shampoos, medicated, 120
Shaving tips, 117
Shift work, 241–242
Shingles, 128
Shin splints, 99
Shock, 11
Shoes, fitting, 104, 222
Shortness of breath, 110

Shoulder pain, 92–93
Sigmoidoscopy, 223
Sildenafil, 143
Simethicone, 60
Simvastatin, 214
Sinuses, *116*
Sinus infection (sinusitis), 116
Skin cancer, 129
Skin care, 117
Skin problems
    acne, 118
    angioedema, 123
    athlete's foot, 122
    boils, 119
    burns, 17–19
    cancer signs, 129
    cellulitis, 119
    corns and calluses, 120
    dandruff, 120
    dermatitis, 121
    dryness, 121
    fungal infections, 122
    hives, 123
    impetigo, 123
    itching, 124
    jock itch, 122
    keloids, 23
    lice, 126
    moles, 127
    psoriasis, 127
    rashes, 124–125
    ringworm, 122
    scabies, 126
    scars, 23
    shingles, 128
    sunburn, 19
    warts, 130
    wrinkles, 130
Skull fracture, 32
Sleep cycle, 44
Sleepiness, excessive, 45
Sleep positions, 54
Sleep problems, 44–45
    insomnia, 44
    obstructive sleep apnea, 45
    in pregnancy, 156
    shift work, 241–242
Sleepwalking, 45
"Slipped" disk, 53
Smell, sense of, 112
Smokeless tobacco, 195
Smoking, 192–195

Italic page numbers indicate illustrations.

TriCor (fenofibrate), 214
Trigger finger, 96
Triggers, headache, 84
Triglycerides, 215
Twitching eyelid, 79
Tylenol (acetaminophen), 258
Type 1 vs. type 2 diabetes, 172
Typhoid vaccine, 283

U

Ulcers, mouth. *See* Canker sores
Ulcers, stomach, 67
Unpasteurized apple cider, 27
Unpasteurized milk, 27
Urge incontinence, 150
Urgent care
    allergic reactions, 12–13
    bites, 14–16
    bleeding, 10
    breathing problems, 2–4
    burns, 17–19
    choking, 4
    CPR, 2–3
    cuts and scrapes, 22–23
    dislocations, 31
    eye injuries, 24–25
    fractures, 31
    frostbite, 20
    head injury, 32
    heart attack, 5–6
    heat problems, 28
    Heimlich maneuver, 4
    hypothermia, 21
    object in eye, 25
    poisoning, 9
    poison ivy, oak, sumac, 29
    puncture wounds, 23
    shock, 11
    sprains, 32
    stroke (brain attack), 7–8
    tooth loss, 30
    trauma, 31–32
    wounds, 22–23
Urinary tract infections
    in men, 142
    in women, 150
Urination problems
    frequent, in men, 141
    frequent, in women, 150
    incontinence, 150
    leakage, 150
    painful, in men, 142

painful, in women, 150
    slow, in men, 141
Uterine fibroids, 152
UV (ultraviolet) radiation
    and cataracts, 80
    and skin cancer, 129
    and sunburn, 19

V

Vaccines. *See* Immunizations
Vaginal bleeding, 147
Vaginal discharge, 150
Vaginal yeast infections, 150
Vaginitis, 150
Valtrex (valacyclovir), 128
Vardenafil, 143
Varicose veins in pregnancy, 155
Varivax vaccine, 224
Vasectomy, 143
Vasomotor rhinitis, 114
Vegetables and fruits, 210
Venereal disease, 184–186
Venlafaxine, 148
Ventricular fibrillation, 5
Vertebrae, 50
Vertigo, 34–35
Viagra (sildenafil), 143
Vibrio vulnificus, 27
Viral conjunctivitis, 78
Vision problems
    cataracts, 80
    contact lenses, 81
    and driving, 80
    farsightedness, 81
    floaters, 77
    glare sensitivity, 79
    glasses, 81
    glaucoma, 80
    macular degeneration, 80
Visual imagery, 227
Vitamin A, 261
Vitamin C, 261
Vitamin E, 261
    and heart attack, 179
Vitamin supplements, 261, 265–267
Voice, loss of, 135–136
Vomiting and nausea, 66
Vytorin, 214

W

Waist circumference, 208
Walking for fitness, 219–222

Walking shoes, 222
Warts
    genital, 186
    hands and feet, 130
Wasp stings, 15–16
Watery eyes, 77
Wax in ears, 73
Web health information, 278
Web travel information, 286
Weight control, 208–209
Weight gain, 47
Weight loss
    tips, 208–209
    unintended, 47–48
WelChol (colesevelam), 214
Well-child immunizations, 224
West Nile virus, 15
Wheezing, 110
Whiteheads, 118
Whooping cough. *See* DTaP vaccine
Witch hazel, 62
Women's health
    birth control, 153
    bleeding between periods, 147
    breast self-exam, 144
    cancer statistics, 168
    endometriosis, 152
    hysterectomy, 152
    irregular periods, 147
    lump in breast, 144
    mammograms, 145
    menopause, 149
    menstrual cramps, 146
    pain in breast, 146
    Pap tests, 151
    pregnancy, 154–156
    premenstrual syndrome (PMS), 147–148
    toxic shock syndrome, 152
    urinary incontinence, 150
    urinary tract infections, 150
    uterine fibroids, 152
    vaginal dryness, 149
    vaginal infections, 150
Wood ticks, 16
Workplace issues
    back care, 53, 238
    carpal tunnel syndrome, 238–239
    computer use, 246

Italic page numbers indicate illustrations.

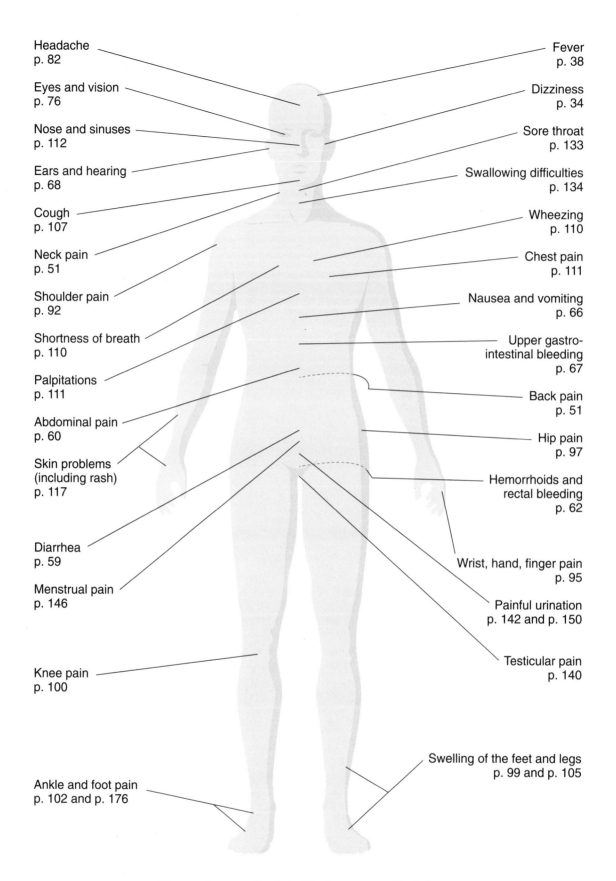

Headache
p. 82

Eyes and vision
p. 76

Nose and sinuses
p. 112

Ears and hearing
p. 68

Cough
p. 107

Neck pain
p. 51

Shoulder pain
p. 92

Shortness of breath
p. 110

Palpitations
p. 111

Abdominal pain
p. 60

Skin problems
(including rash)
p. 117

Diarrhea
p. 59

Menstrual pain
p. 146

Knee pain
p. 100

Ankle and foot pain
p. 102 and p. 176

Fever
p. 38

Dizziness
p. 34

Sore throat
p. 133

Swallowing difficulties
p. 134

Wheezing
p. 110

Chest pain
p. 111

Nausea and vomiting
p. 66

Upper gastro-
intestinal bleeding
p. 67

Back pain
p. 51

Hip pain
p. 97

Hemorrhoids and
rectal bleeding
p. 62

Wrist, hand, finger pain
p. 95

Painful urination
p. 142 and p. 150

Testicular pain
p. 140

Swelling of the feet and legs
p. 99 and p. 105

Symptoms Quick Reference Guide